Latin America Since the Left Turn

DEMOCRACY, CITIZENSHIP, AND CONSTITUTIONALISM

Rogers M. Smith and Mary L. Dudziak, Series Editors

# Latin America Since the Left Turn

*Edited by*

## Tulia G. Falleti

*and*

## Emilio A. Parrado

UNIVERSITY OF PENNSYLVANIA PRESS

PHILADELPHIA

Published by
University of Pennsylvania Press
Philadelphia, Pennsylvania 19104-4112
www.upenn.edu/pennpress

Printed in the United States of America on acid-free paper
10 9 8 7 6 5 4 3 2 1

Library of Congress Cataloging-in-Publication Data

Names: Falleti, Tulia Gabriela, editor. | Parrado, Emilio A., editor.
Title: Latin America since the left turn / edited by Tulia G. Falleti and
    Emilio A. Parrado.
Other titles: Democracy, citizenship, and constitutionalism.
Description: 1st edition. | Philadelphia : University of Pennsylvania Press, [2017] |
    Series: Democracy, citizenship, and constitutionalism | Includes bibliographical
    references and index.
Identifiers: LCCN 2017010470 | ISBN 9780812249712 (hardcover)
Subjects: LCSH: Latin America—Economic conditions—History—21st century. |
    Latin America—Politics and government—History—21st century. |
    New Left—Latin America.
Classification: LCC F1414.3 .L38 2017 | DDC 980.04—dc23
LC record available at https://lccn.loc.gov/2017010470

# CONTENTS

Introduction
*Tulia G. Falleti and Emilio A. Parrado* 1

## PART I. NATIONAL AND REGIONAL MODELS OF DEVELOPMENT

1. Latin American Development: Perspectives and Debates
*Maristella Svampa* 13

2. Fiscal Policy, Income Redistribution, and Poverty
Reduction in Argentina, Bolivia, Brazil, Mexico, Peru,
and Uruguay: An Overview
*Nora Lustig and Claudiney Pereira* 33

3. Social Investment in Latin America
*Evelyne Huber and John D. Stephens* 47

4. Debt, Democracy, and Post-Neoliberalism: Thirty Years
of Regional Integration in Latin America
*Isabella Alcañiz* 68

5. Mercosur and Regional Migration: A Human Rights Approach
*Marcela Cerrutti* 88

## PART II. DEMOCRACY AND ITS DISCONTENTS

6. Venezuela Between Two States
*George Ciccariello-Maher* 113

7. From Partial to Full Conflict Theory: A Neo-Weberian
   Portrait of the Battle for Venezuela
   *David Smilde*                                                    138

8. Populism or Democracy? Reexamining the Role of "the People"
   in Twenty-First-Century Latin American Politics
   *Paulina Ochoa Espejo*                                           165


PART III. CITIZENSHIP, CONSTITUTIONALISM, AND PARTICIPATION

9. Constitutional Changes and Judicial Power in Latin America
   *Roberto Gargarella*                                             189

10. Agents of Neoliberalism? High Courts, Legal Preferences,
    and Rights in Latin America
    *Sandra Botero*                                                 214

11. Experimenting with Participation and Deliberation
    in Latin America: Is Democracy Turning Pragmatic?
    *Thamy Pogrebinschi*                                            241

12. The *Gattopardo* Era: Innovation and Representation
    in Mexico in Post-Neoliberal Times
    *Gisela Zaremberg, Ernesto Isunza Vera, and Adrian Gurza Lavalle*   264


PART IV. RACE, DECOLONIZATION, AND VIOLENCE

13. Anti-imperial, But Not Decolonial? Vasconcelos on
    Race and Latin American Identity
    *Juliet Hooker*                                                 285

14. Decolonization and Plurinationality
    *Oscar Vega Camacho*                                            308

15. Postwar El Salvador: Entangled Aftermaths
    *Irina Carlota (Lotti) Silber*                                  326

List of Contributors                          353

Index                                         357

Acknowledgments                               375

# Introduction

Tulia G. Falleti and Emilio A. Parrado

If the ideas and policies of the Washington Consensus, such as achieving macroeconomic stability, pursuing free-market economic reforms, and increasing trade openness, dominated much of Latin America at the turn of the twentieth century, the onset of the new millennium found the region swerving left. Jorge Castañeda (2006) described the experience as "Latin America's Left Turn." It included openly rejecting the premises of the Washington Consensus as well as reorienting toward alternative policies that stressed social improvements, a more egalitarian distribution of wealth, political mobilization, and independence from international economic organizations (Castañeda 2006).

However, the Left Turn was not uniform or homogeneous. At one extreme, the election of left-wing parties in Argentina, Bolivia, Brazil, Ecuador, and Venezuela triggered programs that attempted to reverse the reforms of the 1990s and pushed the countries into what was sometimes considered a post-neoliberal or progressive phase. At the other extreme, in Chile, Colombia, Mexico, and Peru, continuity and even extension of the neoliberal agenda remained the norm. Today, the return of the political right to power through democratic elections in Argentina in 2015 and its imposition through the impeachment and outing of leftist president Dilma Rousseff in Brazil in 2016, as well as prior attempted institutional coups and changes in Honduras and Paraguay, raise the question of the likely continuity, attained effects, and projected legacy of the Left Turn.

Considerable research has been devoted to the political forces and socioeconomic conditions prompting the leftist reorientation (e.g., Cameron and

Hershberg 2010; Cleary 2006; Levitsky and Roberts 2011; Weyland et al. 2010). Excellent single-country study analysis of the rise of the left also exist (Anria 2010; Ciccariello-Maher 2013; Hunter 2010). However, less is known about the particular character that the region has assumed since the Left Turn. The political reorientation that started at the inception of the new century triggered considerable changes in the democracy, citizenship, and constitutional arrangements in the region. Evaluating these changes is the main objective of this volume. In doing so, the authors ask specific questions: What were the social, political, and economic consequences of the partial unmaking of the neoliberal consensus in Latin America? Why did some countries stay on the neoliberal course? Were the left-leaning governments that came to power in the 2000s a throwback to the pre-neoliberal consensus? What was new and what remained unchanged in terms of economic development, social policies, regional integration, political representation, constitutionalism, and participation? Have ideas of race and decolonization changed in the region? What are the new challenges regarding violence and security? Discussing these questions helps us analytically frame and understand the major transformations experienced by Latin America in the first two decades of this century, evaluate those changes and continuities, and provide some insights into the region's future direction.

In selecting the contributors and topics included in this volume, we had several goals in mind. First, we aimed for an interdisciplinary approach to the study of Latin America. Thus the contributors to this volume have been formally trained and/or conduct research and teaching in an array of disciplines, including philosophy, economics, political science, sociology, and anthropology. We strongly believe this interdisciplinary collaboration provides the reader with the best approach to understand contemporary Latin America. Second, alongside contributions from eminent Latin Americanists working in U.S. academia, we sought to give voice to the work of outstanding scholars who write from Latin America, such as Maristella Svampa, Marcela Cerrutti, and Roberto Gargarella, from Argentina; Thamy Pogrebinschi and Adrian Gurza Lavalle, from Brazil; Oscar Vega Camacho, from Bolivia; Gisela Zaremberg and Ernesto Isunza Vera, from Mexico; and David Smilde, who lives in between Caracas and New Orleans. In some cases, we are proud to say this is the first time their scholarship is published in English, providing the reader with an original and firsthand analysis of ongoing processes in the region. Finally, we aimed to cover the current trends in the region with regards to the domestic and regional political economy, democracy, institutions (such as constitutions, the judiciary, and participatory innovations), and the perennial issues of race, decolonization, violence, and migration to the United States. These topics structure the four parts of the volume, as described in what follows.

## National and Regional Models of Development

The first part of this volume centers on alternative models of development found in Latin America since the Left Turn, which started with the 1998 election of Hugo Chávez in Venezuela and continued with leftist national victories in Chile, Brazil, Argentina, Uruguay, Bolivia, Nicaragua, Ecuador, and Paraguay during the first decade of the new century.

In Chapter 1, Maristella Svampa analyzes extractivism as the emergent model of development and accumulation in Latin America—whether by governments on the right (Colombia, Mexico, Peru) or left of the political spectrum (Brazil, Bolivia, Ecuador, Venezuela, and Argentina). As Svampa explains, the transition from the Washington Consensus to what she calls the "Commodity Consensus" has implied the "reprimarization" of Latin American economies. As it had been the case over a century earlier, during the period of export-led growth that characterized the economies of the region from the time of their insertion in the international economy in the late nineteenth century until the Great Depression (from circa 1880 to 1930), the economies of the region—riding on the commodity boom of the early 2000s—once again relied heavily on the exports of primary products, including nonrenewable resources. But as Svampa notes, the extractivist model can be interpreted in terms of departures from as much as continuities with past economic models. Extractivism has created conflicting narratives of economic development, particularly in countries ruled by the Left (such as in Bolivia under Evo Morales or in Ecuador under Rafael Correa), between the national governments, which emphasize extraction for economic development, and the indigenous and environmental social movements, which seek to preserve their territories and way of life (at times referred to as "Living Well" or "Buen Vivir"). Thus conflicts have increased over the control and use of the territory and the environment, especially in ecologically preserved areas (such as the Tipnis National Park in Bolivia) and in the Amazonia (as in the case of the Yasuni National Park in Ecuador). Svampa also documents the changes in trade that have taken place during the first fifteen years of the twenty-first century, noting the shift in Latin America's trade dependency from the United States toward China.

Different models of economic development are also analyzed through the lens of fiscal policy and public spending. In Chapter 2, Nora Lustig and Claudiney Pereira provide a comprehensive comparative analysis of the effects of fiscal policy and social spending. They measure the direct and indirect taxes and government subsidies, as well as the conditional cash transfer programs and social spending in health and education in Argentina, Bolivia, Brazil, Mexico, Peru, and Uruguay in the late 2000s. The authors analyze the effect of these fiscal and spending policies on poverty reduction. The countries that collect the most revenue and spend the most achieve the greatest equalizing effect through direct taxes and transfers (Argentina and Brazil). However, when transfers in-kind such as quasi-free services in education and health are included, inequality declines substantially in all six countries, irrespective of levels of revenue and total spending. With regard to poverty reduction, Uruguay stands out as having reduced poverty the most, after taking into account all direct and indirect transfers, cash transfers, and indirect subsidies. The authors present a set of caveats having to do with size of economies of compared countries and raise warnings regarding the sustainability of the redistributive model in Argentina—particularly relevant since the election of right-wing President Mauricio Macri at the end of 2015. They also point to the disturbing fact that consumption taxes in Brazil offset the poverty-reducing effect of direct cash transfers, making the moderately poor net-payers into the Brazilian fiscal system. Interestingly, however, once in-kind transfers in education and health are included, reduction in inequality is observed across the six countries—albeit by one quarter of the equivalent rate in advanced OECD countries.

Evelyne Huber and John D. Stephens, in Chapter 3, focus on the study of social investment (namely, cash transfers and social spending in education) and its impact on income inequality and poverty reduction. They arrive at a clear policy prescription: spending on education cannot substitute for spending on social assistance. Social investment in education must be complemented with targeted cash transfers that will lift the poor out of poverty. As Huber and Stephens show, cash transfers to the poor are a prerequisite to building the human capital of the future. Parents need to be lifted out of poverty for their children to attend school, raise their expectations about educational attainment, and successfully develop cognitive skills. They prove their argument by analyzing the development of cognitive skills, among other education variables, in fourteen countries of South and Central America.

Moving to the regional level, in Chapter 4, Isabella Alcañiz provides a political economy analysis to compare the effects of debt, democracy, and economic crises in the 1980s and in the 2000s. She argues that the incentives created by debt crises and democratization led to the creation of the Common Market of the South (Mercosur) in the 1980s, which built on shared conceptions of economic development, as well as on prior bilateral trade and nuclear agreements between Argentina and Brazil. During the 2000s, economic crisis and the ongoing institutionalization of democratic regimes led to the creation of other regional institutions, such as Unasur, and, paradoxically, to the demise of the role of Mercosur in the region.

However, looking through the lens of intraregional migration, Marcela Cerrutti argues in Chapter 5 that Mercosur has played a pivotal role in migration policy. She shows that since the crisis of neoliberalism and the advent of leftist governments, migration has been increasingly linked to issues of human rights and citizenship, particularly among the countries constituting Mercosur. Thus, the Residence Agreement of 2002 grants equal treatment and recognition of equal rights among natives and migrants in Argentina, Brazil, Bolivia, Chile, Paraguay, and Uruguay. Cerrutti provides a detailed account of the adoption of this agreement in Argentina, which was the first Mercosur country to incorporate many of the Agreement's provisions in its new migration law.

Jointly, the five chapters that constitute the first part of the volume provide the reader with an in-depth account of the main futures of the national economic models adopted in Latin America since the Left Turn, the consequences of their taxation and redistributive policies on poverty and income inequality, and the international and domestic politics that led to the formation and subsequent evolution of regional international organizations such as Mercosur.

## Democracy and Its Discontents

Since the turn to the left in the region, many social scientists have criticized the increased centralization of power in the national executives and the detrimental effects this has had on democracy. Venezuela is possibly the country in the region that has seen the most dramatic social, economic, and political changes in the first two decades of the twenty-first century. It has been the fiercest critic of neoliberalism, putting forward the "Socialism of the Twenty-First Century" instead. It is also a country where constitutional and political institutional changes have led critics to dub its political regime "competitive authoritarianism," (Mainwaring 2012) and where the worsening economic crisis is contributing to heightened social protest and government repression.

Unpacking political transformation in Venezuela, in Chapter 6, George Ciccariello-Maher studies the Bolivarian Revolution, initiated by Hugo Chávez, through three moments, beginning with the movement away from the liberal and representative components of democracy. In this moment, Chávez called into question the separation of powers and promoted a participatory and social conception of democracy, which, according to Ciccariello-Maher, had long roots in Venezuela's history. The second moment is the adoption of the 1999 Constitution, where constituent and constituted powers interact with one another. The third moment is the centripetal movement toward dispersed forms of communal power. According to Ciccariello-Maher, the process of transformation initiated by Chávez builds on the existing history of social movement activism. However, the extent to which dispersed communal power could be compatible with President Nicolás Maduro's poor handling of the economy, concentration of power, and cracking down on the political opposition should invite further analysis and future research.

To such end, the neo-Weberian full conflict theory of David Smilde, in Chapter 7, provides an excellent analytical framework. Smilde depicts the ideological, economic, military, and political power networks present in Chavismo and in the opposition camps. Smilde's nuanced approach to conflict allows him to examine the tensions inherent in the Chavista project, while explaining its main sources of support. In highly politically polarized countries, such as Venezuela, the neo-Weberian full conflict theory is a suitable tool to analyze conflicts and tensions and better understand the complexities of national politics.

The discussion of political arrangements emerging in Latin America continues in Chapter 8, where Paulina Ochoa Espejo, changing the focus to the case of Mexico, asks provocatively, "Are the New Left movements democratic or populist?" She answers the question by focusing on the meaning of "the people" (el pueblo). She proposes a different criterion for demarcating populism and liberal democracy: self-limitation. From this perspective, populists defend their policies by the claim that people want them. Liberal democracy, in her view, also appeals to the people, but to signal that their claims are fallible, and thus limit their reach. She applies this criterion to the contested 2006 elections in Mexico.

As the parties in power and the political regimes in the region continue to change, it will be interesting to see the extent to which the Ochoa Espejo's criterion to distinguish between democratic and populist democracies can be further validated and extended to other contexts and historical events. We also wonder whether Ochoa Espeho's normative framework could be productively combined with the sociological neo-Weberian full-conflict theory advanced by Smilde, and/or complemented with the ideas of communal democracy presented by Ciccariello-Maher, to more comprehensibly study the social bases of support of ruling and opposition coalitions and their standing vis-à-vis the political regime claims these groups support and legitimize.

## Citizenship, Constitutionalism, and Participation

The study of political regimes, which are the main object of analysis in the second part of the book, is complemented in the third part of the volume with the study of political institutions and their historical and recent transformations. This section opens with two chapters devoted to Latin American constitutions and judiciaries, followed by two chapters that focus on the new forms of citizen participation, promoted by recent legal reforms and institutional innovations.

In Chapter 9, Argentine constitutional expert Roberto Gargarella reviews Latin American constitutional history from its origins in the nineteenth century to the present, focusing on the main transformations: from the division of powers within government at the moment of state building, to the declaration of rights in the early twentieth century, to the promotion of human and social rights in the late twentieth century, to the arrival of new experiments on what he calls "dialogic constitutionalism." However, Gargarella remains skeptical about the reach of these reforms, positing that the hyperpresidentialism of the nineteenth century (or what he calls the "engine room" of Latin American constitutions) has not changed. Is it possible to make constitutional changes when the main features of Latin American constitutions remain practically the same? Gargarella sees a tension between the new participatory, more democratic constitutional reform initiatives and judiciaries of the recent past and the hierarchical organization of power still prevalent in the region's constitutions and governments.

Shifting her focus to the last quarter century, Sandra Botero, in Chapter 10, analyzes the constitutional courts of the region in terms of neoliberal and social constitutional reforms. What are the political dynamics triggered by the active exercise of judicial power? In Botero's view, neither path dependence nor ideology can account for the activist role of judges. Focusing on the case of Colombia's constitutional court, Botero argues that the type of appointments to constitutional courts affects their future activism, which she analyzes in the areas of women's reproductive and sexual rights and lesbian, gay, bisexual, and transgender rights.

Chapters 11 and 12 focus on relatively recent institutional creations that seek to promote citizens' participation and deliberation in public policy decision-making and in the distribution of social services and public goods. Interestingly, the authors provide contrasting interpretations regarding the vitality of these participatory institutions and their effects on democracy. In Chapter 11, drawing from a comparative analysis of institutional innovations for participation created throughout Latin America, Thamy Pogrebinschi argues that the new forms of participation and deliberation we see in the region amount to a "pragmatic turn" for democracy, which deepens the meaning and substance of the social component of democracy. In her analysis, this pragmatic turn is intrinsically linked to the rise of the Left in the governments of the region after 1999 and to the constitutional reforms that followed.

Drawing from an analysis of public opinion surveys carried out in Mexico, in Chapter 12 Gisela Zaremberg, Ernesto Isunza Vera, and Adrian Gurza Lavalle provide a less optimistic view of the effects of participatory institutional innovations on democracy. In their assessment, these new institutions have been weakly implemented and have little impact on people's life or their access to the state. Instead, Mexican individuals, they argue, continue to rely on political parties as their main intermediaries with the state.

## Race, Decolonization, and Violence

The final section of the volume discusses race, decolonization, and the urgent problems of violence, security, and international migration. In Chapter 13, Juliet Hooker adds to the extensive literature on the meaning of *mestizaje* by elaborating a very original and refreshing interpretation of the work of José Vasconcelos. By carefully grounding Vasconcelos's work in space and time, especially within the concrete political context in which they emerged, Hooker constructs a Vasconcelos who is clearly anticolonial in his rejection of U.S. ideas about race and U.S. imperialism. She argues that while Vasconcelos's philosophical and political valorization of mestizaje is a clear anticolonial answer to global white supremacy and U.S. imperialism, the vision cannot be considered fully de-colonial. His rejection of U.S. imperialism and white supremacy was limited, in that it did not fundamentally challenge the reification of racial hierarchies in Latin America.

In Chapter 14, Oscar Vega Camacho revisits the meaning of decolonization in South American politics and thought. In his words, decolonization is "the struggle against and resistance to colonial power relations on multiple scales in a historical process for emancipation and liberation." Vega Camacho analyzes the demand from social and indigenous movements for decolonization in relation to the ideas and political projects of plurinationality and "Buen Vivir," particularly as they have developed in Bolivia since 2006. In order to map the main conflicts that lie ahead in Bolivia's process of democratization, he then introduces three topics closely linked to decolonization and plurinationalism: social movements, constitutional politics, and social economy efforts.

Irina Carlota Silber, in Chapter 15, brings us closer to the everyday and personal consequences of war and instability in El Salvador, a country suffering, as are other Central American countries, from violence and insecurity. However, the situation as experienced in the everyday lives of residents remains underexplored. More importantly, the implications for migration, especially the push for families to cross into the United States, raise humanitarian concerns that transcend national boundaries. Building on over twenty years of longitudinal, ethnographic research in the District of Chalatenango, a former war zone, and with the Salvadoran diaspora, Silber argues in favor of a critical anthropology of security and illuminates the insecure and precarious lives of Salvadoran citizens and their interpersonal and structural connections.

## Conclusion

As the second decade of the twenty-first century comes to a close, significant political change in the ideological orientation of the democratically elected governments of Latin America is taking place, with swings to the center-right in highly polarized countries such as Argentina, Paraguay, Peru, and Brazil, and increased tensions affecting continuity of the leftist projects in countries such as Bolivia and Venezuela. Violence, meanwhile, remains high in Central America and Mexico and has spiked in Venezuela.

While we cannot provide definitive answers on the direction that Latin America will take in the twenty-first century, our hope is that the highly insightful chapters that follow and that analyze the main economic, social, institutional, and political transformations that have taken place since the Left rose to power at the beginning of this century will shed light on why some Latin American countries broke with the neoliberalism of the previous era while other countries experienced more continuity than change in the realm of economic policies, as well as in their institutional creations and reforms. Overall, we are confident this volume will contribute to a better understanding of the tensions and contradictions that are the current signature of Latin American societies and politics.

## References

Anria, Santiago. 2010. "Bolivia's MAS: Between Party and Movement." In *Latin America's Left Turn: Politics, Policies, and Trajectories of Change*, edited by M. A. Cameron and E. Hershberg, 101–25. Boulder, Colo.: Lynne Rienner Publishers.

Cameron, Maxwell A., and Eric Hershberg, eds. 2010. *Latin America's Left Turn: Politics, Policies, and Trajectories of Change*. Boulder, Colo.: Lynne Rienner Publishers.

Castañeda, Jorge G. 2006. "Latin America's Left Turn." *Foreign Affairs* 85 (3): 28–43.

Ciccariello-Maher, George. 2013. *We Created Chávez: A People's History of the Venezuelan Revolution*. Durham, N.C.: Duke University Press.

Cleary, Mathew. 2006. "Explaining the Left Resurgence." *Journal of Democracy* 17 (4): 35–49.

Hunter, Wendy. 2010. *The Transformation of the Workers' Party in Brazil, 1989–2009*. New York, N.Y.: Cambridge University Press.

Levitsky, Steven, and Kenneth M. Roberts. 2011. "Latin America's 'Left Turn': A Framework for Analysis." In *The Resurgence of the Latin American Left*, edited by S. Levitsky and K. M. Roberts, 1–28. Baltimore, Md.: Johns Hopkins University Press.

Mainwaring, Scott. 2012. "From Representative Democracy to Participatory Competitive Authoritarianism: Hugo Chávez and Venezuelan Politics." *Perspectives on Politics* 10 (4): 955–67.

Weyland, Kurt, Raúl L. Madrid, and Wendy Hunter. 2010. *Leftist Governments in Latin America*. New York: Cambridge University Press.

# PART I

## National and Regional Models of Development

# Latin American Development: Perspectives and Debates

Maristella Svampa

## Introduction: The Latin American Scene

One of the recurring topics in Latin American debates refers to the dynamics of accumulation and current models of development. Critical categories such as extractivism and neoextractivism, as well as positive ones such as Buen Vivir, Common Goods, Rights of Nature, and postextractivism, traverse social struggles and debates and are generating a new political grammar that questions the sustainability of current development models and poses different relationships among society, economy, and nature.

These discussions originated mainly in Ecuador and Bolivia, two countries where the anti-neoliberal social movements of the late twentieth and the early twenty-first centuries were accompanied not only by the emergence of new governments (progressive or popular) but also by constituent processes explicitly aimed at rethinking or reestablishing the social pact. It was in this period of radical openness when categories such as those of the plurinational state, Rights of Nature, and Buen Vivir ceased to be concepts exclusively associated with theoretical schools of thought and entered the field of political dispute.

Over the years, however, as progressive governments consolidated, these debates became increasingly complex. On the one hand, given the comparative advantages derived from the commodities boom, progressive Latin American governments gradually reinforced a view of development linked to the growth of exports based on primary products. On the other hand, as territorial and environmental conflicts sprung up, and as projects to exploit natural resources for exportation proliferated, extractivism and neoextractivism were increasingly criticized.

Finally, over the past decade quite a few Latin American governments considered to be progressive or popular have developed strong populist traits. These governments have been reinforcing a dynamic grounded in strong personal leadership, the subordination of social and political organizations to that leadership, the strengthening of the state's capacities (as compared to in neoliberal times) grounded in fiscal enhancement, the policy of social expenditure (social policies or bonds addressed to the most vulnerable sectors), and the consumption subsidy. An additional factor is that in Latin America, more than elsewhere, the Left, whether in its anticapitalist or its national-popular matrix, has maintained a strong developmental standpoint, tending to emphasize a reading of history that exalts the expansion of productive forces within the framework of an industrialist or laborer-centered model.

In this chapter, I propose an approach to the debate about development and the intensification of the extractive model, in terms of political economy, in four different instances. First, I present two general concepts that are a framework for our proposal: the Commodities Consensus and extractivism. Second, I describe a recursive, dynamic approach to the different phases of the Commodities Consensus. Third, I explore the conflicting narratives and perspectives on development in the current phase of accumulation. Finally, I discuss the progressive shift toward new forms of dependency, especially in relation to China.

## Framework Concepts

Latin America has recently transitioned from the Washington Consensus, based on financial valorization, to the Commodities Consensus, based on the large-scale exportation of raw materials such as hydrocarbons (gas and petroleum), metals and minerals (copper, gold, silver, tin, bauxite, zinc, and so forth), agricultural products (corn, soy, and wheat), and biofuels. The Commodities Consensus is a complex, fast-paced, recursive process that must be read from an economic and a social point of view. From the economic point of view, it has involved a process of "reprimarization" of Latin American economies, emphasizing their reorientation toward mainly extractive or rent-based activities with little added value. According to the United Nations Conference on Trade and Development (UNCTAD, n.d.), agricultural, mineral, and commodity raw materials represented 76 percent of Union of South American Nations (Unasur) exports in 2011, compared to only 34 percent for the world as a whole. The manufacture of advanced technology, in comparison, represented 7 percent and 25 percent respectively (UNCTAD, n.d.). The situation is compounded by the entry of China, a country that is quickly imposing itself as an unequal partner in commercial exchange with countries in the Latin American region (Rodriguez 2014).

From the social point of view, the Commodities Consensus deepens the dynamic of dispossession—to use the expression popularized by David Harvey (2004)—which is the dispossession and accumulation of land, resources, and territories, principally by large corporations in multiscalar alliances with governments. It is not by chance that the critical literature on Latin America considers these processes to consolidate neoextractivist development (Acosta 2010; Gudynas 2010; Machado Aráoz 2012; Svampa 2011; 2013a), which is usually defined as a pattern of accumulation based on the overexploitation of generally nonrenewable natural resources, as well as the expansion of capital's frontiers into territories previously considered to be nonproductive. Developmentalist neoextractivism is characterized by large-scale enterprises, a focus on exportation, and a tendency toward monoproduction or monoculture. Its emblematic figures include strip mining, the expansion of the petroleum and energy frontier (which also includes the exploitation of nonconventional gas or shale gas, using the questionable methodology of hydraulic fracturing, or fracking), the construction of large hydroelectric dams, the expansion of the fishing and forestry frontier, and the generalization of the agribusiness model (soy and biofuels).

A key feature of neoextractivism is the immense scale of the projects, which tells us about the size of the investment: they are capital-intensive activities, not labor-intensive. For example, in the case of large-scale mining, for every one million dollars invested, between 0.5 and 2 jobs are directly created (Colectivo Voces de Alerta 2011). In Peru, mining employs a mere 2 percent of the economically active population, compared to 23 percent in agriculture, 15 percent in retail, and almost 10 percent in manufacturing (Permanent Working Group on Alternatives to Development 2013).

In relation to the Washington Consensus, the Commodities Consensus can be read as a rupture with the Washington Consensus as much as it can be seen as a continuity of it. The Washington Consensus placed financial valorization at the center of its agenda and included policies of adjustment and privatization that redefined the state as a metaregulating agent (Santos 2007). The Commodities Consensus focuses on the implementation of massive extractive projects oriented toward exportation, establishing greater flexibility in the state's role. This allows for progressive governments that question the neoliberal consensus to coexist with governments that continue to deepen a neoliberal, conservative political framework.

Finally, the Commodities Consensus is built on the idea that there is agreement—tacit or explicit—about the irrevocable or irresistible character of the current extractivist dynamic, resulting from the growing global demand for raw materials. The aim is to limit collective resistance and close off the possibility of thinking of other notions of development, and to install a comprehensive historical threshold in regards to alternatives. Consequently, critical discourse or radical opposition is considered in terms of antimodernity, negating progress, "pachamamism," "infantile ecologism," or even "colonial environmentalism" promoted by NGOs and foreign agents.

In the vision of the progressive governments that support it, the Commodities Consensus is associated with the state's action as producer and regulator, as well as with funding social programs for the most vulnerable from extractivist rent. The state installs itself within a variable geometry, which means within a multiactor scheme marked by a civil society complexified through social movements, NGOs, and other actors. At the same time, it operates in tight association with multinational capital, which plays an increasingly important role in Latin American economies. This places clear limits on the state's action and an inexorable threshold on the very demand for democratization of collective decision-making by communities and populations affected by large extractive projects.

The Latin American setting illustrates the coupling not only of neodevelopmentalist extractivism and neoliberalism, as seen in the paradigmatic cases of Peru, Colombia, and Mexico, but also of neodevelopmentalist extractivism and progressivism, further complicating the current problem. The most paradoxical scenarios of the Commodities Consensus are those presented by Bolivia and Ecuador. In these countries, which have strong participatory processes, new concept horizons have been generated, such as the plurinational state, autonomy, Buen Vivir, and the Rights of Nature, which appear in the Ecuadoran and Bolivian constitutions. However, as these regimes consolidate, other questions, questions linked to the deepening of neoextractivism, become central.

Whether in the crude language of dispossession (liberal neodevelopmentalism) or in pointing to the state's control of the surplus (progressive neodevelopmentalism), the current development model is based on an extractivist paradigm. It draws from the idea of "economic opportunities" and "comparative advantage" provided by the Commodities Consensus and deploys social imaginaries around the magical enrichment resulting from the exploitation of natural resources (Zavaletta Mercado, 2009) that overstep the political-ideological borders constructed in the 1990s. These positions reflect the tendency to consolidate a model of appropriation and exploitation of the commons, which advances on populations through a top-down logic, threatening improvements in participatory democracy and inaugurating a new cycle of criminalization and violation of human rights.

On the other hand, neoextractivism presents a specific territorial dynamic that tends toward the intensive occupation of a territory through ways related to monoculture or monoproduction, which displaces other forms of production (local/regional economies). The advance over the territory, in most cases, combines the dynamics of enclave or territorial fragmentation (low production of relevant endogenous chaining that could benefit a model of territorial and regional integration) with the dynamics of displacement (dislocation of traditional local economies and expulsion of populations). This tends to cast big companies, which have a global outreach, in the role of absolute social actors within local societies. At the same time, these processes impact the condition of citizenship and the violation of human rights. In other words, the dynamics of dispossession unfold in various directions, vertically imposing megaprojects without consulting affected populations; tending toward intensive land use, competition, and progressive displacement of other productive activities; inflicting long-term socioenvironmental and health impacts on inhabitants; handling institutional arrangements available (direct and semidirect democracy); and progressively closing channels for expressing dissent by stigmatizing, criminalizing, and violently repressing social resistance.

Thus defined, neoextractivism encompasses more than the activities traditionally considered as extractive. In addition to involving open-pit megamining, expanding the petroleum and energy frontier (by exploiting non-conventional gas and oil via fracking), and constructing large hydroelectric dams (usually at the service of extractive production), neoextractivism includes expanding the fishing and forest frontier, as well as generalizing the agribusiness model (transgenic crops, such as soy and biofuels).

## Phases of the Commodities Consensus and Conflicts Around Development

The expansion of neoextractivism and the high level of conflict associated with it during the Commodities Consensus present various phases or moments. The Commodities Consensus must be approached as a process, because progressive governments have consolidated (second terms in office) and a developmental hegemony with an extractive basis has emerged.

We must remember that, in political and ideological terms, approaching the year 2000 Latin America underwent a change upheld by an intense social mobilization that denatured and questioned the Washington Consensus. The subsequent emergence of different popular or progressive governments in Venezuela, Bolivia, Ecuador, and Argentina, among other countries, pointed to the state's gradually recovering its institutional capacities so it could become a major economic actor and, in some cases, an agent of redistribution. This state transformation, which was accompanied by an important integrationist (inward) and Latin Americanist (for the region) narrative, gave rise to high political expectations regarding the extension of rights and forms of popular participation (constituent assemblies and new constitutions in Bolivia, Venezuela, and Ecuador). Over the years, however, this widening of the bounds of rights (environmental, collective rights) found severe limitations in the expansion of capital's frontiers. Far from the "creative tension" proposed by Bolivia's Vice President Garcia Linera, it seems that Latin America has entered a period of intense socioterritorial conflicts and colliding narratives of emancipation.

Since 2003, due to the boom in international prices for raw materials, governments have benefited from a very favorable economic situation, a new cycle based on the massive exportation of commodities, which brought large profits and comparative economic advantages. In this new scene, regardless of the nationalist rhetoric in vogue, the state has come to occupy a space of variable geometry, where one of the key factors has been its association with multinational private capital, whose weight on national economies, far from diminishing, has increased as extractive activities have expanded and multiplied. A new developmentalism, more pragmatic and prone to extractivism, not necessarily linked to the forms of statism that prevailed from the 1950s through the 1970s, appeared as a central feature of the dominant practice, configuring what some authors have called "developmental hegemony" (Feliz 2012).

This first phase of the Commodities Consensus, a period of economic growth and reformulation of the state's role, as well as nonrecognition of the conflicts associated with extractive dynamics, lasted until about 2008–10. During this first phase, progressive governments, with consolidated administrations (many having renewed their presidential terms), began to admit and affirm an explicitly extractive matrix, due to the increased hostility of certain territorial and environmental conflicts (such as the Tipnis conflict in Bolivia, the Belo Monte mega-dam in Brazil, and the different projects of mega-mining in Argentina and Ecuador, among others). The increase of conflicts linked to extractive activities (megamining, megadams, petroleum, and, to a lesser extent, agribusiness) revealed both the dimensions and alliances of the hegemonic developmentalism and the limits imposed on the processes of citizen participation. It also opened the door to conflict criminalization.

The second stage is a period of officialization of the Commodities Consensus and of open conflict in the territories. Progressive governments doubled their bets by greatly increasing extractive projects while, paradoxically, using an industrialist discourse. In the case of Brazil, the Growth Acceleration Plan is a project to build a great number of dams in Amazonia. In Bolivia, there is the promise of a Big Industrial Leap, a plan launched by the Bolivian vice president in 2010 that fosters extractive projects (gas, lithium, iron, and agribusiness, among others). In Ecuador, the government is advancing megamining and has ended the moratorium on the Yasuni project (2013). Venezuela, in turn, in 2012 formulated the Strategic Plan for the Production of Petroleum, which implies extending the boundary for exploitation into the Orinoco Belt, where there are reservoirs of extra heavy (nonconventional) crude oil. Argentina launched the 2010–20 Agrifood Strategic Plan, which projects a 60 percent increase in grain production and is also moving forward in exploiting unconventional hydrocarbons via fracking (it also promoted expropriation of the oil company in the hands of Repsol in 2012, a new national law of hydrocarbons, and the subsequent signing of a deal with Chevron Company in 2013). Nevertheless, many of these projects have been delayed since the drop in the international price of petroleum and other minerals in mid-2014.In this phase, numerous socioenvironmental and territorial conflicts emerged from their local confines to gain nationwide visibility: the project to build a road crossing the Tipnis area (Bolivia), the construction of a megadam in Belo Monte (Brazil), the revolt in Famatina and the resistance movements against megamining (Argentina), the end of the moratorium on the Yasuni project (Ecuador), and the unrest caused by the Aratirí megamining project (Uruguay).

Similarly emblematic conflicts occurred in countries with neoliberal or conservative governments, among which: in Peru, an undefined number of people were killed by repressive forces at the Conga mine (Observatorio de conflictos Cajamarce, 2015) under the administration of Ollanta Humala; in Colombia, there was opposition to the La Colosa mining megaproject; and in Chile, the Pascua-Lama binational mining project was suspended as a result of legal actions brought before the courts.

Progressive governments have frequently responded to these conflicts by stigmatizing environmental protests and attributing to them a conspiratorial nature. In fact, wherever there are environmental and territorial conflicts, publicized and politicized, that expose the blind spots of progressive governments regarding the dynamics of dispossession, the reaction is usually the same. It has happened in Ecuador since 2009, especially in reference to megamining; in Brazil, with the conflict of Belo Monte; and in Bolivia concerning the Tipnis. In all three cases, the governments chose to emphasize the nationalistic discourse and overlook the issue, denying the legitimacy of the claim and attributing it either to "infantile environmentalism" (Ecuador), to the ulterior motives of foreign NGOs (Brazil and Bolivia), or even to "colonial environmentalism" (Bolivia).

Much of the same has been happening in Argentina, though without major debates: the term "neoextractivism" itself is far from the government's rhetorical horizon. This is illustrated by the revolt against megamining in Famatina. The subsequent realignment between national political power and economic power (mining corporations) culminated in President Cristina F. Kirchner's legitimizing megamining as an integral part of the official project.

The Economic Commission for Latin American and the Caribbean (ECLAC) is now upholding the extractivist pact throughout Unasur. Its report on natural resources in Latin America, presented in Caracas in June 2013, constituted a sort of clean-up or officialization of the Commodities Consensus. Thus the regional agenda is being updated so as to consider the issue of strategic natural resources from a developmental viewpoint. As Antonelli (2014) pointed out: "This process has two key points accepted by the members in 2013, namely, the water governance, that is, the management of water resources for extractive models, and the regional government's control of mining conflicts. The 'infinite wealth' is directly related to the 'new technologies' (fracking) for non-conventional extractions (mining, gas, petroleum), and agreements are made with regional universities and scientific-technological systems to 'inventory' the wealth that is still unknown to us." Unlike in the first phase, the Commodities Consensus is no longer a tacit agreement shamefully linking neoliberal and conservative governments with progressive ones. The matching between discourses and practices, as well as the strong stigmatization of environmental criticism that occurs even in those countries with the highest expectations of political change—such as Bolivia and Ecuador—illustrates how progressive governments have evolved toward more traditional models of domination linked to the classical national-popular or national-developmentalist model. It must, thus, be recognized that these governments are entering a disturbing phase characterized by limited democracy. The governments are curbing civil and political rights, both collective and individual, by modifying and manipulating the available institutional arrangements that link semidirect and direct democracy. An example for countries with large indigenous populations is the case of the right of free, prior, and informed consultation established by ILO Convention 169. This right is present in the constitutions of all countries in the region, but it has been reduced and constrained by various Latin American governments to prevent it from leading to a right of veto of extractive projects. That is, beyond their political and ideological orientation, governments favor a weaker version of the right of inquiry, contrary to the strong guarantor proposed by the Interamerican Court of Human Rights.

Another case of manipulation concerns semidirect democracy. In late 2014, citizens in Argentina gathered signatures and pushed for a bill of popular initiative to ban megamining in all its stages, which required 3 percent of the electoral roll. The provincial ruling party (then, Kirchner and her allies) took up that popular initiative to enact a law adopted in precisely the opposite direction to that which had been urged by citizens, that is, the ruling party ended up enacting a law that opened the way for megamining in the province. Finally, social and environmental struggles have been criminalized across the continent, from Mexico to Argentina. This criminalization is

visible in the hardening of criminal offenses (including the charge of terrorism, as in the emblematic case of Ecuador), imprisonment (Peru, Mexico, and
Nicaragua, among others), murder as a result of repression (the most dramatic case is Peru), or suspect mining deaths in border areas (as in the case
of Argentina, in areas of expansion of the soya frontier).

## Narratives of Development and Colliding Views

We find, among the principal narratives about development underlying the
Commodities Consensus, the neoliberal (or orthodox) narrative, the neostructuralist narrative, and the socioenvironmental narrative. Development
was one of the cornerstones of Latin American thinking. For ECLAC, development was connected to economic structure and the international division
of labor. Therefore, Latin America had to reject the formulations of classical
economy that subjected the subcontinent to economic specialization by
country (the "comparative advantages" of primary export production) and
build up its own way to industrialization. Developmentalism was the result
of this innovative proposal, which generated intense theoretical debate
about the limits and the possibilities of industrialization in the capitalist
periphery.

In recent decades, however, the crisis of the idea of modernization and,
therefore, the criticism of the development-as-powerful-homogenizer narrative, gave new space to other political and philosophical perspectives. The
objections to the productivist view, which identifies development with economic growth, called for new elaborations, which began to consolidate in the
1990s. One of them, "sustainable development," was introduced into the international agenda following the publication of "Our Common Future," in
1987, and the Summit in Rio in 1992, where weak visions about sustainability triumphed.

In fact, there are two distinct versions of sustainable development: a
strong version, according to which growth is seen as a means not as an end,
thus emphasizing both a commitment to present and future generations and
also respect for the integrity of the natural systems that support life on the
planet (political ecology, ecological economics, and deep ecology, among
others); and a weak version, which does not challenge the classical idea of
development, and which views sustainability from the perspective of the
advancement and efficient use of technology. While social organizations

and environmental sectors hold by the strong version, the weak version is often expressed in the discourse of corporations and high-level government officials.

Accordingly, by the 1990s the view of development as a "grand narrative"—that is to say, as both an organizing framework and a promise of emancipation—had disappeared from the political and academic agenda in Latin America and elsewhere. But this eclipse of the development category was transitory, because today we are witnessing its forceful return to the agenda; although, of course, it has a different sense than it had before. In this new phase of asymmetric globalization, the idea of development appears linked to the extractivist paradigm, which previously had been strongly questioned by developmentalists, and has also incorporated some misleading notions of widespread repercussions, such as those of sustainable development (in its weak version), corporate social responsibility (CSR), and governance.

## The Orthodox or Neoliberal View

The Commodities Consensus updated the neoliberalists' basic guidelines. In this framework, the central concepts of the neoliberal narrative are: First, the vision of a state that is subordinated to the market and mainly to the present supranational instances of regulation (that is to say, a "metaregulating state"). Second, natural common goods are seen as commodities, that is, primary products or products of low added value, the price of which is determined by market forces. Third, the idea of CSR (or corporate social responsibility) is central to the neoliberal narrative, promoted by large corporations and nation-states. CSR is based on two principles: on the one hand, that corporations are the quintessential actors of globalized economies; and on the other hand, that they must confront conflicts with local populations relating to the social, economic, and environmental impact and risks generated by their economic activities. CSR comes together with the concept of governance, as a micropolitical conflict resolution device of a multiactor nature. Moreover, CSR is combined with other actors who are involved—specialists, journalists, and symbolic mediators, among others—to contribute to the process of sociodiscursive production with the purpose of gaining community acceptance and social license. Finally, the neoliberal narrative favors a weak view of sustainable development much criticized by various social organizations

(Saguier 2014). Such a "weak" view implies obliterating the very idea of sustainability by promoting an efficiency-oriented outlook that confirms the notion of nature as capital (now linked to overexploitation and to the expansion of the boundaries of exploitation) while leaning on a "clean" solution to each "problem," supposedly provided by new technologies (Martínez Alier 2002). For example, in 2012, the paradigm of the Green Economy presented in the Rio +20 Summit has been embraced.

## The Neostructuralist Vision

The neostructuralist perspective is based on recognizing that accumulation is sustained by increasing exports of commodities or primary products. In 2010, Bresser Pereira of Brazil wrote about neodevelopmentalism, noting that "in the era of globalization, growth led by exports is the only sensible strategy available to developing countries" (Feliz 2011, 158). As we have pointed out, this is the position held by ECLAC and officially presented within Unasur (June 2013). Neostructuralism thus appears as the conceptual basis of progressive governments with respect to their conception of development. This emphasizes the privileged conditions that Latin America offers in the present phase in terms of "natural capital," or strategic natural resources, demanded by the international market, especially by Asia.

Overall, neostructuralism conceives of natural goods in such a way that creates an area of ambiguity between the notions of commodities and of strategic natural resources. Although development policy is oriented toward growing exports and partnerships with large transnational corporations, it also aims for greater state control over extractive revenue, especially revenue from hydrocarbons and energy.

In spite of the increasingly "reprimarizing" scene, it has been proposed as a policy to industrialize natural resources, which some believe could be carried out through a strategic relationship with China (Bruckmann 2012). Some authors believe that in the early twenty-first century it is no longer possible to talk about the deterioration of trade terms (as Prebisch, from ECLAC, did some decades ago when he criticized the productive structure of Latin American countries and pointed at the asymmetrical commercial exchange relations with developed countries). Today there are several advocates of the extractive model that bypasses traditional criticism realized in other times by ECLAC deterioration of trade terms. Others argue that the export of primary products is what enables countries to generate foreign exchange that they can redistribute and grow based on an internal market strategy or redirect toward activities with higher value-added content.

Like neoliberalism, the neostructuralist vision is based on the principle of "weak sustainability" and the notion of CSR. There is little or no interest in establishing a diagnosis of environmental crisis, even if mention is made of the need for models of governance that allow an improvement in "the public management of socioenvironmental conflicts that arise in the development of natural resources sectors" (NU, CEPAL 2013, 8).

To sum up, liberal neodevelopmentalism and progressive neodevelopmentalism have some topics and frameworks in common as regards the conception of development, even if they also show clear differences in relation to the role of the state and the areas of democratization.

## The Critical Perspective on Extraction

There are numerous critical views throughout Latin America nowadays regarding current development models. For example, a comprehensive environmental perspective emphasizes the Buen Vivir; an indigenist perspective is oriented to the community; an eco-feminist perspective emphasizes the ethics of care and the criticism of patriarchy; and an ecoterritorial perspective is linked to social movements that have been developing a political grammar focused on the notions of environmental justice, Common Goods, territoriality, food sovereignty, and Buen Vivir.

One of the most innovative approaches is political ecology. There are various authors in the region, including Enrique Leff, for whom political ecology poses a question about the most recent mutation processes, not only regarding ecological distribution conflicts but also on relations between the life of people and the globalized world. As Leff argues, political ecology's fundamental contribution is not just epistemological, because it aims not only to distort "natural" conditions giving rise to "natural" disasters but also to green social relations (Leff 2014). In sum, for Leff, political ecology is a disputed territory in which they are building new cultural identities around the defense of nature, culturally re-signified through the struggles of resistance existing today, struggles that are defined against the developmentalist ideology and different forms of extractive activities. Finally, political ecology proposes a new environmental rationality centered on defending the

production and reproduction of life, challenging and exploring the sociological imagination of social sustainability, and confronting the knowledge
established through a change in beliefs and values after other ways of understanding the world and habitability (Leff 2014, 136).

The contributions of critical geographers, among which we highlight the
Brazilians Milton Santos, Carlos Porto Goncalves, and Bernardo Mancano
Fernandes, are inserted in a nearby line of thought, which appears compromised by the issue of space, territory, and social relations. As the latter said:
"We live with different types of territories, which are produced by different
social relations" (Mançano Fernandes 2008). This is done in a complex space,
in which logic and rationales of different assessment carriers intersect. The
expansion of the mining frontier, through large-scale metals mining, the
advance of hydrocarbons, and agribusiness in its various forms, among
others, can be thought of as a paradigmatic example that generates not only
a "tension of territoriality" (Porto Gonçalvez 2001) but also a vision of territoriality presented as excluded (or potentially available).

In line with these policy perspectives is critical sociology, which aims to
develop the concepts of intermediate range and is necessary for studying the
dynamics established between social structures and social subjects, that is,
between forms of accumulation of capital and changes in social subjectives,
changes in the role of the state, the characteristics and dynamics of the
political system, and sociodiscursive production from positions of power.
In this line of interpretation are inserted various critical contributions,
which include in their analysis the importance of territory and territoriality,
both in urban and rural movements, as the territory appears as a space of
resistance and also, increasingly, as a place of significance and in creating
new social relations. Thus Latin American social movements are understood
as socioterritorial movements. From this perspective, "the greening process
of social struggles" (Leff 2014) can be read in terms of rotation of the ecoterritorial struggles (Svampa 2012). Nor can we ignore that this analytical
approach to social movements must be linked to the prospect of autonomy,
referring to the demand for "self-determination," which in contemporary
parlance means central recognition of diversity and difference, but also the
possibility of building a realm of common distance between the market and
the state.

Finally, these views converge in a postdevelopmentalist perspective. This
line was opened by Arturo Escobar, who proposed an original line that
opens the door to other viewpoints and languages of valuation, to think

about possible transitions to postextractivism through an alternative epistemological framework to a ruling that investigates and brings together powerful concepts such as Buen Vivir and Rights of Nature with those of sustainability, environmental soundness, and environmental ethics (Gudynas 2010).

In short, political ecology, critical geography, sociology, and political perspective converge in the commitment to build a critical paradigm of hegemonic vision of development based on a different relationship between society and nature, between space and social relations, and between subjects and collective democracy. In my view, this multidisciplinary field under construction, which undoubtedly is built on confrontation with other key prospects (those who advocate both neoliberalism and progressive neodevelopmentalism), has great potential, for example, for articulated critical thinking, advocacy groups, and individual lives.

## Toward a New Phase: From the Commodities Consensus to the Beijing Consensus?

Latin America seems to be heading toward a new phase in which not only extraction and commodities exports but also relations with China have acquired an irrevocable status and are referred to as "comparative advantages." Certainly, with its 1.3 billion people, China has been increasing its share in the global consumption of many basic products, including numerous metals, soy, petroleum, and timber. Also, China has become the great factory of the world, and its commercial integration no longer depends on exporting low technology, but rather on advanced technology. In step with the growth of consumption, its increasingly technified industry is demanding more energy resources and basic inputs. For this reason, China has become the world's leading consumer of the vast majority of commodities, increasing prices.

Far from its self-definition as a developing country, China is today a major economic power with a fast-paced rise and a diversified global presence. In the emerging multipolar world, therefore, China is one of the strongest candidates to become a hegemon in the modern world system. According to the National Intelligence Council of the United States, by 2030 Asia will have surpassed North America and Europe combined in terms of overall power, based on GDP, population, military expenditure, and technological investment. China will have the largest economy, surpassing the United States a few years before 2030, which will imply a shift in hegemony. In recent years trade between Latin America and China has noticeably intensified, so much so that China is the main importer of goods from Brazil, Chile, and Peru; the second largest importer of goods from Uruguay, Venezuela, and Colombia; and the third largest from Argentina. It is also the largest exporter to Brazil and Paraguay and the second largest to Argentina, Bolivia, Chile, Colombia, Costa Rica, Ecuador, Honduras, Mexico, Peru, Panama, and Venezuela.

Some examples will help us illustrate Chinese capital in Latin America. In the hydrocarbons sector, for instance, the four big Chinese companies (Sinopec, National China Petroleum Corporation [CNPC], the China National Offshore Oil Company [CNOOC], and Sinochem) are present in the region. In Venezuela, CNPC operates jointly with Petroleos de Venezuela (PDVSA). I must also mention the joint exploitations of Sinopec with Repsol Brazil, and of Sinochem with Statoil Brazil (both of European origin), as well as the acquisition of 50 percent of the Bridas group (Argentina) by CNOOC. Bridas owns 40 percent of the shares of Pan American Energy and operates the largest oilfield in Argentina, Cerro Dragon, in the province of Chubut. Chinese capital is also present in Vaca Muerta for the exploitation of unconventional hydrocarbons (fracking)—although due to the drop in the international price of petroleum, specific projects have been delayed.

As regards mining and metals, mineral prices were most affected by China's demand. The main destination for mining investment has been Peru and, more recently, Ecuador. China is also present in the agriculture, fishing, and forestry sectors, especially in Peru. In 2015, Chinese capital has bought one of the largest multinational companies in grain production, Nidera, which has its headquarters in Argentina. In this country, a space station is being built in the province of Neuquén, ostensibly for "civilian purposes," but legislators approved the agreement without making public all the clauses they signed, which casts a cloud of suspicion about its potential military use.

In summary, investments from China in Latin America mainly fund extractive activities. In some cases, they are directed to the tertiary sector to support the former. In general, these are payments for acquiring or licensing the exploitation of natural resources. When infrastructure work is required, it is commissioned to Chinese companies run by Chinese nationals. The arrival of huge Chinese transnational corporations (TNCs) also poses a threat to the clusters of small and medium-sized enterprises (SMEs), either due to environmental contamination or to the possibility of directly exporting to China products that were previously transformed by local SMEs.

In conclusion, the investment that Latin America receives from China tends not to develop local capacity or intensive activities in terms of knowledge or productive chains. The location of Chinese TNCs tends to enhance extractive activities at the expense of those with a higher added value, which generates a reprimarizing effect in Latin American economies. Despite the wistful expressions we can find in ECLAC documents or in pronouncements by some left-wing analysts (such as Monica Bruckmann), we are far from attaining South–South cooperation. Rather, we are witnessing the emergence of new, fast-paced, asymmetrical relations between Latin America and China. To this, we must add that according to various analysts, we are coming to the end of the "commodities super cycle" (Canutto 2014), which some link especially to slowing growth in China. Few Latin American governments are prepared for the fall in commodity prices or for the consequences, and tend to fall into a trade deficit (Martínez Alier 2015). In other words, Latin American countries export much to China, but this fails to cover the cost of imports from China, leading not only to more debt but also to an exacerbation from extraction, that is, to an upward trend in exports of primary products in order to cover trade deficits, which would enter into a sort of downward spiral (multiplication of extractive projects, increased environmental conflicts, population displacements, and so forth).

## Conclusions

Both in political-ideological and in social terms, the Commodities Consensus (2003–14) has to be read as a process, and within the reference frame of a recursive dynamic. Thus extractivism is inserted into Latin America in the context of a change of time that indicates the passage to a political-economic scenario where the main features are the consolidation of the Commodities Consensus based on the large-scale export of primary goods; the updating of the national-popular matrix expressed by progressive governments; and the emergence of a new dependency on China.

The expansion of the boundary of rights (collective, territorial, environmental) encountered a limit in the growing expansion of the frontiers of capital exploitation in search for goods, lands, and territories, and knocked down those narratives of emancipation that had raised high expectations, particularly in Bolivia and Ecuador. This collision between narratives about development was expressed in the outburst of environmental conflicts, several of which had high visibility in the public-political sphere (emblematic conflicts) and forced governments to "clear up" the extractive discourse strongly condemned by territorial and socioenvironmental mobilizations.

The stigmatization and criminalization of environmental protest endangered democratization and respect for human rights. In turn, as a response to objections raised by social movements against the extractive matrix, progressive governments sought to regain the initiative in the discussion about development through the Unasur.

Finally, the emergence of a new dependency, with guidelines—in terms of juridical and economic order—and conditions of subordination (and development) that will probably be defined in the next few years, lends plausibility to the hypothesis of a transition from the Commodities Consensus to the Beijing Consensus (Slipak 2014; Svampa and Slipak 2015), which will entail new political, social, environmental, and cultural consequences.

## References

Acosta, Alberto. 2009. *La maldición de la abundancia*. Quito: Abya Yala.

———. 2010. "El Buen Vivir en el camino del post-desarrollo. Una lectura desde la Constitución de Montecristi." Edited by Friedrich Ebert Stiftung. *Policy Paper* N° 9. http://library.fes.de/pdf-files/bueros/quito/07671.pdf.

Antonelli, Mirta. 2014. "Megaminería transnacional e invención del mundo cantera." *Nueva Sociedad* 252:72–86. www.nuso.org/upload/articulos/4042_1.pdf.

Bruckmann, Monica. 2012. "Recursos naturales y la geopolítica de la integración sudamericana." Presentación Theotonio dos Santos. Lima: Instituto Perumundo; J. C. Mariátegui.

Canutto, Otaviano. 2014. "The Commodity Super Cycle: Is This Time Different?" World Bank. *Ecomomic Premise*, no. 150, June.

Colectivo Voces de Alerta. 2011. *15 mitos y realidades sobre la minería transnacional en Argentina*. Buenos Aires: El Colectivo-Herramienta.

Feliz, Mariano. 2011. "Neoliberalismos, neodesarrollismos y proyectos contrahegemónicos en suramérica." *Astrolabio: Nueva Epoca* 7. http://www.trabajosocial .unlp.edu.ar/uploads/docs/neoliberalismos__neodesarrollismos_y_proyectos _contrahegemonicos_en_suramerica_.pdf.

———. 2012. "Proyecto sin clase: Crítica al neoestructuralismo como fundamento del neodesarrollismo." In *Más allá del individuo: Clases sociales, transformaciones económicas y políticas estatales en la Argentina contemporánea*, edited by Mariano Feliz, 13–44. Buenos Aires: El Colectivo.

Gudynas, Eduardo. 2010. "The New Extractivism of the 21st Century: Ten Urgent Theses About Extractivism in Relation to Current South American Progressivism." *Americas Program Report.* Washington, D.C.: Center for International Policy.

Harvey, David. 2004. "The 'New' Imperialism: Accumulation by Dispossession." *Socialist Register* 40:63–87. Socialistregister.com/index.php/srv/article/view/5811# .U17RffldU2s.

Leff, Enrique. 2014. *La apuesta por la vida: Imaginaciòn sociológica e imaginarios sociales en los territorios ambientales del sur.* Mexico: Vozes.

Machado Aráoz, Horacio. 2012. "Naturaleza mineral: Una ecología política del colonialismo moderno" PhD dissertation, National University of Catamarca, Argentina.

———. 2014. *Potosí, el origen: Genealogía de la minería contemporánea.* Buenos Aires: Mardulce.

Mançano Fernandes, Bernardo. 2008. "Sobre la tipología de los territories," http://web .ua.es/es/giecryal/documentos/documentos839/docs/bernardo-tipologia-de -territorios-espanol.pdf.

Martínez Alier, Joan. 2002. *The Environmentalism of the Poor: A Study of Ecological Conflicts and Valuation.* Northampton, Mass.: Edward Elgar.

———. 2015. "Sudamérica: El triunfo del post-extractivismo en el 2015." *La Jornada*, February 21. www.jornada.unam.mx/2015/02/21/opinion/022a1mun.

NU, CEPAL. 2013. *Recursos naturales en Unasur: Situación y tendencias para una agenda de desarrollo regional.* Santiago: CEPAL. www.cepal.org/publicaciones /xml/3/49893/RecursosNaturalesUNASUR.pdf.

Observatorio de conflictos Cajamarca. 2015. *Conflicto minero Conga.* Grufides. http:// www.grufides.org/sites/default/files/Documentos/fichas_casos/CONFLICTO%20 MINERO%20CONGA.pdf.

Permanent Working Group on Alternatives to Development. 2013. "Alternativas al capitalismo/colonialismo del siglo XXI." Quito: Rosa Luxemburg Foundation. www.rosalux.org.ec/attachments/article/727/Alternativas%20al%20capitalis- moimprenta.pdf.

Porto Gonçalvez, Carlos. 2001. *Geografías, movimientos sociales: Nuevas territoriali- dades y sustentabilidad.* Mexico: Siglo XXI.

Rodriguez, José Luis. 2014. "Coyuntura económica y social de América Latina y el Caribe," Cubadebate, February 2. http://www.cubadebate.cu/opinion/2014/02/02 /coyuntura-economica-y-social-de-america-latina-y-el-caribe/#.WMlZj9I1_IU.

Saguier, Marcelo. 2014. "Minería para el desarrollo integral en la estrategia de Unasur: A Unasur strategy for mining and development." *Conjuntura Austral* 5 (21–22): 2178–8839.

Santos, Boaventura de Sousa. 2007. *La reinvención del estado y el estado plurinacional.* Cochabamba: Centro de Comunicación y Desarrollo Andino.

Slipak, Ariel. 2012. "Las relaciones entre China y América Latina en la discusión sobre el modelo de desarrollo de la región: Hacia economías reprimarizadas." *Iberoamérica Global* 5 (1).

———. 2014. "América Latina y China: ¿Cooperación sur-sur o 'Consenso de Beijing'?" *Nueva Sociedad* 250:102–113. www.nuso.org/upload/articulos/4019_1.pdf.

Svampa, Maristella. 2011. "Modelo de desarrollo y cuestión ambiental en América Latina: Categorías y escenarios en disputa." In *El desarrollo en cuestión: Reflexiones desde América Latina*, edited by F. Wanderley. La Paz: Plural.

———. 2012. "Pensar el desarrollo desde América Latina." In *Renunciar al bien común: Extractivismo y (pos)desarrollo en América Latina*, edited by G. Massuh. Buenos Aires: Mardulce.

———. 2013a. " 'Consenso de los *Commodities*' y lenguajes de valoración en América Latina." *Nueva Sociedad* 244:30–46. www.nuso.org/upload/articulos/3926_1.pdf.

———. 2013b. "Commons Beyond Development: The Strategic Value of the Commons as a Paradigm Shift." Summary of keynote presentation given at the Economics and the Common(s) Conference, "From Seed Form to Core Paradigm," Berlin, Germany, May 22–24.

Svampa, Maristella, and Ariel Slipak. 2015. "China en América Latina: Del Consenso de los Commodities al Consenso de Beijing." *Ensambles* 3:34–63.

Svampa, Maristella, and Enrique Viale. 2014a. *Maldesarrollo: La Argentina del extractivismo y el despojo*. Buenos Aires: Katz.

———. 2014b. "Commodities Consensus: Neoextractivism and Enclosureof the Commons in Latin America." *South Atlantic Quarterly* 114 (1): 65–82.

UNCTAD. n.d. "Statistics." http://unctad.org/en/Pages/Statistics.aspx.

World Bank. n.d. "Data Catalog." http://datacatalog.worldbank.org/.

Zavaletta Mercado, René. 2009. *Lo nacional-popular en Bolivia*. La Paz: Plural.

# CHAPTER 2

# Fiscal Policy, Income Redistribution, and Poverty Reduction in Argentina, Bolivia, Brazil, Mexico, Peru, and Uruguay: An Overview

Nora Lustig and Claudiney Pereira

## Introduction

Although inequality in Latin America has been falling since 2000, Latin America is still the most unequal region in the world, and poverty rates are high for Latin America's GDP per capita (Lustig, López-Calva, and Ortiz-Juarez 2013). Given these facts, the extent to which governments use fiscal policy to reduce inequality and poverty is of great relevance. This chapter summarizes the results of applying a standard benefit-tax incidence analysis to estimate the effect of taxes and social spending on inequality and poverty in six Latin American countries: Argentina (Pessino and Lustig 2014), Bolivia (Paz Arauco et al. 2014), Brazil (Higgins and Pereira 2014), Mexico (Scott 2014), Peru (Jaramillo 2014), and Uruguay (Bucheli et al. 2014). Depending on the country, the household surveys utilized in the incidence analysis are for 2009 or 2010. It should be noted that the study for Argentina does not include the impact of taxes.

The main contribution of this article is twofold. First, in contrast to other work, the analysis is comprehensive: it includes the effect of direct taxes, indirect taxes and subsidies, and social spending (that is, cash transfers and the monetized value of public spending on education and health). Second, the six studies apply a common methodology (Lustig and Higgins 2012), so results are comparable across countries. As is common in most benefit-tax incidence analyses, the studies do not incorporate behavioral, lifecycle, or general equilibrium effects. These limitations notwithstanding, they are among the most detailed, comprehensive, and comparable tax-benefit incidence analyses available for Latin American countries to date. In addition, compared to some of the existing publications, reliance on secondary sources is kept to a minimum.

How much redistribution and poverty reduction is being accomplished through fiscal policy in Latin America? Argentina, Brazil, and Uruguay reduce inequality and poverty by nontrivial amounts and Bolivia has the lowest reduction in the Gini coefficient. Net indirect taxes are equalizing only in Mexico and Peru. Public spending on education and health has higher equalizing effects than net direct transfers and net indirect taxes combined. While net direct transfers lower poverty in all six countries, adding the effect of net indirect taxes leaves poverty higher than market income poverty in Bolivia and Brazil.

## Concepts, Definitions, and Data

### Market, Net Market, Disposable, Post-fiscal, and Final Income: Definitions and Measurement

We use five income concepts in our incidence analyses: market, net market, disposable, post-fiscal, and final income (Lustig and Higgins 2012). Market income is total current income before direct taxes, equal to the sum of gross (pre-tax) wages and salaries in the formal and informal sectors (also known as earned income); income from capital (dividends, interest, profits, rents, and so forth) in the formal and informal sectors (excluding capital gains and gifts); autoconsumption (except in the case of Bolivia); imputed rent for owner-occupied housing; private transfers (remittances and other private transfers such as alimony); and old-age and other pensions from the contributory social security system. Net market income equals market income minus direct personal income taxes on all income sources (included in market income) that are subject to taxation and all

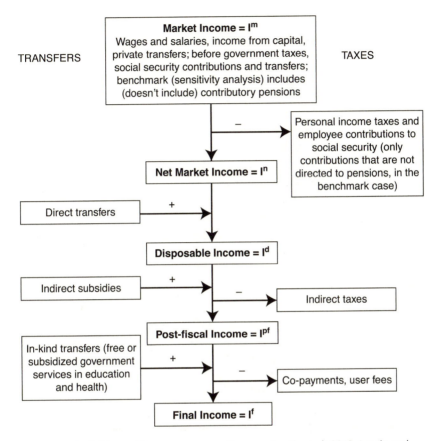

Figure 2.1. Definitions of income concepts. Sources: Lustig et al. 2013; Lustig and Higgins 2012. In some cases we also present results for "final income,*" which is defined as disposable income plus in-kind transfers minus co-payments and user fees.

contributions to social security except for the portion going toward pensions. Disposable income is equal to the sum of net market income plus direct government transfers (mainly cash transfers but can include food transfers). Post-fiscal income is defined as disposable income plus indirect subsidies minus indirect taxes (for example, value-added tax, sales tax, and so forth). Final income is defined as post-fiscal income plus government in-kind transfers in the form of free or subsidized services in education, health, and housing minus co-payments or user fees. The definitions are summarized in Figure 2.1. For a detailed description of how each income concept was constructed in the six countries see the Statistical Appendix, available on request.

## Tax Shifting Assumptions

Consistent with other conventional tax incidence analyses, here we assume that the economic burden of direct personal income taxes is borne by the recipient of income. The burden of payroll and social security taxes is assumed to fall entirely on workers. Consumption taxes are assumed to be shifted forward to consumers. These assumptions are strong because, in essence, they imply that labor supply is perfectly inelastic and consumers have perfectly inelastic demands for goods and services. In practice they provide a reasonable approximation.

## Incidence of Public Services

The approach to estimate the incidence of public spending on education and health followed here is the so-called "benefit or expenditure incidence" or "government cost" approach. In essence, we use per beneficiary input costs obtained from administrative data as the measure of average benefits. This approach—also known as the "classic" or "nonbehavioral approach"— amounts to asking the following question: How much would the income of a household have to be increased if it had to pay for the free or subsidized public service at full cost?

## Allocating Taxes and Transfers at the Household Level

Information on direct and indirect taxes, transfers in cash and in kind, and subsidies cannot always be obtained directly from household surveys. When it can be obtained, we call this the direct identification method. When the direct identification method is not feasible, one can use the inference, simulation, or imputation methods, or an alternate source. As a last resort, one can use secondary sources. The methods one can use to allocate taxes and transfers are described in detail in Lustig and Higgins (2012).

The most frequent method was direct identification, especially for cash transfers. Direct personal income taxes and indirect consumption taxes were simulated (including assumptions for evasion) in all cases except for direct taxes in Brazil. In-kind transfers were imputed using the government cost approach.

## Main Results

Table 2.1 presents taxes and spending as a share of GDP and identifies which taxes and transfer programs were included in the incidence analysis. As noted by Lustig et al. (2013), one cannot really speak of a "Latin American" prototype. As one can see, the six countries are quite heterogeneous in terms of government size as well as spending and revenue-collection patterns. Government spending as a share of GDP in Argentina and Brazil, for example, is similar to that found in OECD countries, while in Mexico and Peru the ratios are half as large. Thus in Argentina and Brazil—and to a lesser extent in Bolivia and Uruguay—the size of the government budget is not a constraint on redistributive and poverty-reducing interventions. In Mexico and Peru, raising enough revenue to increase social spending as a percentage of GDP would be a relevant option.

### Inequality

Of the six countries, and using the Gini coefficient as an indicator, Argentina, Brazil, and Uruguay achieve a higher reduction in income inequality through direct taxes and transfers (8.6 percent, 6 percent, and 7.3 percent income inequality reduction respectively). Mexico and Peru reduce inequality but to a lesser degree (4.5 percent and 2 percent respectively). In Bolivia, inequality remains essentially the same (see Table 2.2 and Figure 2.1). When compared with disposable income inequality, net (of indirect subsidies) indirect taxes are slightly unequalizing in Bolivia and Brazil but slightly equalizing in Mexico and Peru. Net indirect taxes temper the redistributive impact of the fiscal system in Bolivia, Brazil, and Uruguay but not in Mexico or Peru. When one adds the effect of transfers in kind (access to free or quasi-free services in education and health), inequality declines substantially in all

Table 2.1. Government Spending and Revenue by Category in Public Accounts (as a percent of GDP)

| Government spending and revenue (as % of GDP) | Argentina (2009) Total | Bolivia (2009) Total | Brazil (2009) Total | Mexico (2010) Total | Peru (2009)[l] Total | Uruguay (2009) Total |
|---|---|---|---|---|---|---|
| **Gross national income per capita (PPP in $US)** | **14,230** | **3,919** | **10,140** | **14,390** | **8,390** | **12,412** |
| **Total government spending[a]** | **43.2%** | **34.8%** | **51.2%** | **25.7%** | **25.5%** | **30.8%** |
| **Primary government spending[b]** | **40.6%** | **33.3%** | **41.4%** | **23.7%** | **24.2%** | **27.9%** |
| **Social spending[c]** | **20.6%** | **14.7%** | **16.2%** | **10.0%** | **8.4%** | **13.0%** |
| **Total cash transfers** | **3.7%** | **2.0%** | **4.2%** | **1.0%** | **0.4%** | **2.3%** |
| Cash transfers (excluding all pensions) | 0.8% | 0.7% | 3.7% | 0.8% | 0.4% | 1.7% |
| Noncontributory pensions[d] | 2.9% | 1.4% | 0.5% | 0.2% | 0.0% | 0.5% |
| **Total in-kind transfers[e]** | **12.9%** | **11.9%** | **10.5%** | **7.7%** | **5.9%** | **8.4%** |
| Education | 6.7% | 8.3% | 5.3% | 4.5% | 2.8% | 3.7% |
| Tertiary | 1.3% | 3.7% | 0.8% | 0.8% | 0.6% | 0.8% |
| Health | 6.2% | 3.6% | 5.2% | 3.1% | 3.1% | 4.7% |
| Contributory[f] | 3.6% | 1.7% | 0.0% | 1.7% | 1.2% | 2.3% |
| Noncontributory | 2.6% | 1.9% | 5.2% | 1.3% | 1.9% | 2.4% |
| **Other social spending[g]** | **4.0%** | **0.8%** | **1.5%** | **1.3%** | **2.1%** | **2.3%** |
| **Non-Social spending[g]** | **12.8%** | **15.0%** | **16.1%** | **11.1%** | **14.9%** | **6.3%** |
| Indirect subsidies | 5.6% | 0.6% | 0.1% | 1.4% | na[m] | 0.0% |
| Other non-social spending[h] | 7.2% | 14.4% | 16.0% | 9.7% | 14.9% | 6.3% |
| **Contributory pensions[i]** | **7.2%** | **3.5%** | **9.1%** | **2.6%** | **0.9%** | **8.7%** |
| **Debt servicing** | **2.6%** | **1.6%** | **9.8%** | **2.0%** | **1.3%** | **2.9%** |
| **Total revenue** | **41.0%** | **31.6%** | **44.0%** | **22.6%** | **24.0%** | **28.8%** |
| **Taxes[j]** | **31.4%** | **26.9%** | **34.4%** | **11.8%** | **16.0%** | **27.0%** |
| **Direct taxes** | **8.1%** | **5.7%** | **12.2%** | **5.2%** | **5.0%** | **4.7%** |
| Personal income tax | 1.7% | 0.2% | 2.1% | 2.3% | 1.5% | 4.7% |
| Corporate income tax | 3.0% | 4.5% | 3.9% | 2.9% | 2.9% | 0.0% |
| Other direct taxes | 3.4% | 1.0% | 6.2% | 0.0% | 0.6% | 0.0% |
| **VAT and other indirect taxes** | **12.8%** | **11.1%** | **15.2%** | **4.3%** | **7.6%** | **12.1%** |

| | | | | | | |
|---|---|---|---|---|---|---|
| **Other taxes** | 10.5% | 10.0% | 7.1% | 2.3% | 3.4% | 10.2% |
| of which social security contributions with pensions (in sensitivity analysis) | 6.7% | 0.0% | 7.1% | 2.3% | 1.9% | 5.6% |
| *Memo: Social Security Contributions without Pensions (benchmark scenario)*[k] | *na* | *0.0%* | *0.0%* | *1.6%* | *1.4%* | *0.0%* |
| **Non-tax revenues** | 9.6% | 4.7% | 9.6% | 10.8% | 8.0% | 1.7% |

Sources: Argentina: Lustig and Pessino (2014); Bolivia: Paz Arauco et al. (2014); Brazil: Higgins and Pereira (2014); Mexico: Scott (2014); Peru: Jaramillo (2014); and Uruguay: Bucheli et al. (2014). GNI per capita from the World Development Indicators: http://data.worldbank.org/indicator/NY.GNP.PCAP.KD.

Note: "-.-": not applicable because the study for Argentina does not include the incidence of taxes; "na": not available.

[a] Total government spending = Primary government spending+Debt services (interests and amortizations).

[b] Primary government spending = Social spending (w/o Contributory pensions)+Non-social spending (w/o Contributory pensions)+Contributory pensions.

[c] Social spending = Total cash transfers+Total in-kind transfers+Other social spending.

[d] For Brazil the figure for noncontributory pensions includes only the flagship noncontributory pension program, *Benefício de Prestação Continuada*, and no other noncontributory pensions programs, such as the Special Circumstances Pensions.

[e] Education spending in Bolivia and education and health spending in Peru in incidence analyses are net of administrative costs (but the totals from public accounts do include them), so shares are not comparable with the other countries; in Bolivia and Peru administrative costs were added to "Other social spending." The incidence analysis for Argentina includes only public spending on noncontributory health. In Brazil all public health is noncontributory. The incidence analyses for Bolivia, Mexico, Peru, and Uruguay include both contributory and noncontributory health. Except for Uruguay, spending on education and health includes both recurrent and capital expenditures; Uruguay includes recurrent expenditures only.

[f] Argentina does not include incidence analysis for public spending on contributory health systems or taxes.

[g] Non-social spending = Indirect subsidies+Other non-social spending. Note that the value under total for Mexico here differs from Scott (2014) because the value here excludes contributory pensions.

[h] Other non-social spending = Government administration+any additional non-social spending not already included. Note that the value under total for Mexico here differs from Scott (2014) because the value here excludes contributory pensions.

[i] "Contributory pensions" reported for Mexico correspond to federal government spending on contributory pensions. This value differs from total pension income reported in the household survey (4.0% of GDP, adjusted to National Accounts). In the sensitivity analysis of Scott (2014), Scott used 4.0%.

[j] Argentina does not include an analysis of taxes. In Bolivia, taxes in the benchmark include: value-added tax (VAT), specific consumption tax (ICE), hydrocarbons tax (IEHD), and transactions tax (IT). Other taxes (not in Incidence Analysis) include other taxes from which 6.7% of GDP corresponds to direct hydrocarbons tax (IDH), and 3% to hydrocarbons royalties and other taxes applied to enterprises and private entities. IDH is a direct tax applied to hydrocarbons production to be distributed to regions. IEHD is a transaction tax applied to individuals and enterprises. Unlike the other countries, the indirect taxes in Brazil are atypical since they consist of different taxes levied at different government levels, and they also vary by type of goods and services considered. Indirect taxes in Brazil include a state tax called ICMS, a federal tax, an industrialized products tax, and a cascading tax that is in the process of changing to a more typical VAT tax, the PIS/COFINS. Mexico includes VAT and other indirect taxes. Peru includes VAT and excise taxes on fuels. Uruguay includes VAT and other indirect taxes.

[k] In Argentina, the values are not available. In Peru, the incidence analysis for the benchmark scenario did not subtract the contributions to social security that were not for pensions (such as contributions for the contributory health system). In the other country studies that include the tax side in the analysis, the benchmark scenario does account for the social security contributions other than the contributions for pensions. In Uruguay, it is not possible to distinguish the portion that goes to pensions, so in the benchmark scenario no contributions were deducted to get net market income.

[l] The incidence analysis for Peru differs slightly from the incidence analysis column from Table 1 from Jaramillo in Scott (2014) because here the data on education and health spending does not include administrative costs, while it does so in Jaramillo. The incidence analysis for education and health spending in Jaramillo was carried out excluding administrative costs.

[m] Peru has a subsidy for gasoline and other oil derivatives; however, the actual numbers spent on this subsidy were not publicly available at the time of the analysis.

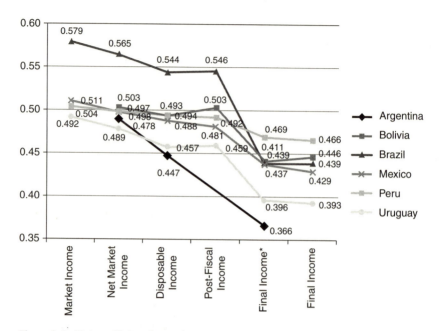

Figure 2.2. Gini coefficient for each income concept. Sources: Lustig et al. 2013. For Argentina, see Lustig and Pessino 2014; for Bolivia, see Paz Arauco et al. 2014; for Brazil, see Higgins and Pereira 2014; for Mexico, see Scott 2014; for Peru, see Jaramillo 2014; and for Uruguay, see Bucheli et al. 2014. For definition of income concepts, see Figure 2.1 and text. The analysis for Argentina does not include the tax side so Disposable Income Headcount is gross of direct personal income taxes. The results are thus not strictly comparable.

countries. But Peru stands out as the least redistributive (see last column of Table 2.2 and Figure 2.2).

## Poverty

The headcount ratio (with the international extreme poverty line of US$2.50/ day in purchasing power parity) is used to estimate the impact of taxes and transfers on poverty. In Table 2.2, one can observe that the combination of net direct taxes and direct transfers (cash and food transfers) lowers poverty the most in Argentina (57.5 percent), Brazil (26.1 percent), and Uruguay (71.5 percent) and the least in Peru (7.3 percent). However, when one adds

Table 2.2. Reduction in Inequality and Poverty

| | Change in Net Market Income wrt Market Income[a] | Change in Disposable Income wrt Market Income[a] | Change in Post-Fiscal Income wrt Market Income[a] | Change in Final Income wrt Market Income[a] | Change in Final Income wrt Market Income[a] |
|---|---|---|---|---|---|
| **Argentina (2009)[b]** | | | | | |
| Gini | -.- | −8.6% | -.- | −25.2% | -.- |
| **Headcount index** | | | | | |
| $2.50 PPP/day | -.- | −57.7% | -.- | -.- | -.- |
| **Bolivia (2009)[c]** | | | | | |
| Gini | -.- | −2.0% | −0.04% | −12.4% | −11.3% |
| **Headcount index** | | | | | |
| $2.50 PPP/day | -.- | −10.4% | 3.3% | -.- | -.- |
| **Brazil (2009)** | | | | | |
| Gini | −2.4% | −6.0% | −5.7% | −24.1% | −24.1% |
| **Headcount index** | | | | | |
| $2.50 PPP/day | 3.8% | −26.1% | 8.1% | -.- | -.- |
| **Mexico (2010)** | | | | | |
| Gini | −2.6% | −4.5% | −5.8% | −14.4% | −15.9% |
| **Headcount index** | | | | | |
| $2.50 PPP/day | 0.6% | −14.9% | −15.1% | -.- | -.- |
| **Peru (2009)** | | | | | |
| Gini | −1.1% | −2.0% | −2.4% | −6.9% | −7.6% |
| **Headcount index** | | | | | |
| $2.50 PPP/day | 0.0% | −7.3% | −4.4% | -.- | -.- |
| **Uruguay (2009)** | | | | | |
| Gini | −2.8% | −7.1% | −6.7% | −19.6% | −20.2% |
| **Headcount index** | | | | | |
| $2.50 PPP/day | 0.7% | −71.5% | −54.1% | -.- | -.- |

Sources: Lustig et al. 2013. Argentina: Lustig and Pessino (2014); Bolivia: Paz Arauco et al. (2014); Brazil: Higgins and Pereira (2014); Mexico: Scott (2014); Peru: Jaramillo (2014); and Uruguay: Bucheli et al. (2014).

Note: "-.-": not applicable.

[a] For definition of income concepts see Figure 2.1 and text.

[b] The analysis for Argentina does not include the tax side so Disposable Income Headcount is gross of direct personal income taxes. The results are thus not strictly comparable.

[c] Bolivia does not tax income, so percentage change is calculated with respect to net market income.

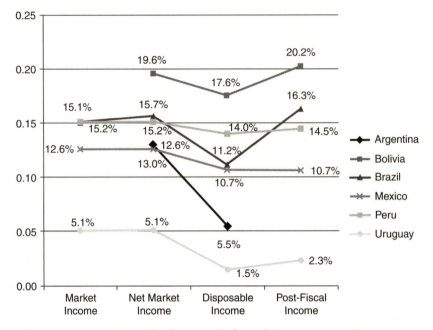

Figure 2.3. Extreme poverty headcount ratio for each income concept. Sources: Lustig et al. 2013. For Argentina, see Lustig and Pessino 2014; for Bolivia, see Paz Arauco et al. 2014; for Brazil, see Higgins and Pereira 2014; for Mexico, see Scott 2014; for Peru, see Jaramillo 2014; and for Uruguay, see Bucheli et al. 2014. For definition of income concepts, see Figure 2.1 and text. The analysis for Argentina does not include the tax side so Disposable Income Headcount is gross of direct personal income taxes. The results are thus not strictly comparable.

the effect of net indirect taxes, the headcount ratio in Brazil is higher than the market income headcount ratio (8.1 percent as compared to 3.8 percent of poverty headcount index). That is, overall, the Brazilian tax and transfers system (excluding public services) increases poverty. The same happens in Bolivia (see Figure 2.2). The country that lowers poverty the most after direct and indirect taxes, cash transfers, and indirect subsidies are taken into account is Uruguay.

A word of caution: The indicators of inequality and poverty have some comparability issues, for two main reasons. First, the assumptions to take into account indirect tax evasion differ across countries. Second, Peru and Uruguay did not include the impact of indirect subsidies in the incidence analysis. Also, as stated above, Argentina is not strictly comparable with the rest, because the study focuses only on the spending side.

## Conclusions

The comparative analysis of the redistributive effects of the fiscal system presented here reveals more variations than a common Latin American welfare state. First, the Latin American states represented here vary significantly in size: total government spending ranges from 25.5 to 51.2 percent of GDP (35 percent on average). Second, the countries vary in terms of the redistributive impact of their fiscal policy, and this variation is not always correlated with size. The six fiscal systems analyzed can be divided into two groups in terms of their total redistributive effect. The first (Argentina, Brazil, and Uruguay) achieves a reduction of final income inequality—that is, including the effect of in-kind transfers—between 20 and 25 percent (and a reduction of disposable income poverty between 26 and 72 percent), while a second group (Peru, Bolivia, and Mexico) reduces final income inequality by 7.6 to 16 percent (and disposable income poverty by 7 to 15 percent). The less redistributive states are so either because they spend significantly less (Mexico and Peru) or because their spending is not targeted to the poor (Bolivia).

There are differences within as well as between these groups. Perhaps the most interesting finding is that equity may matter more than size. Bolivia achieves only half the inequality reduction of Argentina despite spending 18 percent more on social transfers (analyzed) in relation to GDP (see Table 2.1). More dramatically, the net effect of all taxes and cash transfers is to increase poverty by 3 percent in Bolivia, while in Uruguay, with similar shares of cash transfers to GDP but significantly higher taxes, the net effect is to reduce poverty by 54 percent (see Table 2.2). However, this is also partly because Uruguay has a higher GDP per capita than Bolivia; hence, the absolute amounts devoted to cash transfers will be higher and divided among fewer people (given that both the population and poverty rates in Uruguay are lower than in Bolivia). At the same time, with similar levels of redistributive effectiveness, the difference in redistributive effect between Mexico and Brazil is explained mostly by the differences in social spending levels. In Peru, the inequality reduction achieved is less than a third that of Brazil. This is partly because it is slightly less effective. More importantly, it is because Peru's social spending is just over a third of Brazil's (analyzed) in relation to GDP.

The comparatively "rosy" redistributive picture of Argentina, Brazil, and Uruguay (by Latin American standards), however, hides some unpleasant facts. As discussed by Lustig and Pessino (2014), the problems with Argentina's redistributive policies are mainly the allocation of nonsocial subsidies and fiscal sustainability. Total government spending on indirect subsidies equaled 5.6 percent of GDP in 2009 (incidence analysis did not include indirect subsidies), compared to the 3.7 percent of GDP spent on progressive cash transfers in the same year. These are primarily subsidies to agricultural producers, airlines, manufacturing, transportation, and energy. The first three are outright regressive (unequalizing), and their budget equaled 1.3 percent of GDP in 2009 (compared to 0.6 percent allocated to the Universal Family Allowance). In addition, the sharp rise in Argentina's public spending during the 2000s has been increasingly financed by distortionary taxes and unorthodox revenue-raising mechanisms. Moreover, the export tax—a major source of revenue—is highly sensitive to commodity prices. All in all, this suggests that the Argentine government has embarked on a redistribution process that to some extent generates unfair losses (to the formal sector retirees) and may not be fiscally sustainable unless subsidies accruing to the nonsocial sectors are significantly curbed.

In the case of Brazil, the most disturbing fact is the significant negative effect of consumption taxes on the poor. Based on a study by Higgins and Pereira (2014), in Brazil 27 percent of the moderate poor are pushed into extreme poverty, and 4.5 percent of the extreme poor are pushed into ultra-poverty when comparing postfiscal income poverty rates with respect to market income poverty rates. Also, consumption taxes more than offset the poverty-reducing effect of direct cash transfers (Figure 2.2), and the moderately poor are net payers to the fiscal system (before imputing the value of in-kind transfers, that is).

The impact of fiscal policy on inequality and poverty can be summarized as follows. Direct taxes and cash transfers reduce inequality and poverty by nontrivial amounts in Argentina, Brazil, and Uruguay but less so in Bolivia, Mexico, and Peru. Although direct taxes are progressive, the redistributive impact is small because direct taxes as a share of GDP are generally low. Cash transfers are quite progressive in absolute terms, except in Bolivia where programs are not targeted to the poor. However, their poverty-reducing impact, as expected, is smaller in countries that spend less as a share of GDP on direct cash transfers targeted to the poor (Mexico and Peru). In Bolivia, Brazil, and Uruguay consumption taxes temper the redistributive impact of the fiscal system, and in Bolivia and Brazil, consumption taxes more than offset the poverty-reducing impact of cash transfers.

When one includes the in-kind transfers in education and health, valued at government costs, they reduce inequality in all countries by considerably more than cash transfers. This result is not surprising given the much larger share of public spending devoted to education and health compared to cash transfers. Care should be taken, however, not to read too much into the redistribution through transfers in kind, because the valuation using government costs may not reflect the actual valuation by the beneficiaries, and because the method used to monetize the transfers in kind does not take into account variations in quality. Furthermore, the progressiveness of the education and health systems could be due to an undesirable underlying phenomenon—that is, the middle class and the rich opting out of the public education and public health systems because of quality concerns.

To put the results for these six Latin American countries in perspective, the average reduction in the disposable income Gini coefficient for advanced OECD countries equals 12 percentage points, while the average for our six countries (which includes Argentina and Uruguay, possibly the most redistributive in the region) equals 3 percentage points. The average reduction in the final income Gini coefficient for OECD countries is 17 percentage points; for the six Latin American countries, it is 9 percentage points. Thus, in spite of the progress witnessed in terms of inequality and poverty reduction in the 2000s, Latin America still significantly lags behind OECD countries in redistribution achieved through taxation and social spending.

## References

Breceda, Karla, Jamele Rigolini, and Jaime Saavedra. 2008. "Latin America and the Social Contract: Patterns of Social Spending and Taxation." Policy Research Working Paper, May 2008. Washington, D.C.: World Bank.

Bucheli, Marisa, Nora Lustig, Máximo Rossi, and Florencia Amábile. 2014. "Social Spending, Taxes and Income Redistribution in Uruguay." In "The Redistributive Impact of Taxes and Social Spending in Latin America," edited by Nora Lustig, Carola Pessino, and John Scott, special issue, *Public Finance Review* 42 (3): 413–33.

Goñi, Edwin J., Humberto López, and Luis Servén. 2011. "Fiscal Redistribution and Income Inequality in Latin America." *World Development* 39 (9): 1558–69.

Higgins, Sean, and Claudiney Pereira. 2014. "The Effects of Brazil's Taxation and Social Spending on the Distribution of Household Income." In Lustig, Pessino, and Scott, "The Redistributive Impact of Taxes and Social Spending in Latin America," 346–67.

Immervoll, Herwig, Horacio Levy, José Ricardo Nogueira, Cathal O'Donoghue, and Rozane Bezerra de Siqueira. 2009. "The Impact of Brazil's Tax-Benefit System on Inequality and Poverty." In *Poverty, Inequality, and Policy in Latin America*, edited by Stephan Klasen and Felicitas Nowak-Lehmann, 271–301. Cambridge, Mass.: MIT Press.

Jaramillo, Miguel. 2014. "The Incidence of Social Spending and Taxes in Peru." In Lustig, Pessino, and Scott "The Redistributive Impact of Taxes and Social Spending in Latin America," 391–412.

Lindert, Kathy, Emmanuel Skoufias, and Joseph Shapiro. 2006. "Redistributing Income to the Poor and Rich: Public Transfers in Latin America and the Caribbean." Social Protection Discussion Paper. Washington, D.C.: World Bank.

Lustig, Nora, George Gray Molina, Sean Higgins, Wilson Jiménez et al. 2013. "The Impact of Taxes and Social Spending on Inequality and Poverty in Argentina, Bolivia, Brazil, Mexico and Peru: A Synthesis of Results." CEQ Working Paper No. 13. New Orleans, La.: Tulane University.

Lustig, Nora and Sean Higgins. 2012. "Commitment to Equity Assessment (CEQ): Estimating the Incidence of Social Spending, Subsidies and Taxes Handbook." Tulane Economics Working Paper Series No. 1219, October 2012. New Orleans, La.: Tulane University.

Lustig, Nora, Luis F. Lopez-Calva, and Eduardo Ortiz-Juarez. 2013. "Declining Inequality in Latin America in the 2000s: The Cases of Argentina, Brazil, and Mexico." *World Development* 44:129–41.

Paz Arauco, Verónica, George Gray Molina, Wilson Jiménez Pozo, and Ernesto Yáñez Aguilar. 2014. "Explaining Low Redistributive Impact in Bolivia." In Lustig, Pessino, and Scott "The Redistributive Impact of Taxes and Social Spending in Latin America," 326–45.

Pession, Carola, and Nora Lustig. "Social Spending and Income Redistribution in Argentina During the 2000s: The Increasing Role of Noncontributory Pensions." In Lustig, Pessino, and Scott "The Redistributive Impact of Taxes and Social Spending in Latin America," 304–25.

Silveira, Fernando Gaiger, Jonathan Ferreira, Joana Mostafa, and José Aparecido Carlos Ribeiro. 2011. "Qual o impacto da tributação e dos gastos públicos sociais na distribuição de renda do Brasil? Observando os dois lados da moeda." In *Progressividade da Tributação e Desoneração da Folha de Pagamentos Elementos para Reflexão*, edited by José Aparecido Carlos Ribeiro, Álvaro Luchiezi Jr, and Sérgio Eduardo Arbulu Mendonça, 25–63. Brasilia: IPEA.

Scott, John. 2014. "Redistributive Impact and Efficiency of Mexico's Fiscal System." In Lustig, Pessino, and Scott "The Redistributive Impact of Taxes and Social Spending in Latin America," 368–90.

CHAPTER 3

# Social Investment in Latin America

Evelyne Huber and John D. Stephens

## Introduction

Social investment has come to mean many things to many people. It is central in the debate about predistribution versus redistribution. Critics of the traditional welfare state have argued that it relies too heavily on redistribution of income through the tax and transfer system. They suggest that instead of providing cash transfers—such as unemployment compensation, family allowances, social assistance, and more—welfare state policy should aim to improve the pretax and transfer distribution of income by raising the labor force's employment levels and skills. Raising the labor force's skill levels requires social investment, most prominently in education and training—from preschool education to lifelong learning, and retraining. Raising employment levels also involves integrating women into the labor market, thus requiring investment in social services that support women in combining work and family.

The main argument we want to develop in this chapter is that predistribution and redistribution need to be treated as complementary approaches not as alternatives. Social investment targeted at all sectors of society reduces market inequality but to be highly effective needs to be accompanied by redistributive measures that reduce poverty and inequality in disposable income. Or, investing effectively in the next generation requires improving the living conditions of the present generation. We want to argue, further, that effective social investment is crucial not just for human welfare but also for economic growth in the new international economy.

We think these arguments are important both from a theoretical and a practical point of view. Theoretically, they allow us to build connections between well-established micro-level relationships that link socioeconomic background to school achievement, and macro-level relationships that link aggregate poverty and inequality to cognitive skills in the population. Practically, the arguments hold lessons for the debate about conditional cash transfer programs. They contradict the notion that cash transfers are a waste of money, if governments want to build the human capital of the next generation, but they also underline how important schools are, in that they are where human capital is developed. These arguments are particularly important in Latin America because both approaches have been neglected, and because a slowing of economic growth might arrest the past twenty years' progress. Specifically, cash transfers to the poor might be vulnerable unless policymakers know that such transfers are integral to investing effectively in human capital and to supporting economic growth in the long run.

There is reciprocal causality between the level and distribution of human capital, measured by cognitive skills, and poverty and inequality. In fact, we explore this two-way causality by examining not only how poverty and inequality impact cognitive skills but also how investment in human capital impacts poverty and inequality. However, by using time lags and by demonstrating how current poverty and inequality levels are connected with the skills of secondary school students, who cannot yet be held responsible for their families' incomes, we can cut into the causal chain analytically.

## Different Conceptions of Social Investment

### The Conception of Social Investment as an Alternative to Redistribution

Some advocates of the "Third Way" exemplified by New Labour in Britain have framed social investment as an alternative to traditional redistributive social policy (for example, Giddens 1998; for a critical discussion see Waring et al. 2001). They see social investment as a path to equality of opportunity, which is preferable to misguided efforts to bring about equality of condition. In their view, traditional redistributive social policy (unemployment compensation, sickness pay, invalidity pensions, social assistance, and so forth) discourages recipients from working and is economically and politically unsustainable. Not only is it an unproductive expenditure, it heavily burdens the budget and lacks political support because hardworking citizens are unwilling to subsidize inactivity. Investing in human capital (for education and training), in contrast, is supposed to help people help themselves and to appeal to notions of fairness. And because better human capital increases productivity, these policies are supposed to pay for themselves. Therefore, they are both economically and politically sustainable.

Jenson (2010) shows that the diffusion of the social investment perspective in Europe and Latin America was a reaction not only against the failures of neoliberalism but also against the perceived failures of the traditional post-World War II welfare state, which emphasized protecting people from social risks that could lead to poverty. "Social policies must be pro-active, stressing investment in people's capabilities and the realization of their potential, not merely insuring against misfortune" (Jenson 2010, 63). Jenson also characterizes the Giddens (1998) and New Labour version of social investment as more supply-side oriented and more limited in interventions than the more comprehensive conceptions promoted by Esping-Andersen and colleagues (Esping-Andersen et al. 2002; Jenson 2010, 73). What this supply-side conception overlooks is whether investment in human capital can, by itself, produce the desired effects.

## The Comprehensive Conception of Social Investment

The comprehensive conception of social investment sees investment in education and training as an essential component of a more encompassing set of policies, including free or subsidized health care and child care, and cash transfers to keep people out of poverty (Esping-Andersen 2002). It is based on social scientific evidence that "has found a pervasive tendency for children born in socially disadvantaged families to have poorer health, education, and general welfare" (Fergusson, Horwood, and Boden 2008). Researchers have also found socioemotional factors that account for the achievement gap of disadvantaged students, such as academic and school attachment, teacher support, peer values, and mental health (Becker and Luthar 2002). Socialization tends to continue to work against educational success, both through inadequate support for learning and peer pressure to reject compliance with expectations and self-discipline. Family-based factors have been found to be the most powerful in predicting achievement and delinquency, followed closely by influence from "best friends" (Duncan, Boisjoly, and Harris 2001). However, school and neighborhood composition matter as well; Van Ewijk and Sleegers performed a meta-regression analysis of thirty studies that found varying degrees of impact of peers' socioeconomic status on students' test scores (2010).

Pressure on students from their peers to not conform with a school's expectations is particularly intense when their prospects for entering the labor market and acquiring a decent career are low. High socioeconomic inequality, high youth unemployment, and large informal sectors lower such expectations, fostering youth subcultures that devalue education. Lacking a decent education bars students from accessing a decent job, reproducing poverty. Child labor is a response to the poverty of families and significantly depresses educational achievement (for example, Psacharopoulos 1997 for Bolivia and Venezuela), helping reproduce poverty across the generations.

These micro-level relationships manifest themselves at the macro level in relationships between levels of poverty and inequality and the level and distribution of cognitive skills. The nature of the school system, tracked versus comprehensive and overwhelmingly public versus strong private participation, can reduce or reinforce the impact of class inequality on educational inequality. Cross-national differences in inequalities in educational achievement have been explained by the level of inequality in a society, the level of modernization of a society, and school systems (Marks 2005). Where school systems are tracked, social selection is biased toward privileged groups and perpetuates or increases class inequality. The same argument can be made about school systems that rely heavily on private schooling.

We adopt the comprehensive conception of social investment and demonstrate that differences in the levels of public investment in education by Latin American countries are related to differences in average years of education and average skill levels, but imperfectly so. Societal poverty and inequality both influence how effective investment in education is. This means that in practice both types of intervention—reducing poverty and inequality, and expanding and improving education—must be made if either of them is to be economically and politically sustainable.

### Evidence from Latin America

We begin by demonstrating that levels of inequality and poverty in a society strongly impact how its population's cognitive skills develop. We do so by analyzing the determinants of average levels of cognitive skills, both over the long run and in the shorter run. Since data on cognitive skills are scarce and only available in a cross-section for the 1990s, we supplement this analysis with an examination of the role of determinants of education completion, measured as average years of education in the adult population, for which we have a longer time series. Here we note the imperfect relationship between public education expenditure and average years of schooling, and between both of these variables and cognitive skills. The effects of educational expenditures and of years of schooling are mediated by other factors, prominent among them levels of poverty and inequality in a society.

Then we analyze how social investment impacts inequality and poverty, controlling for other factors that have been shown to be predictors of these dependent variables. After presenting our own analysis, we discuss analyses done by López-Calva and Lustig (2010) on microdata, which show that increasing investment in education during the 1990s was associated with a declining skill premium and declining inequality during the 2000s. We finally show that cognitive skills have a stronger impact on economic growth than capital investment.

## Data

Our data all come from the Social Policy in Latin America and the Caribbean Dataset, 1960–2006, and updates of that dataset. The measurements and original sources of the data are documented there. Given how important data on education are, it is worth commenting on them. Since the advent of new growth theory, with its emphasis on human capital, the measures of formal education in the Barro-Lee Educational Attainment Dataset, 1950–2010 (Barro and Lee 2013), have been used as measures of human capital in most quantitative studies of economic growth. The Barro-Lee dataset contains measures of education completion at seven levels (no schooling, some primary, completed primary, some secondary, completed secondary, some tertiary, completed tertiary) and an estimate of average years of education based on the completion data of the population ages 15 years and older, and the population ages 25 years and older, for 140 countries at five-year intervals from 1960 to 2010.

The Barro-Lee dataset measures the stock of human capital in the adult population and thus is conceptually superior for studies of economic growth or income distribution to measures of flows of students through the educational system, such as primary or secondary school enrollment rates. Enrollment rates tell us only what proportion of relevant age cohorts are in school; they do not tell us what the skill levels of the working-age population are. The relationship between average level of education and its distribution needs clarification. One could argue that if one raises the level of education of the privileged only, average years of education will rise yet inequality will also rise. Conceptually this is a valid argument but empirically it is not a problem, because educational inequality and average years of education are very highly negatively correlated. Thomas, Wang, and Fan (2001) calculate educational Ginis for the 140 countries in the Barro-Lee dataset and find that average years of education explains 91 percent of the variation in educational inequality. Thus we treat average years of education as an indicator for educational completion among all sectors of the population.

The best comparable data on skills in the adult population come from the International Adult Literacy Survey (IALS) (OECD 2000). The same tests for literacy and numeracy skills were administered to samples of the adult population in twenty-four countries. Thus the IALS has produced the best measures of the stock and distribution of human capital in the working-age population, but it unfortunately includes only one Latin American country—Chile. Hanushek and Woessmann (2009) collected and standardized a large number of tests administered to secondary school students in Latin America in the mid-1990s and produced the only comparable measure for cognitive skills. It measures cognitive skills among the teenage school population and is available as a cross-section. This is the measure we use here.

Analytic Techniques

For the cross-sections/time-series data, we use Prais-Winsten regressions (panel-corrected standard errors, first order autoregressive corrections, and imposition of a common rho for all cross-sections) because they take care of problems with these kinds of data, such as serial correlations, better than other estimation techniques. Where there are significant gaps in the data, Prais-Winsten regressions cannot be used. There we use OLS regressions with panel-corrected standard errors. Panel-corrected standard errors correct for correlations of errors within the units. They do not correct for unmeasured factors that might affect the dependent variable in all units at the same point in time. Global economic fluctuations, such as the debt crisis period in Latin America in the 1980s, could produce such contemporaneous effects. To evaluate the potential impact of such unmeasured, period-specific factors we estimated the models with indicator variables for the debt crisis and the recovery period; the baseline category corresponds to the period before 1982. For the analyses of the cross-sectional data, we begin by examining correlation matrices and scatter plots, and then we use simple OLS regressions.

## Exploring Factors That Shape Cognitive Skills

We hypothesize that high degrees of inequality and high levels of poverty in a society depress the quality of human capital. We measure human capital using the average test scores of secondary school students. We assume that high poverty and inequality depress test scores at the bottom, and that low test scores at the bottom depress the overall average (OECD 2000). We control for the history of educational spending, measured by the average expenditure on education over that period.

The mechanisms that translate high degrees of inequality into low cognitive skills are the lower classes having low expectations and preparation, and the government's skewed allocation of expenditure. The social distance between classes in highly unequal societies deters educational aspirations among the lower classes. High socioeconomic inequality also directly translates into high inequality in the quality of education available to different social classes, beginning at the preschool and primary levels. Both of these factors, educational aspirations and quality of education, are sticky—they change only very slowly. This means that high inequality when parents grew up will depress their children's human capital.

The mechanisms that translate past and present poverty into low educational achievement are similar. The quality of education available to the poor is lower than that available to the rest of society, be it due either to skewed allocation of public education expenditure or to private expenditure supplementing or substituting for public funds. In addition, the opportunity costs of education are important for the poor; when children are in school, they cannot be sent to hustle to help support the family.

In order to explore whether high inequality has a lasting impact on cognitive skills, we regress the test scores from the mid-1990s on the average of

Table 3.1. Determinants of Cognitive Test Scores—Mid-1990s

| | | | |
|---|---|---|---|
| Gini index, pre-1991 | −10.450 | [3.211] | ** |
| Average spending on education, 1970s to mid-1990s | 42.156 | [19.003] | * |
| Constant | 804.291 | [175.651] | *** |
| $R^2$ | .48 | | ** |
| Observations | 15 | | |

Note: Standard error in brackets.
*Significant at .05.
**Significant at .01.
***Significant at .001.

Ginis available for the pre-1991 period, controlling for average education spending from the 1970s to the mid-1990s. We exclude Venezuela from the analysis because of its outlier status. As Table 3.1 shows, high inequality before the 1990s depresses the cognitive skills of secondary school students in the 1990s, controlling for educational expenditures. As Table 3.1 further shows, educational expenditure does improve cognitive skills, once we control for early inequality.

The effect of education spending, then, is strongly influenced by socioeconomic conditions. In fact, the zero-order correlation between average educational spending in roughly the quarter century before the tests are administered to the students and those students' cognitive skills is only 0.28. Our Figure 3.1, which plots test scores and average educational expenditure, shows how some countries achieve results from their educational expenditure that are dramatically better than the results of other countries. It also shows how some countries do much worse than expected. The leaders are Uruguay and Costa Rica. Both of them have long had among the lowest levels of inequality in Latin America. At the other end is Venezuela, with exceptionally low scores given its comparatively high level of education expenditure. Inequality in Venezuela has been moderate, but poverty has been high (see below).

We get a similar picture when we examine the relationship between average years of education in the adult population and cognitive skills among secondary school students (Figure 3.2). The zero-order correlation between average years of education and cognitive test scores is only 0.43. In some countries, the education provided by schools and the absorption of this education by students are apparently much better than in others, as their students acquire better cognitive skills in the same number of or in fewer years. Figure 3.2 plots

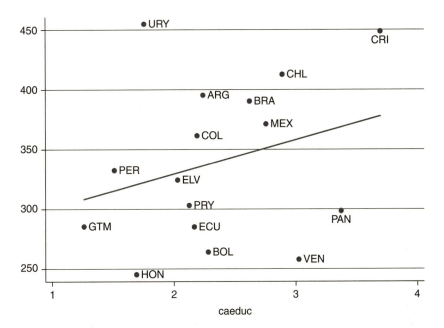

Figure 3.1. Mean cognitive test scores mid-1990s and average spending on education, mid-1970s to mid-1990s. (r=0.28)

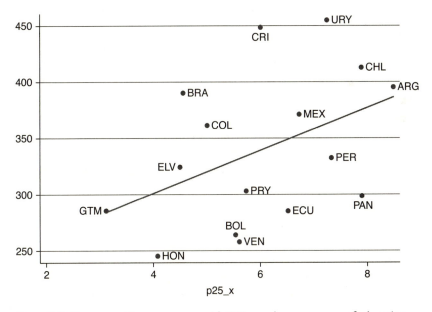

Figure 3.2. Mean cognitive test scores, mid-1990s, and average years of education, 1995. (r=0.43)

Table 3.2. Determinants of Cognitive Test Scores—Mid-1990s

| | | | |
|---|---|---|---|
| Gini index, 1990–97 | −7.581 | [3.422] | * |
| Average spending on education, 1970s to mid-1990s | 44.515 | [25.273] | * |
| Constant | 637.762 | [180.162] | *** |
| $R^2$ | .28 | | |
| Observations | 14 | | |

Note: Standard error in brackets.
*Significant at .05.
**Significant at .01.
***Significant at .001.

average years of education and cognitive skills and shows that Costa Rica and Uruguay are again the greatest overachievers and that Venezuela, Bolivia, Honduras, Ecuador, and Panama are considerable underachievers.

When we examine the impact of inequality in the 1990s on test scores from the same period, we find that the impact is significant and educational expenditure continues to matter. Early and contemporaneous poverty have even stronger effects on test scores than inequality. The zero-order correlation between pre-1990s poverty and test scores is −0.62, and between contemporaneous poverty and test scores it is −0.79. In our regressions, we find significant negative relationships between both early and contemporaneous poverty and test scores, and we find a stronger relationship for contemporaneous than for early poverty and test scores. This makes sense, because poverty has varied tremendously over time in Latin American countries, much more so than inequality. Thus parents who grew up in poverty may be lifted above the poverty line by changing economic conditions and social policies, in which case the opportunity costs of education for their children will be lower than they were for the parents when the parents were children. Table 3.3 shows that contemporaneous poverty has a very strong negative effect on test scores. It also shows that educational expenditures do not matter once we control for poverty.

Of course there is also reverse causality between cognitive skills and poverty. An individual with higher skills is more likely to get a higher paying job, and a labor force with higher cognitive skills is more productive and able to generate higher average earnings. However, the measure for cognitive skills here is of secondary school students, so the people whose skills are measured are not yet in the labor force and cannot be the cause for lower poverty in the society.

Table 3.3. Determinants of Cognitive Test Scores—Mid-1990s

| | | | |
|---|---|---|---|
| Poverty (1990–97) | −3.245 | [.669] | *** |
| Average spending on education, 1970s to mid-1990s | 1.515 | [18.417] | |
| Constant | 469.771 | [59.632] | *** |
| $R^2$ | .67 | | *** |
| Observations | 14 | | |

Note: Standard error in brackets.
*Significant at .05.
**Significant at .01.
***Significant at .001.

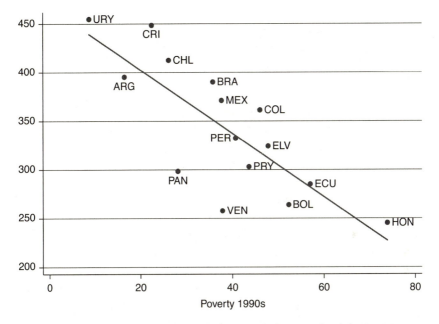

Figure 3.3. Mean cognitive test scores, mid-1990s, and poverty levels, 1990–97.
(r= −0.79)

Figure 3.3 illustrates the relationship between contemporaneous poverty and test scores. The zero order correlation is a high −0.79. Despite the close fit of the cases with the regression line, we see still the better-than-predicted performance of Uruguay and Costa Rica, and the comparatively very poor performance of Venezuela.

Since we only have cross-sectional data for cognitive skills but want to pursue the exploration of determinants of human capital further, we turn to

Table 3.4. Determinants of Average Years of Education (PCSE)

| | | | |
|---|---|---|---|
| Employment in industry | .056 | [.027] | * |
| Stock of FDI | .038 | [.006] | *** |
| Female labor force participation | .079 | [.011] | *** |
| Ethnic diversity | −.532 | [.182] | ** |
| Trade openness | .004 | [.002] | * |
| GDP per capita | .000 | [.000] | |
| Average spending on education (mid-1970s to year of observation) | −.196 | [.129] | |
| Poverty | −.029 | [.007] | *** |
| Constant | 2.086 | [1.028] | * |
| $R^2$ | .64 | | *** |
| Observations | 129 | | |

Note: Standard error in brackets.
*Significant at .05.
**Significant at .01.
***Significant at .001.

average years of education in the adult population as an indicator (albeit an imperfect one) for which we have cross-section/time-series data. We regress average years of education on poverty and average education spending and on a number of control variables that can theoretically be expected to be related to educational levels of the population: employment in industry, stock of foreign investment, female labor force participation, ethnic division, trade openness, and GDP per capita.

Table 3.4 shows that poverty has a highly significant and substantively strong negative effect on average years of education. Again, educational expenditure does not have an effect on average years of education once these other variables are controlled for. A society's level of affluence, as measured by GDP per capita, does not have an impact either once the level of industrialization and the other variables are controlled for. Higher levels of industrial employment and higher levels of integration into the world economy, as measured by accumulated foreign investment and trade openness, are associated with more years of schooling in the population, as is female labor force participation. Of course we acknowledge the reciprocal causality here: more industrialization and integration into the world economy require more schooling. Also, a more educated population is more attractive to foreign investors, making an economy better able to industrialize and compete in international trade, and women are more likely to enter the labor force as they become more educated. The point we want to emphasize is that once we control for these mutually reinforcing relationships, poverty retains a strong negative effect on average years of schooling in the adult population. High levels of poverty work against mass education as poor people in more and less industrialized societies alike are less likely to keep their children in school.

## Exploring the Impact of Human Capital on Human Welfare

We now turn to exploring the impact of human capital on poverty and inequality. We begin with poverty, focusing on the impact of policies, operationalized as different kinds of social expenditure, and on the impact of the results of these policies, operationalized as average years of education in the adult population. Our measure of poverty is an absolute one: it measures the percentage of total households living below the poverty line as defined by the Economic Commission for Latin America and the Caribbean (ECLAC) based on the cost of a basket of basic goods (*Statistical Yearbook of Latin America* and *Social Panorama of Latin America*, various years). This value includes households living in extreme poverty.

We would expect spending on health and education to improve human capital in the long run and thus to have a dampening effect on poverty. Short-run fluctuations in health and education spending should not have any significant effects—a one-year increase will not significantly improve education and health services. To capture the importance of long-run commitments to education and health services, we measure the average spending in the period up to the year of observation. If education expenditures are allocated correctly over the long run, we would expect an increase in the average years of education in the adult population. Thus entering average years of education in the same model should absorb the effect of well-allocated education spending, rendering spending insignificant.

Spending on social security and welfare should have a more immediate effect on poverty. Social security denotes mandatory public contributory programs, the bulk of which are pensions. Welfare denotes noncontributory cash transfers, which are overwhelmingly income or means tested. Clearly, welfare expenditures are highly redistributive and directly aimed at poor people. Social security expenditure in Latin America is regressive in the sense that higher income groups get virtually all of it. However, it tends to be less unequal than market income distribution, and is contributory, which means that the beneficiaries pay for it unless the benefits are subsidized by

Table 3.5. Determinants of Poverty (PCSE)

| | | | |
|---|---|---|---|
| GDP per capita (1000) | −.687 | [.276] | ** |
| Stock of FDI | .082 | [.042] | * |
| Informal sector employment | .485 | [.088] | *** |
| Ethnic diversity | 5.983 | [2.086] | ** |
| External debt | .052 | [.016] | *** |
| Average years of education | −2.879 | [.662] | *** |
| Social security and welfare spending | −1.306 | [.190] | *** |
| Democracy | −.149 | [.037] | *** |
| Constant | 38.249 | [4.846] | *** |
| $R^2$ | .85 | | ** |
| Observations | 112 | | |

Note: Standard error in brackets.
*Significant at .05.
**Significant at .01.
***Significant at .001.

general tax revenue. Moreover, the higher social security and welfare expenditure, the more likely it is that the coverage is larger, including lower income groups. Unfortunately, there are no data separating out social security from welfare spending before the 1990s, so we use the combined measure from the IMF (*Government Finance Statistics*). We expect this measure to reduce poverty in the short run, so we use the country/year observation, not an average over the previous period.

We controlled for a number of variables that we expected to impact poverty and present a reduced model in Table 3.5, with only the significant variables. Given that we use an absolute measure of poverty, it is not surprising that GDP per capita has a statistically significant negative effect on poverty (i.e. as GDP increases, poverty decreases). In contrast, stock of foreign investment, external debt, size of the informal sector, and ethnic diversity are all positively related to poverty. As we have argued previously, the length of a society's democratic record influences poverty and inequality (Huber and Stephens 2012). It does so by allowing civil society groups and political parties that represent the interests of the underprivileged to organize. As these forces grow in strength, they are able to influence policy. We can capture part of this influence through our policy variables, but there are many policy instruments other than social expenditure that influence policy and inequality, such as minimum wage legislation

Table 3.6. Determinants of Inequality (Prais Winsten Regressions)

| | | | |
|---|---|---|---|
| Gross income | 2.410 | [.506] | *** |
| No adjustment for household size | −3.069 | [.689] | *** |
| Youth population | −.404 | [.096] | *** |
| FDI inward | .372 | [.109] | *** |
| Industrial employment | −.452 | [.073] | *** |
| Ethnic diversity | 4.369 | [.688] | *** |
| Democracy | −.192 | [.035] | *** |
| Average years of education | −1.049 | [.235] | *** |
| Social security and welfare spending | .160 | [.101] | |
| Democracy* social security spending | −.010 | [.004] | ** |
| Education spending | 1.726 | [.436] | *** |
| Constant | 79.491 | [5.578] | *** |
| Common ρ | .29 | | |
| $R^2$ | .85 | | *** |
| Observations | 252 | | |

Note: Standard error in brackets.
*Significant at .05.
**Significant at .01.
***Significant at .001.

and labor market regulation, that we do not catch. Therefore, we expect a statistically significant negative effect of cumulative years of democracy on poverty, and this is indeed what we find.

Only two of our three policy variables of interest have statistically significant negative effects (i.e. decreasing poverty); health spending was not significant. Social security and welfare spending reduces poverty, as do average years of education in the adult population. Thus investment in broad-based education clearly has a beneficial effect on human welfare by reducing poverty levels in a society, as does spending on social transfers. Extrapolating to the individual level makes this effect highly intuitive—higher levels of education enable individuals to perform better in the labor force, which reduces the probability that they will live in poverty.

Human capital also significantly shapes income inequality. We proceed as above—controlling for methodological and substantive variables and showing only the significant variables in Table 3.6. To begin with a variable that is significant for poverty but not for inequality, GDP per capita does not have an impact on inequality. Economic development only reduces inequality under the influence of appropriate public policies. Length of the democratic record does have a statistically significant negative effect on inequality, partly through transfer spending and partly through other kinds of policies. Based on Lee's (2005) and our own work (Huber and Stephens 2012), we expect that social security and welfare expenditure will be more redistributive in democracies, and we do find the expected statistically significant negative effect of an interaction term between democracy and social security and welfare spending on income inequality. With democracy set at zero, social security and welfare spending loses its significant effect and even has a positive sign. We do find a highly significant human capital effect: higher average years of education are negatively associated with income inequality, as expected. However, once average years of education are controlled for, education spending assumes a statistically positive and significant effect on income inequality. In other words, if higher levels of education spending do not translate into broad-based education and higher average human capital, as captured by the indicator of average years of education, it goes to privileged groups and thus aggravates income inequality.

The evidence for the importance of education in shaping income inequality is strong in the analyses of microdata for Argentina, Brazil, Mexico, and Peru published in Lopez-Calva and Lustig (2010). These four countries experienced increasing inequality in the 1980s and early 1990s due to a combination of economic crisis and austerity, followed by structural adjustment according to the neoliberal Washington Consensus. The combination of cuts in public expenditures, the liberalization of trade and financial markets, privatization, and antilabor policies resulted in deindustrialization, the growth of the informal sector, the weakening of organized labor, and skill-biased technological change. These changes caused an increase in the skill premium and a fall in labor and nonlabor income for the poorer sectors.

These trends were arrested at different time points in different countries between the mid-1990s and early 2000s. As structural adjustment was completed, the process of skill-biased change was arrested or slowed, and the upward pressures on the skill premium weakened. Where governments promoted educational expansion in the 1990s, the greater supply of semiskilled and skilled workers brought down the skill premium after the turn of the century. In all four countries, a declining skill premium contributed to declining income inequality. The same is true for Chile (Eberhard and Engel 2009).

Important additional factors contributing to the decline in inequality were cash transfers to the poor in all cases, and increases in the minimum wage in Argentina (Gasparini and Cruces 2010) and Brazil (Barros et al. 2010). Cash transfers made an important contribution to declining poverty and inequality in Uruguay as well. In sum, the evidence from country studies supports the general argument that it is important for governments that are committed to reducing inequality to expand education, and that the most effective approaches combine expanding children's education with improving parents' living conditions.

## Human Capital and Economic Growth

For roughly the past twenty-five years endogenous growth theorists have argued that human capital has a strong effect on economic growth (Barro 1991; Aghion and Howitt 1998; Helpman 2004). As noted above, the improvement in data availability—moving from school enrollment rates to average years of education completed (Barro-Lee 2011) and ultimately cognitive skills (Hanushek and Woessmann 2008; 2012)—has strengthened the empirical results. Hanushek and Woessmann (2012, 275) showed that substituting a measure of skills for average years of education in a growth model, controlling for initial level of GDP per capita (to control for the catch-up effect), raised the variation explained from 25 percent to 73 percent.

Elsewhere (Evans, Huber, and Stephens 2014), we used Hanushek and Woessmann's (2008) data to analyze the impact of cognitive skills on growth from 1960 to 2000 in a sample of fifty countries, controlling for initial level of GDP per capita, income inequality, land inequality, fertility, and investment share of GDP 1960–2000. Both cognitive skills and investment share were statistically significant, but cognitive skills were stronger. Here we use Hanushek and Woessmann's (2009) data on cognitive skills for Latin America to analyze the impact of cognitive skills on average economic growth 1960–2000, controlling for initial level of GDP per capita and average investment share of real GDP between 1960 and 2000. As Table 3.7 shows, we obtain the same results: both cognitive skills and capital investment are significant, but cognitive skills are stronger.

Given the data limitations, that is, the fact that we have only cross-sectional data for fourteen countries for the 1990s, each regression alone is more suggestive than conclusive. However, it is the consistency of the results for both the worldwide sample and the Latin American sample and the

Table 3.7. Determinants of Economic Growth

| | | | |
|---|---|---|---|
| GDP in 1960 (1000) | −.205 | [.089] | * |
| Cognitive scores | .009 | [.003] | ** |
| Investment | .081 | [.045] | * |
| Constant | −2.163 | [1.477] | |
| $R^2$ | .42 | | * |
| Observations | 14 | | |

Note: Standard error in brackets.
*Significant at .05.
**Significant at .01.

theoretical grounding in endogenous growth theory that strengthen confidence in these findings.

## Conclusion

We started from the theoretical notion that, in order to be effective, investment in human capital needs to be accompanied by policies that combat poverty and support individuals and families in upgrading their skills. In other words, policies that improve predistribution cannot replace policies that bring about redistribution through the tax and transfer system. Spending on education and training cannot substitute for spending on social assistance, unemployment compensation, and so forth; such spending needs to be complemented by cash transfers. It also needs to be complemented by services that enable individuals to participate in education and training. This is as true for investment in the human capital of the present generation as it is for that of future generations. If adults need to find work at any cost to feed their families, or if mothers have no safe place to leave their children, they will not be able to participate in adult education and training to upgrade their skills. If children grow up in poor households, they will lack the support to take advantage of educational opportunities. In the long run, effective investment in human capital will reduce poverty and inequality. It will do so by improving the distribution of human capital and by promoting economic growth.

We have presented evidence from Latin America to support these theoretical expectations. High levels of inequality in the previous generation depress test scores of secondary school students, regardless of average educational expenditure over the period. High levels of poverty and inequality in the period when cognitive tests are administered do the same, and high levels of contemporaneous poverty even render educational expenditure statistically insignificant as a predictor of test scores. Average poverty in a society and average test scores of secondary school students are very closely related. We got the same results when we analyzed data for average years of education in adult populations in the long run; high levels of poverty depress school completion. Thus relying on investment in education of future generations as a substitute for investing in the living conditions of the underprivileged in the present generation is a very ineffective way of improving human welfare.

We have further presented evidence that antipoverty policies and higher average levels of education are effective in lowering poverty, controlling for a number of variables, including levels of affluence and industrialization. Social security expenditure, welfare expenditure, and broadly allocated educational expenditure are essential to an integrated social investment approach to lowering poverty. The evidence for inequality is similar: mass education—indicated by high average years of education—and democratically determined, broadly allocated social security and welfare expenditure reduce income inequality.

Elsewhere (Huber and Stephens 2012, 138–47), we have shown that length of the democratic experience is an important predictor of expenditure on education, health, and social security and welfare. In addition, strength of democracy and the political presence of left parties are strong predictors of the allocation of such expenditure and thus of levels of poverty and inequality in society. We suggest that it is precisely the simultaneous pursuit of investment in health and education and in antipoverty policies by left parties that produces these results.

Finally, we have presented evidence suggesting that human capital is more important for economic growth than physical capital. This evidence puts into question the "grow first and distribute later" principle that has guided so much policy in Latin America. In contrast, "distribute now (in combination with investment in health and education) and grow more strongly" would be a more effective guiding principle. Of course, this is not a prescription for irresponsible deficit spending. In order to ensure sustainability, this principle needs to be pursued within the parameters of macroeconomic stability. Within these parameters, though, there is room for political action.

## References

Aghion, Philippe, and Peter Howitt. 1998. *Endogenous Growth Theory.* Cambridge, Mass.: MIT Press.

Barro, Robert J. 1991. "Economic Growth in a Cross Section of Countries." *Quarterly Journal of Economics* 106 (2): 407–43.

Barro, Robert, and Jong-Wha Lee. 2013. "A New Data Set of Educational Attainment in the World, 1950–2010." *Journal of Development Economics* 104:184–198. Barro-Lee Educational Attainment Dataset, 1950–2010. http://www.barrolee.com.

Barros, Ricardo, Mirela de Carvalho, Samuel Franco, and Rosane Mendonça. 2010. "Markets, the State, and the Dynamics of Inequality." In *Declining Inequality in Latin America: A Decade of Progress?*, edited by Luis Felipe López-Calva and Nora Claudia Lustig, 134–74. Washington, D.C.: Brookings Institution Press.

Becker, Bronwyn E., and Suniya S. Luthar. 2002. "Social-Emotional Factors Affecting Achievement Outcomes Among Disadvantaged Students: Closing the Achievement Gap." *Educational Psychologist* 37 (4): 197–214.

Duncan, Greg J., Johanne Boisjoly, and Kathleen Mullan Harris. 2001. "Sibling, Peer, Neighbor, and Schoolmate Correlations as Indicators of the Importance of Context for Adolescent Development." *Demography* 38 (3): 437–47.

Esping-Andersen, Gøsta, Duncan Gallie, Anton Hemerijck, and John Myles. 2002. *Why We Need a New Welfare State.* Oxford: Oxford University Press.

Fergusson, David M., L. John Horwood, and Joseph M. Boden. 2008. "The Transmission of Social Inequality: Examination of the Linkages Between Family Socioeconomic Status in Childhood and Educational Achievement in Young Adulthood." *Research in Social Stratification and Mobility* 26:277–95.

Gasparini, Leonardo, and Guillermo Cruces. 2010. "A Distribution in Motion: The Case of Argentina." In López-Calva and Lustig, *Declining Inequality in Latin America*, 100–133.

Giddens, Anthony. 1999. *The Third Way: The Renewal of Social Democracy.* Cambridge: Polity Press.

Hanushek, Eric A., and Ludger Woessmann. 2008. "The Role of Cognitive Skills in Economic Development." *Journal of Economic Literature* 46 (3): 607–68.

———. 2009. "Schooling, Cognitive Skills, and the Latin American Growth Puzzle." NBER Working Paper Series No. 15066, June. Cambridge, Mass.: National Bureau of Economic Research. http://www.nber.org/papers/w15066.

———. 2012. "Do Better Schools Lead to More Growth? Cognitive Skills, Economic Outcomes, and Causation." *Journal of Economic Growth* 17:267–321.

Helpman, Elhanan. 2004. *The Mystery of Economic Growth*. Cambridge, Mass.: Belknap Press of Harvard University Press.

Huber, Evelyne, and John D. Stephens. 2012. *Democracy and the Left: Social Policy and Inequality in Latin America*. Chicago, Ill.: University of Chicago Press.

Huber, Evelyne, John D. Stephens, Thomas Mustillo, and Jennifer Pribble. 2008a. Latin America and the Caribbean Political Dataset, 1945–2001. http://huberandstephens .web.unc.edu/common-works/data/.

Huber, Evelyne, John D. Stephens, Thomas Mustillo, and Jennifer Pribble. 2008b. Social Policy in Latin America and the Caribbean Dataset, 1960–2006. http:// huberandstephens.web.unc.edu/common-works/data/.

Jenson, Jane. 2010. "Diffusing Ideas for After Neoliberalism: The Social Investment Perspective in Europe and Latin America." *Global Social Policy* 10 (1): 59–84.

Lee, Cheol-Sung. 2005. "Income Inequality, Democracy, and Public Sector Size." *American Sociological Review* 70 (1): 158–81.

López-Calva, Luis Felipe, and Nora Lustig. 2010. *Declining Inequality in Latin America: A Decade of Progress?* Washington, D.C.: Brookings Institution Press.

Mark, Gary N. 2005. "Cross-National Differences and Accounting for Social Class Inequalities in Education." *International Sociology* 20 (4): 483–505.

OECD (Organisation for Economic Co-operation and Development). 2000. "Literacy in the Information Age: Final Report of the International Adult Literacy Survey." Paris: OECD.

Psacharopoulos, George. 1997. "Child Labor Versus Educational Attainment: Some Evidence from Latin America." *Journal of Population Economics* 10:377–86.

Thomas, Vinod, Yan Wang, and Xibo Fan. 2001. "Measuring Education Inequality: Gini Coefficients of Education." World Bank Policy Research Working Paper No. 2525, January 2001. http://papers.ssrn.com/sol3/papers.cfm?abstract_id=258182.

Van Ewijk, Reyn and Peter Sleegers. 2010. "The Effect of Peer Socioeconomic Status on Student Achievement: A Meta-Analysis." *Educational Research Review* 5:134–50.

Waring, Peter, Shane Ostenfeld, John Lewer, and John Burgess. 2001. "The Third Way, Employment and the Workplace in Australia." *Economic and Labour Relations Review* 12:174–92.

CHAPTER 4

# Debt, Democracy, and Post-Neoliberalism: Thirty Years of Regional Integration in Latin America

Isabella Alcañiz

## Introduction

The Southern Common Market, known as Mercosur, is faltering. For a little over a decade, the largest regional trade scheme of Latin America, made up of Argentina, Brazil, Paraguay, Uruguay, and Venezuela, has been seen as losing its way and exhibiting symptoms that resemble more a process of "disintegration" than of integration (Sáenz 2008). Since the 2000s, Mercosur has struggled to find a clear mandate and a unified voice as a somewhat imperfect customs union and common market. Intraregional trade imbalances and increased commercial exchanges with nonmember states are two key challenges to Mercosur (Malamud 2005; Carranza 2006; Christensen 2007; Baumann 2009). Even as a shared political platform for the subregion to deal with the new giants of the Global South (in other words, China, India, and Russia), Mercosur fails to offer a common strategy. Commercial gains made by China and the EU with the Mercosur economies seem to entail losses for intraregional trade, especially when we focus on Brazil and its rising non-Mercosur commerce (Baumann 2009; Polaski et al. 2009). Under the weight of a founding member's foreign debt crisis, the rise of new commercial partners in the global economy, and protracted intraregional conflicts, South American leaders in the twenty-first century seem less invested in Mercosur than ever. Even the outgoing president of Uruguay, in his last days in office, recently declared that "Argentina forgets about integration . . . as does Brazil."[1]

Paradoxically, the conditions hindering the deepening of Mercosur also existed at the time of its creation. In the second half of the 1980s, akin to the 2000s, Latin American economies were shattered by foreign debt crises, early globalization was quickly raising the costs of trade isolation, and the two largest economies of South America—Argentina and Brazil—appeared engulfed in a dangerous competition for nuclear supremacy. A key difference between these two periods, which I discuss below, is that in the 1980s country leaders were reeling from the political turmoil caused by democratization. The new democracies of the Southern Cone sought refuge from these conditions by embarking on a regional process as a strategy to deal with competing domestic and international demands (Malamud 2005; Carranza 2006; Von Bülow 2010; Oelsner 2013). Surprisingly, regionalization in the Southern Cone began in the security field, after Argentina and Brazil signed a series of agreements institutionalizing technical, commercial, and even political cooperation in nuclear energy, science, and technology. The decision to tackle integration first in a military-dominated field with a major international perception problem stemmed from the new civilian leadership's need—under severe debt negotiations—to send a positive signal to the international community while simultaneously attempting to reduce its dependence on the industrial North (Carasales 1997; Alcañiz 2012). The nuclear treaties between Argentina and Brazil constitute the direct antecedent to the trade agreements that culminated in the 1991 signature of the Asunción Treaty, thus creating Mercosur.

This chapter examines two periods of regionalization in South America experiencing similar debt crises: the mid-1980s immediately after democratization, and the 2000s, characterized by post-neoliberalism responses. In the following pages, I explore how debt, democracy, and economic crises shaped the incentives for country executives to invest in regional integration but not necessarily in the same institution. This chapter seeks to answer the question of why similar politico-economic conditions led toward Mercosur in the 1980s but away from it the 2000s. I find that the first regionalization process was driven by a critical need for the new democracies of Latin America to be recognized internationally and integrated into the world economy, whereas in the second period, the now consolidated democracies of the region sought increased autonomy from the industrial North and a greater presence in South–South cooperation.

## Some Benefits and Limitations of the Latin American Regional Integration Strategy

There is no simple answer to the question of why South American leaders do not continue to invest in Mercosur to further regional integration. After the market-friendly policies of the 1990s, when its founding membership endowed Mercosur with functional institutional capabilities, South Americans have embraced regionalization, just not within the institutional structure of Mercosur (Malamud 2005). In fact, the first years of the twenty-first century in Latin America have been characterized by a number of new regional institutions created with the explicit mission of minimizing dependency on the financial North and strongly dominated by a statist model (Oelsner 2013). This new wave of regionalization harks back to the first attempts at integration in Latin America. In other words, the new Union of South American Nations (Unasur) created in 2008 has a lot in common with the old Latin American Free Trade Association (ALALC) of the 1960s (Sanahuja 2011). As I discuss below, ALALC was founded on the principles of economic structuralism made popular in the region by the UN Economic Commission for Latin America (more commonly known by its Spanish acronym, CEPAL). Structural economics conceives of global trade as a result of the division of labor between the peripheral economies in the South and the industrial core in the North. The terms of trade that result from this division of labor tend to be detrimental to the periphery, and consequently, CEPAL advocated a central (and centralized) role for political institutions in economic development (Stallings and Peres 2010).

After a decade of substantial structural reforms adopted by the countries of the Southern Cone, with a Mercosur reflecting the prominence of market actors in the 1990s, the 2000s brought back a renewed commitment to statism in the subregion. Once again the policies advocated by CEPAL are shaping regional integration (Christensen 2007). Recent (re)nationalization and (re)regulation policies adopted in South America (especially in Bolivia and Venezuela) do not help Mercosur to function smoothly. But the return of the state-centered paradigm is not the only challenge Mercosur faces (Malamud 2005; Oelsner 2013): in the first decade of the new century, Mercosur has received less attention from its main stakeholders. This disinvestment is revealed in the lack of development and deepening of common institutions and minimal enforcement mechanisms of regional norms at the domestic level (Christensen 2007; Levi Coral 2011). Furthermore, Mercosur's political principals are investing efforts in regional cooperation elsewhere, such as the new Unasur, BancoSur; the Bolivarian Alliance for the Peoples of Our America (ALBA); and the cross-regional New Development Bank (also known as the development bank of the Brics countries, Brazil, Russia, India, China, and South Africa).

To illustrate the challenges facing Mercosur, consider the growing trade presence of China in South America: "The participation of Brazilian products in the Argentine market reached a maximum of 36.4% in 2005, and was only 30.8% in 2008. In the same period the Chinese presence went up from 5.3% to 12.4%. A comparison between 2003 and 2008 shows that Brazil lost market-share in 19 of the 30 groups of products most relevant for her exports to that market; in the same period China increased her participation in all 30 groups" (Baumann 2009, 13).

Dual themes traverse the two periods of regional institution building analyzed in this chapter. First, as the description of the integration endeavors in the 1980s and the 2000s will show, debt and regionalization are connected, in that South American countries seek to depend less on OECD-dominated finance by creating common institutions. These new institutions tend to be endowed with scarce resources, and often their creation is the low-cost signal the founders are after. This relates to what many scholars have observed: that Mercosur's external agenda—through which its members jointly deal with third parties—receives more attention from its stakeholders than its internal agenda does, which requires country members to make policy and trade concessions in order to deepen integration (Carranza 2006; Oelsner 2013). Mercosur's internal agenda requires much costlier investments than its external agenda does to function properly.

Similarly, creating a new regional institution can send a clear, albeit low-cost, signal to the intended audience (for example, international financial institutions) without investing significantly in resources (Schiff and Winters 2002; Cernat 2003). Indeed, using regional institutions as signaling devices to the international (financial) community is less costly than moving toward a perfect customs union and a real common market. On the other hand, prioritizing external objectives over internal ones seems to doom Mercosur to chronic stagnation. Here I pay attention to what new regional treaties signal to the international community (Simmons 2000). Treaties are "designed, by long-standing convention, to raise the credibility of promises by staking national reputation on adherence to them" (Simmons 2000, 821). I find that the first regional project of the democratic era, as well as the more recent regionalization of the post-neoliberal era, sends similar (low-cost) signals of a need to reduce financial dependence and mitigate exposure to international markets.

There is no unifying theory to explain the genesis and evolution of a regional integration scheme (Sbragia 2008). Undoubtedly, regional institutions are better fitted to address the common problems of neighbors; in contrast to global institutions, which by necessity follow a "one size fits all" design, regional schemes are more flexible and allow greater direct policy management to all stakeholders (Schiff and Winters 2002; Cernat 2003; De Lombaerde et al. 2012). In other words: "There is a growing understanding that the regional level, between the national and global ones, provides an adequate and sometimes optimal level of governance to address a variety of problems of cross-border nature" (De Lombaerde et al. 2012, xv).

## Debt, Democracy, and Regional Integration in the South

In the mid-1980s the majority of South American states were leaving behind the military rule that for years had driven their countries to increasing international isolation and indebted economics. Democratization of the region was in part triggered by the militaries' inability to weather the foreign debt crises. The new civilian leaderships in South America faced the harsh prospect of restoring trustworthy relations with the rest of the world, sustaining domestic democratic transitions, and refinancing the debt accrued by the departing military regimes. For the new civilian leaderships, economic growth was critical. As Raul Alfonsín, the first democratic president of Argentina, stated: "Today, we are all convinced that growth is the solution. High interest rates and the fall in international commodity prices make it clear that austerity cannot solve the debt crisis. Only strong and growing economies can meet their obligations. But growth requires a coordinated effort by all: creditor nations, financial institutions, and debtor nations."[2]

One way the South American governments coordinated their efforts to repair the disastrous economic situation and defend their fragile democracies was the Cartagena Consensus (1984), a Latin American intergovernmental forum led by Mexico to pressure international creditors on the foreign debt issue (Roett 1985). Its main goal was to approve the rejection of payment to international creditors by regional consensus. This goal was not reached, but what was achieved was the politicization of the issue, which to a certain extent questioned the legitimacy of the foreign debt. Increasingly, South Americans realized that the negotiation was as much political as it was economic. Again, President Alfonsín: "Joint action with other debtor nations, such as Brazil and Mexico, is both possible and desirable. Together we can explain how the debt crisis, and more specifically the transference of domestic savings to foreign countries, is at the root of problems that transcend economics and become political."[3]

The new regional order hoped for by South Americans was thus one where the solutions to shared problems were tackled together. In a sense, it recalled the situation in Europe after 1945, as President Alfonsín stated: "After WWII, the exhausted European countries faced the task of reconstructing their democracies. Today, Latin America and Argentina, devastated by years of authoritarianism, are faced with the same task. In 1948 the European countries benefited from the Marshall Plan, an imaginative and generous response from the rest of the world which helped consolidate democracy and secure liberty in Europe. Today, in Argentina and Latin America, democracy is again flourishing. But unlike postwar Europe we have not benefited from a Marshall Plan."

Argentina and Brazil, the Southern Cone's two largest economies, found themselves on the same side of the negotiating table regarding the debt issue. But in their recent past there was a troubling history of rivalry in nuclear development. For Argentines and Brazilians the nuclear issue was as much an international problem as it was a bilateral concern. The quest for advanced nuclear technology had increased distrust between the neighbors and, moreover, had raised suspicions from the international community regarding their motives in pursuing nuclear energy. Argentina and Brazil rejected the attempts made by the United States and its nuclear power allies to regulate and set terms for technology transfers to non-nuclear countries via the nonproliferation regime, made up of a number of multilateral security treaties designed to stop the proliferation of nuclear weapons (Alcañiz 2012). Specifically, the two countries refused to sign the 1968 Nonproliferation Treaty (NPT), claiming its backers used it as an excuse to curb their right to explore and develop new technologies, while countries with nuclear weapons, such as the United States, were not affected. Anti-NPT feelings ran deep in the Southern Cone. As a Brazilian diplomat explained it: "We saw the NPT not only as a way of avoiding the proliferation of nuclear weapons, but also as preventing knowledge."[4]

Even though Argentina and Brazil had most of their nuclear facilities under international safeguards established by the International Atomic Energy Agency (IAEA), they refused to sign on principle the NPT or the 1967 Latin American Tlatelolco Treaty (Tlatelolco) that declared Latin America a nuclear weapons–free zone. The two countries expressed concerns with on-site inspections that could be justified solely if it was suspected that nuclear material was being diverted, contemplated in both the NPT and Tlatelolco, which they argued might reveal industrial secrets (Carasales 1997). This anti-NPT sentiment became official nuclear policy in both countries.

Sharing Brazil's position, Argentina also refused to sign the NPT. The international community interpreted this refusal as evidence that Argentina and Brazil were leaving the weapons option open and could become involved in a nuclear arms race (for a discussion, see Levethal and Tanzer 1992). Argentina and Brazil were deemed countries to be monitored for their nuclear activities and were often compared to India and Pakistan as potential nuclear enemies (Carasales 1997; Alcañiz 2000; Kassenova 2014). When the countries democratized in the mid-1980s, their refusal to comply with all international nonproliferation norms became a major liability. U.S. warnings that economic aid would be partly conditioned on the review of the two countries' nuclear foreign policy exacerbated their nuclear problem (Carasales 1997; Alcañiz 2000).[5]

## Regionalization and Economic Structuralism in Latin America

Latin American countries' search for economic development through regional strategies began with the creation of CEPAL in 1948, which embodied structural theories of economic development advanced by the Argentine economist Raúl Prebisch. As well as shaping domestic growth models, these theories also shaped regional integration models, such as the 1960 Latin American Integration Association (ALADI), the 1969 Andean Community, and the 1980 Latin American Free Trade Association (ALALC) (Axline 1994; Van Klaveren 2001). Because the developing economies of Latin American countries suffered increasingly unfavorable terms of exchange in their trade with industrial states, the CEPAL formula centered on import-substituting industrialization (ISI) and inward-oriented models of development that relied on protectionism (Axline 1994; Van Klaveren 2001). Commodities, Latin America's chief export, increasingly lost their value relative to manufactured goods imported from central economies. Prebisch's solution, which came to be known as the Cepalian paradigm, was a model of inward-looking development whose main principle was an ISI strategy (Iglesias 2006). As described by CEPAL economist Osvaldo Sunkel: "Inward-looking development places the emphasis on demand, on the expansion of the domestic market, and on replacing previously imported goods with locally produced goods, instead of placing the emphasis on accumulation, technical progress, and productivity" (Sunkel 1993, 46).

The first major agreement on regional integration, the Montevideo Treaty, was signed in 1960 by the majority of Latin American countries, including Argentina and Brazil. It established the Latin American Free Trade Association (ALALC), which sought to integrate local economies and liberalize intraregional trade by applying ISI strategies under CEPAL development models.[6] Participating countries, however, failed to eliminate existing protectionist measures or agree on common external tariffs. Not surprisingly, ALALC did not produce the expected economic boom for the region. Twenty years later, ALALC was transformed into ALADI, the Latin American Integration Association. In contrast to its predecessor, the much more flexible ALADI allowed for subregional preferential treatment and did not establish an integration schedule (Pecequilo and Carmo 2013). Yet despite its flexibility, ALADI also failed to have a lasting effect on regional integration in Latin America (Albuquerque 2000).

Two years after the signing of ALADI, Mexico defaulted on its foreign debt, setting off one of the greatest economic crises the region had ever seen, hitting Argentina and Brazil especially hard (Roett 1983; Frieden 1991). The first coordinated response to this crisis by the countries of the region was the Cartagena Consensus, discussed earlier. But given Latin America's debt and political vulnerabilities, it was not surprising that the initiative lost steam before it could achieve its objectives (Roett 1985). Latin Americans were caught in a delicate dilemma: on the one hand, they had to pay for the massive debt acquired by the departing military regimes; on the other hand, they had to manage difficult democratic transitions at home. Funds were scarce yet desperately needed, and the viable policy options were few and politically costly.

## Nuclear Integration in South America: Atoms for Dollars

Given the demands of regime transition and the economic crisis, Argentina and Brazil worked on improving diplomatic ties with the international community.

One common problem the two countries inherited from their military governments was the nuclear problem, which the debt crisis exacerbated by forcing
ever greater budget reductions in the sector (Madero and Takacs 1991; Solingen 1996; Carasales 1997). Thus Presidents Alfonsín of Argentina and Sarney
of Brazil were pressured from abroad to open up to the international community, and pressured also by the nuclear sector's scientists and by the military to
stop the downsizing and budget cuts. In other words, the civilian leaders faced
conflicting demands: from above, to internationalize and from below to na-
tionalize (even more) their nuclear programs (Alcañiz 2000). Facing a common nuclear problem, the leaders of Argentina and Brazil, backed by diplomats
and nuclear bureaucrats, worked toward a regional solution.

Regional nuclear integration would help deflect accusations from the international community of a hidden weapons agenda and keep the now severely impoverished nuclear programs running. As the head of the Argentine
National Commission of Atomic Energy (CNEA) stated: "We reached the
conclusion that a government can show that it has a program without strategic diversions by opening it, but on equal standing. That's why the agreements with Brazil were made. Nobody can say you haven't opened up, but
you disclose to whom discloses in turn. On equal standing. That is the reason for the agreements."[7]

Regional integration also delayed domestic reactions against the impend-
ing restructuring of the nuclear sector, given that the two countries were nearly
bankrupt and could not keep up with their prior pace of nuclear development.
Indeed, regionalization has been recognized as one way to avoid internal conflict (Mansfield and Milner 1999): "Although governments may choose to join
regional agreements to promote domestic reforms, they may also do so if they
resist reforms but are anxious to reap the benefits stemming from preferential
access to other members' markets" (Manfield and Milner 1999, 605).

In 1985, regionalization in nuclear energy, science, and technology between Argentina and Brazil began with a joint declaration on nuclear policy
signed by Presidents Alfonsín and Sarney. This was the first regional agreement in the democratic era between the two countries. The joint declaration
asserted twice in its brief text the wish to extend "this cooperation to all of
the other Latin American countries that share the same objectives" (Carasales 1997, 144). In 1986, the two countries signed the Treaty for Integration,
Cooperation, and Development, seen as the immediate predecessor of the
Treaty of Asunción. In this comprehensive agreement, Argentina and Brazil
committed to consolidating "the process of integration and economic coop-

eration" initiated with the "historical landmark represented by the Declaration of Iguaçu, dated November 30, 1985" and greatly based on the 1986 "Act for Brazilian-Argentine Integration," which established a number of protocols for trade and nuclear cooperation between the two countries.

Presidents Alfonsín and Sarney and their top diplomats favored political coordination and an international agenda that would signal to the nonproliferation community that Argentina and Brazil were not diverting nuclear material for strategic uses. The political leadership wanted to improve political relations with the United States and its western allies and refinance foreign debt (Alcañiz 2000). To accomplish this, they set about establishing trust mechanisms between the two states that would unequivocally indicate transparency and openness in their nuclear dealings. Thus the presidents scheduled a number of high-profile meetings at previously covert nuclear facilities, such as the Pilcaniyeu uranium enrichment plant (in Argentina) and the Aramar Experimental Center (in Brazil). This carried great political weight; the invitations were to facilities that were not under IAEA full-scope safeguards.

The technical staff of the two nuclear programs, on the other hand, were more concerned with economic cooperation and the domestic agenda of regional integration (Carasales 1997; Ornstein and Carasales 1998). Their preferences were clearly oriented toward finding common solutions to the financial crisis, which was hindering the nuclear sector's development (Wrobel and Redick 1998). The CNEA, the Brazilian National Commission of Nuclear Energy (CNEN), and industrialists prioritized the completion of the nuclear power plants already under construction—Atucha II (in Argentina) and Angra II (in Brazil) (Ornstein and Carasales 1998). For them, integration was a viable local alternative to seeking out international sources of technology, know-how, and above all financing from the industrial North, which was not always receptive. State experts on both sides of the border believed in complementing their industries in order to reap economic rather than political benefits.[8] Yet they understood that if industrial cooperation were to advance, their governments must first crystallize a political agreement that would serve as an institutional framework for future commercial exchanges, and improve general international conditions for nuclear transfers from the North to the South.

The Coordinating Committee of Argentine–Brazilian Business in the Nuclear Field (1986, CEABAN) was very active in pushing the domestic agenda of Argentine–Brazilian nuclear integration, and in the Permanent Committee they found support with the expert bureaucrats of CNEA and

CNEN, as they too preferred technical and industrial cooperation to political coordination (Ornstein and Carasales 1998). CEPAL principles found their way into the domestic agenda of CEABAN as ISI was the key strategy proposed by them, but their economic proposals went mainly unanswered: "The CEABAN has still not received a clear answer. If this does not occur in the near future, the initiatives of industrialists in both countries, oriented towards integrating the existing capabilities and supplying goods and services, will frustrate beyond repair and will only have served to feed empty political declamation without any real base."[9]

While the domestic agenda of nuclear integration stalled, the international agenda advanced swiftly. In 1990 the presidents of Argentina and Brazil (Carlos S. Menem and Fernando Collor de Mello) met in the city of Foz de Iguazú to sign a new joint declaration more groundbreaking than its 1985 predecessor. This agreement established the Common System of Accounting and Control of Nuclear Materials (SCCC), which had been negotiated by the Permanent Committee, and sought to keep tabs on all nuclear energy, science, and technology facilities on both sides of the border. The SCCC instituted cross-national inspections and comprehensive sharing of inventories of nuclear materials. In addition, Presidents Menem and Collor de Mello approved the start of negotiations with the IAEA to reach a safeguard agreement between the two countries and the international organization, and committed to ratifying together the Tlatelolco Treaty once the safeguard agreement with the IAEA was concluded (Carasales 1997).

In 1991, Argentina and Brazil signed the Bilateral Agreement in Mexico, which institutionalized the resolutions of the joint declaration and created the Brazilian–Argentine Agency for Accounting and Control of Nuclear Materials (ABACC) to administer and implement the SCCC. The agency has the power to implement inspections of all nuclear facilities in the two countries, to represent Argentina and Brazil before third parties with regards to the SCCC, and to sign international agreements with the approval of the Argentine and Brazilian governments (Carasales 1997). Only a few months after its creation, ABACC became party to the Quadripartite Agreement, a comprehensive safeguard agreement signed with Argentina, Brazil, and the IAEA that regulates the overlapping functions of ABACC and IAEA (Ornstein and Carasales 1998). After ratifying the Quadripartite Agreement, Argentina and Brazil together ratified the Tlatelolco Treaty in 1994. In 1995, Argentina finally adhered to the Nonproliferation Treaty, and Brazil followed in 1998.

In conclusion, in only six years Argentina and Brazil integrated their system of control, verification, and accountability of nuclear material and activities. During that short time, the two countries established a regional system of safeguards and opened up their programs to the international community and the IAEA. The domestic agenda of nuclear integration lagged behind political integration, though. Lack of funding remained the key obstacle to furthering commercial integration. The nuclear experts of Argentina, Brazil, and CEABAN considered alternatives to external funding—unavailable due to the debt crisis—such as a "compensated exchange" regime by which services rendered by one country would be paid in kind by the other. Still, this system of bartering was completely ineffective in helping with the construction of Atucha II and Angra II/III due to the massive financing required for such projects.

## Debt and Regionalization in the Post-Neoliberal Era

Thus the origins of Mercosur were shaped by the new civilian leaderships' need to depend less on international financial markets while sending a clear signal to the international community that the countries of the region were committed to ending the isolation of the military juntas of the 1970s. These political goals shaped, more so perhaps than the trade objectives of the South American states, the creation and evolution of Mercosur. As Oelsner has argued: "The project of Mercosur was born out of political as much as—if not more than—economic motivations. The weight of its political dimension explains at least in part why its initial design was based on gradualism (sectoral agreements), and why cooperation included most sensitive areas, such as nuclear technology and biotechnology" (Oelsner 2013, 119).

Concerns with foreign debt, economic development, and democracy informed regionalization in the 1980s. Political executives adopting the early nuclear and trade protocols of 1986 drew from the conflictive experience of dealing with international financial institutions dominated by stakeholders from OECD countries. The fiscal crises of the 1980s (as well as those of the late 1990s and early 2000s) led Latin American executives to approach integration as a safeguard against too much exposure to the international market. South American decision-makers also drew from historically dominant antimarket beliefs (Christensen 2007; Stallings and Peres 2010). As discussed above, Latin

America's suspicion of unfettered markets, stemming from successive economic crises, was reinforced in part by CEPAL.

In the 1990s, the countries of Latin America embraced significant market-friendly policies, adopting programs that privatized and deregulated the state. Regionalization also followed the paradigm of "open regionalism"— regional integration that furthered domestic economic liberalization. Mercosur and the proposed Free Trade Association of the Americas (FTAA) reproduced at the regional level some of the key tenets of neoliberalism implemented domestically: less state, less protectionism, and more multilateralism (Van Klaveren 2001). Oelsner explains it best when she states: "In contrast to the economic and foreign policies implemented during the 1990s, in the late 1980s both Brazil and Argentina still followed heterodox economic recipes and sought to keep aside the strategic and ideological components of the East–West confrontation. However, rather quickly the actual content of the bloc identity adapted to post-Cold War and Washington consensus circumstances, replacing the defensive and protectionist model of integration with the concept of open regionalism" (Oelsner 2013, 123). The neoliberal paradigm in South American regionalization, namely Mercosur, was radically disrupted by the 1999 Brazilian fiscal crisis, with the devaluation of the real, and in particular by the latest foreign debt crisis affecting Argentina.

## Argentina's Sovereign Debt Crisis, the Rise of Brazil, and the Stagnation of Mercosur

As stated in the introduction, disinterest in Mercosur has not entailed an abandonment of active regional institution building in the Southern Cone. The presidents of Mercosur—both jointly and unilaterally—have founded major regional and interregional schemes. Unasur, created in 2008, unites Mercosur both with the customs union of the Andean Community (Bolivia, Colombia, Ecuador, and Peru) and with Chile, Guyana, and Suriname, and seeks eventually to expand regional integration to all of South America. Its political rationale is to help increase the region's economic independence from the industrial North, especially from the United States (Sanahuja 2011). BancoSur, founded by the center-left governments of Argentina, Bolivia, Brazil, Ecuador, Paraguay, Uruguay, and Venezuela in 2009, has a similar mission to the World Bank's—to lend for social and infrastructure programs—but without conditionality clauses requiring market reforms.

Outside of Mercosur, Brazil and its Brics partners signed the founding treaty of the Brics Development Bank in 2014. This financial institution, which shares the development objectives of BancoSur, clearly seeks to challenge the dominance of OECD countries in multilateral lending and signal a new order, dominated by the so-called emerging markets. Finally, less institutionalized but politically relevant to Brasilia, is the IBSA Dialogue Forum, created in 2003 by Brazil, India, and South Africa to promote South–South cooperation and policy coordination in key areas such as pharmaceuticals, patent disputes, and science and technology.

What explains the flurry of new regional and cross-regional institutions? Argentina's sovereign default at the beginning of the new millennium brought to the heart of Mercosur the problem of foreign debt and the relationship between developing countries and multilateral financial institutions such as the IMF. Argentina's financial collapse, which led to the most important political crisis of its postdemocratic history, resulted from its currency having been long overvalued, its economy's having become less competitive, its failure to invest domestically, and a recession that had dragged on since the late 1990s (Weyland 2002; Huber and Solt 2004; Walton 2004; Alcañiz and Hellwig 2011). The December 2001 crisis caused the government of President de la Rúa (1999–2001) to fall and a series of short-lived interim governments to follow. One of the provisional governments, lasting only one week, declared a unilateral moratorium on all of Argentina's U.S. $155 billion public debt, earning the infamous distinction of presiding over the largest sovereign default in history (*Economist* 2002). The Argentine economy's meltdown was directly triggered by the decision of the then Minister of Economy Domingo Cavallo to limit significantly all cash withdrawals in order to curb rampant capital flight. These restrictions placed extreme stress on an already recessive economy, bringing it to a sudden halt. Unemployment increased rapidly, income contracted, and the devaluated peso lost well over half of its value (Weyland 2002).

Argentinians blamed not just the political leadership for the debacle; they placed almost as much blame on international multilateral financial institutions, especially the IMF (Alcañiz and Hellwig 2011). This resulted from political scapegoating as national politicians sought to transfer blame to outsiders, as well as from the entanglement of the IMF in the country in the months preceding the crisis (Alcañiz and Hellwig 2011). In effect, the final desperate measures taken by the de la Rúa administration appeared to come with the blessing of the international financial community as they were enacted on the heels of a record-breaking billion-dollar loan package granted by the IMF to Argentina. The perception of responsibility was strong in the country: in 2002 and 2003 Latinobarómetro surveys, 30 percent of Argentine respondents blamed the IMF for the economic problems of their country; 16 percent of those surveyed found the general category of "banks" responsible (Alcañiz and Hellwig 2011, 398). This perception of responsibility was shared by Argentina's Mercosur partners, with almost 20 percent of Brazilians and a quarter of surveyed Uruguayans blaming the IMF; 12 percent of respondents in Brazil and 18 percent of Uruguayans found banks responsible for the bad economy (Alcañiz and Hellwig 2011, 398).

As Argentina's 2001 collapse came after a decade of neoliberal reforms in all of Latin America, characterized by the deep involvement of the IMF and the World Bank and the use of conditionality loans, Argentina's downfall was seen as a cautionary tale to its neighbors. Analysts expected the crisis to irreparably damage Mercosur (Feldstein 2002): "The current crisis will weaken the prospects for the Mercosur trading arrangement among Argentina and its neighbors (Brazil, Paraguay, and Uruguay) and may kill any chance of a general Free Trade Area of the Americas" (Feldstein 2002, 8). Indeed, the following years were particularly stagnant for Mercosur, which was already reeling from Brazil's 1999 devaluation of the real (Malamud 2005; Mera 2005).

Scholars agree that Mercosur's external agenda—through which members coordinate negotiations with third parties such as international organizations or other countries—is its raison d'être and in all likelihood explains its survival over the past decade and a half (Carranza 2006; Gomez Mera 2005; Oelsner 2013). Increasingly, Mercosur serves as a defensive platform, sheltering member states from markets and foreign institutions. Gomez Mera argues that this common external focus "can be understood by examining the persisting convergent foreign policy or 'strategic' incentives faced by Argentina and Brazil, given shared perceptions of external (and to some extent also internal) vulnerability. Defensive strategic considerations, ultimately reflecting the partners' awareness of their relative weakness within a highly asymmetrical international system, have constituted a major force motivating their willingness to overcome crises and further the integration process" (Gomez Mera 2005, 110).

The Latin American governments' goals of minimizing exposure to international actors and of signalling collectively that, when possible, they will choose regional alternatives to international resources, is reflected in their creating the region's new institutions (Sanahuja 2011). In the 2000s, the political leadership of Mercosur states became urgently concerned with depending less on foreign finance and minimizing the chances of another financial catastrophe. Negotiations for the (now failed) FTAA, headed by Brazil, served as a strong focal point against full integration with the markets of the North and brought closer the center-left leadership of South America (Von Bülow 2010). It also highlighted some of the political obsolescence of Mercosur, given the growth of Brazil as a world trade power and the lack of achievements within the common market. Mercosur, in this sense, can be said to be at "a real danger of becoming irrelevant if it remains suspended in its present 'transition' phase, without taking significant steps to implement its internal agenda by completing the custom union and moving towards a common market" (Carranza 2006, 805).

The new regional institutions of Latin America reveal the limitations of the "external agenda" as a survival strategy and the unwillingness of the South American leadership to invest in Mercosur and develop it. Tellingly, Unasur seeks to supersede Mercosur, an effort that BancoSur would help fund, and which the many cross-regional integration initiatives in which Brazil is involved—such as the Brics New Development Bank or the IBSA Dialogue Forum—could kill. Evidently, formal regional integration in the Southern Cone has benefited little from the leading challenges of the current post-neoliberal period: namely, increased (re)nationalization of some of the region's economies, especially in Bolivia and Venezuela; the rise of China as a major commercial stakeholder; the Argentine–Uruguayan conflict over the shared Uruguay River; and Brazil's new position as a world economic power. At present, it is too early to know if regionalization in the 2000s will accomplish the goal of decreased dependence on international finance and markets or even if some of these endeavors—in their initial phases of development—will survive the eventual ideological shift of the subregion's political leadership. Still, they clearly indicate what the priorities are for these South American countries regarding access to trade and, above all, international finance.

## Conclusion

The relationship between debt and the stagnation of regional integration is not surprising. What is more unusual, I argue, is the relationship between debt and the creation of new regional institutions. Yet, as this chapter shows, again and again Latin American governments have responded to common debt crises by investing in regionalization. Interestingly, these investments tend to be low cost, and thus focus more on the "external agendas" of new institutions than on the "internal agendas" of old institutions. Low-cost investments translate into low-cost signals to international market actors. This rationale, I claim, explains in part why Mercosur appears to have been abandoned by its larger members. It should be said, however, that the incentives to deepen regional integration vary cross-nationally and differ greatly for the smaller economies of Mercosur, like Uruguay and Paraguay.

Latin American governments have a strong tradition, starting in the nineteenth century with the first attempts to create a united Latin America, of embarking on regionalization projects. Simón Bolívar's ideals of a Pan-American union—based on his call for continental solidarity and strength in numbers—shaped the negotiations for a (failed) integration of the region in 1826. More often than not, unfortunately, these efforts have failed, in all likelihood because the search for independence from the industrial world has been imbued with economic nationalism (Sanahuja 2011). Perhaps the reason is that these regional projects are frequently born out of crises and deficits rather than out of surplus. This chapter has examined some of the conditions that have led to Latin American regionalization in the early democratic and post-neoliberal eras. A next step would be to examine the agency—the main groups—driving regional integration in Latin America. Scholars and practitioners seem to agree that business tends to be underrepresented in most of these endeavors, which are top-down and state-centered. But bureaucrats, especially those with the technical skills needed to advance interstate cooperation, offer a promising line of inquiry. Indeed, Latin American bureaucrats in the nuclear energy, science, and technology, environmental, and water policy sectors are increasingly active regionally to access resources unavailable at home. These state experts create dense regional networks through which many shared problems (such as budgetary cuts triggered by their indebted governments) are tackled by pooling scarce resources (Alcañiz 2010).

## Notes

1. See Carlos Gabetta, "Mujica, sin filtro: 'Argentina no acompaña un carajo la integración con el Mercosur,'" Perfil, February 22, 2015, http://www.perfil.com /elobservador/Si-uno-esta-lloriqueando-por-lo-que-le-paso-vive-en-el-pasado -20150222-0055.html.

2. President Raul R. Alfonsín quoted in 1987 in *New Perspectives Quarterly* 4 (3), http://www.digitalnpq.org/archive/1987_fall/saving_argentina.html.

3. Ibid.

4. Interview with the Brazilian ambassador to Argentina, Dr. Rego Barros, Buenos Aires, July 2000.

5. Interviews with CNEA's former president Dr. Emma Perez Ferreira, March 2001; Dr. Jorge Coll from CNEA, July 1997 and December 1998; and the director of International Cooperation of CNEN, Dr. Laercio Vinhas, 2000 and 2006.

6. See Carlos Quintas, "La reciente reunión de la CEPAL en Lima y su relación con la CECLA; exposición en la Quinta Reunión de la Comisión Especial de Coordinación Latinoamericana a Nivel Ministerial, Viña del Mar, mayo 1969," CEPAL Digital Repository, http://repositorio.cepal.org/handle/11362/35044.

7. Interview with Dr. Emma Perez Ferreira, Buenos Aires, March 2001.

8. Interviews with CNEA's former president Dr. Emma Perez Ferreira, March 2001; Dr. Jorge Coll from CNEA, July 1997 and December 1998; the director of International Cooperation of CNEN, Dr. Laercio Vinhas, 2000 and 2006, and the director of International Cooperation of CNEA, Roberto Ornstein, 2006.

9. Declaración de Comité de Empresarios Argentinos y Brasileros del Area Nuclear (CEABAN) a la 6ta Reunión del Grupo de Trabajo sobre Política Nuclear, March 1, 1988.

## References

Albuquerque, J. A. G. 2000. *Sessenta anos de política externa brasileira: Prioridades, atores e políticas*. São Paulo: Annablume.

Alcañiz, I. 2000. "Slipping into Something More Comfortable: Argentine-Brazilian Nuclear Integration and the Origins of the MERCOSUR." In *Questioning Geopolitics: Political Projects in a Changing World-System*, edited by G. M. Derluguian and S. L. Greer, 155–68. Westport, Conn.: Praeger.

———. 2010. "Bureaucratic Networks and Government Spending: A Network Analysis of Nuclear Cooperation in Latin America." *Latin American Research Review* 45 (1): 148–72.

———. 2012. "Democratization and Multilateral Security." *World Politics* 64 (2): 306–40.

Alcañiz, I., and T. Hellwig. 2011. "Who's to Blame? The Distribution of Responsibility in Developing Democracies." *British Journal of Political Science* 41 (2): 389–411.

Axline, W. A. 1994. *The Political Economy of Regional Cooperation: Comparative Case Studies*. Madison, N.J.: Fairleigh Dickinson University Press.

Baumann, R. 2009. "Some Recent Features of Brazil-China Economic Relations." Report LC/BRS/R.209 prepared for the Economic Commission for Latin America and the Caribbean (ECLAC/CEPAL), April.

Carasales, J. C. 1997. *De rivales a socios: El proceso de cooperación nuclear entre Argentina y Brasil*. Buenos Aires: Grupo Editor Latinoamericano.

Carranza, M. E. 2006. "Clinging Together: Mercosur's Ambitious External Agenda, Its Internal Crisis, and the Future of Regional Economic Integration in South America." *Review of International Political Economy* 13 (5): 802–29.

Cernat, L. 2003. "Assessing South–South Regional Integration: Same Issues, Many Metrics." Policy Issues in International Trade and Commodities, Study Series No. 21 (UNCTAD/ITCD/TAB/22), prepared for the United Nations Conference on Trade and Development.

Christensen, S. F. 2007. "The Influence of Nationalism in Mercosur and in South America: Can the Regional Integration Project Survive?" *Revista Brasileira de Política Internacional* 50 (1): 139–58.

De Lombaerde, P., R. Flores, P. Lelio Iapadre, M. Schultz, eds. 2012. *The Regional Integration Manual: Quantitative and Qualitative Methods.* Abingdon, U.K.: Routledge.

*Economist.* 2002. "Argentina's Collapse: A Decline Without Parallel." Special report, February 28. http://www.economist.com/node/1010911.

Feldstein, M. 2002. "Argentina's Fall: Lessons from the Latest Financial Crisis." *Foreign Affairs* 81 (2): 8–14.

Frieden, J. A. 1991. *Debt, Development, and Democracy: Modern Political Economy and Latin America, 1965–1985.* Princeton, N.J.: Princeton University Press.

Gomez Mera, L. 2005. "Explaining Mercosur's Survival: Strategic Sources of Argentine–Brazilian Convergence." *Journal of Latin American Studies* 37 (1): 109–40.

Huber, E., and F. Solt. 2004. "Successes and Failures of Neoliberalism." *Latin American Research Review* 39 (3): 150–64.

Iglesias, E. V. 2006. "Economic Paradigms and the Role of the State in Latin America." *CEPAL Review* 90 (12): 7–14.

Kassenova, T. 2014. "Brazil's Nuclear Kaleidoscope: An Evolving Identity." Study prepared for the Carnegie Endowment for International Peace, Washington, D.C.

Levi Coral, Michel. 2011. "La Unión Europea y la nueva integración latinoamericana." *Comentario Internacional* (Quito) 11:217–51.

Madero, C. C. and E. A. Takacs. 1991. *Política nuclear argentina: Avance o retroceso?* Lima: El Ateneo.

Malamud, A. 2005. "Mercosur Turns 15: Between Rising Rhetoric and Declining Achievement." *Cambridge Review of International Affairs* 18 (3): 421–36.

Mansfield, E. D., and H. V. Milner. 1999. "The New Wave of Regionalism." *International Organization* 53 (3): 589–627.

Oelsner, A. 2013. "The Institutional Identity of Regional Organizations, Or Mercosur's Identity Crisis." *International Studies Quarterly* 57 (1): 115–27.

Ornstein, R., and J. C. Carasales. 1998. "La complementación con Brasil." In *La cooperación internacional de la Argentina en el campo nuclear,* edited by J. C. Carasales and R. M. Ornstein. Buenos Aires: Consejo Argentino para las Relaciones Internacionales.

Pecequilo, C. S., and C. A. d. Carmo. 2013. "Regional Integration and Brazilian Foreign Policy: Strategies in the South American Space." *Revista de Sociologia e Política* 21 (48): 51–65.

Polaski, S., J. B. de Souza Ferreira Filho, J. Berg, S. McDonald, K. Thierfelder, D. Willenbockel, and E. Zepeda. 2009. "Brazil in the Global Economy: Measuring the Gains from Trade." Study prepared for the Carnegie Endowment for International Peace, Washington, D.C.

Roett, R. 1983. "Democracy and Debt in South America: A Continent's Dilemma. " *Foreign Affairs* 62 (3): 695–720.

———. 1985. "Latin America's Response to the Debt Crisis." *Third World Quarterly* 7 (2): 227–41.

Sáenz, M. S. D. 2008. "Los complejos caminos del Mercosur: ¿Integración o desintegración sudamericana?" *Sociedad Global* 2 (2): 37–62.

Sanahuja, J. A. 2011. "Multilateralismo y regionalismo en clave suramericana: El caso de Unasur." *Pensamiento Propio* 33 (7): 115–58.

Sbragia, A. 2008. "Review Article: Comparative Regionalism: What Might It Be?" *Journal of Common Market Studies* 46 (1): 29–49.

Schiff, M., and L. A. Winters. 2002. "Regional Cooperation and the Role of International Organizations and Regional Integration." Policy Research Working Paper No. WPS2872, prepared for the World Bank, Washington, D.C., July 31, 2002.

Simmons, B. A. 2000. "International Law and State Behavior: Commitment and Compliance in International Monetary Affairs." *American Political Science Review* 94 (4): 819–35.

Solingen, E. 1996. *Industrial Policy, Technology, and International Bargaining: Designing Nuclear Industries in Argentina and Brazil.* Palo Alto, Calif.: Stanford University Press.

Stallings, B., and W. Peres, 2010. *Growth, Employment, and Equity: The Impact of the Economic Reforms in Latin America and the Caribbean.* Washington, D.C.: Brookings Institution Press.

Sunkel, O., ed. 1993. *Development from Within: Toward a Neostructuralist Approach for Latin America.* Boulder, Colo.: Lynne Rienner.

Van Klaveren, A. 2001. *Chile, el Mercosur y la Unión Europea.* Lisbon: Instituto de Estudos Estratégicos e Internacionais (IEEI). Working Paper #11.

Von Bülow, M. 2010. *Building Transnational Networks: Civil Society and the Politics of Trade in the Americas.* New York: Cambridge University Press.

Walton, M. 2004. "Neoliberalism in Latin America: Good, Bad, or Incomplete?" *Latin American Research Review* 39 (3): 165–83.

Weyland, K. G. 2002. *The Politics of Market Reform in Fragile Democracies: Argentina, Brazil, Peru, and Venezuela.* Princeton, N.J.: Princeton University Press.

Wrobel, P. S., and J. R. Redick. 1998. "Nuclear Cooperation in South America: The Role of Scientists in the Argentine-Brazilian Rapprochement." *Annals of the New York Academy of Sciences* 866 (1): 165–81.

CHAPTER 5

# Mercosur and Regional Migration:
# A Human Rights Approach

Marcela Cerrutti

## Introduction

International migration within South America is a long-standing tradition. Despite losing relative importance since the 1980s compared to movement to countries forming the industrialized North, particularly to the United States and Spain (Villa and Martínez Pizarro 2000; Pellegrino 2003; Reher and Requena 2009; Durand and Massey 2010), such migration has regained relevance and dynamism over the last decade (Cerrutti 2014). The growing numbers of intraregional migrations are linked to processes that have been taking place in both industrialized receiving countries and, to a lesser extent, in South American countries. On the one hand, the intensification of migration barriers and controls in northern receiving countries have made these countries less attractive and more insecure for migrants, particularly for the undocumented; on the other hand, the severe international economic crisis has meant less demand for immigrants' labor in specific sectors (Aysa-Lastra and Chacón 2011).

Meanwhile, South American countries have adopted more socially inclusive policies. These policies have improved their populations' standards of living, and in most such countries the demographic pressures have decreased. After a decade of neoliberal experiments that had devastating social results (Portes and Roberts 2005), many countries have implemented redistributive policies to reduce poverty and improve access to basic human rights (CEPAL 2012a; CEPAL 2012b). At the same time, and to a large extent promoted by regional integration agreements, countries have been improving legal standards governing international migrations in accordance with human rights principles.

This situation may help to explain why emigration to the North has decreased while intraregional migration has increased. For the last decade or so, regional movements have reinvigorated and diversified, not only regarding countries of origin and destination but also motivations. Besides the widely known traditional motives for migration, such as the search for better labor opportunities and the reunification of families, new stimuli are emerging, promoted to a great extent by changes in migration legislation, such as the quest for improved public policy support, the pursuit of academic degrees (university education), and short-term academic circulation.

This chapter analyzes the normative and policy context of intraregional migration in South America. It also explores intraregional migration's implication for a more general discussion on international migration, migrants' rights, and citizenship. The purpose is three-fold: first, to describe how the crisis of neoliberalism in South America and changes in government political orientations brought about a significant shift in the way migration was perceived and linked with human rights and citizenship within the Common Market of the South agreement (Mercosur); second, to depict advances made and difficulties encountered by the Mercosur countries in promoting free circulation of nationals within the region; and finally, to discuss in more detail the recent process undergone by Argentina, the most important immigrant-receiving country in the region and first in line in the advance of immigrant rights. This last part examines progress made in legal provisions regarding migrant rights. It also explores the implications for social and economic integration of migrants and their citizenship practices. The chapter starts with a brief description of the nature and characteristics of intraregional migration flows in Latin America—that is, magnitude, traits, and recent evolution—to provide context to the discussion that follows.

## Intraregional Migration: Trends and Traits

Migration characterizes the lives of many South Americans. Frontiers imposed by decolonization and the formation of nation-states separated people who had shared territories, cultures, and ethnicities (Hinojosa Gordonava 2008). Cross-border movement was common, and the seasonal migration of agricultural workers was a common feature of the first half of the twentieth century (Balán 1985; Reboratti 1986; Villa and Martínez Pizarro 2000). Since the 1950s, divergent processes of economic development in the region and specific linkages between countries have determined the upsurge of two main migration systems. One of these systems, continuing to the present, is centered in Argentina; the other, no longer dynamic, is centered in Venezuela (Massey et al. 1998).

While searching for better opportunities has been recognized as a main migration motivation in migration studies, and the case of intraregional South American migration is not an exception, several additional explanations aside from the existence of wage differentials are useful to understand these dynamics. These include historical factors, sociopolitical situations and violence, access to public services and goods, and the existence of porous borders that facilitate movements across countries. Even key economic motives that explain the majority of moves are based not on wage differentials but on structural deficits of labor markets and labor demand in countries of origin and destination (Cerrutti and Parrado 2015).

Immigration to Argentina from countries that border it, the core of the Southern Cone migration system, is a long-standing tradition. Regional immigration has significantly increased since the 1950s (Marshall and Orlansky 1981; 1983), although inflows were sensitive to both macroeconomic and political conditions. More recently, from 2001 to 2010—when the economy began growing at high rates and labor demand expanded—the number of regional immigrants increased by 40 percent, reaching more than 1.4 million people, and there are strong indications that the number is still increasing (INDEC 2010).

Argentina is not the only country in the region to have received increased numbers of migrants from the region. Chile, after restoring democracy and experiencing high rates of economic growth, also started receiving regional inflows (mainly from Peru and to a lesser extent from Argentina, Bolivia and Colombia). Although not traditionally a country of immigration, in the last decade the number of immigrants into Chile almost doubled (reaching approximately 340,000 in 2012), even though the proportion of migrants in the entire population is still low (Arias, Moreno, and Nuñez 2010; Texidó and Gurrieri 2012). Ecuador has also been attracting regional migrants. Largely originating in Colombia and to a lesser extent from Peru, in the last decade the number of immigrants practically doubled (from 104,130 in 2001 to 194,398 in 2010). Colombian citizens represent 49 percent of the total foreign

population and 98 percent of refugees recognized by the Ecuadoran government (Herrera Mosquera, Moncayo, and Escobar García 2012). These could
be considered mixed flows—that is, flows that are partly in response to forced
migration and partly for economic reasons (Courtis 2011). Thus what can be
observed in recent years is an intensification of migration movements within
the region.

## Economic and Social Integration of Immigrants

Despite regional migrants being very heterogeneous in term of countries of
origin, ethnicity, social and economic background, and migration motivations, a significant portion are in vulnerable positions. Those with indigenous or rural backgrounds or from low socioeconomic positions have
frequently been discriminated against in many spheres of social life. This
marginalization also excludes them from civic and political participation
and often makes them targets for scapegoating by the public, mass media,
and far-right parties. This lack of migrant integration goes against the ideal
of social inclusion with participation, a sense of belonging, and equality.

The process of social integration of immigrant populations strongly depends on how well the host country—its native population and institutions—
receives them, and there are different models of integration around the
world.[1] By no means does this integration imply assimilation in its traditional sociological version; rather, it involves a dynamic process of mutual
adaptation between host population and immigrants. This interaction presupposes stable and cooperative relations that demand certain preconditions. It greatly depends on immigrants' ability to acquire and use new skills
and their willingness to actively participate in social life. Yet receiving countries play a central role in the process of immigrant adaptation, particularly
in the case of more vulnerable or minority groups. The structure of opportunities immigrants encounter greatly determines the possibilities for their
social, economic, and political participation. This structure of opportunities
is shaped by access to rights, equal treatment, the nature and characteristics
of labor demand, public opinion, and attitudes toward immigrants, as well
as the capacity of public institutions to adapt to the specific needs of migrants (including their respect for cultural diversity).

For a long time in South America, and as a relic of past dictatorships,
migration policies were understood as part of national security policy so

were very restrictive both toward granting residency and irregular migration (Novick 2012). The fact that vast proportions of immigrants were of low socioeconomic status, with indigenous or rural backgrounds, placed them in a vulnerable situation.

For example, in Argentina, intraregional labor migrants have traditionally been employed in more disadvantaged and precarious sectors of the economy, in many instances earning lower wages than natives for equal work (Cerrutti and Maguid 2007) and occupying the lowest segment of the labor market (Maguid 1995a; 1995b; 2004). Women are particularly vulnerable because they are highly concentrated in one of the least protected sectors of the labor market—domestic services and caregiving. About six out of ten Paraguayan women and seven out of ten Peruvian women work in domestic services in Argentina (Cerrutti 2009). The demand for these services grew as native women increasingly participated in the labor force, a process also found in the developed world and referred to as global chains of care (Ehrenreich. and Hochschild 2004; Herrera 2005; Pérez Orozco 2007; 2009; Cerrutti and Maguid 2010). Although immigrant men enjoy a somewhat wider range of labor opportunities, these opportunities are also concentrated in specific sectors of the economy, particularly in construction, manufacturing, repair services, and informal commerce. This pattern of immigrant-segmented integration and precarious labor conditions is also found in other countries, such as Chile (Stefoni 2002), Brazil (Baeninger 2012), Ecuador (Herrera Mosquera, Moncayo, and Escobar García 2012), and Uruguay (Koolhaas and Nathan 2013).

Immigrants are discriminated against not only in labor markets but also in other social spheres, such as the housing market. In Argentina, studies show that migrants experience significant spatial segregation in poverty-stricken areas (Mera 2013; 2014) and face more difficulties in renting than natives because they cannot fulfill contract requirements (for example, to provide proof of earnings or rental collateral). In the past they have also suffered discrimination in health care (Mombello 2006; Caggiano 2006; 2007; 2008; Cerrutti 2011; Torres and Garcés 2013) and education (Nobile 2006; Novaro et al. 2008; Beheran 2009).

Access to basic rights is therefore crucial to improving the process of civic and political integration of international migrants in the region. Considering the difficulties encountered by European countries, Rudiger and Spencer (2003) have argued that policies must address institutional barriers to integration, particularly regarding discriminatory practices, and avoid pointing only to migrants' need to adapt and develop their skills. They argue that to effectively address migrant integration, steps should be taken to formalize the legal status of long-term residents and nationals combined with targeted policies oriented toward certain disadvantaged groups. Participation in civic and political decision-making—that is, exercising the rights and responsibilities of residency and citizenship—appears to be a vital, albeit neglected, integration goal.

For more than a decade now, and with some heterogeneity among countries, particularly within the context of the Mercosur agreement, South America has undergone considerable efforts to grant and equalize the rights of citizens of Mercosur countries. As will be shown, agreements and commitments have been made to move toward free circulation and, more controversially, to the constitution of a regional citizenship. In this process, some countries have moved faster than others, as is clearly the case with Argentina.

## Migration, Rights, Citizenship, and Transnational Contexts

International migration motivates crucial debates around the idea of citizenship, particularly in its liberal version. Since a legal status is linked to the nation-state, citizenship and migration legislation are central to the definition of who is entitled to the status of citizen. Only under certain conditions (that vary considerably among countries) can migrants acquire citizenship through naturalization based on legal residency in host countries (Olmos Giuponni 2011). The ability to attain citizenship is central in the current global system of sovereign nation states because it obliges a state to protect an individual. Therefore, nationality is, as Arendt put it, "the right to have rights" (Arendt 1968).

Yet citizenship is not just a matter of formal legal status; it is also a matter of belonging that implies recognition by other members of the community. The law and legal rulings are significant aspects in the granting or denial of recognition; yet the maintenance of boundaries between social groups relies on enforcement, not only by designated officials but also by so-called members of the public (Nakano Glenn 2002).

According to Bloemraad and Provine (2013), in each country the political struggle over the civil rights of its members and who counts as a member makes civil rights a measure of immigrant inclusion. These authors argue that in North America, immigration law has been shaped by domestic politics—beliefs about economic and foreign policy—with only occasional detours for humanitarian considerations, and that the rights of immigrants have been, at most, a minor concern. In Europe the situation is not much different, and the greater attention to immigrant rights has come from domestic court cases and international institutions pressing governments for more considerate treatment of immigrants.

The relationship between citizenship and immigration has been extensively studied in the case of European and North American countries, although no extensive research has been carried out in other countries (Olmos Giupponi 2011). Meanwhile, interesting developments are taking place in South America that could contribute to the debate about immigrant rights, immigration policies, and citizenship. One such development is the ongoing process of regional integration, the so-called Mercosur, which opens a series of questions and challenges regarding the link between citizenship and nationality, particularly because the agreements include commitments to foster a regional citizenship that transcends the boundaries of nation-states. Mercosur developments, as well as significant ongoing changes that are taking place in individual countries regarding the rights of migrants, may serve as contrasting examples of increasingly restrictive paradigms of migration governance.

## Migration and the Mercosur Agreement

Mercosur was created by Argentina, Brazil, Paraguay, and Uruguay in 1991 with the intention of reaching a common market. Over time, it expanded by establishing associated free trade agreements with Chile, Bolivia, Peru, Venezuela, Ecuador, and Colombia, with Mexico given observer status. Venezuela applied for full membership, which it achieved in July 2012. Since its initial stage (the Treaty of Asunción [1991]), labor mobility among member states (Argentina, Brazil, Paraguay, and Uruguay) was included as a topic of concern, although it was problematic. The treaty stated that the main purpose of the agreement was to reach "free movement of goods, services, and factors of production between countries through, among others, the elimination of customs duties and tariffs on the movement of goods, and any other equivalent restrictions" and the signing countries agreed to establish a common external tariff, adopt a common trade policy towards third countries, coordinate macroeconomic and sector policies, and commit to harmonizing legislation in pertinent areas. These were considered the first steps toward the constitution of a common market.

However, as some scholars have argued, the formation of an integrated regional block of countries in the Southern Cone in the early 1990s was a response more to neoliberal globalized trends seeking the liberalization of trade in goods and movement of capital. From its institutionalization as Mercosur, there was a struggle between a purely commercial vision to serve the interests of transnational entrepreneurs and a more social and politicized vision that integration should be motivated by cooperation and solidarity among peoples of different countries defending against globalizing actors (in other words, the transnational corporations and international financial institutions) and generating a space to improve economic, social, cultural, and political relations (Taks 2010).

The treatment of the migration issue within Mercosur was changing in accordance with a different political climate in member states. Granting migrants rights has been promoted by the steady struggle of civil society organizations (particularly human rights movements and migrant associations), progressive center/left political parties and governments. Regional integration agreements as well as bilateral agreements between countries have also played a role in pushing this matter on to the agenda. In the context of Mercosur significant progress has been made, although migration was not a key issue during the first years of the agreement. Over time migration gained relevance, not only because labor mobility was considered along with other production factors but also because member states became increasingly interested in protecting human rights and promoting similar legal standards and control mechanisms. In fact, it was not until 2002 that the region made significant progress in protecting the fundamental rights of migrant persons, with the Residence Agreement for the Mercosur States, the main treaty for migration issues. This agreement, signed by Argentina, Brazil, Bolivia, Chile, Paraguay, and Uruguay, is based on equal treatment and recognition of equal rights between natives and immigrants. It promotes regular migration by recognizing the fundamental rights of foreigners, regardless of their migration status.

The spirit of the Residency Agreement is to allow nationals of a signatory state to reside in the territory of another signatory state. Citizens of signatories may obtain legal residency through the accreditation of nationality and by fulfilling simple requirements (such as possessing a certified ID, a birth certificate, and clear police and judicial records), and are able to do so without having to return to their country of origin. Those with temporary or permanent residence in another Mercosur country will receive the same treatment as country nationals, including in the labor sector. Immigrants with residency and their families have the same civil, social, cultural, and economic rights and freedoms as the nationals of the host country. These immigrants will receive the same treatment as nationals in all matters related to the application of labor legislation, wages, working conditions, and social security.

This Mercosur agreement regarding migrant rights within the region has passed a first major hurdle in general terms with its ratification, in some cases very time-consuming, by six signatory states; it has yet to be fully applied in all countries. Despite its progress as a space of regional integration, Mercosur is still far from the European Union experience, particularly in terms of institutional consolidation and policy. In this context, development of a notion of community citizenship is still embryonic (Aguirre, Mera, and Nejamkis 2008). Yet in the treatment of migration within member states, the issue of free circulation has arisen strongly, and the notion of free movement contains elements that favor the formation of community citizenship over any other circumstances.

As will be further explained, the Argentine government was the first to report the adoption of the agreement on residence and incorporate many of the provisions of this document into its new migration law, passed in December 2003 and enacted in January 2004. It was not until July 2009 that Paraguay ratified the agreement, and only in December 2009 did it enter into force. According to Muñoz Bravo (2010), the delay in ratification and entry into force was due to the fact that countries have differing immigration laws and types of institutions involved in ratification of the agreement.

Mercosur countries have made significant efforts in this area, enacting laws that are international models. However, the need to harmonize the domestic legislation of countries with multilateral and international agreements can still be brought to the regional level (IPPDH 2012). For example, some countries have adapted their migration legislation according to international standards in the field and have ensured the right to migrate, as well as the protection of certain rights regardless of the person's migration status; this is the case in Argentina, Uruguay, and more recently Bolivia. Other countries are still debating adapting their migration laws to meet these standards (for example, Brazil and Paraguay).

## Migration as a Human Right: The Argentina Experience

Argentina is the major immigrant-receiving country in the region and has moved fastest to recognize migrants rights and a regional citizenship. In January 2004, Argentina enacted a new migration law that was a turning point in the way migration was perceived in normative terms. Law 25.871 replaced a law enacted in 1981, during the last military dictatorship. Hines (2010, 472–73) writes: "The new law establishes that migration is a human right—a principle that is not found in the immigration laws of any other large immigrant-receiving country nor explicitly in any international human rights conventions. Law 25.871 extends constitutional and human rights protections to all immigrants within the country, regardless of their legal status, and guarantees immigrants the rights to equal treatment, non-discrimination, and access to educational, medical, and social services."

It took a long time to change the regulatory framework that was enacted to prevent undesirable immigration from neighboring countries, which provided meager legal protection to foreigners, particularly if undocumented. This previous law, the Videla Law, allowed deportations in many circumstances with minimal due process. Furthermore, only permanent residents were allowed to access health services, rent or buy property, or enroll in secondary education. Even after Argentina restored democracy in 1983, the law continued to determine migration matters. This was reflected in case law decided against migrants by the Argentine Supreme Court during the 1980s and 1990s (Olmos Giuponni 2011). In terms of access to other basic rights, such as health care, many of the restrictions were not applied, although treatment of undocumented migrants depended on the discretion of public servants, allowing for discriminatory practices (Cerrutti and Parrado 2002; Jelin, Grimson, and Zamberlin 2006).

The new law was approved in 2004 with strong political support not only from the government but also from all political parties. The need to adapt migrant legislation to Argentina's constitution and international agreements, the strong pressure of human rights advocacy groups, and the reality of a growing number of undocumented migrants in the country largely explain the approval of this law. The activism of human right groups in Argentina should not be underestimated. They gained social legitimacy and public support by litigating against human rights violations on the basis of both the Argentine constitution and international human rights law (Hines 2010). In fact, throughout the 1990s leading human rights organizations took over several cases involving immigrants, and some were even brought before the Inter-American Commission on Human Rights.

It should be pointed out that in contrast to industrialized immigrant-receiving countries, Argentina has adopted the International Convention on the Protection of the Rights of All Migrant Workers and Members of Their Families (United Nations 1990). The new Argentine law went further than the convention and included substantial provisions regarding equal treatment and prohibiting discrimination, deportations, and cancellations of residency. Particularly important are those articles that grant labor, social (including health and education), and economic rights to migrants, irrespective of their migration status. For example, the law establishes that the state in all jurisdictions has to ensure equal access for immigrants and their families to the protections and rights enjoyed by nationals, particularly in reference to access to social services, public goods, health, education, justice, labor, employment, and social security (Article 6). In no event shall a migration irregularity of a foreign national preclude admission as a student at an educational institution, whether public, private, national, provincial, municipal, primary, secondary, tertiary, or university. Educational institutions shall provide guidance and advice on the formalities required to remedy the effects of irregular migration (Article 7). Access to social assistance and health care cannot be denied or restricted in any case to foreigners in need, regardless of their status. Healthcare facilities shall provide guidance and advice on the formalities required to remedy the effects of irregular migration (Article 8).

The new law constitutes an exceptional case where compared to other immigrant-receiving countries, and it has been argued that the law is the product of specific legal circumstances (in other words, human rights are included in Argentina's constitution), that immigration policy is less politicized than in other countries, and that anti-immigrant movements are smaller and have less power in political terms than in other countries (Hines 2010).

Something important to mention about this law is that it provides citizens from Mercosur differential treatment. In accordance with integration principles and the Residency Agreement, the law seeks to facilitate attainment of residency status. This new perspective was confirmed by a decree prepared by the executive branch in 2004 through a massive regularization program. For government officials, the law and the special provisions for Mercosur nationals are based on the recognition that migration restrictions generally have deleterious and unforeseen effects because they cannot modify the forces behind migration, and on the recognition of migration as a human right. The current secretary of the National Office of Migration has stated:

> We should ask at this point if a law can change reality; if the law is one hundred percent fit to motivate behavior as we say as men of law, or if the laws must be appropriate responses to preexisting social phenomena that need to be addressed, sorted, and channeled. . . . Our current view is based on the finding that human mobility is a natural phenomenon. . . . [M]igration always existed in every corner of the planet. . . .
>
> One may wonder what interests are served by restrictive migration policies. In my opinion, they only promote irregularity, informal work, labor and sexual exploitation, smuggling of migrants, and corruption of public officials. . . .
>
> It is noteworthy that Law 25.871 explicitly recognizes the positive contribution of migrants to the host society, and conflates the political conviction about the need to achieve full integration of migrants within the territory with a solid social cohesion, which cannot be achieved if there are no roads to regularization. This latter objective requires public policies to accompany the integration process. Consequently, the law expresses the obligation of the state to guarantee certain basic rights, regardless of the migration condition, such as equal treatment of migrants and their families, access to health, education, justice, and protection of labor rights. (Arias Duval 2010, 100, 102)

The number of residence permits granted during the last 10 years has grown from 40,039 in 2004 to 304,251 in 2012. Between 2004 and 2014, 2,222,462 petitions for residence were initiated. The most important groups were Paraguayans (40 percent), Bolivians (25 percent), and Peruvians (14 percent), followed distantly by Colombians (4 percent). The number of residence permits (temporary and permanent) granted over this period reached 2,007,836.[2]

One significant question to answer in the specific context of Argentina, where considerable advances in granting equal rights to immigrants have been made, is whether those who were in the most vulnerable positions in the past have experienced changes in their social integration and in their civic engagement. This question demands a multifaceted approach to monitor access to rights using both empirical indicators from hard data as well as qualitative data from key social actors, particularly migrants themselves.

## Lights and Shadows in the Implementation of the Law

So that states are accountable for the legal responsibilities they assume toward immigrants, control mechanisms are clearly established. In the human rights protection system, these mechanisms are both internal and external, and procedures for complaining or petitioning international supervisory bodies are available in case states violate their legal responsibilities.

In the case of national, as well as regional, obligations to immigrants, a system to monitor and control actual access to rights should be designed by governmental and nongovernmental organizations. If migrant integration policies are being developed, their success must be assessed, not only to evaluate improvements but also to provide information useful in pointing out difficulties, redefining strategies, and empowering social actors.

Since the new migration law in Argentina, a series of initiatives have been undertaken to regularize migrants and improve the enjoyment of their rights, particularly those related to their access to basic needs and equal treatment before the law. Areas of government have developed mechanisms to accelerate regularization, train public servants on migrant rights, adapt health-care provision to migrant needs, include issues of multiculturalism in schools, penalize migrant slave labor and migrant labor exploitation, protect migrant children, and prevent sex trafficking. Many of these initiatives have been promoted by human rights organizations and academic institutions devoted to human rights research with the support of international organizations (such as OIM, Unicef, and UNFPA) and public funding.

However, the scope and impact of these valuable initiatives are difficult to assess; multiple public institutions are involved and they differ in the level of commitment and resources invested in this particular matter. Most of them have not designed specific monitoring mechanisms, and do not gather systematic follow-up information. A recent study, conducted in Buenos Aires province and aimed at assessing migrants' actual access to rights, found advances in some areas but persistent vulnerabilities in other areas (IPPDH and Buenos Defensor del Pueblo de la Provincia de Buenos Aires-Buenos Aires Ombudsman 2014). Combining quantitative indicators with in-depth interviews, the study found that migrants exhibit worse socioeconomic indicators than natives, as was shown previously, but there have been improvements in several areas of their social lives, particularly in access to health care, education, social programs, and labor markets. Data show that regional migrants' access to primary education is universal, although high-school attendance rates drop, mainly because migrants start work earlier than natives. Parents do not have specific complaints about access to public schools, and most students argue they do not feel discriminated against by teachers or principals. However a significant proportion stated they do feel mistreated and discriminated against by Argentine students, which should be of institutional concern (Cerrutti and Binstock 2012).

In terms of labor incorporation, the new law and the regularization program seem to have had a positive effect. Even though, as stated before, protected jobs are more common among native workers, after the massive program of regularization the percentage of migrant workers without benefits has dropped at a higher rate than that of natives (Baer et al. 2011).

Despite these positive outcomes, there other areas in which migrants have been left behind compared to natives. One area is housing. Some specific but large immigrant groups (such as Bolivians and Paraguayans) show significant spatial segregation in areas with poor urban infrastructure and services. This situation is not only due to their low socioeconomic status; it is also because they face limitations on renting or buying properties and in accessing housing plans (Gallinati 2014; Mera 2014). This situation has surely worsened since 2010 as the numbers of migrants have continued to increase.

Another area that remains problematic is residency requirements for access to some social programs. This is the case, for example, in the imposition of a length of stay in order to enroll in the Universal Child Allowance program (Asignación Universal por Hijo [AUH]). Human rights advocates have argued that this situation is illegal and arises from a lack of harmonization between norms, regulations, and administrative procedures.

Finally, studies have shown that many migrants are not fully informed of their rights, making migrants easy targets for abuse. The situation is even worse when public servants or administrative personnel who deliver services to migrant populations are not aware of norms and procedures regarding the rights of migrants.

## Integration and Regional Citizenship:
## A Struggle for Recognition

In Argentina there is a long-standing tradition of struggle for migrants' rights. As pointed out before, human rights groups and immigrant advocacy groups promoted the new migration law. At the time of writing, there are hundreds of migrant associations pursuing different goals and responding to a variety of social, ethnic, and political groups, with various interlocutors within the state, political parties, other NGOs, and even international organizations (Morales 2012). Many of these associations connect local and national government with migrant communities. Some of these institutions have collaborated in initiatives to promote regularization of migrants and to inform their constituencies of their rights. They also ally with nongovernmental organizations monitoring enforcement of the law.

The radical change in governmental perspective toward immigrants has partly altered the relationships that these associations have had with the government. Such associations display an array of strategies to improve their situation, depending on the specific goal they pursue. In some instances they stress their status as migrants, particularly when this is the criteria defined by policy requirements. For example, in their struggle for making health services more sensitive to their needs, or when in search of unrestricted access to social programs (which impose length of stay as a requirement), they appeal to their migrant status to avert discrimination. In these cases, they appeal to the rights conferred by the Constitution and the new migration law. The granting of these rights has empowered them in their struggle for social inclusion.

The relationship of migrant groups to political power is heterogeneous; however, their appreciation for the legal recognition of their rights is clear. For some leaders, having achieved the recognition of rights puts them now in a different position than when they have to fight recognition. As an interviewee once told me, "We should now pass from a confrontational demand phase (toward political power) to a new one of co-responsibility (in the implementation of policies toward immigrants)."

Interestingly, studies have shown that some immigrants in Argentina who now possess rights consider themselves part of the "poor" population, forgotten by society in general and by political power in particular. This happens when demands are shared by nonmigrant groups, as has been the case in the struggle for access to housing and urban infrastructure. Interestingly, they appeal to their status as regional citizens and not as much as to that of migrants. Gallinati (2014), in her ethnography of the practices of citizenship among immigrants in a shanty town in Buenos Aires, shows that even though Bolivians and Paraguayans were the majority of inhabitants in the neighborhood, they opted to struggle jointly with Argentines, who were in a similarly precarious situation and with whom they shared chronic structural problems, appealing to their subordinate position in the social structure. By a complex process of network building, training in norms and regulation, as well as various paths of political participation, they found it more effective to leave aside their migrant identity and to struggle as subordinate citizens of a regional space.

Gavazzo (2011) posed a very interesting question in her study: Can the Argentine state, with various institutional mechanisms, activate, promote, and facilitate valid forms of participation in the national political arena? By examining how Bolivian and Paraguayan organizations work, she concludes that the structure of political opportunities can be enlarged so long as a number of conditions are met: migrants must recognize themselves as subjects with rights; migrant associations must be able to settle internal conflicts; migrant leaders must be able to represent collective interests; migrant organizations must be acknowledged and named as partners by the state; and public policies must be designed not only to improve knowledge among migrant communities but also to generate debate over migration issues in the general public. She also argues that migrants can be political actors only if Argentine society accepts them as citizens and not merely as immigrant residents who are socially integrated but politically excluded.

## Conclusion

Since the first years of the 2000s, migration within South America has been reinvigorated at a time when migration barriers and controls, particularly for undocumented migrants, have intensified in Northern receiving countries. South America for the first years of the 2000s has made considerable efforts to grant and equalize the rights of citizens of Mercosur countries. The region is trying to attain a free circulation space and, within this context, to discuss a regional citizenship. Yet this process has just begun, with some countries having moved faster than others, and many questions remain.

This chapter has examined the questions and challenges posed by Mercosur, including developments in migration rights, integration, and regional citizenship, with specific emphasis on the case of Argentina, which is the main immigrant-receiving country and the one that has changed more dramatically in its perspective on migration issues. The regional processes and discussions taking place may serve as a contrasting example of increasingly restrictive paradigms of migration governance, particularly in North America.

Current stands on migration issues are the result of historical processes in the region. Progressive governments have since about 2000 onwards (depending on the country) contested the dark legacies of a past that has linked migration regulations to national security policies, followed by the promotion of neoliberal free circulation policies restricted to capital and goods. A renewed political climate has contributed to advances in the rights of migrants in national legislation and regional agreements. In this process, civil society organizations (particularly human rights movements and migrant associations), progressive center/left political parties, and governments have all played a significant role.

Considerable efforts have been made to grant and equalize the rights of citizens of Mercosur member states. In the treatment of migration within member states, free circulation has arisen strongly as a goal, and this notion contains elements favoring the formation of community citizenship over any other circumstances. Some countries have adapted their migration legislation according to international standards in the field, establishing migration as a human right regardless of the person's migration status (Argentina, Uruguay, and more recently Bolivia).

Argentina has enacted a migration law that goes further than international conventions on the matter, and includes substantial provisions regarding equal treatment and prohibiting discrimination, deportations, and cancellations of residency. The law grants labor, social (health and education), and economic rights to migrants, irrespective of their migration status. Compared to other immigrant countries, Argentina constitutes an exceptional case, and it is for this reason that its progress should be scrutinized.

Compared to other immigrant-receiving countries, Argentina possesses three advantageous traits: human rights are included in its constitution; immigration policy is less politicized; and anti-immigrant movements are less powerful (Hines 2010).

However, Argentina is still a young democracy that needs to advance mechanisms of control and accountability. For this reason, states must be monitored in how they fulfill their responsibilities to immigrants. It seems reasonable to design a system with the participation of governmental and nongovernmental organizations. If migrant integration and actual access to rights constitute key policy goals for the state, then monitoring must be established to assess their accomplishments and difficulties. This process will redefine strategies and empower social actors. Furthermore, it will constitute a test case for many other countries of the region that are adapting their normative frameworks to Mercosur agreements.

## Notes

1. See Rudiger and Spencer 2003 for the European case.
2. Dirección Nacional de Migraciones, "Sintesis estadistica de radicaciones: Informe especial del año 2014," www.migraciones.gov.ar/pdf_varios/estadisticas/Sintesis%20 Estadisticas%20Radicaciones%20a%20Diciembre%202014.pdf.

## References

Aguirre, O., G. Mera, and L. Nejamkis. 2008. "Ciudadanía y libre circulación en el Mercosur." *Revista Umbrales* 6:73–80.

Arendt, H. 1968. *The Origins of Totalitarianism*. New York: Harcourt.

Arias, S. G., R. M. Moreno, and D. G. Nuñez. 2010. "Inmigración Latinoamericana en Chile: Analizando perfiles y patrones de localización de la comunidad peruana en el Area Metropolitana de Santiago." *Tiempo y Espacio* 25.

Arias Duval, M. A. 2010. "Política migratoria y derechos humanos." In *Migraciones Internacionales en el Siglo XXI*, 100–107. Buenos Aires: Ministerio del Interior, Dirección Nacional de Migraciones.

Aysa-Lastra, M. and L. Chacón. 2011. "El impacto de la crisis global en el mercado de trabajo de los inmigrantes latinoamericanos en Estados Unidos y en España." *Revista del Ministerio de Trabajo e Inmigración de España. Migraciones Internacionales* 95:47–82.

Baeninger, R. 2012. *Imigracao Boliviana no Brasil*. Campinas, Braz.: NEPO.

Baer, G., N. Benitez, D. Contartese, and D. Schleser. 2011. "El trabajo inmigrante en una etapa de recuperación del empleo e integración sudamericana in Ministerio de Trabajo, Empleo y Seguridad Social y Organización Internacional del Trabajo." *La Inmigración Laboral de Sudamericanos en Argentina.* Buenos Aires: Ministerio de Trabajo, Empleo y Seguridad Social y Organización Internacional del Trabajo.

Balán, J. 1985. *Las migraciones internacionales en el Cono Sur.* Buenos Aires: Comité Intergubernamental para las Migraciones.

Beheran, M. 2009. "Niños y niñas bolivianos en la Ciudad de Buenos Aires: Escolaridad y experiencias formativas en el ámbito familiar." *Estudios Migratorios Latinoamericanos* 22/23 (67): 375–95.

Bloemraad, I., and D. M. Provine. 2013. "Immigrants and Civil Rights in Cross-National Perspective: Lessons from North America." *Journal of Comparative Migration Studies* 1 (1): 45–68.

Caggiano, S. 2006. "Fronteras de la ciudadanía: Inmigración y conflictos por derechos en Jujuy." In *Migraciones regionales hacia la Argentina: Diferencia, desigualdad y derechos,* edited by A. Grimson and E. Jelin, 237–84. Buenos Aires: Prometeo.

———. 2007. "Madres en la frontera: Género, nación y los peligros de la reproducción." *Iconos, Revista de Ciencias Sociales* 28:94–106.

———. 2008. "Qué se haga cargo su país: La cultura, los estados y el acceso a la salud de los inmigrantes bolivianos en Jujuy." In *Hegemonía e interculturalidad: Poblaciones originarias e inmigrantes,* edited by C. García Vázquez, 243–79. Buenos Aires: Prometeo.

CEPAL. 2012a. *Estudio económico de América Latina y el Caribe 2012.* Santiago de Chile: CEPAL.

———. 2012b. *Panorama social de América Latina 2012.* Santiago de Chile: CEPAL.

Cerrutti, M. 2009. "Gender and Intra-regional Migration in South America." *Human Development Research Papers 2009/12.* United Nations Development Program.

———. 2011. *Salud y migración internacional mujeres Bolivianas en la Argentina.* Buenos Aires: Fondo de Población de las Naciones Unidas.

———. 2014. "Migración internacional en América Latina: Tendencias y retos para la acción." In *Cairo+20: perspectivas de la agenda de población y desarrollo sostenible después de 2014,* organized by Laura Rodríguez Wong, José Eustáquio Alves, Jorge Rodríguez Vignoli, and Cássio Maldonado Turra. *Serie Investigaciones* 15. Río de Janerio: Asociación Latinoamericana de Población.

Cerrutti, M., and G. Binstock. 2012. *Los Estudiantes Inmigrantes en la Escuela Secundaria. Integración y Desafíos.* Buenos Aires: UNICEF

Cerrutti, M., and A. Maguid. 2007. "Inserción laboral e ingresos de migrantes limítrofes y del Perú en el Área Metropolitana de Buenos Aires, 2005." *Notas de la Población (CEPAL)* 83:75–98.

———. 2010. "Familias divididas y cadenas globales de cuidado: La migración sudamericana a España." *Serie Políticas Sociales No. 163. División de Desarrollo Social.* Santiago de Chile: CEPAL.

Cerrutti, M., and E. Parrado. 2002. "The Health Needs of Migrants in a Context of Economic Integration: The Case of Paraguay and Argentina." Final Research Report, CENEP/Pan American Health Organization.

———. 2015. "Intraregional Migration in South America: Trends and a Research Agenda." *Annual Review of Sociology* 41:399–421.

Courtis, C. 2011. "Marcos institucionales, normativos y de políticas sobre migración internacional en Argentina, Chile y Ecuador." In *Migración internacional en América Latina y el Caribe: Nuevas tendencias, nuevos enfoques*, edited by J. Martínez Pizarro, 99–207. Santiago de Chile: CEPAL.

Durand J., and D. Massey. 2010. "New World Orders: Continuities and Changes in Latin American Migration." *Annals of the American Academy of Political and Social Science* 630 (1): 20–52.

Ehrenreich, B., and A. R. Hochschild. 2004. *Global Women: Nannies, Maids and Sex Workers in the New Economy*. New York. Henry Holt.

Gallinati, C. 2014. "Migración, vivienda e integración regional: Un abordaje desde la villa miseria." Ph.D. dissertation, Facultad de Ciencias Sociales, Universidad de Buenos Aires.

Gavazzo, N. 2011. "Oportunidades políticas para la participación de los migrantes: El caso de las organizaciones de latinoamericanos en Argentina?" *Migración, Cohesión Social y Gobernabilidad*. Lisboa: Instituto de Ciencias Sociais, Universidade de Lisboa.

Herrera, G. 2005. "Mujeres ecuatorianas en las cadenas globales del cuidado." In *La migración ecuatoriana: Transnacionalismo, redes e identidades*, edited by Giaconda Herrera, María Cristina Carrillo, and Alicia Torres, 281–303. Quito: Facultad Latinoamericana de Ciencias Sociales, FLACSO.

Herrera Mosquera, G., M. I. Moncayo, and A. Escobar García. 2012. *Perfil migratorio del Ecuador*. Quito: Organización Internacional para las Migraciones.

Hines, B. 2010. "The Right to Migrate as a Human Right: The Current Argentine Immigration Law." *Cornell International Law Journal* 43 (3): 471–511.

Hinojosa Gordonava, A. 2008. "España en el itinerario de Bolivia: Migración transnacional, género y familia en Cochabamba." In *Las Migraciones en América Latina: Políticas, culturas y estrategias*, edited by Novick Susana, 93–112. Buenos Aires: CLACSO-Catálogos.

INDEC. 2010. Censo Nacional de Población y Vivienda 2010. Instituto Nacional de Estadísticas y Censos, República Argentina.

IPPDH. 2012. "La implementación de los acuerdos de residencia del Mercosur relativos a la protección de los derechos de los niños, niñas y adolescentes: Diagnóstico y lineamientos para la acción." *Estudios e Investigaciones, Instituto de Políticas Públicas en Derechos Humanos Mercosur*. Buenos Aires: IPPDH.

IPPDH and Defensor del Pueblo de la Provincia de Buenos Aires. 2014. *Informe: Acceso a derechos de migrantes en la Provincia de Buenos Aires*. Buenos Aires: IPPDH-DFP.

Jelin, E., A. Grimson, and N. Zamberlin. 2006. "¿Servicio? ¿Derecho? ¿Amenaza? La llegada de inmigrantes de países limítrofes a los servicios públicos de salud." In *Salud y migración regional: Ciudadanía, discriminación y comunicación intercultural*, edited by Elizabeth Jelin, 33–46. Buenos Aires: Instituto de Desarrollo Económico y Social.

Koolhaas, M., and M. Nathan. 2013. *Inmigrantes internacionales y retornados en Uruguay: Informe de Resultados de Censo 2011*. Montevideo: UNFPA-OIM-INE.

Maguid, A. 1995a. "Migrantes limítrofes en la Argentina: Su inserción en el mercado de trabajo." *Estudios del Trabajo* 10:47–76.

———. 1995b. "L'immigration des pays limitrophes dans l'Argentine des années 90: Mythes et réalités." *Revue Européenne des Migrations Internationales* 11 (2).

———. 2004. "Immigration and the Labor Market in Metropolitan Buenos Aires." In *International Migration: Prospects and Policies in a Global Market*, edited by Douglas Massey and Edward Taylor. New York: Oxford University Press.

Marshall, A. 1979. "Immigrant Workers in the Buenos Aires Labor Market." *International Migration Review* 13 (3): 499–501.

———. 1983. "Inmigración de países limítrofes y demanda de mano de obra en la Argentina 1940–1980." *Desarrollo Económico* 23 (89): 35–58.

Marshall, A., and D. Orlansky. 1981. "Las condiciones de expulsión en la determinación del proceso emigratorio desde países limítrofes hacia la Argentina." *Desarrollo Económico* 20 (80): 491–510

———. 1983. "Inmigración de países limítrofes y demanda de mano de obra en la Argentina 1940–1980." *Desarrollo Económico* 23 (89): 35–58.

Massey, D., J. Arango, G. Hugo, A. Kouaouci, A. Pellegrino, and E. Taylor. 1998. *Worlds in Motion: Understanding International Migration at the End of the Millennium*. Oxford: Clarendon Press.

Mera, G. 2013. "Migraciones y espacio urbano: Distribución de los migrantes paraguayos en la ciudad de Buenos Aires: Procesos de diferenciación y segregación especial." Ph.D. dissertation, Facultad de Ciencias Sociales, Universidad de Buenos Aires.

———. 2014. "Migración paraguaya en la ciudad de Buenos Aires (2010): Distribución espacial y pobreza." *Revista Latinoamericana de Población* 8 (14): 57–80.

Mombello, L. 2006. "Alternativas de atención en salud basadas en la interculturalidad: La cercanía barrial y la acción institucional." In Jelin, *Salud y Migración Regional*, 103–16.

Morales, O. G. 2012. "Asociacionismo y formas de visibilización/participación en la arena pública." *Tram[p]as de la Comunicación y la Cultura* 70:119–32.

Muñoz Bravo, M. 2010. "El proceso de internalización del Acuerdo sobre Residencia en el Mercosur: Una evaluación del compromiso de seis estados de crear un área de libre residencia y trabajo" (mimeo).

Nakano Glenn, E. 2002. *Unequal Freedom: How Race and Gender Shaped American Citizenship and Labor*. Cambridge, Mass.: Harvard University Press.

Nobile, M. 2006. "La discriminación de los inmigrantes en la escuela media: Un análisis de los discursos, las prácticas y los condicionantes legales." Final Report, Regional Fellowship Program, Consejo Latinoamericano de Ciencias Sociales, CLACSO, Buenos Aires.

Novaro, G., L. Borton, M. L. Diez, and A. C. Hetch. 2008. "Sonidos del silencio, voces silenciadas: Niños indígenas y migrantes en escuelas de Buenos Aires." *Revista Mexicana de Investigación Educativa* 13 (36): 173–201.

Novick, S. 2012. "Transformations and Challenges of Argentinean Migratory Policy in Relation to the International Context." *Migraciones Internacionales* 6 (3): 205–36.

Olmos Giuponni, M. B. 2011. "Citizenship, Migration and Regional Integration: Reshaping Citizenship Conceptions in the Southern Cone." *European Journal of Legal Studies* 4 (2): 104–36.

Pellegrino, A. 2003. "La migración internacional en América Latina y el Caribe: Tendencias y perfiles de los migrantes." *Serie Población y Desarrollo* 35. Santiago de Chile: Centro Latinoamericano y Caribeño de Demografía, CELADE, División de Población.

Pérez Orozco, A. 2007. "Cadenas Globales de Cuidado." Working Paper No. 2, "Género, Migración y Desarrollo" Series, UN-INSTRAW, Santo Domingo.

———. 2009. "Miradas globales sobre la organización social de los cuidados II: Qué retos políticos debemos afrontar?" *Serie Género, Migración y Desarrollo.* Santo Domingo: UN-INSTRAW.

Portes, A., and B. Roberts. 2005. "The Free Market City: Latin American Urbanization in the Years of the Neoliberal Experiment." *Studies in Comparative International Development* 40 (1): 43–82.

Reboratti, C. 1986. "Migración y trabajo estacional en la Argentina." In *Se fue a Volver,* PISPAL, CENEP, CIUDAD. Mexico City: El Colegio de México.

Reher, D., and M. Requena. 2009. "Introducción: El impacto de la inmigración en la sociedad española." In *Las múltiples caras de la inmigración en España,* edited by D. Reher and M. Requena, 7–19. Madrid: Alianza Editorial.

Rudiger, A., and S. Spencer. 2003. "Social Integration of Migrants and Ethnic Minorities: Policies to Combat Discrimination." *Economic and Social Aspects of Migration,* Conference jointly organized by the European Commission and OECD.

Stefoni, C. 2002. "Mujeres inmigrantes peruanas en Chile." *Papeles de Población* 8 (33): 117–45.

Taks, J. 2010. "Antecedentes y desafíos de las políticas de migración en Uruguay." In *Estado actual y perspectivas de las políticas migratorias en el Mercosur,* edited by C. Zurbriggen and L. Mondol, 151–79. Montevideo: FLACSO Uruguay.

Texidó, E., and J. Gurrieri. 2012. "Panorama migratorio de América del Sur 2012." Buenos Aires: International Organization for Migration.

Torres, G. O., and H. A. Garcés. 2013. "Representaciones sociales de migrantes perua-
nos sobre su proceso de integración en la ciudad de Santiago de Chile." *Polis, Revista Latinoamericana* 12 (35): 309–34.

Villa, M., and J. Martínez Pizarro. 2000. "Trends and Patterns in the Americas." In
*International Migration and Development in the Americas. Symposium on Inter-
national Migration in the Americas* 15. Santiago de Chile: Comisión Económica
para América Latina y El Caribe, CEPAL, Seminarios y Conferencias.

# PART II

## Democracy and Its Discontents

CHAPTER 6

# Venezuela Between Two States

George Ciccariello-Maher

## Introduction

As the title of this chapter suggests, while contemporary Venezuela may be considered post-neoliberal, it is not yet postliberal. Much less is it what some, in an unfortunate turn of phrase, have called "postdemocratic" (Levine 2002, 261). In fact, it is in the easy slide between postliberal and postdemocratic that we can locate the questions animating many contemporary debates, including the intervention that follows. Instead of being comfortably "post-," Venezuela stands at something of a tipping point: situated tensely between capitalism and socialism, between liberal democracy and . . . something else. That "something else" is increasingly denoted in terms of the "communal state," a grassroots and radically democratic alternative to both liberal democracy in the political sphere and the oil export-driven and consequently import-addicted economic sphere. This is an alternative, in other words, that aspires to a postliberal future that is not postdemocratic but in fact *more* democratic.

It is from this space between the existing and the not-yet that many misunderstandings arise, however willfully. Despite widespread laments about the dismantling, unraveling, and even destruction of Venezuelan democracy, what is too often neglected is that such concerns center on a particular form of liberal-representative democracy.[1] In other words, most contemporary criticisms of Venezuela's Bolivarian government leverage their opposition on the basis of a specific understanding of what democracy means but, more often than not, this is not a view of democracy that is either reflected in the existing institutional apparatus or shared by its constituents, and specifically the popular organizations that form the backbone of Bolivarian movement. As a result, supporters and opponents of Chavismo more often than not speak past one another through the opaque conceptual veil of democracy.

I do not expect to bridge this most insurmountable of political and interpretive gaps in a single chapter, especially because this gap is simultaneously a partisan one, and its partisan nature is inseparable from both the perspectival view it embodies and the dynamic it helps to set in motion. But what I do hope to do is at least clarify the theoretical and practical terrain by counterposing the broad dynamics of the Bolivarian Revolution to purportedly unassailable assumptions regarding the inevitability and universality of liberal-representative democracy. This, however, is no easy task in and of itself: if there exists a multitude of different interpretations of liberal democracy, each with their own centers of gravity and points of emphasis, the same is true of Bolivarian socialism. Simply recalibrating our concept of democracy, however, is not sufficient either, since neither democracy nor Bolivarianism is simply a theory, but both are practices informed by contested theories, practices that then circle around to inform the theories themselves.

The practice of the Bolivarian Revolution, moreover, is that of a project and a process of transformation, rather than a steady-state regime of government (Denis 2004; Fernandes 2010). I have shown previously how this process itself predates, coexists tensely with, and far exceeds the realm of the government in *sensu stricto*, embodying instead a dynamic tension between constituted power from above and constituent power from below (Ciccariello-Maher 2013a). Something strange happens indeed when we attempt to view such dynamic processes—much less combat formations—either through the lens of or in counterposition to fixed political forms. As a result, many opponents of the process—and even some supporters—misunderstand (or choose to misunderstand) it not only synchronically (by incorrectly holding it up against liberal democracy) but also diachronically (by viewing it as a stable form of government rather than as something in motion and possessing of a direction).

The resulting analytic difficulties are obvious: many more variables than could plausibly be held constant—or even slowed sufficiently—and all in motion and operating incessantly one upon the other. But however difficult the analytic task or imperfect the result, we must attempt to sketch its rough parameters, and in what follows I do so by tracking three rough moments in the Bolivarian process that constitute a sort of boomerang swing. In the first, taking cues from Carl Schmitt and Antonio Gramsci's critiques of liberalism, I show how the Chávez government and the social movements that it comprises press away from liberal-representative democracy toward popular unity by breaking decisively with what many consider the fundamental aspect of liberal democracy: the separation of powers. In the second moment, the 1999 Constitution stands as a momentary congealment or condensation of forces that accordingly looks both backward (toward liberalism) and forward (toward a new, participatory state). Finally, through Enrique Dussel's combative and ruptural notion of the people, I show that instead of settling on unity (as Eurocentric conceptions of the popular would have it), the Bolivarian process is instead pressing outward toward the consolidation of a dispersed form of communal power that coexists tensely and, increasingly, in open antagonism toward the liberal-representative apparatus.

However, my goal is to contribute not only to concrete interpretation of Venezuelan history and politics, but to political thought as well, in which static conceptions—quasi-Aristotelian ideal states and best regimes—weigh heavily on theorizing even today. Such static conceptions prove woefully insufficient for grasping both, in a general sense, the real contradictions and real movement they set into motion, and in particular the sort of counterintuitive, inverse transition through centralization to decentralization that we find in contemporary Venezuela. Moreover, when these static conceptions are drawn from the arsenal of liberal-representative democracy, this difficulty is redoubled. Liberal-representative concepts do not help us to grasp dynamic political motion, precisely because they were designed to do just the opposite: to check power by dividing it, and to privilege stability over change. While this may be obvious, few appear willing to admit the corollary: that any effort at radical change will inevitably confront the separation of powers as a barrier to be rightly overcome.

## Against Liberalism

Much contemporary political debate, discussion, and theorizing is grounded in the unstated assumption that there is no alternative to liberal-democratic political forms. Even those who reject the quasi-Hegelianism of Fukuyama's "end of history" nevertheless tend to concede his normative point: that liberal-democratic institutions are the safest, most stable, and most trustworthy institutional arrangements for political life today. Contemporary

Venezuela is no exception and, if anything, it is there that such claims are expressed most shrilly, thereby providing a transparent example of what David Scott calls the "blackmail" of (liberal) democracy (2012, 223). However, the idea that liberal democracy is not an inherently stable institutional order, and instead one rife with deep and irreconcilable contradictions, has a long and critical pedigree on both extremes of the political spectrum. In what follows, I turn briefly to both Schmitt and Gramsci, who in different ways draw out irreducible and fatal tensions within liberalism, tensions that invariably center on the separation of powers.

As implausible as it may seem in retrospect, the interwar period of the 1920s and 1930s—so rife with apparent contradiction—did not escape the same presumption that reigns today: that liberalism represented a safe and stable alternative to threats on the Left and the Right. As the conservative jurist Carl Schmitt cautioned, "discussion cannot content itself with repeating the question: 'Parliamentarism, what else?' and insist that at present there is no alternative" (1988, 76). Similarly, we need only scratch the surface to see that Venezuelan history has not been particularly kind to liberal democracy. Instead, and despite its own pretenses, Venezuelan liberalism has never managed to escape Schmitt's famous dictum that, "Sovereign is he who decides on the exception" (1985, 5). In fact, the four decades of liberal-representative democracy prior to Chavismo were bookended by brutal resort to the sovereign exception: the ostensible founder of Venezuelan democracy, Rómulo Betancourt, presided over a near-constant state of exception between 1959 and 1962 as those radicalized by the democratic opening demanded more than he was willing or able to give, and the liberal state was later forced, when mortally wounded, to resort to yet another state of emergency to quell the anti-neoliberal Caracazo rebellion of 1989 at the cost of hundreds or even thousands of lives.

As many grassroots revolutionaries and organizers will tell you, even the period between those emergencies was not characterized by the universal enforcement of liberal protections; hundreds or thousands were disappeared and tortured, with revolutionary and grassroots movements alike persecuted, repressed, and subject to increasingly severe massacres as the system entered its terminal phase. The claim, so frequent today, that recent years in Venezuela have seen a privileging of second-wave social rights over first-wave political rights[2] is thus little more than smoke and mirrors, since for Venezuela's persecuted and disappeared these first-wave protections were simply never a reality. From this perspective, liberal democracy as either a safe or a stable form of government loses its easy credibility, its end-of-history pretense of being the only real option.

Furthermore, radical voices in Venezuela have long aspired not to perfect liberal democracy but to replace it. Fabricio Ojeda, one of the central figures in toppling the dictator Marcos Pérez Jiménez on 23 January 1958, was quick to denounce the dangers of merely formal democracy in a speech that marked his own transition into the armed struggle: "On January 23—this I confess as creative self-criticism—nothing happened in Venezuela . . . only names were changed. . . . The Venezuelan people are already tired of promises that cannot be fulfilled and disappointed with a democracy that never arrives, but in whose name they are mistreated, persecuted, and misled" (Ojeda 1962). In so doing, Ojeda set the tone early on for those later generations that would struggle for a different democracy, a democracy that exceeds and transcends its merely liberal or representative forms, and this demand has been a continuous thread uniting struggles spanning the past five decades, as first guerrillas, then dispersed movements across excluded social sectors demanded—while practicing—more direct and unmediated, participatory forms of democracy that sought not only political equality but social equality as well. The Bolivarian Revolution, as a long trajectory that predated Hugo Chávez himself and has continued beyond his death, was never about building a better liberal democracy, but about replacing that system with a different, better, and more direct form of democracy altogether.

This demand for a better and more radical democracy, not to mention the institutions that have developed to put this vision into practice, are often erased and obscured in the present by the very same conflation of democracy with its liberal variant. The Chavistas, we are told, are undemocratic for failing to uphold a preordained image of what democracy is. And if there is a single complaint from which all others spring, it centers on the single idea that is almost synonymous with liberal democracy itself: the separation of powers. With good reason: as Gramsci insisted, the separation of powers encapsulates "the entire liberal ideology . . . and its weaknesses" (1971, 246). Democracy is liberal democracy, and liberal democracy is the separation of powers, or so it would seem.

Opponents of the Chávez and now Maduro governments have consistently portrayed liberal democracy as though under a mortal threat, with the separation of powers the proverbial canary in the coal mine. We have been informed on many occasions for more than fifteen years that the separation of powers was finally dead, only to be newly informed, at a later date, that it had in fact survived only to then suffer the same fate. This complaint then opens organically onto all others: just as the autonomy of the legislature and judiciary is threatened by a creeping executive power, so too the fiscal autonomy of the central bank and the national oil company, PDVSA, the regional and municipal autonomy of elected officials, and even the prized autonomy of the ostensibly professional and apolitical armed forces. Such anxieties, which also manifest in the temporal separation of term limits, inevitably point to the broader concern to preserve Venezuela's liberal-representative democracy as a sort of safe and stable fallback.

This perceived trampling over legislative and especially judicial power by the executive creates a peculiar situation in which every executive action serves as further proof of this cardinal violation, just as every sign of legislative deference to the executive merely confirms what it would seem to contradict: the quasi-dictatorial power of a caudillo. Here I refer in particular to the legislative approval of enabling laws that allow the president to issue decrees for a specific time and to specifically limited ends. Even though enabling laws are issued by the legislature itself, and although such laws have been a common currency of Venezuelan politics—Chávez was the fifth president in as many decades to be granted such powers (Wilpert 2007, 289n24)—one law article goes so far as to deem Chávez's first enabling law in 2001 "the demise of the separation of powers" (García-Serra 2001).[3]

Chavistas tend to respond to such concerns from a perspective that does not reject democracy but in fact prioritizes democratic claims over a formally institutionalized separation of powers, embodying the future transcendence of liberal democracy in the process: Isn't democracy about the people, the poor and dispossessed above all, making decisions for themselves rather than ceding those decisions to the cold sterility of technocratic institutions? If the people serve as the final instance of sovereignty for rewriting the constitution—hardly a controversial opinion—then why does that popular sovereignty dissipate once the words are laid to paper? This points directly to the unresolved paradox of democratic founding: If the people make institutions, then surely they can unmake them as well.

In the Venezuelan context, these point to a permanent and irreducible transcendence of the law, and raise a series of other, more specific questions: How can a government of the people, much less a process of transformation, possibly relinquish control over both oil income (PDVSA) and broad macroeconomic policies (the central bank) to the technicians? Where the military is historically characterized as apolitical and excluded from political

participation, others ask (with the experiences of Southern Cone dictatorships in mind): What politics are already always latent in the armed forces?
And whereas the Venezuelan opposition ferociously opposed the elimination
of term limits, many Chavistas wondered aloud at the time: What could be
less democratic than preventing the population from electing the leader of
their choice?

Many Chavistas, moreover, point to the bad faith of self-styled liberal opposition forces that are liberal only as long as it suits them, that claim today
to defend a constitution they once opposed, and that support the separation
of powers above all else, but did not hesitate to dissolve those same powers
during the 2002 coup against Chávez and the Constitution. This, too, emerges
most clearly when viewed as a process: it was precisely the furious reaction
to Chávez's enabling law of 2001, which critics tarred as unconstitutional or
even dictatorial, that set into motion a dynamic that eventually led to the
short-lived coup. It was during the coup that many vociferous proponents of
liberal democracy—including one of the harshest critics of the "dismantling"
of Venezuelan democracy and the separation of powers, Allan Brewer-
Carías—nevertheless found themselves implicated in and actively supporting
a concrete break with the constitutional order that saw dozens shot dead in
the streets.

On the tensely partisan terrain of contemporary Venezuela, such patently
selective liberalism should not surprise in and of itself, but such tensions do
nevertheless point to theoretical contradictions to be drawn out. Nor would
this bad faith prove surprising to liberalism's theoretical critics, for whom
the internal contradictions of liberalism render resort to emergency measures all but inevitable. According to Schmitt, the liberal separation of powers is marked by a faith in a banal bipartisan "metaphysic," which assumes
that unity can emerge from even the internally divided legislative talking-
shop (1988, 41). For Schmitt, this system—characterized by "a threefold division of powers, a substantial distinction between the legislative and the
executive, the rejection of the idea that the plenitude of state power should
be allowed to gather at any one point"—is in fact "the antithesis of a democratic conception of identity" (36). The gap between democratic identity and
liberalism will in fact prove to be the latter's Achilles' heel, and Schmitt insists that liberalism "seems fated then to destroy itself in the problem of the
formation of a will" (1988, 28). Dictatorship, a category Schmitt is ambiva-
lent about at best, is accordingly not the suspension of democracy per se
but the suspension of (the) constitution qua division between legislative

and executive. This division is not sustainable, as liberals would like to think, but instead ultimately self-abolishing.

While insightful as a critic of liberalism, Schmitt nevertheless falls short as a guide to grasping either the objectives of the Bolivarian Revolution or the dynamic role it has granted to the 1999 Constitution. We can see this when Schmitt cites Article 16 of the Rights of Man to insist that "a constitution is identical with division of power" (1988, 41). In doing so, he neglects even the tensions within that document: the Rights of Man was itself the product of a specific and momentary balance of forces, in which Rousseau's general will (Article 6) cohabitates uncomfortably with Montesquieu's separation of powers. As a result, Schmitt cannot explain the much more dynamic function of the Venezuelan Constitution as a tense snapshot of political forces at a particular moment in time. After all, just as 1789 was not 1791, 1999 is not 2002, and much less 2017.

Moreover, where Schmitt resolves the contradiction of liberal separation of powers through a resort to absolute, national unity, this hardly characterizes the dynamic currently playing out in Venezuela or the grassroots forces driving that dynamic forward. Instead, Gramsci proves a more useful alternative: a thinker similarly critical of the separation of powers, but one that instead pushes us in a very different direction. Gramsci historicizes the separation of powers as "a product of the struggle between civil society and political society in a specific historical period," thereby emphasizing that it reflects an "unstable equilibrium between the classes." Despite its historical nature, liberalism nevertheless seeks through the separation of powers to "crystallize permanently a particular stage of development," declaring that there is no alternative while actively attempting to prevent any alternative from being able to emerge (1971, 245).

This effort is as self-defeating for Gramsci as it was for Schmitt, because while the liberal state is revolutionary for declaring universal inclusion, it quickly becomes "saturated," unable to concretely include as many as it promises (1971, 260). Instead of its vaunted universality, it is instead the case that the bureaucracy—traditional intellectuals and leading sectors with their hands on the instruments of coercion—inevitably separates and "becomes a caste" (246). As we will see, the detachment of the bureaucracy is painfully relevant for a petro-state like Venezuela. In viewing the separation of powers as embedded within a class project, and in emphasizing the emergence of a political caste, Gramsci grants the liberal state more autonomy of maneuver than Schmitt, who, criticisms aside, ironically gives liberals too much credit by presenting them as acting more on principle than brute self-interest.

For Gramsci, by contrast, liberalism is a massive exercise in bad faith in which liberals themselves are far from liberal and the separation of powers only goes so far. Indeed, no description would seem more apt for the Venezuelan opposition today, which has proven itself liberal and democratic only when convenient, than the judgment Gramsci reserves for Catholics, who "would like the State to be interventionist one hundred per cent in their favor; failing that, or where they are in a minority, they call for a 'neutral' state, so that it should not support their adversaries" (1988, 262). Here the counterproof—as it was for Marx in his origin story of capitalism—is the very real role of the state as a heavy-handed interventionist force: "civil society and State are one and the same" and "*laissez-faire* too is a form of State 'regulation' . . . a deliberate policy, conscious of its own ends, and not the spontaneous, automatic expression of economic facts" (160).

Gramsci's solution is neither the minimal liberal state, which "has never existed except on paper" (1971, 261), nor Schmitt's recourse to the absolute unity of the sovereign will. Instead, he points to the possibility of a political state "tendentially capable of withering away" and leaving in its place a paradoxical "State without a State." Here, "pure science" and "pure utopia" coincide, "since based on the premise that all men are really equal and hence equally rational and moral, i.e., capable of accepting the law spontaneously, freely, and not through coercion" (263). While such a state—which is no more and no less than the commune—might appear to be an "extreme liberalism," Gramsci insists that it is in reality and "at the same time its dissolution" from within, a process through which apparently liberal demands give way to what he calls—cryptically but suggestively in a contemporary Venezuelan context—"the permanent Constituent Assembly" (246).

### Coalescing Popular Sovereignty

In an attempt to introduce necessary nuance into discussions around Venezuelan democracy, Coppedge (2002, 1) rightly suggests that we "sharpen the distinction between democracy, narrowly defined as popular sovereignty, versus the more conventional notion of liberal democracy," and that we furthermore "look beyond the rules and institutions of Venezuela's 1999 Constitution to consider the way they were used." Coppedge defines popular sovereignty as "the idea that a government should do what most citizens want it to do," considering it a necessary but not a sufficient condition for democracy. Against this, he understands liberalism as urging "limits on the sovereignty of a popular majority," while viewing contemporary Venezuela "as a paradigmatic illustration of the tension between [these] two standards for democracy" (3, 14).

For Coppedge, the claim to popular sovereignty as the basis of political legitimacy found its highest expression in the National Constituent Assembly (ANC), which was empowered to write the 1999 Bolivarian Constitution, and to which Chavistas won 93 percent of the seats. From this starting point, and arguably misled by the framing of popular sovereignty as a narrower form rather than a legitimate alternative to liberal democracy, Coppedge reaches untenable conclusions: that Venezuela has become "a case form of delegative democracy . . . in which there is no 'horizontal accountability.'" In fact, the best check on governmental power comes from a more horizontal source than Coppedge wants to consider—the popular grassroots movements that brought Chávez to power and returned him to power during the coup— and Maduro's relative immobility in recent years is a testament to the fact that the institutional power of the presidency is not the problem. But his cues to both distinguish popular sovereignty from liberal democracy and to consider democracy as both dynamic and as exceeding the formal structures of government remain useful and necessary.

As I have suggested, one of the sharpest ironies of liberal criticism of the Bolivarian process today is that those who today criticize the government's behavior as unconstitutional are often the very same people who originally opposed the Constitution and cheered its abrogation by force during the 2002 coup. While this is an understandable rearguard tactical maneuver, it also points to the nature of the Constitution—and any constitution—as a momentary condensation of a political balance of forces. Not only does an understanding of the Boliviarian Revolution as a process undermine static criticism based on liberal representative democracy, and not only is it the case that such criticism ring hollow given the actual history of Venezuela's liberal democracy, bookended as it was by states of emergency, but it is also true that for the 1999 Constitution to even be written, and indeed for the Bolivarian Revolution to become a process, to enter into motion, required first overcoming the self-imposed stasis of the balance of powers. I mean this very concretely, beginning with the constituent (or better, the constitutional) moment itself.[4] When the new Constitution was ratified, Venezuela, like Ecuador and Bolivia, confronted a standoff between constituted power (the existing Congress) and the ANC, which eventually opted to cut the Gordian knot by dissolving the Congress and the Supreme Court. As Coppedge puts it, in what is apparently meant as a criticism: "By the time the ANC ended its functions, there was not a single national power, other than President Chávez himself, that had not been appointed by a body that was 93 percent Chavista" (Coppedge 2002, 31).[5]

These moves were justified by appeals to popular sovereignty: that the people are the ultimate legislators, and the ANC their clearest voice, albeit a temporary one. This radical decision to make the ANC the highest embodiment of popular sovereignty would be followed in short order by increasingly ambitious and capacious breaks with the separation of powers. These included the new Constitution's establishment of a powerful and unicameral National Assembly; a reining in of the autonomy first of PDVSA (which was retaken by the government after the disastrous lockout that shut down the national economy between December 2002 and January 2003) and later the central bank and even the armed forces; and the creation of the Mission System to funnel oil money around existing state institutions and toward social programs, which was itself only made possible by the reclamation of oil revenue.

The progressive transformation of the judiciary stands out for both its importance to the Bolivarian process itself and to opposition claims that Chávez was threatening to undermine the separation of powers. But as is the case in most circumstances, the Supreme Court had served as a brake on the Bolivarian process: for example, ruling that the 2002 coup was not a coup at all, but a "power vacuum," and thereby preventing the purging of the military; or around the same time striking down key aspects of the land reform law (TSJ 2002; Wilpert 2006, 256). All of these breaks with the liberal separation of powers have been, strictly speaking, extralegal, and certainly extraliberal, but nevertheless served as unavoidable preconditions for what was to come.

On the basis of this deference to notions of popular sovereignty over separation of powers, both the 1999 Constitution and the conception of constitutionalism that has emerged in contemporary Venezuela reflect not Schmitt's equivalence of constitution with separation but instead a far different approach to constitution as generative dynamic. While the drafting of the Bolivarian Constitution is proudly understood by many to have been a heroic collective task (involving the deputies in the assembly working amid the echoing din of movements in the streets, and everyday Venezuelans in thousands of study groups known as Bolivarian Circles), it nevertheless remains just that: the mortal product of particular human hands at a specific moment, and therefore subject to constant constituent pressure and indeed inevitable transformation. After all, 1999 was a long time ago already: many—notably Luis Miquilena, a close advisor to Chávez who presided over the constituent assembly—have since "jumped the divider" to join the opposition, and Chavismo's electoral base in 1999 was more urban and more middle-class than it is today (Wilpert 2007, 18–19).

Concretely speaking, what is important for our purposes is that the 1999 Constitution both concentrates and deconcentrates power, empowering the executive and a newly unified legislature as it enshrines in principle popular participation from below.[6] It extends presidential terms and expands executive authority, while similarly expanding the power of the legislature and the autonomy of the military, which could be seen as countervailing powers. At the same time, the Constitution also provides for greater protection of human rights, adding two branches of government—electoral power (in the National Electoral Council) and a Simón Bolívar-inspired citizen (or "moral") power, consisting of the attorney general and comptroller general—to supplement the executive, legislative, and judiciary (Wilpert 2007, 37). Finally, and most importantly, it enshrines popular participation and oversight in ways that do not delineate but open up the possibility of the future revision of the document itself.

These tensions do not simply reflect an "internally contradictory" document (Levine 2002, 265). Nor do they result from the refusal of the ANC to deliver to Chávez the full centralization he demanded (Coppedge 2002, 30). Instead, the tension is a dialectical one in which the two aspects—centralization of popular power and the eventual deconcentration of state institutions—coexist in Bolivarian thought and enter into a specific dynamic relation, the former laying the groundwork for the latter. In other words, while the composition of the ANC and the document it drafted pertained to a specific moment in the Bolivarian process, this moment points to the radical boomerang of first unifying popular power and then using that unity to transform the state. It consequently represents a dialectical congealment, not a halting of motion, but a pausing or momentary freezing over that gives way to further motion, to borrow Fredric Jameson's terms (2010, 27). But if we are to understand the broad and paradoxical movement of the Bolivarian Revolution—toward unity and then away from it—we must understand that this was moreover a necessary moment, which drew power together in order to disperse existing institutions, hardening around a notion of popular sovereignty as a momentum-gathering precondition to then radically transforming the state.

This appeal to a political dynamic that reaches beyond the existing institutional structure—creating a gap is in some senses extralegal—would be built into the Constitution itself and the power dynamics it unleashes. As Wilpert describes it, not only did the constituent process embody the freedom of all founding moments, it also opened up a constituent dynamic from the outset: by declaring itself a document founded not merely on the rule of law but on "law and justice," it "highlights the potential differences between law and justice, implying that justice is just as important as the rule of law, which might not always bring about justice" (2007, 31). The extralegal space opened up in the Bolivarian Constitution and enacted in the process of its drafting and ratification is clearest in the role it envisions for popular and participatory power.

According to the Latin American philosopher of liberation, Enrique Dussel, the Venezuelan Constitution represents an unprecedented attempt to incorporate participatory, constituent power from below into the institutional apparatus of the state, one that might be able to overcome or at least mitigate a classic problem of political thought: the problem of constitution or democratic founding. Dussel emphasizes in particular the importance of Articles 62 and 70, which, respectively, enshrine and delineate an ambitious role for popular participation:

> *Article 62*: All citizens have the right to participate freely in public affairs, directly or through their elected representatives. Popular participation in the formation, execution, and control of public management is the necessary means to achieve a protagonism which guarantees full development, individually and collectively.
>
> *Article 70*: The following are means for the participation and protagonism of the people in exercising its sovereignty in the political realm: elections to public posts, referenda, popular consultations, revoking mandates, and legislative, constitutional, and constituent initiative, open councils, and citizen assemblies whose decisions will be binding. (cited in Dussel 2008, 127)

These articles remain vague, as with any constitution, and while Dussel observed at the time that participatory democracy "still lacks powerful organization *from below*" (2008, 133), this has since emerged in the spiral of spontaneous organizing and government legislation that gave rise first to the communal councils and more recently to the communes. Taken together, the concrete provisions of the Constitution—for example, revocable mandates for all elected posts—and its promise of increasingly ambitious participation, all point toward what Dussel calls a "new political spirit . . . of *citizen participation* in a democracy in which the *people* have sovereignty that they can exercise permanently, and not only in those volcanic eruptions that are the elections every six years. *Representative* democracy (which tends to be a movement *from the top down*) needs to be linked with *participatory* democracy (as a movement exerting control *from the bottom up*)" (128). But the real subversiveness of Dussel's formulation lay partially concealed in his concept of the people ("el pueblo") itself.

This moment of gathering, unifying, and hardening oppositions at the threshold of the Manichaean and the dialectical opens onto the fraught question of the status of populism, while exceeding most definitions of the term and stretching the concept of the people in radically creative directions.[7] Whereas some thinkers, notably Paolo Virno (2004) and Hardt and Negri (2004), reject the concept of the people as inherently conservative, unitary, and unifying, this is not at all how popular identity functions in Dussel's thought or in Venezuelan reality. Dussel's account of popular identity, which parallels Laclau's discussion of populism (2006) in many aspects while exceeding it in others, understands the people as a dynamic and ruptural concept of generative combat that "establishes an internal frontier or a fracture within the political community" between the poor and the oligarchs, oppressed and oppressor (2008, 74–75).

Furthermore, if Dussel's people sets into motion a transformative dynamic in which constituent and constituted powers interact with one another, in which popular forces unify not as an end in itself but toward permanent transformation, this is very much the same dynamic at play in the Bolivarian process. The perennially incomplete people draws together the oppressed and excluded and places these constituent forces into a permanent and combative contestation of the constituted power of the state, dissolving outward toward an unattainable horizon that Dussel describes in terms that sound a lot like Gramsci's permanent constituent assembly: as a "*permanent* praxis of Civil Society and social movements through the creation of parallel institutions from the bottom up" that "tend[s] toward the (empirically impossible) identity of representation with the represented" (Dussel 2008, 132–33).

It would be no coincidence when Reinaldo Iturriza, former Venezuelan Communes Minister, chose almost the same words to describe the challenges of the present, insisting that "the imperative continues to be: to progressively reduce the distance between the institutions and the organized people. To hurry up and walk to the rhythm of the real movement" (2013). And it is no coincidence that Marx and Engels (1970, 57) had chosen those same words—"the *real* movement which abolishes the present state of things"—to describe communism itself.

## Toward the Commune

In the Venezuelan context, this unattainable horizon pushes us beyond the 1999 Constitution, as popular movements have already done, using the participatory leverage of Article 62 to lay the groundwork for a new, radically democratic communal state that currently coexists with the liberal state. It is a peculiar characteristic of the Bolivarian process that, while the transformation of the institutions of constituted power has provided crucial leverage for continued progress, this transformation often arrives late, confirming in law what already exists in practice. "Phases of a revolution," as C. L. R. James once insisted, "are not decided in parliaments, they are only registered there" (James 1963, 81).

Prior to Chávez's emergence on the political stage, residents of Venezuela's poorest barrios had established grassroots popular assemblies that would later take on a more institutional form in the communal councils (that were not officially legislated until 2006). Almost immediately after the communal councils were formalized from above, there emerged in practice from below broader configurations known as communes, to be in turn retroactively enshrined in a 2010 law. Thus while many opposition critics are correct to say that these revolutionary institutions have emerged and are today coalescing in a way that is, strictly speaking, illegal (or at least not yet legal), most remain so blinded by paranoia as to neglect the fact that these are the creation, originally, not of a government but rather of revolutionary grassroots sectors.[8] In fact, while the councils and communes as a whole emerge from that extralegal space opened for participation in the Constitution—the space between law and justice, the space for participatory oversight, and more recently, the space opened by the Communes Law itself—one of Chavismo's most radical voices even goes so far as to insist that the communes must emerge "without the law" (Denis 2010).

Concretely speaking, a commune brings together dozens of communal councils, but also socialist productive units, in a given territory, with the communal parliament, the sovereign instance ultimately empowered to make decisions about who produces what, working how many hours for what salary, and how the final product is distributed. More recently, these communes have themselves been integrated into broader state and national confederations that rise all the way to the level of what are called presidential councils, in which, as a sort of radical inverse of the downward distribution of resources in the mission system, representatives of the communes interface directly with Nicolás Maduro.

One of the earliest theorists of the communal state, or what he termed the "commoner state," was the late guerrilla comandante Kléber Ramírez Rojas (who played a key role in Chávez's failed 1992 coup). He described this new, commoner state as emerging out of the "liquidation and burial" of the existing liberal state, a phrase that prefigures what Chávez and Maduro would term the "demolition of the bourgeois state" (2006, 34). According to Kléber, the abolition of the existing state was not foreseen as the abolition of democracy, but instead its radicalization, deconcentration, and deepening: "We advocate a broadening of democracy in which the communities will assume the fundamental powers of the state, electing and recalling their own authorities. . . . The community constituted in a sovereign fashion as the Communal Constituent" (122). As perhaps the tensest imaginable unity of constituent mobility with constituted stasis, Kléber even provocatively deemed this future, commoner state a "government of popular insurgency" (207).

Despite this apparently decentralizing vision, however, Kléber himself was acutely aware of the boomerang swing of popular unity necessary to make it possible, foreseeing the dynamic that has since emerged in the Bolivarian process. On the one hand, he was sharply critical of the horizontalism predominant among popular grassroots movements in the mid-1990s, which he argued needed to transcend their localism in order to constitute a broad and unified movement in the struggle (Ramírez Rojas, 203). On the other hand, he saw the threat of centralism as a paradoxical one, a consequence of the political structure and not the cause, arguing that a future commoner state would only transcend "messianic" presidentialism—a phenomenon that long preceded Chávez—when such messianism becomes unnecessary, and that "centralism as such will collapse when organized communities choose and recall their own authorities, formulate and prioritize their own plans for the development of their well-being" (47).

This new communal state is, in other words, an attempt to do what is nearly impossible in dependent economies, and in oil economies in particular: to break with the centralization imposed not by particular policies but by a global economic structure, and to build a new, deconcentrated, and directly democratic state alongside and as the eventual replacement for the existing liberal-representative state. It is therefore with good reason that this inverse movement parallels the dialectic of decolonization sketched by Fanon in the Algerian context, in which dispersal and decentralization counterintuitively follow tightly on the heels of a necessary unifying moment, both in terms of identity and geography.

As to the first, Fanon insists that the initial stage of decolonization is one of unification, and even homogenization, that consolidating national consciousness in opposition to the colonizer creates the necessary momentum for both victory and a future proliferation of difference. It could not be any other way for Fanon, since the dialectical weight of this boomerang swing is what matters most. Geographically, such decentralization is inherent in the decolonial project, to combat what Fanon calls the "urban macrocephaly" implanted by colonialism, and in particular to demystify the capital (a task even more urgent in Venezuela than elsewhere). Where decentralization once facilitated colonial domination, as it has facilitated neoliberalism in Venezuela and elsewhere, the future is one in which party and society "must be decentralized to the limit" (2004, 128). In this process, unity is not the end but the means to an ever-flourishing multiplicity.

The paradoxical transition through unity to multiplicity, through centralism to a radically deconcentrated form of direct democracy, is, as we have seen, partially resolved in Dussel's concept of the people (in other words, in the fact that what is unified is an exceptionally mobile, dynamic, and divisive people, a people in motion comprising the oppressed and excluded). In the Venezuelan context, this insight only predictably fuels other, inverse criticisms. María Pilar García Guadilla, for example, has criticized the emerging communal state not for threatening a totalizing—and totalitarian—future but for the intrinsic exclusion she sees built into the communal project. If the Bolivarian Revolution is a response to the exclusion of the poor, the argument goes, then is not the task one of ever-more-universal inclusion? And if the communal state fails the test of universality, does it not fail in toto?

García Guadilla is among those who admit the exceptional inclusiveness of the 1999 Constitution, but she insists that "praxis" does not meet this standard, reflecting instead a "selective inclusion" or what she calls a paradoxical "inclusive exclusion." She even goes so far as to deem the Venezuelan government an "exclusionary and classist one" for excluding the wealthy (and here, I think the claim of a reverse classism merits comparison to the similarly imaginary and absurd phenomenon of reverse racism) (García Guadilla 2015).[9] Moreover, the promotion of parallel participatory institutions has come, she insists—although here I would agree—at the expense of existing representative institutions but, as we have seen, this is precisely the point.

To point to exclusion is to both neglect the unavoidable dynamic whereby this communal state has emerged—one marked by partisan combat and divisive struggle—and to hold the bar of legitimacy far too high, in a way that both upholds a straw man of presumably universal liberal democracy and blinds us to the increasing inclusiveness that the Bolivarian process has generated. No system is universally inclusive in practice, and here liberalism falls as short or shorter, establishing its purported universalism only through a blinkered insistence on formal equality and the systematic evacuation of all else—the excision of the social from the political—to produce a universal in words only.

Hegel himself set the bar of the universal to the highest level when he insisted, in the *Phenomenology*, that all government that is merely a victorious "faction"—in other words, the rule of a part over the whole—would ultimately need to be overthrown (2008, §591). In setting the bar so high, he paved the way for his own supersession by Marx, who identified in the existence of the poverty inevitably bred of capital accumulation the real and concrete nonuniversality of Hegel's own approach. By grounding his system on the mediating function of civil society, Hegel posed the separation of the social from the political as a problem that he himself could not solve. Social (in other words, economic) inequality would prove to be the Achilles' heel of Hegelian universality, revealing it too as mere faction worthy of overthrow, and the same can be said of liberal-representative democracy today.

Liberalism can only claim the most threadbare universality by excising entirely the social from the political, segregating out the economic effects of capitalism and narrowing its definition of equality—and democracy—to purely formal aspects: rights, elections, and of course, the separation of powers. Crucially, however, this separation of the social from the political itself tends historically to undermine even these most formal aspects of liberal equality in practice, giving rise to the striation of political access on the basis of race and class that extends—as it did for decades in Venezuela and as we see today in the United States—to limiting even the most basic element of suffrage. While especially poor Venezuelans, but also many others, were structurally excluded from substantive participation in a rigid, two-party political system, this exclusion extended even to their formal exclusion from any participation in elections: for decades of Venezuelan democracy, millions lacked the resources and access to acquire the identity card (*cédula*) necessary to register to vote.

According to liberalism's own minimal criteria, the Bolivarian governments have been concretely the most inclusive the country has ever seen, in part through the constitutional enshrinement of electoral power and the guarantee that voter registration be provided universally and free of charge (Article 56). As late as Chávez's 1998 election, the electoral registry contained a mere 47 percent of the population (and 80 percent of those eligible), a number that by 2012 reached nearly 65 percent of the population (more than 95 percent of those eligible). In concrete terms, this meant more than seven million new participants were included in the electoral process. If Bolivarian socialism has proven more liberally inclusive than even liberal democracy—and we could add to this the increased inclusion of women, Afro and indigenous Venezuelans, and LGBTQ people—it aspires to something much more substantive and participatory, raising questions of what limits might exist to its own project of inclusion.

This, in a way, is to return to Gramsci's own diagnosis of the limits of liberal inclusivity, which promises universal inclusion, albeit in formal terms, and yet becomes inevitably "saturated" and fails to deliver on even that narrow promise. Is there a threat that Bolivarianism as it currently exists has reached a similar saturation point? For some on the radical Chavista Left, the answer appears to be yes. The internal dynamics of the process, and in particular, its reproduction of petro-rentism, have dramatically improved the well-being of certain newly included sectors, but in so doing, the Bolivarian process may have produced its own gravediggers in a new middle class that fears the urban poor of the barrios just as its enemies had (Antillano et al. 2016; López 2015). It is this continued exclusion of those most historically excluded, not the pseudo-exclusion of the upper classes, that poses the most serious threat to the legitimacy, and indeed the survival, of the Bolivarian process today.

This does not mean the process is doomed to reproduce liberal exclusion. At least in theory, the commune—as a territorial government grounded in local production and direct participation—poses the potentially universal in a way that liberalism never could by overcoming the most significant barrier to liberal inclusivity: the exclusion of the socioeconomic from the political. Such a potentially universal order, however, could only plausibly emerge as a process (in other words, as an inherently partisan instrument of struggle, as an active alternative presenting a real contradiction to be confronted and overcome). If we attempt to judge a process by the criteria of a government, if we expect that it look like anything but confrontation and contestation, if we interpret any perceived political slight, every hurt feeling as an exclusion and thus a blow to the universal, then we are doomed to eternally miss the point.

After all, the inclusiveness that even García Guadilla recognizes in the 1999 Constitution was only possible at the expense of dissolving the Congress, a gesture she would certainly see as exclusionary. As though intent on proving this point, García Guadilla homes in on a particular statement by Atenea Jiménez of the National Commoners' Network, in which Jiménez insists that "the bourgeoisie can't be in the commune unless they assume class consciousness, the economic, political, and cultural principles of the commune, because the commune is more than a large communal council—it's the government in that territory, and that government has a political orientation. And that orientation is socialism" (Velasco 2013). Through a simultaneous misinterpretation of this quotation and of the Bolivarian process as process, García Guadilla reads Jiménez's words as straightforwardly exclusionary.

But on a most basic level, Jiménez's statement expresses a clear-cut tautology: how on earth could the bourgeoisie *as* bourgeoisie play any role whatsoever in a commune? In other words, what must be excluded from the commune (and in fact ultimately abolished) is not a group of concrete persons but instead a social position, one that, if included, would of course mark the demise of the commune. On a second level, moreover, what García Guadilla misses is precisely this play between the part and the whole that is characteristic not only of the Bolivarian process but also of Dussel's concept of the people as a combative part, and indeed of the Marxian concept of revolution from which it draws its prototype: the coalescence of the oppressed and excluded part, its unification in combat, as a necessary precondition for the transformation of the whole of society in ever more universal directions.

## Conclusion

Political thinking has for too long been dominated by a search for fixed forms and ideal regimes, generating a built-in bias toward those institutional arrangements that are themselves geared to dividing and separating power, slowing the momentum of the demos in search of change. Contemporary Venezuela, perched as it is between two different forms of government, provides a useful lens not only for assessing those clashing forms but also for taking stock of what is necessary for any change to occur to begin with. From this perspective, the separation of powers so often synonymous with liberal-representative democracy appears as a barrier to change that must necessarily be overcome if any real progress is to be made in achieving real inclusion and equality promised by the communal state as a radical grassroots alternative to the existing liberal state.

Today, this communal future is far from certain, but the tipping point that characterizes all dual power situations seems closer than ever (Lenin 1964). The perceived unresponsiveness of the Maduro government to the creeping economic crisis led the anti-Chavista opposition to victory in the December 2015 National Assembly elections. While this momentous defeat momentarily mobilized Chavismo from the grassroots to the leadership, the underlying difficulties are far from resolved and a persistent economic crisis grounded in the perennial dangers of the oil economy saps the resolve of the grassroots as it throws wind in the sails of the Right. Today, opposition control over the legislature has set existing liberal institutions against the emerging communes and even against one another. For Chavismo to survive, it will soon need to choose between these two states, retreating into a contradictory liberalism or pressing forward toward the commune.

## Notes

1. Perhaps the best example is Brewer-Carías's *Dismantling Democracy in Venezuela* (2010), which even one well-known opposition blogger deems a "remarkably ill-tempered screed . . . a kind of archaeology of an entire displaced elite's wounded sense of entitlement" that conveniently elides "his own role in the comedy of errors"

that was the 2002 coup (Toro 2011). Toro is right to point to the centrality of the question of "supra-constitutionality," although he neglects the fact that this question is perennial and intrinsic to the constitution and founding of all regimes, one addressed notably by thinkers from Jean-Jacques Rousseau to Hannah Arendt. While Levine (2002) is apparently more nuanced, his narrative of the "decline and fall of democracy in Venezuela" is not. McCoy and Myers, by contrast, clarify that the "unraveling of representative democracy" they speak of "did not signal the end of democracy per se but of one variant of limited democracy"; a slipperiness nevertheless persists in their volume as a whole, in part through the editors' resorting to the idea of a "hybrid regime" (and the implication that the prior limited democracy was not itself "hybrid") (McCoy and Myers 2004, 2). It would appear that only Ellner and Tinker Salas (2007) resort to a narrative of decline in a wholly consistent way, their object being the "exceptional democracy" of the past.

2. See, for example, Vivas 2013.

3. Enabling laws are approved and passed by three-fifths majority in the National Assembly, which since 2005 has been facilitated by opposition abstention in legislative elections (in a characteristically circular way, the absence of opposition deputies as a result of their own terrible decisions was often cited as proof that the separation of powers had been compromised). It matters little to García-Serra that enabling laws are fairly common in Venezuela, or that Carlos Andrés Pérez issued thousands of decrees. As though sensing he is on weak ground, he supplements his dubious claim that the enabling law is "inconsistent with Venezuela's constitution" by denouncing the measure as an "effective tool to chip away at the economic base of the Venezuelan upper class" and dedicating an entire section to the concern that it may prove "inimical to foreign investment" (García-Serra 2001, 266). It is incomprehensible that a law review, even in Miami, would publish such an article.

4. While the ANC might often be considered a reflection of the constituent moment par excellence, I have elsewhere argued for a more radical conception of constituent power that would find better exemplification in the 1989 Caracazo rebellion (Ciccariello-Maher 2013b).

5. It is difficult to see how this could be otherwise. Even for Arendt, the constituent moment was characterized by a leap into the unknown. While it is excessive to say, as Coppedge does, that the true enemy was not the 1961 Constitution but the Congress itself—the last stronghold of the traditional parties—there is truth to this statement nevertheless.

6. "Deconcentration" is the term Chávez himself deployed to distinguish the Bolivarian project of dispersing and restructuring power—rebuilding a different form of power from below—from what many perceived to be the neoliberal decentralization carried out before he was elected (Chávez and Harnecker 2005, 114–15). Today this view, which reflects the importance of early movements and thinkers like Alfredo Maneiro of Radical Cause on Chavismo, is often echoed by grassroots organizers, who insist that the communal councils and communes do not decentralize power, but instead rebuild it from the bottom up.

7. One recent defense of liberal-representative democracy worth noting is that of Urbinati (2014), which views populism as a "disfiguration" of democracy, but this view neglects the dynamic aspect of many populisms (not to mention polarization and Manichaeism) as—for example, in the Venezuelan case—the only possible path toward a better democracy (even if understood in terms of the 1999 Constitution as an improved liberal democracy). Jason Frank is right to respond that, "Urbinati's polemical account of populism closes down more radically democratic alternatives for confronting these pressing problems than the liberal proceduralism for which she advocates" (2015, 226). I defend polarization and Manichaeism in the Venezuelan context in Ciccariello-Maher (2010; 2016).

8. See, for example, the critiques put forward by Margarita López Maya in González 2013, 23.

9. See similar arguments in Silva Michelena 2014, 35; González 2013; Servigna 2015.

## References

Antillano, Andrés, Iván Pojomovsky, Verónica Zubillaga, Chelina Sepúlveda, and Rebecca Hanson. 2016. "The Venezuelan Prison: From Neoliberalism to the Bolivarian Revolution." *Crime, Law and Social Change* 65 (3): 195–211.

Brewer-Carías, Allan R. 2010. *Dismantling Democracy in Venezuela: The Chávez Authoritarian Experiment*. Cambridge: Cambridge University Press.

Chávez, Hugo, and Marta Harnecker. 2005. *Understanding the Venezuelan Revolution: Hugo Chávez Talks to Marta Harnecker*. Translated by Chesa Boudin. New York: Monthly Review Press.

Ciccariello-Maher, George. 2010. "Jumpstarting the Decolonial Engine: Symbolic Violence from Fanon to Chávez." *Theory & Event* 13 (1).

———. 2013a. *We Created Chávez: A People's History of the Venezuelan Revolution*. Durham, N.C.: Duke University Press.

———. 2013b. "Constituent Moments, Constitutional Processes: Social Movements and the New Latin American Left." *Latin American Perspectives* 40 (3): 126–45.

———. 2016. *Decolonizing Dialectics*. Durham, N.C.: Duke University Press.

Coppedge, Michael. 2002. "Venezuela: Popular Sovereignty Versus Liberal Democracy." Working Paper No. 294 prepared for the Helen Kellogg Institute for International Studies, April 2002.

Denis, Roland. 2004. *Rebelión en proceso: Dilemas del movimiento popular luego de la rebelión del 13 de Abril*. Caracas: Ediciones Nuestra América Rebelde.

———. 2010. "Por unas comunas 'sin ley.'" Aporrea, October 19, 2010, www.aporrea .org/ideologia/a110539.html.

Dussel, Enrique. 2008 (2006). *Twenty Theses on Politics*. Translated by G. Ciccariello-Maher. Durham, N.C.: Duke University Press.

Ellner, Steve, and Miguel Tinker Salas, eds. 2007. *Venezuela: Hugo Chávez and the Decline of an "Exceptional Democracy."* Lanham, Md.: Rowman and Littlefield.

Fanon, Frantz. 2004 (1961). *The Wretched of the Earth.* Translated by R. Philcox. New York: Grove Press.

Fernandes, Sujatha. 2010. *Who Can Stop the Drums? Urban Social Movements in Chávez's Venezuela.* Durham, N.C.: Duke University Press.

Frank, Jason. 2016. "Populism, Polarization, and Praxis." In "Critical Exchange: Debating Representative Democracy." *Contemporary Political Theory* 15 (2): 205–42.

García Guadilla, María Pilar. 2015. "Exclusionary-Inclusion and the Incorporation of Popular Sectors in Venezuela Under Chavismo." Presentation at "Venezuela in Crisis and Context" symposium, New York University, February 20.

Garcia-Serra, Mario J. 2001. "The 'Enabling Law': The Demise of the Separation of Powers in Hugo Chavez's Venezuela." *Inter-American Law Review* 32 (2): 265–93.

González, David. 2013. *El estado descomunal: Conversaciones con Margarita López Maya.* Caracas: El Nacional.

Gramsci, Antonio. 1971. *Selections from the Prison Notebooks.* Edited by Q. Hoare and G. Nowell Smith. New York: International Publishers.

Hardt, Michael, and Antonio Negri. 2004. *Multitude: War and Democracy in the Age of Empire.* New York: Penguin.

Hegel, G. W. F. 2008 [1807]. *Phenomenology of Spirit.* Translated by T. Pinkard. N.p.: N.p.

Iturriza, Reinaldo. 2013. "Desear la comuna." *El otro saber y poder* (blog), August 22. https://elotrosaberypoder.wordpress.com/2013/08/22/desear-la-comuna/.

James, C. L. R. 1963 [1938]. *The Black Jacobins: Toussaint L'Ouverture and the San Domingo Revolution.* New York: Vintage.

Jameson, Fredric. 2010. *Valences of the Dialectic.* London: Verso.

Laclau, Ernesto. 2006. *On Populist Reason.* London: Verso.

Lenin, V. I. 1964 [1917]. "The Dual Power." In *Lenin: Collected Works* 24, 38–41. Moscow: Progress.

Levine, Daniel H. 2002. "The Decline and Fall of Democracy in Venezuela: Ten Theses." *Bulletin of Latin American Research* 21 (2): 248–69.

López, Ociel Alí. 2015. *¡Dale más gasolina! Chavismo, sifrinismo y burocracia.* Caracas: Fundación Casa Nacional de las Letras Andrés Bello.

Marx, Karl, and Friedrich Engels. 1970. *The German Ideology.* New York: International Publishers.

McCoy, Jennifer, and David Myers, eds. 2004. *The Unraveling of Representative Democracy in Venezuela.* Baltimore, Md.: Johns Hopkins University Press.

Ojeda, Fabricio. 1962. "Carta de renuncia de fabricio ojeda." Centro de Documentacion de los Movimientos Armados, June 30. www.cedema.org/ver.php?id=2105.

Ramírez Rojas, Kléber. 2006 (1998). *Historia documental del 4 de febrero.* Caracas: El Perro y la Rana.

Schmitt, Carl. 1985 (1922). *Political Theology: Four Chapters on the Concept of Sovereignty.* Translated by G. Schwab. Cambridge, Mass.: MIT Press.

———. 1988 (1923). *The Crisis of Parliamentary Democracy.* Translated by E. Kennedy. Cambridge, Mass.: MIT Press.

Scott, David. 2012. "Norms of Self-Determination: Thinking Sovereignty Through." *Middle East Law and Governance* 4 (2/3): 195–224.

Servigna, Ana. 2015. "Whose Plaza Is It, Anyway? Chávez's Bolivarianism and Contested Public Spaces in Caracas." *Journal of Latin American and Caribbean Anthropology* 20 (3): 475–95.

Silva Michelena, Héctor. 2014. *Estado de siervos: Desnudando el estado comunal.* Caracas: UCV/Ediciones del Rectorado.

Smilde, David A. 2013. "Hello Lenin: Socialism and Students in Venezuela." Paper presented at the Conference of the Latin American Studies Association, May 30, 2013.

Toro, Francisco. 2011. "The Useless Old Guard." *New Republic,* January 24. https://newrepublic.com/article/79544/dismantling-democracy-venezuala-allan-brewer-carias.

Tribunal Supremo de Justicia (TSJ). 2002. Expediente No. AA10-L-2002-000029, August 14, 2002. http://historico.tsj.gob.ve/decisiones/tplen/Septiembre/SENTENCIA%20DE%20LOS%20MILITARES.htm.

Urbinati, Nadia. 2014. *Democracy Disfigured: Opinion, Truth, and the People.* Cambridge, Mass.: Harvard University Press.

Velasco, Alejandro. 2013. "Communes in Progress: An Interview with Atenea Jiménez." *NACLA Report on the Americas* 46 (2): 31–34. https://doi.org/10.1080/10714839.2013.11721993.

Virno, Paolo. 2004 (2001). *Grammar of the Multitude: For an Analysis of Contemporary Forms of Life.* Translated by I. Bertoletti, J. Cascaito, and A. Casson. New York: Semiotext(e).

Vivas, Leonardo. 2013. "Some Human Rights at the Expense of Others: The Case of Freedom of the Press in the Bolivarian Revolution." Comments made at the Venezuela: Change or Continuity conference, University of Massachusetts, Amherst, April 19, 2013.

Wilpert, Gregory. 2006. "Land for People Not for Profit in Venezuela." In *Promised Land: Competing Visions of Agrarian Reform,* edited by P. Rosset, R. Patel, and M. Courville. New York: Food First.

———. 2007. *Changing Venezuela by Taking Power: The History and Policies of the Chávez Government.* London: Verso.

# CHAPTER 7

# From Partial to Full Conflict Theory: A Neo-Weberian Portrait of the Battle for Venezuela

David Smilde

## Introduction

Most analyses of contemporary Venezuelan politics comes from what might be called *partial* conflict theories—theoretical perspectives that critically examine some areas of social life but systematically ignore others. Perhaps the leading perspective used to understand Venezuela is a contemporary descendant of classic liberalism. Pluralist political theory serves not only as the paradigmatic perspective of Anglophone political science but also as the tacit framework for most journalistic commentary. Indeed, sociologist Michael Mann says, "Pluralism is liberal democracy's (especially American democracy's) view of itself" (Mann 2012, 46).

Pluralist political theory suggests that there are multiple sources of social power that compete for dominance—such as religious, legal, ethnic, and labor groups—and looks at the way political systems can ensure a polyarchy, a relative balance of interest groups (Dahl 1971). As it is generally used in Latin American scholarship, it is a normative theory that looks at political institutions and whether they ensure a democratic equilibrium between competing groups (good) or end up allowing one group to attain hegemony over others (bad). In this view the democratic institutions of the state are ultimately decisive.[1]

In the case of Venezuela, scholars and commentators working from the pluralist perspective have been remarkably insightful in criticizing the progressive concentration of power occurring during the Chávez and now Maduro governments. Yet they also tend to ignore social, economic, and cultural inequalities. They ignore them as causes for the rise of Chavismo and also ignore Chavismo's achievements in reducing them. Instead they provide analyses that begin with politics and end with politics. For example, a recent article by leading political scientist Kurt Weyland (2013) perspicaciously traces all of the ways in which liberal democratic institutions have declined in the governments led by Hugo Chávez, Evo Morales, and Rafael Correa. They have: increased executive powers, allowed for presidential reelection, weakened checks and balances, and engaged in "discriminatory legalism." And these leaders are not alone. Before he was ousted, writes Weyland, Honduras's Manuel Zelaya was "preparing his own perpetuation in power" (19). And Argentina's Cristina Kirchner is "eyeing constitutional changes" in a "push for entrenchment" (19). But perhaps more interesting are the motives Weyland projects onto these leaders. The decline in liberal institutions is not portrayed as a lamentable means to noble ends, nor as the unintended or even secondary consequence of policies intending to address the inequalities of the globe's must unequal region. Rather, these leaders' "progressive rhetoric" is simply used by them to justify a "quest for personal power" (Weyland 2013).

In action-theoretic terms, all of the motivations Weyland projects onto the actors he describes are political. The story begins with a will to power and ends with the concentration of power, and actual achievements in addressing social, economic, and cultural inequalities are not even mentioned. This perspective makes it virtually impossible to understand why Chavismo has won so many elections and indeed obliges Weyland to suggest that Chávez's 2012, eleven-point electoral victory (accurately predicted by Venezuela's most reliable pollsters) was unfair and only confirmed that Venezuela "had already fallen under non-democratic rule."

Most sympathetic treatments of Chavismo come from descendants of classic Marxism. Contemporary neo-Marxists provide insightful criticism of the effects of global capitalism and the way it can exacerbate economic, social, and cultural inequalities. In the case of Venezuela they have provided perspicacious analyses of the rise of Chavismo, its achievements and the clear class nature of Venezuela's conflict. Nevertheless, neo-Marxists become Pollyannaish when it comes to the concentration of power in a revolutionary state. In the Venezuelan case this is especially striking given that the original key metaphor of the Chavista project was participatory democracy. Yet almost every reform over the past sixteen years has served to centralize and concentrate power in the executive branch of the government. Even participatory instruments like communal councils are centralized and depend on the executive branch instead of local governments. Neo-Marxists systematically ignore how similar the concentration of power and its effects are to the centripetal forces that plagued twentieth-century socialist projects. For example, Juan Carlos Monedero (2013), one of the leading theorists of twenty-first-century socialism, clearly identifies problems such as "hyper-leadership," centralism, clientelism, and corruption. However, he does not see these as ironic tendencies inherent to socialism so aptly described by Roberto Michels (1962), Gaetano Mosca (1939), and others. Nor are they the fault of a government that has been in power for a decade and a half. Rather, he portrays them as carryovers from the atomization of Venezuela's neoliberal 1990s.

In the rest of this chapter, I will use the neo-Weberian perspective of Michael Mann to develop a fuller version of conflict theory, a perspective that can conserve the insights of pluralist and neo-Marxist perspectives, yet set aside their myopias. This portrayal will show the Venezuela conflict to be a clash of rival constellations of power networks vying for monopoly power. We do not need to choose between seeing it as a political conflict or as an economic conflict. It is both at the same time and is oriented by an ideological struggle. I will also show how this perspective can be used as a normative base of critique.

### Full Conflict Theory

The key to neo-Weberian conflict theory is the idea of "multiple, conjunctural causality." Of course, most social and political theories include the idea of multi-causality. John Locke (1986) spoke of the state, economy, and public opinion. Karl Marx (Tucker 1978) analyzed state, economy, and culture. Max Weber's (1968) classic, if brief, formulation looked at party, class, and status. Contemporary neo-Weberian Michael Mann (2012) has modified Weber's formulation to include four basic "sources of social power": political, economic, ideological, and military.

But where these social theories actually differ is on the issue of causal primacy. Marxism, of course, sees the means of production as the most basic cause. While some variants of neo-Marxism give the state and culture relative autonomy, they still give the economic base ultimate primacy "in the last instance" or through the notion of "totality" (Jay 1984). Liberalism, especially in its contemporary pluralist variant, does not really provide a clear theory of causal primacy. But in practice it clearly regards the state as having analytic primacy, as being the most fundamental and important factor for understanding social and political life. In classic Lockean terms the realms of economy and public opinion have a natural virtue, and if left to their own devices will grow and address human needs. The institutions of collective life (in other words, of the state) can successfully regulate social life if kept to a minimum, but can also impede and suppress. Hence it is here that liberalism generally focuses its analytic attention, on the structures that facilitate or impede the natural virtue of the market and public opinion.

What is different about neo-Weberian conflict theory is that none of the sources of social power are ultimately decisive or somehow more fundamental. In this sense it is a truly multi-causal perspective. Mann puts forward four ideal-typical sources of social power. These are all emergent phenomena that address certain human needs. This is not action theory. It is not needs but power networks that are motors of history. Needs are universal and relatively unchanging, but power networks that form to meet them vary and give shape to history. These power networks are not "layers" of social reality in the Parsonsian sense. All power networks are "social"; the four sources of social power refer to the types of needs that they address. Ideological power comes from the human need to impose concepts on perceptions and provide ultimate meaning to life (Mann 2012, 22); economic power refers to the satisfaction of subsistence needs through production, distribution, and consumption of goods (24); military power, to the necessity of organized defense and aggression (25); and political power, to "the usefulness of centralized, institutionalized, and territorialized regulation of many aspects of social relations" (26).

A second important aspect of neo-Weberian theory is the idea of conjunctural causality—the idea that the causal efficacy of a particular factor depends on particular historical conjunctures. Michael Mann (2013), for example, ended his four-volume *Sources of Social Power* by suggesting that while in any given historical context research can show one of the sources of social power to be causally dominant, no one of these causes is ultimately determinative in human history. In one context or period economics can be decisive; in another, ideology (or military power, or political processes) can be more fundamental. It is important to realize that a multi-causal theory does not necessarily entail a concept of conjunctural causality. Talcott Parsons's (1951) structural functionalism worked with a notion of constant association, the idea that all of the basic sources of causal power are at play at every moment and in every context. Much social science still does work with the idea of constant association; indeed, the very idea of linear regression is based on it (Ragin 1987).

An emphasis on multiple, conjunctural causality also generates a relatively more open-ended research agenda. While there can be repeating regularities in history, there is no preestablished causal primacy or direction. Thus research necessarily becomes more inductive than deductive, prioritizing empirical engagement. This does not mean the researcher comes to the empirical field a tabula rasa—the conceptualization of four sources of social power combining and generating social networks that struggle for dominance provides a clear orientation. But how these networks play out and what factors predominate in a given context are always empirical questions.

A fuller conflict theory can also help us move to a fuller critical theory. Constellations of power networks can be evaluated in terms of their performance and criticized in terms of their tendency to seek monopoly. First, the sources of social power all address human goals and can be evaluated in terms of how well they perform. Ideological power networks seek to make meaning of the world. While some meanings about the ultimate significance of life are probably beyond scholarly analysis, most meanings can indeed be critically engaged.[2] Taken on their own terms, do they provide adequate orientation to life-in-the-world? Put differently, do they deliver what they promise? Claims of eternal life are beyond confirmation, but many cultural visions of the nature of social relations and the good life can in fact be evaluated. Economic power networks are oriented toward providing subsistence through production, distribution, and consumption. How well does a given economic articulation do this? Military power networks seek to organize violence to provide physical security; in many cases they do just the opposite. Political power networks seek to institutionally regulate social relations in a given territory. The analyst can ask whether they achieve that task. This focus on the way power networks can actually provide for human needs and facilitate human goals means that full-conflict theory engages in "criticism" in the literary sense, providing not just jeers but also applause when merited.

Second, the conflict in Weberian conflict sociology comes from Weber's portrayal of power networks as inherently oriented toward monopoly (Collins 1994). No sooner do ideological power networks make meaning of the world than members of the network seek to protect those meanings from competitors and develop for themselves special positions of authority. No sooner do economic power networks make profits than members of the network seek to ensure stable and consistent profits into the future by restricting the competition and seeking to colonize other sources of social power, just as neo-Marxist theory would suggest. Any military power network that achieves predominance seeks to monopolize the means of violence by defeating "irregular" military forces. And of course, no sooner does a political power network get a grasp on power than it seeks to perpetuate itself in that power, just as liberal theory would predict. Monopolistic ambitions are part of the consolidation of any network and create social power. However, monopolies can stifle the creativity and interstitial emergence of new forms of social organization. Full-conflict sociology can help detect and criticize these monopolistic tendencies beyond the blind spots of neo-Marxist and pluralist perspectives, pointing out the injustices they cause and the atrophic deterioration to which they lead.

Finally, the notion of conjunctural causality can help us move past any abstract obligation to "balance" in our critical analyses, as there is no guarantee of equilibrium in social life. While the goal of social science should always be to portray actors as fully human rather than engaging in the strategic "othering" typical of political communication, this does not oblige us to strike diplomatic compromises between social actors. Nor does it require a misrepresentation of "objectivity" as neutrality or a lack of value commitments. It is entirely possible that in any given historical context, one articulation of overlapping power networks achieves overwhelming power, institutionalizes inequality, violates human rights, and systematically undermines the possibility of network creativity. If so, it deserves more critical scrutiny. Just as often, however, societies look like battles between titans struggling for dominance while average people pay the price.

### The Venezuela Conflict

In Table 7.1, I have laid out a portrait of the Venezuelan conflict in terms of the ideal-typical sources of social power. As Mann suggests, "real institutionalized networks of interaction do not have a simple one-to-one relationship to the ideal-typical sources of social power" (Mann 1986, 17). Most actual, concrete social networks (including institutions and organizations) appeal to multiple sources of social power. For example, almost all of the power networks on the Chavista side of the table have a strong ideological component, giving them a common language and means of coordinating with other networks. Most all of them have some relationship to political power as well. However,

Table 7.1. Chavista Versus Opposition Power Networks Organized
by Ideal-Typical Sources

| Chavismo | Opposition |
|---|---|
| **Ideological power networks** Bolivarian ideology (Third-worldism, postliberalism, developmentalism) pushed forward through: | **Ideological power networks** Liberalism, globalism, Catholicism pushed forward through: |
| • State media complex <br> • Primary and secondary education <br> • Bolivarian universities <br> • Progovernment churches, priests, and pastors <br> • International solidarity groups | • Private media companies <br> • Private and autonomous universities <br> • Catholic hierarchy and diocesan churches <br> • Global networks of media, education and travel |
| **Economic power networks** <br> • The state oil company (PDVSA) <br> • The state mining and hydroelectric company (CVG) <br> • Venezuelan Central Bank <br> • Exchange control board (CENCOEX) <br> • State tax collecting agency (SENIAT) <br> • Boliburgueses <br> • Missions <br> • Progovernment unions | **Economic power networks** <br> • Private enterprise (banks, commerce, transportation, agroindustry) <br> • Chambers of commerce (such as Fedecamaras) and sectorial organizations (Fedeindustria, more) <br> • Leisure consumption organizations (commerce, shopping malls, entertainment, leisure clubs, travel industry) |
| **Military power networks** <br> • Armed Forces: Army, Air Force, Navy, National Guard | **Military power networks** <br> • Discontent of active and retired military officers <br> • Un Nuevo Orden |
| **Political power networks** <br> • Through 2015, all five powers of the central government: Executive, Legislative, Judicial, Electoral and Moral <br> • Majority of state and municipal governments <br> • Socialist Party (PSUV) <br> • Government-sponsored participatory groups (communes, communal councils, water committees, and urban land committees) <br> • Collectives <br> • New multilateral institutions (Unasur, CELAC) <br> • International solidarity groups | **Political power networks** <br> • Opposition coalition (MUD) <br> • From 2016, legislative power (i.e., National Assembly) <br> • Some state and municipal governments <br> • A little less than 40 percent of the National Assembly <br> • Student movements <br> • National and international NGOs <br> • Traditional union movement <br> • Expat networks <br> • Fringe radicals |

I have arranged them in terms of their primary ideal-typical source of social power. The horizontal division separates the networks into two constellations of power: "Chavismo" versus "opposition." In what follows I will work through each side to develop a sense of this conflict that goes beyond a reductionist focus on political actors and the state to a broader view of the networks involved.

## The Power Networks of Chavismo

### Ideological Power Networks

Gaining public recognition in the 1990s through the failed 1992 coup, the Bolivarian movement tapped into a broad "Polanyian" resistance to marketization of society resulting from neoliberal reform (Silva 2009). They channeled this sentiment through a "third-worldist" appropriation of Leninism that blames underdevelopment on imperialism and promotes the struggle for national liberation as the key strategy for a transition to socialism. Bolivarian ideology is postliberal, not illiberal, insofar as it does not reject the liberal discourse of rights but expands it to include economic, social, and cultural rights (Arditi 2010). Bolivarian ideology is also developmentalist in its view that modernity can be pushed forward through large-scale development projects. Finally, it emphasizes a civilian role for the military. There is a strong tradition in Venezuela of seeing the armed forces as an example of order, rectitude, and moral authority, and Bolivarian ideology taps into this.

These ideological configurations can be pushed forward through a massive state media complex as well as through government control over private media. From the time he was a presidential candidate in 1997 and 1998, Hugo Chávez sought power without the support of a real political party, unions, or articulated social movements. Media was his way of overcoming the problem of coordination this presented. His hallmark policy as president was a television call-in show named "Aló Presidente" that would last hours. His government transformed state-owned, Channel 8 from a marginal station few people watched to a state-of-the-art media facility getting out the government's message. This has been followed by the development of new state radio networks, web pages, newspapers, and more television networks, complemented by many community radio and television stations and newspapers, all of which are funded by the government and wholeheartedly support it.

The one part of the public sector over which Chavismo has not been able to gain significant control is Venezuela's public autonomous universities (more on these below). The government has responded by creating its own network of "Bolivarian Universities" as well as by dramatically expanding universities associated with the armed forces (UNEFA). These universities openly reject the idea of autonomy and trumpet the fact that they are part of a revolutionary project. They train students in occupations that are consistent with the government's development model—such as community doctors and popular educators. These universities have seen hypertrophic growth and do not come close to the academic standards of Venezuela's other universities. However, they have enrolled hundreds of thousands of students who otherwise would not have been able to study and are grateful for the opportunity.

Throughout the Chávez period some evangelical churches and pastors, as well as Catholic priests and nuns, have strongly promoted the government's message (Smilde 2013). Evangelical churches such as Centro de Cristo para las Naciones and Iglesia Renacer have collaborated directly with the government on social service projects and provide a message based in "dominion theology" compatible with Chavismo's nationalism. Likewise, numerous Catholic priests actively support Chavismo in their work with communities.

Representation and messaging is also carried out by international solidarity groups. Over the past fifteen years, Venezuela has become a destination for "revolutionary tourism" by leftists from other countries who want to understand more about Chavismo. There are also numerous blogs and publications, such as Venezuelanalysis.com, that provide progovernment messaging. In addition, social media initiatives such as Hands Off Venezuela, Real News Venezuela, and the Venezuela Solidarity Network work to monitor the media for what they see as unfair representations.

Of course, these are not the totality of Chavismo's sources of ideological power. Virtually every participatory movement and government organization does significant ideological work with discourses, chants, logos, songs, T-shirts, hats, billboards, stories, and more. Indeed, probably the most distinctive aspect of Chavismo is the amount of ideological work it does.

Economic Power Networks

What puts the Venezuelan government in a unique position is the fact that it controls a state oil company (PDVSA) that brings in tens of billions of dollars in revenue every year. Scholars no longer assume that there exists a "resource curse" that condemns countries rich in commodities to underdevelopment and dictatorship (Dunning 2008). Indeed, much of the Chavista government's success comes from the extraordinary resources it had to pursue its goals, control its opposition, and garner the support of the population. Oil allowed the Chávez government to carry out a form of "export-oriented populism" (Richardson 2009), a non zero-sum form of spending benefiting urban as well as rural sectors. This is not to say that oil is simply a resource blessing. It can indeed lead to economic dysfunction through "Dutch disease" and complicate democratic competition by giving the executive branch an overwhelming advantage.

PDVSA is involved not only in the extraction, processing, and delivery of hydrocarbons (oil, coal, natural gas) but also in food imports, building homes, and many other parts of the government's social programs. The government uses PDVSA resources in this way to circumvent the normal budget process and exercise more discretion over its spending. One result of this expanding vocation is that PDVSA has fallen seriously behind in investment. While projections were that it was supposed to be producing six million barrels of oil per day by 2014, it currently produces less than three million, less than it did when Chávez took office.

Another formerly autonomous economic institution that has come under direct governmental control is the Venezuelan Central Bank. It controls reserves of foreign currency and gold, as well as the monetary supply. Since President Maduro has taken office they have expanded the monetary supply by at least 60 percent each year at the same time that the economy has contracted, leading to inflation that reached triple digits in both 2015 and 2016 and has the potential for four digits in 2017. Perhaps even more important is the Ministry of Economy and Finances, which controls concessions of wildly overvalued official-rate dollars and thereby has ample discretion to pick winners and losers. Of course, this has given rise to corruption networks that create fictitious "briefcase businesses" that apply for and obtain official-rate dollars, then sell them on the black market for windfall profits. Frequently those close to the government are in the best position to engage in foreign exchange scams. Some big players in the government have used this mechanism to generate parallel budgets with which they can carry out government projects and develop their own personal networks of patronage. This is large part explains the government's resistance to modifying a foreign exchange regime that is obviously undermining the government's viability.

One of the government's signature initiatives is the institution of "missions." These are, in essence, a social policy delivery mechanism whereby the government attends to urgent needs through newly created, flexible institutional arrangements. In all of them, the employees that work with the missions have a serious interest in their continuance.

Increasing state control over the economy has not done away with the private sector, as the government has needed it for its projects. Private companies have carried out everything from construction projects to food distribution, and private banks hold much of the government's cash. This has provided endless opportunities for insider contacts, kickbacks, and other rackets, creating a class of wealthy entrepreneurs referred to in Venezuela as *boliburgueses*. These people have a strong interest in the continuation of the government and frequently contribute to its causes.

As will be mentioned below, one power network that the government has not been able to control is the preexisting union movement. However, through a number of changes in the laws governing union creation and elections, it has been able to diversify the field, and there are now numerous progovernment unions that vie for power in labor relations.

## Military Power Networks

Of course, his past as a soldier was Hugo Chávez's most important biographical characteristic. The attraction this held for Venezuelans is indicative of the high esteem in which they hold the armed forces. In the minds of average Venezuelans the military is characterized by discipline, rectitude, order, power, and moral authority. While democracy is inevitably messy and exposes all sorts of conflicting interests and unintended consequences, to the average Venezuelan, the military appears to work through an understandable moral economy of authority, responsibility, and concerted execution of tasks. As commander in chief, Chávez rolled back decades of professionalization and depoliticization of the military by increasing the military's role in the exercise of governance and in the government itself. This tendency has been dramatically expanded, however, by his civilian successor. Weakened by a squeaker of an electoral victory in April 2013 and an immediate protest movement, Nicolas Maduro seems to have identified the military as the security blanket. He has increased the number of active and retired military officers in the government, turned over citizen security to them, and given them a larger profile in the importation of basic goods, as well as a bank and even a television network. The military controls Venezuela's borders as well as its airspace. Some sectors are involved in drug trafficking. The armed forces also control arms imports and the manufacture of ammunition, both of which seriously compromise its role in citizen security. In 2016 journalists uncovered massive corruption in the military's role in food distribution (Dreier and Goodman 2016)

## Political Power Networks

The central political characteristic of Chavismo is the degree of control it has had over all five powers of the central government: executive, legislative, judicial, electoral, and moral. It has held both the presidency and legislature since 1999. In 2004 it pushed through a judicial reform that expanded the number of judges in the Supreme Justice Tribunal (Supreme Court). The judicial branch has also run seriously behind in naming judges. Roughly 80 percent of Venezuela's judges are provisional. As a result, the courts are squarely in the government's corner and do not exercise any type of counterweight or veto power on the government. After the opposition boycotted the 2005 legislative elections, the government had five years of free rein, during which time it installed progovernment rectors in the electoral authority as well as a new People's Ombudsman who is squarely progovernment. The opposition participated in the 2010 legislative elections and controlled roughly 40 percent of the seats, which is enough to block some government initiatives. The electoral authority has run clean election days, but is incapable of exercising any control over campaign conditions, giving the government an unfair advantage in electoral competition. This was not enough to prevent the government from losing its legislative majority to the opposition in 2015. But subsequently, the Electoral Authority more squarely took the side of the government as it indefinitely postponed the push for presidential recall referendum in October 2016 and the regional elections that were supposed to take place in 2016.

The United Socialist Party of Venezuela (PSUV) is the largest party in Venezuela. PSUV was created in 2007 after Chávez was elected to a second term and said he wanted all parties supporting him to merge into one. Most complied, but several, for example the Partido Comunista de Venezuela and Patria Para Todos, declined. Now PSUV brings together roughly 90 percent of progovernment support, while other parties combine for another 5–10 percent. However, the process of party "revalidation," taking place in spring 2017, seems destined to eliminate smaller pro-government parties.

A good deal of attention was paid in 2014 to progovernment collectives. These are community groups, many of which predate Chávez, that see themselves as defenders of the revolution. Some of them are armed. Chávez himself encouraged them in the early years of his presidency with the idea of "the people in arms." However, in the last couple of years of his presidency he created the militia, which is an actual citizen body of the armed forces, and pushed forward a plan for gun control that pointed toward the need for these *colectivos* to lay down their arms. Most of them refused, and the government in recent years has lived in tense coexistence with them. Government-sponsored participatory groups, such as communes, communal councils, water committees, and urban land committees, can be mobilized to support the government and carry out projects (Garcia-Guadilla 2011).

Hugo Chávez considered himself, and is considered by his movement, as a modern-day Simon Bolivar, not only for liberating his country but also for seeking regional unity. Chávez was one of the regional leaders who worked to create and strengthen the Union of Southern Nations (Unasur) and the Community of Latin American and Caribbean States (CELAC). These are meant to create alternative multilateral institutions not dominated by the United States. So far these organizations have focused almost exclusively on strengthening the sovereignty of member nations. But slowly they are putting human rights and issues of citizenship on their agendas.

## Opposition Power Networks

### Ideological Power Networks

The opposition movement is guided by a classic liberal perspective that sees the distinction between tyranny and liberty as the central element of democracy and human dignity itself. It connects this with a discourse of universal human rights, but is largely restricted to civil and political rights. Rather than "nation," it affirms modernity and the global economic, social, cultural, and political networks that represent it. In Venezuela this liberalism has a particular cast through the values of Catholic Neo-Scholasticism (Levine 1981). Catholic culture is strong in Venezuela's upper and upper-middle classes, as it valorizes the life of the mind and reason as that which gives access to the immutable, essential, and universal, and provides control over the body and lower passions. In neo-scholastic culture it is spirituality and cultivation of higher faculties that underlie human dignity and provide the grounds for liberty, autonomy, and democracy. This is the standpoint from which the populism, clientelism, and instrumentality of Chavismo are frequently signified as undignified and barbaric. The Catholic Church in general and the Catholic hierarchy most particularly have been some of the most effective critics of the Chávez government, sparring with it regarding democracy and human rights from the beginning. In 2014 the Church released a document called "Dialogue and Political Pluralism," stating that "no social or political model has the right to be imposed on others. The Venezuelan Constitution guarantees a pluralist society and its different visions" (Conferencia Episcopal Venezolana 2014).

Venezuela's private media were once the strongest bastion of opposition to the government, serving a more important aggregating and coordinating function than political parties in the first five years of Chavismo. However, here as well, the government has increasingly gained the upper hand. In 2007 the government refused to renew the airwave concession of fierce anti-Chávez network RCTV. More recently, the Maduro government has removed from the air NTN24—a channel focusing on Venezuelan news but transmitting from Colombia—and CNN en Español. These and other actions led other private networks such as Globovisión, Venevision and Televen to self-censor, seriously toning down their criticism. There is still a robust representation of antigovernment opinion, but it is increasingly confined to online publications and has a reduced presence on the airwaves or newsstands. In this situation, social media services like Facebook, Twitter, and Zello have become the most important means of staying informed and organizing political action.

Venezuela's public autonomous universities are funded by the government but have far-reaching institutional autonomy. During the eighteen years of Chavismo these universities, along with private universities, have been the most solid bastion of intellectual criticism of the government. Chavismo has tried to gain control of university administration repeatedly but never succeeded. It has attempted to change the electoral rules so that university presidents are elected not just by students and university professors but by all personnel, including maintenance, in the hope that this will tip the balance in favor of progovernment candidates. In lieu of this, the government has progressively suffocated the university sector in multiple ways. It has reduced their budgets, changed the terms of funds for research and attending conferences, allowed inflation to diminish faculty salaries. Most recently it took control of the process of student admissions (Pérez Hernáiz and Smilde 2015).

The opposition ideological perspective has a strong elective affinity with global networks of media, education, and travel. International journalists who cover Venezuela not only tend to live in the affluent areas of Eastern Caracas, they are very similar in human, social, and cultural capital to the opposition, relate to their situation, and feel their pain. Only the most conscientious international journalists travel to the interior or to a poor *barrio* to interview people and try to understand their situation. People allied with the opposition are more likely to speak with them and know the vocabulary of the international media. Members of Venezuela's former political elite now have teaching positions at top universities abroad, or head NGOs and foundations, giving them a disproportionate voice in international discussion. They edit journals, have newspaper columns, give lectures, and fund other scholars. In addition, there is still a strong bias toward affluent opposition members among those who have the opportunity to travel abroad for work, study, or pleasure, and share their stories.


## Economic Power Networks


While the size of the Venezuelan government grew dramatically during the Chávez period, the private sector did as well, and still accounts for approximately half of the economy in the Maduro years. For the past eighteen years, private agroindustry, commerce, and finance have all vigorously opposed the Chavist governments. In recent years, through expropriations, exchange control, and business regulation, the government has clearly gained the upper hand over the private sector, and most entrepreneurs live uncertain lives. The Venezuelan Federation of Chambers of Commerce (Fedecamaras) was once a fierce and formidable opponent of the government—indeed its president, Pedro Carmona, was named interim president during the 2002 coup— but is now a less vocal critic and over the past three years has successfully held dialogues with the government over concrete impediments to production. Food giant Polar Industries controls a large percentage of food production and distribution in Venezuela and frequently finds itself accused and threatened by the government. Leisure consumption institutions (commerce, shopping malls, entertainment, leisure clubs, travel industry) are still dominated by the urban middle classes and prioritize their needs.

Another once formidable adversary, the labor movement, has been seriously weakened. The Confederación de Trabajadores de Venezuela (CTV) was, along with Fedecamaras, one of the leading forces in the 2002–4 conflict that had Chávez on the ropes. Since then its own corruption and dysfunction, combined with the government's assiduous efforts to weaken the movement through electoral laws and by preferring progovernment unions, has reduced its effectiveness. However, the labor unions in heavy industry in Guyana are still strong and some of them are militantly antigovernment.

## Military Power Networks

The Venezuelan opposition does not hold executive power in the central government and therefore does not have a hold on military power networks. However, many retired military officers actively oppose the government. Over the second half of the twentieth century Venezuela's military significantly professionalized and came to see itself as under civilian control and separate from politics (Trinkunas 2005). The increasing incorporation of the armed forces into Chavismo's socialist project has caused discontent among active and retired military officers, who see it as a regression. Many such officers received training in U.S. military programs and have long-term ties to the U.S. military. One group, calling itself Un Nuevo Orden (UNO), consists of radicalized retired military officers operating abroad and working for a military-civilian overthrow of the government (mainly through social media).

## Political Power Networks

The leading force in the opposition is the coalition of opposition parties called the Mesa de la Unidad Democratica (MUD). The MUD has brought together parties mainly for electoral purposes. One of the main explanations for the rise of Chavismo was the implosion of Venezuela's party system in the 1990s. A lack of internal democracy and connection to the broader public undermined the legitimacy of parties in the electorate and led them to a series of self-defeating decisions. Indeed, analysts frequently suggest that Acción Democrática (AD) and Comité de Organización

Política Electoral Independiente (COPEI) weren't killed by Chávez; they committed suicide. The MUD brings together a diverse set of parties and many leaders with aspirations and has had a difficult time presenting a unified alternative to Chavismo.

With the central government dominated by Chavismo, the highest profile positions for opposition leaders through 2015 were governorships and mayoralties. And indeed the opposition controls the better part of Venezuela's major cities and states. For example, Henrique Capriles is the governor of Miranda State; Henri Falcon is the governor of Lara; and Carlos Ocariz is the mayor of the Sucre municipality in Caracas. These positions gave space to opposition leaders to cultivate followers and policy profiles. In 2015 they overcame their divisions long enough to go to the December legislative elections in united form and reaped enormous benefits, winning an ample majority of the seats. However, in 2016 their divisions reemerged and impeded strategic action.

One of the most important opposition actors in Venezuela is what is known as the "student movement." These are actually student movements from Venezuela's public autonomous and private universities, which now represent a minority of all higher education students. University student movements have had a long-term role in Venezuela's democratic movements going back to the nineteenth century. These universities have electoral processes for student government; being student body president is a time-honored stepping stone to a political career. Such student leaders tend to emphasize local issues such as university budgets and conditions, as well as broader national issues. However, these latter tend to reveal their origins in the urban middle classes, focusing on issues of civil, political, and economic liberties.

Much of the most credible and informed criticism of Chavista governments comes from NGOs focused on human rights monitoring. The NGOs making up "Foro por la Vida" monitor different aspects of human rights and publish reports criticizing the government. These organizations are often articulated into international networks, such as Transparency International, and present their findings in international forums, such as the Inter-American Commission on Human Rights (IACHR) and the United Nations Human Rights Council. As human rights are "universal"—in other words, they are not subject to national sovereignty—they present an attractive discourse for opposition groups to seek international intervention in Venezuela that could tip the balance in their favor. Thus these groups, their reports, and their claims are frequently instrumentalized by opposition figures and parties who make political battles into human rights battles.

Much of this task is taken on by networks of Venezuelan expatriates in the United States and elsewhere. In South Florida, which has the single largest community of Venezuelan immigrants, they have pressured representatives and senators to push for sanctions. Some even organized a Caravan for Freedom to Washington in July 2014 to demand passage of a bill calling for targeted sanctions on Venezuelan leaders. Marco Rubio's sanctions bill is called the Venezuela Defense of Human Rights and Civil Society Act of 2014. Expatriates networks are facilitated by social media inside and outside of Venezuela. *Caracas Chronicles* is a widely read English-language blog that, along with other blogs and Twitter accounts, mobilizes international opinion through expatriates networks. One video portraying a violent government ruthlessly victimizing students, made during the crisis of Spring 2014 (but duplicitously using many clips from ten to twelve years earlier) by a Venezuelan American at the University of Florida, went viral on YouTube. It should be mentioned that these networks can dip into radical fringe groups that seek the overthrow of the Venezuelan government, such as Lord Rebel and Un Nuevo Orden. It is not clear if these movements are simply the social media expressions of youth bravado, or actual organizational efforts.

Traditional multilateral organizations have not (at last update in March 2017) had an effective role in Venezuela. The government regards the Organization of American States as a tool of U.S. hemispheric dominance and has done what it can to undermine the latter's importance. The U.N. likewise, other than occasional criticism of specific issues, has not intervened in Venezuela. Both bodies have asked to send human rights representatives to Venezuela but have been rebuffed. The IACHR and the Inter-American Court on Human Rights have repeatedly criticized Venezuela, and Venezuela has responded in kind. In 2012, after IACHR demanded the release of a prisoner convicted for placing a bomb in the Spanish Embassy in 2003 because of mistreatment, Hugo Chávez announced they would be denouncing the court, a process which takes a year. Indeed, Venezuela finally withdrew from the court in 2013.

But perhaps the most important multilateral agencies are those that have to do with international commerce. The International Chamber of Commerce, the World Bank, and other bodies are overseeing a number of arbitration cases between Venezuela and international oil and mining companies. Venezuela, with refineries and assets in the United States as well as ships that sail the world to deliver oil, is highly vulnerable to having assets embargoed.

## Venezuela Post-Chávez

As any sociologist can tell you, the Achilles heal of charismatic leadership is always succession. Hugo Chávez personally designated Nicolás Maduro as his successor and left him with a 15–20 percent lead in March 2013. When Maduro almost lost the election only one month later, it not only animated the opposition; it also raised doubts within his own coalition regarding his viability as the new leader of the revolution. Maduro responded by prioritizing the solidity of the Chavista political coalition—no small task since it was put together by Chávez and fits his profile, consisting of nationalist military sectors, progressives, radical leftists, and popular sectors. As mentioned above, topping Maduro's list of priorities was to shore up his support in the military. Beyond this, Maduro's strategy seems to be to maintain equilibrium by balancing sectors off of each other. In October 2013 Maduro marginalized pragmatist Nelson Merentes, generating speculation of a leftward direction. In May of 2014 Maduro removed the architect of Chavista economic policy, Jorge Giordani, suggesting a more pragmatic direction. But in September 2014, he sidelined pragmatist Rafael Ramirez from the economic team and then later Nelson Merentes (Smilde and Pantoulas 2014).

Perhaps Maduro's biggest deficit is his lack of charisma in a government designed by, institutionalized around, and requiring a charismatic figure. Maduro has addressed this by calling himself the "son of Chávez" at every opportunity and through a continual flow of ritual events to try to infuse his government with Chávez's charisma. This in some part explains how Maduro's popularity lasted as long as it did. However, even Chávez's popularity levels were highly dependent on economic performance. The centerpiece of Chávez's ideology was the idea that the people could live well if a truly revolutionary government administered the country's oil wealth. When things went well, it was evidence that Chávez was right. When things went poorly, it raised doubts.

But this is precisely Chavismo's weakest link: Maduro inherited from Chávez an unsustainable economic policy. A budget deficit running around 20 percent of GDP leads the government to print local currency not backed by foreign hard currency. An ever-expanding supply of local currency accompanied by fixed foreign exchange rates creates increasing demand on available dollars. Unable to supply the demand for dollars because of stagnant or reduced foreign currency earnings from oil sales, the government needs to restrict dollar allocations. The excess demand creates a parallel market for those who need dollars but cannot get them at the official price. The large, often dramatic difference between the official and parallel exchange rates creates an irresistible incentive for dollars to be siphoned off into corruption and capital flight. And the dollar crunch creates scarcities both directly (by making it harder to import finished goods) and indirectly (by making it harder to import inputs and machinery needed for manufacture) (Smilde and Sánchez Montañés 2013). Thus the Venezuelan economy has a lot of local currency, but not enough things to buy. Goods whose prices are effectively controlled are scarce; the prices of everything else are soaring.

When he took office, analysts predicted that Maduro would make reforms quickly, assuming the political costs early in his term before significant electoral events. But Maduro has consistently put off reform, choosing instead to emphasize an "economic war" supposedly being waged against his government by merchants and industrialists in cahoots with the domestic and international political opposition. This in itself caused the widespread scarcities and inflation that were partial causes of the 2014 protests. But it only became worse in 2015 as the decline in the price of oil, which provides over 95 percent of Venezuela's hard currency revenue, has continued its precipitous drop from $99 in June 2014 to close to $30 a barrel in December 2015. The massive decline in income has led to an economic contraction of around 5 percent, as well as triple-digit inflation. In 2015 and 2016, radical Spanish economist Alfredo Serrano has taken the lead in Maduro's economic policy, rebuffing even friendly efforts at reform, such as that recommended by the Union of Southern Nations in mid-2016. Serrano believes that prices are largely irrelevant and that if well organized, the government should be able to distribute goods purchased with petrodollars to those who most need them.

There are a couple of reasons that it has been so difficult for Maduro to push forward with reform. First, anti-neoliberalism is one of the cornerstones of Chavismo (French 2010). Hugo Chávez catapulted himself to the public stage in February 1992 through a coup against Carlos Andres Pérez, whose government had implemented a radical structural adjustment package three years earlier. That package led to *el Caracazo*, three days of rioting and violence in February 1989 that Chávez and other coup leaders said led them to decide to enact their coup. Within Chavismo, February 27 is still portrayed as the day "the people of Bolivar woke up." Therefore, taking on significant economic reform would generate significant pushback among the leftmost elements of the coalition. Second, as much as average people are suffering today from inflation and scarcities, significant economic reform would cause a short-term shock that could affect the stability of an already weak government. Perhaps most importantly, the enormous distortions created by having a currency whose black market rate is hundreds, even thousands of times the official rate creates stakeholders in and around the government who reap windfall profits. There are likely key players within the government who actively prevent reform because they benefit from the status quo.

One of the main ways the Maduro government has sought to keep control of a failing model has been through increasing authoritarianism. The past 3 years have also seen the government turn the corner in its consolidation of control over Venezuelan media. During 2013, once fervent opposition television news channel Globovisión was domesticated. While the change in ownership in 2013 was obscure, the results since then have been clear. Globovisión showed serious signs of self-censorship during the 2014 protests, providing no coverage of conflicts in the streets and softball coverage of the politics around the protests. A similar process is currently occurring in the largest newspaper conglomerate. *Cadena Capriles* was sold in 2013 and is also undergoing serious turmoil as opposition journalists buck an effort to control their writing. Finally, on the most serious day of protests, February 12, the government removed Colombia-based NTN24 from the air, arguing that it was fomenting chaos. The government is also slowly strangling independent newspapers by restricting their ability to import newsprint. In 2015, the president of the National Assembly, Diosdado Cabello, sued three Venezuelan newspapers for reprinting a story from ABC of Spain suggesting that Cabello was involved in drug trafficking. This lawsuit has led a court to place travel restrictions on twenty-two directors and administrators of these news outlets.

The government's crackdown on protest in 2014 is also notorious. Most critical attention has focused on the number of deaths in the protest. However, just as important is the indiscriminate use of tear gas and rubber bullets, as well as the mass detentions without proper judicial orders or procedure. This led to the arrest of around three thousand protestors. Many of them were given conditional release with unconstitutional restrictions on their ability to continue participating in protests (Centro de Derechos Humanos 2015). In early 2015 the Ministry of Defense issued controversial Resolution 8610, which allowed the military to participate in policing protests (Smilde and Pérez Hernáiz 2015). As a result of these measures, and because the 2015 legislative elections provided an escape valve for opposition energies, street protest has significantly declined in 2015 and 2016 despite objectively worse social and economic conditions.

In 2015 we saw the progressive self-destruction of Chavismo. Regional uproar over the United States' designation of Venezuela as a threat to national security—a requirement for implementing its package of targeted sanctions—led the United States to change course a month later and send senior diplomat Thomas Shannon to engage Maduro and other government leaders (Smilde 2015). This largely removed the United States as the primary focus of Maduro's international conspiracy theories. The government went to the December 2015 elections with only exhausted claims of an economic war to show for its efforts and without signs of any new thinking or projects on the horizon. Chavismo was castigated by the voters. With 57 percent of the vote, the opposition obtained 67 percent of the National Assembly seats, giving them a large majority that put them in position to wield considerable power. In 2015 the opposition largely played the electoral game, focusing on its own unity and allowing the government to self-destruct. Polls shortly before the elections showed that, for the first time in many years, the population had higher levels of trust in the opposition than in the government. The opposition also showed some signs of increased engagement with the population and attention to the ground game of democratic politics: mobilizing voters and poll witnesses to maximize and secure their vote (Ulmer 2015).

The December 2015 legislative election sent Venezuela into uncharted waters. The opposition had not controlled a branch of government during the entire Chávez period and most of the checks and balances in the constitution—including such routine tasks as interpellation of government officials—had never been tested. Furthermore, the electoral loss still left the Maduro government with control over four branches of the government, most importantly the Supreme Court (TSJ), the Armed Forces, and the state oil company. Already in December 2015 the TSJ suspended the election of four deputies from the Amazon State, three of which were from the opposition, which put them below the two thirds of the seats they needed for a super-majority. In the coming months the opposition-controlled National Assembly indeed passed a number of pieces of legislation, all of which were declared unconstitutional by the TSJ. When, in July, the opposition reseated the Amazon deputies whose elections had been suspended, the TSJ declared the AN in official disobedience and suggested that none of their projects would be constitutionally valid. In 2017 Maduro actually gave his State of the

Nation Address to the TSJ instead of the AN. Currently the AN serves the opposition as a meeting space and to get their message out through speeches and resolutions, but there is little it can do institutionally.

While the Maduro government is unpopular it retains considerable power when thought of in terms of ideological, economic, military and political networks. Probably the only thing that would loosen its grip would be some sort of economic crisis or international intervention. This is not unlikely as, despite its power, what the Maduro administration lacks is a viable model of governance. Having sacrificed its citizens' well-being to keep afloat economically, it has little chance of winning presidential elections in 2018. And postponing them indefinitely as it did with the recall referendum would surely generate international diplomatic reaction. It looks like Venezuela will be able to make its debt payments in 2017, but an economic crisis could happen any time, and that too could shake Maduro's hold on power.

In June 2016, Secretary General of the Organization of American States Luis Almagro invoked the Inter American Democratic Charter on Venezuela, a move that could eventually lead to its being suspended from the body. However, after three discussions, member states decided not to proceed with the Democratic Charter and give the dialogue pushed forward by UNASUR a chance to succeed. That dialogue floundered but was revived by the Vatican in the days after the suspension of the recall referendum in October. The Vatican dialogue achieved some important agreements that were subsequently ignored by the Maduro government. Currently dialogue is paralyzed but there is increasing movement in the Organization of American States for taking up the Democratic Charter again. Trading block Mercosur has already marginalized Venezuela from full membership and could also invoke their own democratic clause. The United Nations has a new secretary general and UNASUR soon will too. These bodies could also take up the case of Venezuela in the coming months and years.

## Post-Neoliberal Latin America

Luna and Filgueira (2009) have argued that the rise of the Left has generated a paradigmatic crisis in "academic interpretations of the political economy of democracy and development for Latin America." Attempts to understand the rise of new Left governments in terms of bounded political actors vying for power in a formal political arena simply do not capture the breadth of the conflict. In most new Left contexts, the Left has arisen as part of "Polany-ian" social resistance to the comprehensive marketization of society in the 1980s and 1990s (Silva 2009). Neoliberalism allowed the retrenchment and, in some cases, creation of extensive social, economic, cultural, and political inequalities, which populations and movements resisted, preparing the way for leftist governing projects. Many of these projects pushed forward far-reaching processes of change, precisely by strengthening the power of the executive branch, reducing checks and balances, and restricting civil and po-litical liberties. This has generated, to varying degrees, processes of class-based polarization and conflict over the very meaning of democracy. Supporters of these leftist governing projects have suggested they are moving to a more comprehensive form of democracy, one that includes economic, social, and cultural rights. Opponents argue that fundamental civil and political liber-ties are being attacked and that this is leading to a new form of authoritari-anism. Unfortunately, both sides are right, and we need to construct social scientific concepts that can more fully capture this conflict.

Working from the assumption of multiple, conjunctural causation, neo-Weberian full-conflict theory can adopt the strengths of both neoliberal and neo-Marxist analysis while setting aside their blind spots. Application to the post-neoliberal Left Turn in Latin America facilitates a move beyond simplistic good left–bad left dichotomies. I agree with French (2010) that the common denominator of these leftist governments is their opposition to neoliberalism. The varying directions of these governments depend largely on the economic, political, and social contexts in which they are elected and construct their governing projects. Eschewing causal primacy allows us to benefit from the critical edges of both the pluralist and neo-Marxist perspectives while avoiding their critical myopia. We can appreciate the way the dramatic inequalities of Latin American societies have led to a demand for change at the same time as we understand the ironies whereby robust efforts at using the state to address inequalities can lead to a concentration of power that can undermine these ef-forts. We can criticize the deterioration of civil and political rights at the same time that we praise a reduction in social, cultural, and economic inequalities.

## Notes

I would like to thank Randall Collins, Emilio Parrado, Rogers Smith, Tulia Falleti, Eduardo Silva, Maria Pilar Garcia Guadilla, Timothy Gill, Philip Lewin, Dillon Nuanes, Kenneth Roberts and commenters in presentations at the University of Georgia, Brown

University, Tulane University, University of Pennsylvania, Universidad Simon Bolivar, the 2015 meetings of the American Sociological Association, and the 2016 Congress of the Latin American Studies Association for their feedback.

1. In its pure form, the pluralist perspective actually deemphasizes state structures, suggesting they are, more than anything else, a function of the social forces in play. But in scholarship on Latin America the basic pluralist outlook of looking at contending forces is generally combined with a state-centered perspective that emphasizes particular constellations of state institutions.

2. With this position I am at odds with Mann's perspective, which tends to follow the classic structuralist position that sees culture as substantially arbitrary or at least not subject to empirical verification. In my pragmatist view (Smilde 2013) meanings are tools for engaging the world and can work better or worse when measured by their own criteria. They do vary according to whether they are relatively more literal or figurative, but the basic process of symbolic predication is the same.

## References

Arditi, Benjamin. 2010. "Arguments About the Left: A Post-Liberal Politics?" In Cameron and Hershberg, *Latin America's Left Turns*.

Baker, Andy, and Kenneth Greene. 2011. "The Latin American Left's Mandate: Free-Market Policies and Issue Voting in New Democracies." *World Politics* 63 (1): 43–77.

Berezin, Mabel. 2009. *Illiberal Politics in Neoliberal Times: Culture, Security and Populism in the New Europe*. New York: Cambridge University Press.

Cameron, M., and E. Hershberg, eds. 2010. *Latin America's Left Turns: Politics, Policies and Trajectories of Change*. Boulder, Colo.: Lynne Rienner.

Centro de Derechos Humanos. 2015. *Hasta que se demuestre lo contrario: Violaciones del debido proceso a personas enjuiciadas por manifestar*. Caracas: Universidad Católica Andrés Bello.

Collins, Randall. 1994. *Four Sociological Traditions*. New York: Oxford University Press.

"Colombia presentará pruebas para ordenar la captura de Nicolás Maduro." 2015. *El Nacional* (Caracas), September 5.

Conferencia Episcopal Venezolana. 2014. "Dialogo y pluralismo politico." Caracas, January 10.

Dahl, Robert. 1971. *Polyarchy: Participation and Opposition*. New Haven, Conn.: Yale University Press.

Dreier, Hannah, and Joshua Goodman. 2016. "Venezuelan Military Trafficking Food as Country Goes Hungry." *Big Story*, Associated Press, December 28.

Dunkerely, James. 2007. "Evo Morales, the 'Two Bolivias,' and the Third Bolivian Revolution." *Journal of Latin American Studies* 39.

Dunning, Thad. 2008. *Crude Democracy: Natural Resource Wealth and Political Regimes*. New York: Cambridge University Press.

French, John D. 2010. "Many Lefts, One Path? Chávez and Lula." In Cameron and Hershberg, *Latin America's Left Turns*.

García Guadilla, María Pilar. 2011. "Urban Land Committees: Co-optation, Autonomy, and Protagonism." In *Venezuela's Bolivarian Democracy: Participation, Politics, and Culture Under Chávez*, edited by David Smide and Daniel Hellinger. Durham, N.C.: Duke University Press.

Jay, Martin. 1984. *Marxism and Totality: The Adventures of a Concept from Lucacs to Habermas*. Berkeley: University of California Press.

Levine, Daniel H. 1981. *Religion and Politics in Latin America: The Catholic Church in Venezuela and Colombia*. Princeton, N.J.: Princeton University Press.

Levitsky, S., and K. M. Roberts. 2011. *The Resurgence of the Latin American Left*. Baltimore, Md.: Johns Hopkins University Press.

Locke, John. 1986. *The Second Treatise on Civil Government*. New York: Prometheus Books.

Luna, Juan Pablo, and Fernando Filgueira. 2009. "The Left Turns as Multiple Paradigmatic Crises." *Third World Quarterly* 30 (2): 371–95.

Mann, Michael. 2012 [1986]. *A History of Power from the Beginning to AD 1760*. Vol. 1 of *The Sources of Social Power*. New York: Cambridge University Press.

———. 2012 [1993]. *The Rise of Classes and Nation-States, 1760–1914*. Vol. 2 of *The Sources of Social Power*. New York: Cambridge University Press.

———. 2013. *Globalizations, 1945–2011*. Vol. 4 of *The Sources of Social Power*. New York: Cambridge University Press.

Michels, Robert. 1962. *Political Parties: A Sociological Study of the Oligarchic Tendencies of Modern Democracy*. Translated by Eden Paul and Cedar Paul. New York: Free Press.

Monedero, Juan Carlos. 2013 "Venezuela y la reinvención de la política: El desafío del socialismo en nuevos escenarios." *Observatorio Social de América Latina* 14 (33): 15–36.

Mosca, Gaetano. 1939. *The Ruling Class*. Translated by Hannah D. Kahn. New York: McGraw Hill.

Parsons, Talcott. 1951. *The Social System*. New York: Free Press.

Pérez Hernáiz, Hugo and David Smilde. 2015. "New Admissions Procedures Further Threaten University Autonomy." *Venezuelan Politics and Human Rights* (blog), May 27. http://venezuelablog.tumblr.com/post/120059922959/new-admissions-procedures-further-threaten.

Ragin, Charles. 1987. *The Comparative Method: Beyond Quantitative and Qualitative Strategies*. Berkeley: University of California Press.

Richardson, Neil. 2009. "Export Oriented Populism: Commodities and Coalitions in Argentina." *Studies in Comparative International Development* 44 (3): 228–55.

Silva, Eduardo. 2009. *Challenging Neoliberalism in Latin America*. New York: Cambridge University Press.

Smilde, David. 2013. "Beyond the Strong Program in the Sociology of Religion." In *Religion on the Edge: Decentering and Recentering the Sociology of Religion*, edited by Courtney Bender, Wendy Cadge, Peggy Levitt, and David Smilde. New York: Oxford University Press.

———. 2015. "Back-and-Forth Thaw with Venezuela Signals U.S. Return to Diplomacy," *World Politics Review*, August 19.

Smilde, David, and Dimitris Pantoulas. 2014. "Did Maduro Miss His Chance?" *Venezuelan Politics and Human Rights* (blog), September 9. http://venezuelablog.tumblr .com/post/97047568604/did-maduro-miss-his-chance.

Smilde, David, and Hugo Pérez Hernáiz. 2015. "Resolution Allowing Venezuela's Armed Forces to Police Protest Creates Alarm." *Venezuelan Politics and Human Rights* (blog), February 6. http://venezuelablog.tumblr.com/post/110248926924 /resolution-allowing-venezuelas-armed-forces-to.

Smilde, David, and Melina Sánchez Montañés. 2013. "The Skinny on Shortages, Part I," *Venezuelan Politics and Human Rights* (blog), June 25. http://venezuelablog .tumblr.com/post/53854360739/the-skinny-on-shortages-part-i.

Trinkunas, Harold. 2005. *Crafting Civilian Control of the Military in Venezuela: A Comparative Perspective.* Chapel Hill: University of North Carolina Press.

Tucker, Robert C. 1978. *The Marx-Engels Readers*, 2nd Ed. New York: W.W. Norton & Co.

Ulmer, Alexandra. 2015. "Raised 'Chavista' in Poor Venezuela, Lawmaker-Elect Jolts Opposition Image." Reuters, December 16.

Weber, Max. 1968. *Economy and Society*. Berkeley: University of California Press.

Weyland, Kurt. 2013. "The Threat from the Populist Left." *Journal of Democracy* 24 (3): 18–32.

Weyland, K., R. Madrid and W. Hunter, eds. 2010. *Leftist Governments in Latin America: Successes and Shortcomings.* New York: Cambridge University Press.

# CHAPTER 8

# Populism or Democracy? Reexamining the Role of "the People" in Twenty-First-Century Latin American Politics

Paulina Ochoa Espejo

## Introduction

"The people" made a comeback in twenty-first-century Latin America. Since the start of the millennium, a wave of popular mobilizations spurred a turn away from neoliberal policies in several Latin American countries. In, Argentina, Bolivia, Brazil, Ecuador, and Venezuela these popular mobilizations also led to changes in fundamental political institutions, all justified in the name of the people. The political and economic transformations of the New Left seem to come hand in hand with the images of crowds taking buildings or occupying squares. These images of the people have been interpreted in different ways, however. For some, the movements are illustrations of revitalized democracy; for others, they are examples of populism.

Are the New Left movements democratic or populist? This question cannot be settled by better observing the facts. The disagreement rests on a conceptual distinction, and the distinction is not as clear-cut as it may appear at first sight. The evaluations of the New Left movements as either democratic or populist depend on an unresolved theoretical question: If democracy is rule by the people, and populism appeals to the people for legitimacy, how can we distinguish a populist movement from one seeking to establish a liberal democracy? Unless our theories of populism can answer this question, the distinction between democracy and populism in Latin America seems to signal nothing but ideological preferences (as one of my colleagues half-jokingly put it: "Populism is the term we use to describe the democratic movements that we don't like").

In the last decades, partially because of the discussions on Latin American politics, there has been a lively debate over the nature of populism (Taggart 2000; Weyland 2001; Panizza 2005; Hawkins 2009; Mudde and Rovira Kaltwasser 2012), and a new definition has clearly become dominant in political science. This new leading definition has many advantages; however, as I will argue below, it also has a problem: it can distinguish populism and liberal democracy within stable electoral systems, but it cannot do so during constitutional crises. And it is precisely constitutional crises that characterize many of the popular movements in twenty-first century Latin America.

This chapter offers a new theoretical lens for examining populism in crisis situations. By examining recent theoretical debates on the nature and composition of the people, the chapter proposes a different criterion of demarcation between populism and liberal democracy: self-limitation. Populists, I argue, defend their policies by claiming that the people want them. By contrast, liberal democrats also appeal to the people, but only to signal that their claims are fallible, and thus to limit the reach of their claims. I illustrate the thesis by applying the criterion to the contested 2006 elections in Mexico. If the definition that I propose can help us to better understand this historical event, where there was a borderline constitutional crisis, then it can also be a good criterion to understand and evaluate other popular movements in the region, where entirely new constitutions were drafted from scratch and new institutions introduced to the countries in question.

## A Blind Spot in Classical Definitions of Populism

In recent years, several scholars have revisited the concept of populism, seeking to clarify both it and its complex relationship with democracy. Out of these proposals, Cas Mudde's definition stands out because it captures what counts as correct usage of the term in politics and the media, and it synthesizes the core elements that appear in most current scholarly definitions of the term. Moreover, the definition lends itself to use in empirical research, and it helps us to think of the phenomenon comparatively (Mudde and Rovira Kaltwasser 2012). According to Mudde, "populism is a thin-centered ideology that considers society to be ultimately separated into two homogenous and antagonistic groups, 'the pure people' and 'the corrupt elite,' and which argues that politics should be an expression of the *volonté générale* (general will) of the people" (Mudde 2004; Mudde and Rovira Kaltwasser 2012).

This definition is useful for our purposes because it contains a criterion of demarcation, which promises to help us distinguish between democratic mobilizations and populist uprisings, and explains why populism does not sit comfortably with the ideology and values of liberal democracy. This definition (and others with a similar criterion of demarcation) can explain that liberal democracy differs from populism because populists hold that politics should be an expression of the *volonté générale* (general will) of the people, while liberal democrats believe that a well-organized polity will constrain the people's will and allow for pluralism (Plattner 2010). The Rousseauian language in the definition conveys the populist idea that the direct, nonrepresented "people's voice" is equivalent to the common good; and so the general will trumps liberalism's legal constraints. The definition thus stresses that, for populists, the popular will has a higher authority than representative mechanisms and institutions, such as constitutional courts, the judiciary, independent electoral courts, and central banks (Mudde 2004). According to this definition, it is by the degree to which a politician or party ideology favors the imputed people's will over liberal principles and independent institutions that we are to determine who is a populist and when this position is a threat to liberal democracy (Rovira Kaltwasser 2012).

This definition is useful when distinguishing among party ideologies within settled electoral systems. But it has a blind spot when dealing with popular mobilizations that challenge the constitutional order. During such mobilizations and uprisings, especially when they successfully create constitutional crises, the distinction between populism and liberal democracy breaks down.[1] The breakdown results because these mobilizations occur outside the legal and recognized channels of an established political system: legislatures, courts, bureaucracies, or ombudsmen. In those circumstances, the sharp distinction between liberal institutions and the populist appeal to the "general will" collapses, because the movement in question challenges the legitimacy of those institutions that judge whether a movement complies with constitutional guarantees. So, for example, during periods of constitutional stability we could confidently say that a movement is populist if its spokesperson appeals to electoral mandates or majoritarian sentiment to undermine the rights of individuals or minorities. In such periods, we can spot a populist when she appeals to the moral superiority of the common people as a reason for questioning constitutional constraints, the decisions of the judiciary, or other independent institutions whose in-principle legitimacy she nevertheless accepts. However, during constitutional crises this criterion is not helpful, because a liberal movement would behave in exactly the same way. Imagine a constitutional system in crisis: a country where a large part of society actively challenges the legitimacy of current institutions. These challengers may be suspicious of institutions because they believe that they are substantively or procedurally unjust. They may believe that judicial decisions are constantly biased against one group in society, that the police and judiciary are easily corrupted, or that the constitutionally enshrined rights of minorities protect a system of privilege for the elite while effectively disenfranchising large parts of the population. In such cases, there is a movement that does not accept the authority of those institutions that the movement believes are causing harm, and thus it does not accept the authority of institutional constraints. Hence, in such cases, a liberal democratic movement would have to appeal to the people and reject established institutions in order to gain the legitimacy required to enact liberal reforms. We would be talking of a moment of "higher" or "exceptional" lawmaking (Ackerman 1991; Kalyvas 2008; Schmitt 2008). By proposing a new order in the name of what is right for all, a liberal democratic movement would also claim "that politics should be an expression of the *volonté générale* (general will) of the people." That is, according to the first part of Mudde's definition, in such cases a liberal democratic movement would also be a populist movement. When a liberal democratic movement is extra-institutional, this definition cannot help us distinguish between liberal democracy and populism.

A liberal critic of the view I am putting forward could object that the entanglement of populism and liberal democracy in such cases is easy to resolve. If liberal principles are universal and thus independent of the uprising's concrete circumstances, an impartial judge could distinguish a liberal leader from a nonliberal. However, the reply to this objection is straightforward: when the coin of legitimacy is in the air, there is no authoritative impartial judge available. Unlike philosophical debate, which allows direct or hypothetical appeals to truth, when it comes to ideological challenges there is no higher authority than the people to judge and decide who has the right reasons. So during a constitutional crisis, there will be appeals to the people, and the relation between populism and liberal democracy will always be ambiguous in this respect (Canovan 2005).

However, the appeal to the "general will" is only one aspect of Mudde's definition of populism. What about the definition's Manichean distinction between "the pure people" and the "corrupt elite"? Upon examination, we can see that in times of crisis this criterion cannot help us to distinguish liberals from populists either. If, during normal electoral periods, a politician claimed that society is separated into two antagonistic groups (the pure people versus the corrupt elite) and only the people deserve to be heard, then she would be threatening liberal principles. Her views would probably be unacceptable within the liberal political system, and it would be easy to recognize her as a populist; liberalism requires the equal recognition of rights and protections for all and does not accept the exclusion of minorities on the basis of nonliberal criteria. However, in times of crisis, a liberal movement must also make sharp distinctions and exclusions: it must clearly distinguish those who are entitled to participate as equals in the polity from those who should be excluded. For on those occasions, in order to preserve pluralism, a liberal movement must also exclude those who do not accept the terms of the liberal constitutional arrangement and have both the power and the will to overthrow it. This is the rationale behind banning the Nazi party in Germany, for example. Liberal institutions also require and allow for a militant defense (Kirshner 2010). Moreover, those excluded may in fact be a corrupt elite: given that liberal democracy seeks to establish equal rights for all, the supporters of the old nonliberal regime (in other words, the old, nondemocratic elite) must either accept the new terms or leave. Thus during constitutional crises, liberal democrats also establish sharp distinctions between "us" and "them." They, too, visualize a pure people (which has the right to establish new institutions) and a corrupt elite (which supports the old ways). In fact, this tendency may also be seen at work during periods of liberal stability: in such periods, liberal democrats often seek to exclude populists and nonliberals from the polity (Mouffe 2005).[2]

A second critic could dismiss the ambiguity between populism and liberal democracy as an anomaly, a problem that arises only so rarely that it does not really challenge the definition of populism. However, even though constitutional crises are called "exceptional" or "extraordinary" in theoretical debates (Kalyvas 2008; Schmitt 2008), they are much more common than they may seem. In fact, such crises preceded most revolutions that instituted the liberal democratic orders in the Western world. At their inception, all current democracies had to appeal to the popular principle to establish their legitimacy (Arendt 1990; Ackerman 1991; Kalyvas

2008). The people, after all, are the constituent power in a democratic state (Yack 2001).

So if the ambiguity between populism and liberal democracy in this type of situation is so deep, why should we try to disentangle the terms? First, without some clarity regarding the object of study, we cannot understand populism in specific circumstances, such as the diffusion of and relations between the New Left movements in Latin America. Second, and most importantly, the ambiguity poses a problem of political morality for liberal democrats. Given that many today hold that liberal democracy is the best form of political organization, describing a movement as populist rather than liberal democratic is a way of smuggling a negative normative judgment into a supposedly neutral description. Conversely, for critics of existing liberal democratic regimes, not distinguishing between types of movements gives a free pass to any movement challenging the current order. Yet to determine whether a movement is worthy of support from a liberal-democratic perspective we can't shirk from making a distinction and an explicit normative claim. To do this, I hold, we should return to the normative core of democratic theory and ask when must a liberal democracy appeal to the people, and how such an appeal differs from the appeal made by populists. The answer to these questions should help us find a normative criterion to distinguish a populist from a liberal democratic mobilization.

## Popular Indeterminacy and Self-Limitation in Liberal Democratic Theory

The criterion of demarcation that I propose is self-limitation. We can see the criterion in action when a popular movement justifies its aims by appealing to the people but depicts the people as open. That is, self-limitation is at work when the movement depicts the people as the framework that guarantees pluralism but also frames any particular cause as fallible, including its own. Self-limitation arises from the implicit acceptance that the people can (and probably will) change, and for this reason the appeal to the people's will is fallible, temporary, and incomplete. Such a movement acknowledges that its claims may be wrong and accepts temporary political defeats. This attitude opens a window for institutionalizing individual rights and creating a working multiparty democracy. By contrast, a populist depicts his movement as necessarily right, claims that the legitimating ground of government lays in the direct appeal to the people's will, and holds that the voice of the people is always indefeasible. In sum, a populist claims to speak in the name of the people, and holds that this justifies refusing any limits on her claims, while a liberal democrat, in the name of the people, accepts limits on her claims.

It is clear that this criterion can help us describe the differences between liberalism and populism in normal times, but its main attraction comes from its ability to tell apart movements during times of crisis. The argument for why it can do this is the following: the essence of liberal democracy is limited government and respect for individual rights. Yet during crises there are no legitimate or universally accepted enforcers of the legal constraints on government. So to be recognized as liberal-democratic, a movement that wishes to reestablish or reform liberal government must impose these limits on its own; it must exercise self-limitation.

However, this last point needs an independent defense. One could object that it may be easy to see that a movement is not liberal when it abuses individual rights, but it is much harder to judge whether a movement is liberal when it is trying to establish a new regime. How can such a movement claim that it represents the people and also limit its reach at the same time? How can a movement claim to be the bearer of the general will of the people, to be the highest source of authority, and also say that these claims should be limited? My argument is that it is possible to do both simultaneously, but this requires that the movement portray the people as open, or unbounded. Moreover, I argue that openness is normative. Conceiving the people as open is required for all democrats because openness is the best response to the paradoxes in the theory of popular sovereignty, which in turn is a necessary part of democratic government. For these reasons self-limitation is possible, and it is also a better criterion of demarcation than that offered by Mudde's definition.

But what, precisely, are the paradoxes that arise when democracies of all stripes appeal to the people to legitimize the state? Populism presents an interesting challenge to democracy. When populists claim to speak for the people they force democratic theorists to clarify what they mean by such technical terms as "demos" and explain how the liberal democratic appeal to the people differs from the populist's. In the last decades political theorists have begun to ask again who are, and who should be, the people who govern themselves in a democracy (Näsström 2007; Abizadeh 2008; Smith 2008; Ochoa Espejo 2011). This question matters in the debate about populism because unless we answer it we cannot know who the people are who ground the legitimacy of the liberal democratic state.

The dominant response today is that in liberal democracies the people's boundaries are indeterminate. This conclusion follows from confronting a difficult and persistent logical problem of self-reference that arises when trying to define the people according to liberal democratic principles. The problem is that if the question of who to include in the demos is politically important, then, in a democracy, the people should decide it at the polls. But if we need an election to delimit the demos, how do we choose the electors? This question generates an infinite regress known as "the boundary problem" (Whelan 1983). In the last decades, similar formulations of the problem have been called "the problem of the unit" (Dahl 1989), "the paradox of founding" (Arendt 1990, 161; Connolly 1995, 138–39), "the democratic paradox" (Mouffe 2000), "the paradox of popular sovereignty" (Yack 2001), "the paradox of democratic legitimacy" (Benhabib 2006), "the paradox of politics" (Honig 2007), and "the problem of constituting the demos" (Goodin 2007). In each of these cases, the theorists find that the principles that justify democracy also lead to the infinite regress.

The regress arises because in order to sustain the principle of equality that animates democracy, all individuals ruled should be able to participate in the creation of the main institutions of rule in the polity. But if the demos is one such institution, then the very group of individuals that sustains the citizenry and the democratic state must be democratically defined. This is, of course, impossible. The individuals of a group cannot all have a say in the making of the group unless the group already exists. For that reason, a people, as an association of individuals, cannot sustain democratic legitimacy. Hence, if democracy depends on the people conceived as a collection of individuals, then democratic theory cannot tell us who the people are without getting into fatal problems. According to some theorists of populism, there is no way out of this indeterminacy. They say that democracy requires a determined group of individuals, even though making the determination means drawing arbitrary lines of exclusion and giving up on universalistic liberal principles (Schmitt 1985; Mouffe 2000).

Now, according to some theorists, the upshot of this view is that democracy is structurally identical to populism: both ideologies use the name of the people to institutionalize a political order and draw a sharp moralized distinction between those who belong (the people) and those who do not (elites or foreigners) (Laclau 2005). Yet, a different approach to the indeterminacy is available. In this approach, we can still tell apart liberal democratic practices of legitimization and governance from those that draw arbitrary exclusions. The solution relies on keeping the people open to change.

## Openness: Popular Sovereignty Beyond Unification

Openness is the main response made by contemporary democratic theory to the paradoxes of popular sovereignty. Openness can be interpreted as an "open space" of power (Lefort 1988), as an ongoing process open to the future (Habermas 2001), as an activity not bounded by set rules (Tully 2008), or as a process of pluralization (Connolly 2005). In eighteenth-century social contract theory, the sovereign people's open-endedness was seen as a problem because a determinate people are needed to sustain the normative claims of social contract philosophy. But since last century, democratic theorists have argued that indeterminacy can itself be normative. Leaving open the possibility of changing course or revising claims is in fact a requirement for establishing liberal democratic legitimacy. The requirement for openness allows us to see why a liberal-democratic appeal to the people must be self-limited, and how this liberal-democratic account of the people and sovereignty differs from a populist view of the general will (Abts and Rummens, 2007).

In the last two decades, several legal scholars have tried to address the paradoxes of popular sovereignty by conceiving the people who ground a constitution as a diffused procedure involving institutions and citizens' interactions, rather than by equating the people with electoral majorities, or as the definite will of a group of individuals (Ackerman 1991; Habermas 1998). This conception holds that the interplay of hypothetical principles embedded in the constitution and the continuous challenge of popular opinion together ground the legitimacy of the liberal democratic state. We do not need to give up on democratic legitimacy if we acknowledge that the people are constituted not by a unified community but by a community that changes over time, lacks a unified voice, and whose democratic institutions are never completely settled.

Moreover, this constitutional process need not be seen only under the lens of an ideal rational consensus, or an agreement closed at a frontier. Popular politics thus conceived "will always be open to question, to an element of non-consensus, and to reciprocal question and answer, demand and response and negotiation" (Tully 2008). To elaborate, openness can help democratic theory if it is understood as unboundedness, pluralization, and change.

## Unboundedness

A people's being open in principle means, first, that it is unbounded. Unboundedness follows from the problem laid down in the previous section. Those who are ruled should be able to participate in creating and governing the institutions that rule them. Yet it is impossible that those who are ruled, or those over whom power is exercised, get to define who they are before they are ruled. This logical problem, however, does not prevent individuals from participating in changing and governing institutions that affect them now. We can thus amend the theory of popular sovereignty such that each individual is considered part of the popular sovereign by participating in an ongoing (or open) process. This amendment to the theory of popular sovereignty makes democratic theory coherent again, but it has a radical conclusion: given that current institutions affect (or could affect) almost everyone in the world, the people could potentially include everyone (Goodin 2007). This means that democracy cannot delimit in advance the precise extent of the demos: the demos is, in principle, unbounded. As formulated by Abizadeh, this thesis provocatively implies not only that a state has no right to unilaterally control its own borders (Abizadeh 2008) but also that, in general, democracy should be practiced in each state with a potentially unbound demos in mind.

## Pluralization

The people who make democracy coherent are also open in a second sense: they are plural rather than homogeneous, or unified in one voice. However, this pluralism is not restricted to the usual sense of the term "pluralism"—namely, a legal umbrella covering the rights of groups and minorities within a state. Pluralism in the sense at issue here encompasses traditional pluralism and extends beyond it. Traditional pluralism is insufficient when it faces popular indeterminacy because, as I argue above, it presupposes a bounded background (the precisely limited shadow of the legal umbrella) for which democratic theory cannot vouch. On the conception of pluralism that arises from an open people then, pluralism can be guaranteed only to the extent that we conceive of the people as embedded in a process of pluralization, where the limits of pluralism are open to contestation. As a result, popular sovereignty (the ground of pluralism in the state) is also open to contestation (Connolly 2005), and the people changing, fragmented, and open. This view then, requires that we acknowledge that pluralism's limits are shifting, and the principles that unify and exclude cannot be drawn once and for all. Hence a view that is consistent with this kind of pluralism cannot equate the people solely with the electoral majority.

In practical terms, the difficulties of conjuring a unified people lead to a pluralized conception of the people but also to a concomitant effort to pluralize the forms of representation and the relations that constitute society and citizens. This means avoiding the equation of people and electorate but also pluralizing or multiplying the people into a "complex sovereign" that occupies different spaces of the political culture and institutions. Thus the people remain the constituent power in the state, but given that they do not speak with one voice the people can challenge institutions without completely rejecting them. If the constitution of the state is not thought of in terms of unification, the challenges to the state are also crosscutting and multiple (Rosanvallon 2011).

## Change

Another aspect of openness is the capacity and tendency of a people to change. This translates in practice as understanding and accepting radical transformations in democratic politics. The people and the institutions that they legitimize transform over time, and this seems to challenge any claim to represent the people. However, this mobility can help legitimize liberal democratic politics and distinguish them from populist appeals. We can do this if we think of the people as an ongoing process, as an unfinished series of institutional events in which individuals partake rather than as a well-defined group of individuals (Ochoa Espejo, 2011).

If we think of the people as a process, it is not only the institutions that change over time; rather, we can incorporate the fact that populations themselves are constructed over time and are never completely finished. Thus we can claim that they are a people, even if never fully determinate and complete. We can also conceive of the people as the subject of civil disobedience and revolutions without falling into contradictions. If the people are ever-changing, the claims to speak in the people's name must themselves be unfinished. This provisional quality of democratic claims distinguishes them from the categorical pretensions of populist claims and practices. Populists claim that they are absolutely and permanently right; liberal democrats, by contrast, acknowledge that their claims may be wrong and thus welcome future challengers and accept temporary defeats.

In sum, thinking of the people as open (unbounded, pluralizing, and changing) allows us to define the subject of popular sovereignty without falling into the indeterminacy problem. Seeing the people as open would help us to differentiate democracy from populism by introducing a specific criterion as a litmus test: self-limitation. If a popular movement acknowledges the unbounded, plural, and changing nature of the people, it will appeal to the people, but only in a negative sense. Given that the people are not complete, the people's decisions and will cannot be absolute and unchallenged. A movement that acknowledges an open people does not claim to know the content of the people's will, and it does not claim to be the final authority regarding the truth or correctness of democratic principles. It offers an admittedly partisan and temporary view of what a group of people within the polity holds to be the common good.

In conclusion, self-limitation works as a criterion of demarcation between populism and liberal democracy because it does not undermine the justifying principles of democracy, and it expresses more clearly than current definitions of populism the concern with the misrepresentation of the popular will.

## "To Hell with Your Institutions!": Mediation or Self-Limitation?

I have argued that during constitutional crises current definitions of populism, such as Mudde's, do not help us differentiate between liberal democrats and populists. By contrast, I claim, a better way to tell whether a leader or a movement has either populist or liberal-democratic tendencies is to look for signs of self-limitation. Populists think that there is no limit to what can be justified in the name of the people. Liberal democrats, instead, also appeal to the people and may even moralize it, but they use it as a way to put a brake on claims—most importantly, on their own claims. Here I provide an illustration of the criterion using the movement to contest the 2006 presidential elections in Mexico.

In 2006, Andrés Manuel López Obrador (AMLO), the candidate of the leftist PRD party and leader of the Coalición por el Bien de Todos, lost the Mexican presidential elections by about one half of one percent and refused to accept the electoral tribunal's ruling to this effect (Tribunal Electoral del Poder Judicial de la Federación 2006). Between the first week of July, when the first tally of votes was published, and the first week of September, when the official results were ratified by the independent Electoral Tribunal, AMLO and his supporters engaged in acts of civil disobedience. For fifty days in July and August they blockaded the center of Mexico City, symbolically and physically. AMLO's supporters set up a tent city in Paseo de la Reforma, which is simultaneously the historic avenue that houses the city's and the country's most recognizable monuments, the main avenue of the city's financial district, and the direct path between the president's official residence and the seat of federal executive power in the city's Zócalo, or central square. In September, after refusing to accept the tribunal's final ruling, AMLO took an alternative oath of office during a rally in Mexico City and assumed the title of Legitimate President (Ramos and Herrera 2006). He went on to organize a shadow government (Reséndiz and Gómez 2006).

These events very nearly precipitated a constitutional breakdown because the country's institutions were unable to solve the standoff between the different factions within the state. A coalition of parties and the acting government of the country's most populous region (the Federal District where Mexico City is located) refused to accept the legitimacy of the court that had jurisdiction in these matters, and claimed that the people's legitimacy gave it a higher authority than did the legality of institutions. To those camped out in the street there was no higher court of appeal than the people, and civil disobedience seemed the best hope for the continuation of the liberal democratic order. Yet others (particularly in the media) did not see this as a democratic revolution; instead, they saw it as an imminent threat to Mexico's budding democracy—a textbook example of populism. How do the criteria at our disposal work when seeking to determine whether the movement was a case of populism or a liberal-democratic cry for electoral justice?

According to many analysts, López Obrador's actions were a clear case of populist leadership. After the elections, most of those who believed that AMLO was a populist characterized him using a metric that fits Mudde's definition, but that introduced new ambiguities. AMLO's critics considered him a populist because of his ideology, which presents politics as a contest between ordinary Mexicans and a corrupt elite, and because he appealed to the "popular will" to establish the legitimacy of his movement and his claims to power. He rejected the limitations that independent liberal institutions put on the mass movement, and he directly challenged the authority of electoral officials and the state (Bruhn 2012). This tendency toward populism, in this sense, reached its highest point in September when, during a rally in Mexico City's main square, he uttered the phrase that has become most closely associated with the crisis: *¡Al diablo con sus instituciones!* (To hell with their institutions!) (López Obrador 2006).

According to Bruhn, who uses Mudde's metric, it was the outright rejection of institutions, coupled with Manichean discourse, which made AMLO a populist. However, these traits alone would not have allowed us to distinguish AMLO from a liberal democrat, given that the state's legitimacy was widely contested after the razor-thin elections. This became obvious in the period of near-constitutional breakdown. In these months, AMLO appealed for his movement's authority to the "people" of Mexico as represented in the public square, contrasting them with the corrupt elites who, he claimed, stole the elections on behalf of the incumbent's party. This division of society into two homogeneous and antagonistic groups is, by Mudde's definition, a sure sign of populism. Yet, in this situation, to appeal to the people was to have recourse to a higher source of legitimacy where no other judge was available, something any liberal democrat under the same circumstances would have done. In such situations, referring to the higher moral standing of "the people" qua electorate would be required by democrats of all stripes. Moreover, appealing to the moral superiority of one's supporters is a typical campaign strategy, not uncommon among liberal democrats. AMLO's appeal to the poor during the campaign is also a normal development of electoral politics in the context of economic inequality (Castañeda 2006; Loaeza 2007; Arditi 2008). Furthermore, the references to the people and their corrupt antagonists are not misplaced in a country where a history of electoral fraud could objectively allow voters and PRD supporters to talk about a corrupt elite (Langston 2009, 183; Morris and Klesner 2010). In these crisis circumstances, the rhetorical use of the people and the elite do not help us decide whether AMLO was a populist, and thus the first part of Mudde's definition would not have been able to determine the movement's character as it was unfolding.

The second part of the definition (the claim that politics should express the people's "general will") seems to hold more promise at first. AMLO appealed directly to the people and scoffed at the alleged independence of key institutions, notably, the independent electoral tribunal. Yet his reliance on plebiscitary acclamation rather than on the official electoral results, and his open rejection of institutions, cannot be used to tell him apart from a liberal democrat. For according to Bruhn: "Any candidate who loses a presidential election by less than one per cent of the vote may be tempted to challenge the results, all the more in a country like Mexico where electoral fraud has been common" (Bruhn 2012). It is by no means obvious that under the circumstances of constitutional crisis a liberal democrat would have acted differently.

There are good reasons and ample evidence to believe that the 2006 elections were in fact clean and fair.[3] However, at the time it was plausible that there had been irregularities in the election or that the electoral tribunal may have harbored illegal biases. Moreover, even though the elections were organized by independent electoral authorities, to his supporters AMLO's allegations of corruption were credible because of the long history of electoral fraud supported by the state (Bruhn 2009). According to Eisenstadt, AMLO's refusal to comply was rational in the context of the prior decade's *concerta-cesiones*, or "gentlemen's agreements," among the Partido Revolucionario Institucional (PRI) and its opposition, by which electoral irregularities had been overlooked and election results decided in the back room and with complete disregard for the ballots (Eisenstadt 2007). In sum, AMLO's moralizing view of the people and his appeal to the general will do not give us enough evidence to prove that his position was not liberal during the crisis. According to other scholars, it was precisely his opposition to less-than-perfect institutions that allowed us to recognize him as a true democrat (Ackerman 2010).

Given these difficulties with Mudde's criterion of demarcation, how can we tell whether AMLO was a populist rather than a radical liberal democrat? According to my self-limitation criterion, AMLO could have been recognized as populist during the crisis because his claims to legitimacy were not self-limited. In fact, they were unlimitable. By portraying the people as bounded, unified, and unchanging, he consolidated the fount of legitimacy into an indivisible, inalienable, eternal source of legitimacy. By appealing to the people as unlimitable, he claimed the moral superiority of his cause and made his claims unquestionable within the frame of his discourse. Pluralistic dialogue became impossible, and with this closure, the possibility of electoral democracy and liberal rights were also shut down. In my view, it was not his denunciation of existing institutions that made him a populist; it was his failure to set self-imposed limits or constraints. We can see this in the way he appealed to a people imagined as bound, unified, and unchanging.

"The people" were bounded in López Obrador's characterization because he used the term to refer to the unified nation (ethnos) rather than to the open liberal demos. López Obrador's dismissal of institutions was set in the context of a nationalistic discourse of renovation and refounding (Hoyo Prohuber 2009). According to Loaeza, the success of AMLO's discourse hinged on his ability to promise "integration and coherence in a society whose relations to the state had been destabilized by democratization"(2007, 411). This promise required the revival of Revolutionary Nationalism, "the ideology associated with the goals and traditions of the Mexican Revolution" (411). That ideology provided the foundation for national identity (it was rife with myths, rituals, and symbols) but it did not encourage active citizenship (413). AMLO appealed to the people as an equivalent of the cultural nation: by so doing, he made his claims irrefutable within his own discourse. For unlike the demos as the citizenry, or the electorate, which is a changing group of individuals whose will shifts over time, the nation is an organic whole whose will cannot be established by an aggregative decision procedure: the national will can only be interpreted and channeled by the leader.

López Obrador's characterization of the people was unified because he portrayed it as one voice, a voice that is always right. This had weighty consequences because according to the terms of his discourse he could not have accepted defeat. According to Bruhn, "López Obrador sought to overturn the election not on the basis of solid proof of irregularities, but on the 'basis' that the people could not have lost an election to the elite" (Bruhn 2012). This reaction was populist not because he rejected the tribunal's decision or appealed to the people. In fact, the cursing of institutions could be seen as antics distracting from his main strategy centered on the recount and the legal challenge to the elections, acts that sat firmly within the bounds of electoral institutions. Instead, it was populist because of the type of people it invoked. The hidden premise in this argument is that the people are always right. In his 6 September speech, AMLO portrayed the people as the classical unified popular sovereign who "will set aside the fake institutions and create an authentic, true Republic" (López Obrador 2006). In his view the people are always right, and thus there can be only one unified voice and will. This means that, in his view, it was "morally impossible" that the opposition could win.

Finally, he portrayed the people as unchanging. In his view, Mexico's political institutions should have molded themselves to accommodate the people, a fixed referent. As a populist, AMLO claimed that the only legitimate institutions were those backing "the people's" rule. A liberal democrat, instead, would invoke the people, but only to show that any particular claim to speak in the people's voice must be partial and incomplete, if only because the people's composition changes together with the population, and popular opinion may shift from one election to the next. For AMLO, the people were always an unchanging referent—the static crowd cheering in front of him—rather than a changing process: the interplay of different claims, institutions, and grassroots movements over time.

In sum, what would have allowed us to recognize López Obrador as a populist during the electoral crisis is not that he appealed to the people or that he cursed Mexico's institutions, but rather that he could not have conceded the election or accepted his defeat without contradicting himself.

## Conclusion

In this chapter, I have argued for a criterion of demarcation between populism and liberal democracy: self-limitation. Popular movements that picture the people as open will limit their claims; popular movements that picture the people as closed will refuse any limits on the authority of what they claim is the people's will. Hence liberal democrats use the people as an ideal referent that reminds them that they cannot use a part in the name of the whole. "The people" of the populists, instead, are defined as unified, unchanging, and bounded, and this will always be a problem for pluralism and liberal-democratic politics.

The Mexican elections of 2006 and the movement led by Andrés Manuel López Obrador illustrate an instance of populism during a borderline constitutional crisis. This is the kind of ambiguous situation where it is both important and difficult to decide whether we are dealing with a case of populism or a radical democratic call for change. Due to its ambiguity, this situation presents an interesting opportunity to test the mettle of a theoretical concept. However, this is a single instance, and the example has many contextual limitations. The hope is that this theoretical tool could also be useful in other situations where the constitutional order has changed, such as

Bolivia, Ecuador, or Venezuela. In each of these cases there is still wide debate on whether the fundamental changes to the law are compatible with
liberal-democratic principles. In each of these cases there still is room to
decide whether we are dealing with democracy or populism.

Populism goes hand in hand with democratic politics: it is its underside, as
Arditi has argued (Arditi 2007). The pervasiveness of populism can be explained by the fact that the legitimacy of democracy does not and cannot rest
only on electoral procedures. The requirement of a people as the foundational
ground of legitimacy in the state and the vicious circle that this requirement
begets create a perennial deficit of legitimacy in constituted states. This means
that democracy will always have a legitimization deficit that expresses itself in
extra-electoral appeals to the people, often in the form of mass mobilizations
and exchanges in the public sphere. However, this does not mean that democracy and populism are the same, or that all popular mobilizations are desirable, or that every appeal to the people absolves a popular uprising from moral
scrutiny. If populism is the underside of democracy, a normative criterion for
identifying populism will not help us banish populism from politics, but it
will allow us to figure out which side is up.

## Notes

Parts of this chapter first appeared in Paulina Ochoa Espejo, "Power to Whom? The People
Between Procedure and Populismo," in *The Promise and Perils of Populism: Global Perspectives*, ed. Carlos de la Torre, 59–90 (Lexington: University Press of Kentucky, 2015).

1. By constitutional crisis, I understand the (temporary or definitive) incapacity of
state institutions to mediate conflict among political elites due to a widespread loss of
legitimacy of the legal process. The source of the legitimation crisis is often related to
a democratic deficit. See Habermas 1996.

2. Mudde also notices populism's "similarity with much of the anti-right wing populist discourse, which opposes in biological terms any compromise or cooperation because
'the populist virus' will 'contaminate' the democratic 'body'" (Mudde 2004).

3. See the TRIFE ruling. For analysis see Eisenstadt and Poiré 2006; Grayson
2007; Klesner 2007; Loaeza 2007; Dominguez 2009.

## References

Abizadeh, A. 2008. "Democratic Theory and Border Coercion: No Right to Unilaterally Control Your Own Borders." *Political Theory* 36 (1): 37–65.

Abts, K., and S. Rummens. 2007. "Populism Versus Democracy." *Political Studies* 55 (2): 405–24.

Ackerman, B. 1991. *We the People: Foundations*. Cambridge, Mass.: Harvard University Press.

Ackerman, J. 2010. "The 2006 Elections: Democratization and Social Protests." In *Mexico's Democratic Challenges: Politics, Government, and Society*, edited by A. Selee and J. Peschard, 92–114. Stanford, Calif.: Stanford University Press.

Arditi, B. 2007. *Politics on the Edges of Liberalism*. Edinburgh: Edinburgh University Press.

———. 2008. "Arguments About the Left Turns in Latin America: A Post-Liberal Politics?" *Latin American Research Review* 43 (3): 59–81.

Arendt, H. 1990. *On Revolution*. New York: Penguin.

Benhabib, Seyla. 2006. "Hospitality, Sovereignty and Democratic Iterations." In *Another Cosmopolitanism*, edited by Robert Post. Oxford; New York: Oxford University Press.

Bruhn, K. 2009. "López Obrador, Calderón and the 2006 Presidential Campaign." In *Consolidating Mexico's Democracy*, edited by J. I. Dominguez, C. Lawson, and A. Moreno, 169–90. Baltimore, Md.: Johns Hopkins University Press.

———. 2012. "To Hell With Your Corrupt Institutions: AMLO and Populism in Mexico." In *Populism in Europe and the Americas: Threat or Corrective for Democracy?*, edited by C. Mudde and C. Rovira Kaltwasser, 88–112. Cambridge: Cambridge University Press.

Canovan, M. 2005. *The People*. Cambridge: Polity.

Castañeda, J. 2006. "Latin America's Left Turn." *Foreign Affairs* 85 (3): 28–43.

Connolly, W. E. 2005. *Pluralism*. Durham, N.C.: Duke University Press.

Dahl, Robert A. 1989. *Democracy and Its Critics*. New Haven, Conn.: Yale University Press.

Dominguez, J. I. 2009. "Conclusion: The Choices of Voters During the 2006 Presidential Election in Mexico." In *Consolidating Mexico's Democracy*, edited by J. I. Dominguez, C. Lawson, and A. Moreno. Baltimore, Md.: Johns Hopkins University Press.

Eisenstadt, T. 2007. "The Origins and Rationality of the 'Legal Versus Legitimate' Dichotomy Invoked in Mexico's 2006 Post-Electoral Conflict." *PS: Political Science and Politics* 40 (1): 39–43.

Eisenstadt, T., and A. Poiré. 2006. "Explaining the Credibility Gap in Mexico's 2006 Presidential Election, Despite Strong (Albeit Perfectable) Electoral Institutions." Working Paper No. 4, School of International Service, American University, Washington, D.C., 2006.

Goodin, Robert. 2007. "Enfranchising all Affected Interests and Its Alternatives." *Philosophy and Public Affairs* 35 (1): 40–68.

Grayson, G. 2007. *Mexican Messiah*. University Park: Pennsylvania State University Press.

Habermas, J. 1996. *Between Facts and Norms: Contributions to a Discourse Theory of Law and Democracy*. Cambridge, Mass.: MIT Press.

———. 1998. "Popular Sovereignty as Procedure." In *Between Facts and Norms: Contributions to a Discourse Theory of Law and Democracy*, 463–90. Cambridge, Mass.: MIT Press.

———. 2001. "Constitutional Democracy: A Paradoxical Union of Contradictory Principles?" *Political Theory* 29 (6): 766–81.

Hawkins, K. 2009. "Is Chávez Populist? Measuring Populist Discourse in Comparative Perspective." *Comparative Political Studies* 42 (8): 1040–67.

Honig, Bonnie. 2007. "Between Decision and Deliberation: Political Paradox in Democratic Theory." *American Political Science Review* 101 (1): 1–18.

Hoyo Prohuber, H. 2009. "Cuando las ideas se vuelven creencias utiles: El nacionalismo como instrumento político." *Foro Internacional* 49 (2): 370–402.

Kalyvas, A. 2008. *Democracy and the Powers of the Extraordinary: Max Weber, Carl Schmitt, and Hannah Arendt*. Cambridge: Cambridge University Press.

Kirshner, A. 2010. "Proceduralism and Popular Threats to Democracy." *Journal of Political Philosophy* 18 (4): 405–24.

Klesner, J. L. 2007. "Editor's Introduction to the Symposium: The 2006 Mexican Election and Its Aftermath." *PS: Political Science and Politics* 40 (1).

Laclau, E. 2005. *On Populist Reason*. London: Verso.

Langston, Joy. 2009. "López Obrador, Calderón and the 2006 Presidential Campaign." In *Consolidating Mexico's Democracy*, edited by Jorge I. Dominguez, Chappell Lawson, and Alejandro Moreno, 152–68. Baltimore, Md.: Johns Hopkins University Press.

Lefort, C. 1988. *Democracy and Political Theory*. Minneapolis, Minn.: University of Minnesota Press.

Loaeza, S. 2007. "Mexico's Dissapointment." *Constellations* 14 (3): 409–25.

López Obrador, A. M. 2006. "Discurso integro de AMLO." *El Universal* (Mexico City), September 8.

Morris, Stephen D., and Joseph L. Klesner. 2010. "Corruption and Trust: Theoretical Considerations and Evidence from Mexico." *Comparative Political Studies* 43 (10): 1258–85.

Mouffe, C. 2000. *The Democratic Paradox*. London: Verso.

———. 2005. *On the Political*. London: Routledge.

Mudde, C. 2004. "The Populist Zeitgeist." *Government and Opposition* 39 (4): 542–63.

Mudde, C., and C. Rovira Kaltwasser, eds. 2012. *Populism in Europe and the Americas: Threat or Corrective for Democracy?* Cambridge: Cambridge University Press.

Näsström, S. 2007. "The Legitimacy of the People." *Political Theory* 35 (5): 624–58.

Ochoa Espejo, P. 2011. *The Time of Popular Sovereignty: Process and the Democratic State*. University Park: Pennsylvania State University Press.

Panizza, F., ed. 2005. *Populism and the Mirror of Democracy*. London: Verso.

Plattner, M. F. 2010. "Populism, Pluralism and Liberal Democracy." *Journal of Democracy* 21 (1): 81–93.

Ramos, J., and J. Herrera. 2006. "Convención elige a AMLO 'presidente legítimo.'" *El Universal*, September 17.

Reséndiz, Francisco, and Ricardo Gómez. 2006. "AMLO presenta 'gabinete.'" *El Universal*, November 4.

Rosanvallon, P. 2011. *Democratic Legitimacy*. Princeton, N.J.: Princeton University Press.

Rovira Kaltwasser, C. 2012. "The Ambivalence of Populism: Threat and Corrective for Democracy." *Democratization* 19 (2): 1–25.

Schmitt, Carl. 1985. *The Crisis of Parliamentary Democracy*. Translated by Ellen Kennedy. Cambridge MA: MIT Press.

———. 2008. *Constitutional Theory*. Durham: Duke University Press.

Smith, R. 2008. "The Principle of Constituted Identities and the Obligation to Include." *Ethics and Global Politics* 1 (3): 139–53.

Taggart, P. 2000. *Populism*. Buckingham: Open University Press.

Tribunal Electoral del Poder Judicial de la Federación. 2006. Dictámen Relativo al Cómputo Final de la Elección de Presidente. Mexico.

Tully, J. 2008. *Public Philosophy in a New Key*. Vol. 1, *Democracy and Civic Freedom*. Cambridge: Cambridge University Press.

Weyland, K. 2001. "Clarifying a Contested Concept: Populism in the Study of Latin American Politics." *Comparative Politics* 34 (1): 1–22.

Whelan, F. G. 1983. "Democratic Theory and the Boundary Problem." In *Liberal Democracy*, edited by J. R. Pennock and J. W. Chapman, 13–47. New York: New York University Press.

Yack, B. 2001. "Popular Sovereignty and Nationalism." *Political Theory* 29 (4): 517–36.

# PART III

## Citizenship, Constitutionalism, and Participation

# Constitutional Changes and Judicial Power in Latin America

Roberto Gargarella

## Introduction

In this chapter I examine the development of Latin America's constitutional life from its origins in the nineteenth century to the present. In particular, I focus my analysis on the organization of the judiciary and how it has evolved under the impulse of different constitutional reforms.

Briefly stated, the view that I present here is the following: the constitutional life of the region, I claim, went through two decisive moments. The first began in the 1850s, and it was then when most countries in the region defined the basic features that, even today, characterize their organization of powers. Since those years, Latin American countries have mainly adopted a strong, vertical presidentialist system. The second moment began in the early 1920s, and it was then when most countries in the region defined the basic features that, even today, characterize their declarations of rights. Since those years, Latin American countries have chosen to incorporate broad declarations of social, economic, and political rights into their constitutions.

The main thesis that I maintain is the following: in spite of the numerous constitutional changes that have taken place in the region in the last decades, we cannot talk, as many scholars would want to, about the new Latin American constitutionalism—that is, a new way of thinking about the constitution, which would have emerged in the region in recent decades. On the contrary, I claim, contemporary Latin American constitutions are still very much the same as before. More precisely, most of the new Latin American constitutions still insist on the two main features that were defined in the two early moments: an organization of powers in nineteenth-century style, and an organization of rights that still resembles that first adopted in the 1910s. Now, the problem that this situation poses is not reduced to the question of whether there is something actually "new" in Latin American constitutionalism in terms of institutional design. The most interesting problem is a different one, and concerns the possibilities of making legal changes effective when the old structures that defined the region's constitutions remain very much the same as before.

More specifically, and taking into account the many initiatives that have recently been adopted in the region to try to improve the democratic, socially inclusive, and participatory aspects of Latin American constitutions, my question is this: Could these new democratic initiatives flourish, while the old, vertical, and hierarchical presidentialist system is not changed accordingly? My intuitive answer is negative, given the enormous impact that the rather authoritarian, nineteenth-century presidentialist system still exercises on the rest of the constitution. The same conclusion applies, I maintain, if we refer to recent changes introduced in those constitutions concerning the judicial branch. In order to ground my claims, let me now explore those legal developments in more detail.

## The Origins of Constitutionalism in the Americas

In Latin America, the earliest constitutions emerged as responses to some fundamental collective "dramas." Examining what he called the "first constitutional law" in Latin America, Juan Bautista Alberdi—one of the main constitutional thinkers of the nineteenth century in the region—wrote that those early documents properly served "the need of their time," which he identified as the process of consolidating independence. As he stated, "All the Constitutions enacted in South America during the war of independence were complete expressions of the needs that dominated their time. That need consisted in putting an end to the political power exercised by Europe in America, which began during the conquest and continued during the time of colonialism. . . . Independence and external freedom were the vital interests that concerned the legislators of the time. They were right: they understood the needs of their time, and they knew what to do" (Alberdi 1981, 26).

During the mid-nineteenth century—probably the most important period of Latin American constitutionalism—Latin American countries had already consolidated their independence. The main regional dramas were different, normally related to the economic difficulties that they confronted. Alberdi compared those periods—the early years and his own time—in the following way: "At that time, what was required was to consolidate independence through the use of arms; and today we need to ensure that independence through the material and moral enhancement of our peoples. The main goals of that time were political goals: today we need to concern ourselves with the economic goals" (Alberdi 1981, 123).

This anxiety for economic development was common in most countries of the region: economic growth seemed both necessary and possible. Partly as a result of this certainty, partly as their common fear of the threats, real or imagined, of unchecked masses or unrestrained passions, liberal and conservative groups began to join forces in different ways after many decades of dire confrontation. This is why most constitutional regimes in Latin America began to show a new face, with features that combined the ideals and aspirations of both groups.

The liberal character of Latin American constitutionalism surfaced through the extended adoption of systems of checks and balances. As in the United States, this initiative, which occupied a central place in the organization of power in the new constitutions, was accompanied on many occasions by declarations of religious tolerance in newly adopted bills of rights.

Now, nineteenth-century Latin American constitutionalism was the product of a convergence of ideologies—mainly liberalism and conservatism. If liberals came to the negotiating table with their initiatives for equilibrium of power and moral neutrality, conservatives arrived to those discussions with almost opposite proposals. Conservatives wanted to replace liberal neutrality with moral perfectionism: they wanted to have a state that was active in the enforcement of the Catholic religion. Perhaps most significantly, conservatives despised the system of mutual controls, preferring to have an unchecked, unaccountable figure in charge of government and endowed with the powers necessary for ensuring order, peace, and stability.[1]

The consequence of the liberal–conservative constitutional compact was the enactment of diverse constitutions that, in more or less innovative ways, combined the proposals of both political traditions. In general, Latin American constitutionalism preferred to accumulate rather than synthesize the initiatives of both sectors. The Argentine constitution represented an excellent illustration of what was then achieved. In the section on rights, for example, it included, at the same time and in the same text, both what liberals wanted (namely, religious tolerance, Article 14) and what conservatives demanded (namely, special status for the Catholic religion, Article 2). More significantly, we find the same strategy of "accumulation" in the sphere of the organization of powers. Since the mid-nineteenth century, what we find in the region are constitutions that, following the desires of liberals, consecrate a system of checks and balances but that, at the same time, and following the demands of conservatives, "unbalance" that purported equilibrium by providing additional, special powers to an overtly powerful executive, thus creating so-called hyper-presidentialist regimes (Nino 1996).

That was, for example, Alberdi's recommended formula for the particular "drama" affecting Latin America during the 1850s. It was necessary to ensure order and progress and, for that reason, the system of equilibrium of powers had to allow the president to become a king so as to be able to face situations of crisis and maintain peace. For Alberdi, the Chilean constitution of 1833 demonstrated that it was a good alternative between "the absolute absence of government and a dictatorial government." This was a model of a "constitutional president who can assume the faculties of a King" in situations of "anarchy" (Alberdi 1981, 181).[2]

## The Organization of Power in Nineteenth-Century Latin American Constitutionalism

This brief historical review allows us to recognize three of the main institutional features that have begun to characterize Latin American constitutions since the mid-nineteenth century.

### A Strict Separation Between Public Officers and the People

The first feature that I would mention is what some authors have called the "principle of distinction" (Manin 1997). The idea was to avoid the possibility of having political representatives dependent on the will of the people at large, and thus fall prey to factional or local politics. The purpose was to ensure a system of strict separation between the people and their representatives, under the assumption that the institutional systems that prevailed locally allowed people to exercise undue pressure on their representatives, who thus tended to become mere mouthpieces of their constituency and forced to represent partial interests rather than the interests of the whole. This decision, based on a profound distrust of the people's political capacities, implied acceptance of a particular understanding of political representation, which Edmund Burke had famously presented at Bristol in 1776 when he defended, through elitist arguments, the independence of political representatives once they were elected. In *The Federalist Papers: No. 10*, James Madison presented a similar view for the United States based on similar assumptions: he did not see political representation as a "second best" or a "necessary evil," but rather as a first desired option given that representatives tended to have a better understanding of politics than the people themselves. In his words, the representative system had to be directed "to refine and enlarge the public views, by passing them through the medium of a chosen body of citizens, whose wisdom may best discern the true interest of their country, and whose patriotism and love of justice will be least likely to sacrifice it to temporary or partial considerations. Under such a regulation, it may well happen that the public voice, pronounced by the representatives of the people, will be more consonant to the public good than if pronounced by the people themselves, convened for the purpose." This organization exemplifies what contemporary political philosopher Roberto Unger defined as a system grounded on "distrust about democracy" and based on a plethora of counter-majoritarian devices.

In Latin America, this "counter-majoritarian" choice was aggravated from the independence period and at least until the beginning of the twentieth century by the restriction of political rights. In addition, the radicalization of politics that had taken place in Europe during the "red revolutions" of 1848 also arrived to the region (particularly to countries such as Chile, Colombia, and Peru) and exercised a profound political impact on local politics. In part, this radicalization is what helps explain the (otherwise difficult to understand) convergence between liberals and conservatives that took place during those years. Obviously, it also explains their coming together in the defense of this approach to public representation.

## A System of "Checks and Balances"

The second institutional feature that I want to highlight is the system of "checks and balances," which implied the creation of different devices for ensuring mutual control between the three branches of power. The significance that the system of "checks and balances" achieved during those years implied the displacement of its main alternative, namely a system where the people at large remained at the center of politics. In other words, the choice of a system of "checks and balances" implied the preference for an "internal" rather than "external" system of controls. Early American politics had experimented with numerous devices for "external" control: from mandatory instructions, to mandatory rotation, to annual elections, to the right to recall, to town meetings, etc. The consolidation of a system of "checks and balances" came together with the reduction of those external controls to their minimal expression: namely, periodic elections. And periodical elections per se—this is to say without the help of other means of "external" control—lost most of the force they could have had in order to favor the prevalence of collective, communal preferences in politics.

## Hyper-Presidentialism

The third institutional feature that I want to stress has to do with the decision to strengthen the powers of the president that, in the end, both liberals and conservatives accepted. In some instances, Latin Americans transferred to the president the power to declare a *state of siege* and thus limit rights and individual guarantees; in others they allowed the president to militarily "intervene" in the affairs of local states; in most cases they allowed the president decisive participation in the legislative process, etc. The choice of having a super-powerful executive had, as anticipated, a strong impact upon the system of "checks and balances," which, for that reason, was born "unbalanced." What Latin Americans did represented a significant departure from the original US model of organizing powers. More radically—one could add—their decision to empower the executive in such a way entailed putting the entire system of "checks and balances" at risk. James Madison would have easily predicted some of the risks that, since those early days, began to menace Latin American constitutional systems: mainly, the "most dangerous branch"—the one that was in control of military powers and growing economic resources—would begin to exercise an undue influence upon the other branches and thus destroy the desired equilibrium of powers.

## The Judiciary in Nineteenth-Century Latin American Constitutionalism

The previous notes allow us to better understand the development of the Latin American judicial branch during the nineteenth century. First of all, in Latin America, as in most countries of the Western World, the judiciary was molded under an assumption of "distrust" toward the people and a symmetrical confidence in the judges' intellectual capacities. This view expressed a particular, although then rather common, approach to legal impartiality. For this approach, the best means for achieving impartial solutions consisted of the isolated reflection of the best-trained specialists. This understanding contrasted with a more "democratic" approach, which was already present and which had begun to gain acceptance since then. According to this conception, impartiality required the collective reflection of all those potentially affected rather than processes of isolated, individual reflection (Nino 1992; Habermas 1996). The limited role of the jury system—or its absence—in the new independent Latin American countries can be seen as one additional example of the then-prevalent view.

A second characteristic of the judicial organization that was then adopted was the incorporation of the judicial machinery within a broader system of "internal" controls, namely the system of "checks and balances." At the judicial level, this choice implied the rejection of numerous alternative devices that could have improved the communication between the judiciary and the people and strengthened the accountability of the former. In other words, the Founding Fathers of American constitutionalism preferred to separate judges from the people and subject the former only to the supervision of the other branches. As Madison put it, the members of the judicial department "by the mode of their appointment, as well as by the nature and permanency of it, are too far removed from the people to share much in their prepossessions" (Hamilton, Madison, and Jay 1982, 10). In Latin America, the consequences of this choice were many: direct elections were not taken as acceptable mechanisms for selecting judges; the people's legal opinions (in other words, through *amicus curiae*) were not seriously considered; and, most significantly, access to justice became extremely difficult, either through definitions of who had standing to litigate in what cases or as a consequence of the economic and symbolic costs of litigation.

The third feature of the Latin American judicial system that I want to mention has to do with the influence of hyper-presidentialism. As anticipated, the choice of a super-powerful executive changed the entire dynamic of checks and balances and thus undermined its main, promised virtues. Undoubtedly, the fact that the institutional system became biased in favor of the executive contributed to the gradual erosion of the ideal of judicial independence. In fact, and at least since the independence period, executive power has developed an enormous influence over the judicial branch. Mainly, the executive began to play a decisive (if not exclusive) role in judicial appointments; it also gained decisive control in the removal or promotion of judges; and it exercised, in numerous ways, pressure on the members of the judicial branch, which was allowed by the executive's almost exclusive control over the economic and coercive resources of the state (Rosenn 1990). For example, according to Article 82 of the enormously influential 1833 Chilean constitution, the president was in charge of appointing all members of the judicial branch, according to a proposal by the Council of the State, over which the president himself presided (the Council comprised his ministers and a few other representatives of the political elite of the time). According to Article 60 of the 1869 Ecuadorian constitution, the president proposed to Congress the candidates for the Supreme Court, which the president could appoint during legislative recess. It goes without saying that in both cases, the executive exercised a decisive influence over Congress, which in addition functioned only during a very limited part of the year.

## The Bill of Rights in Twentieth-Century Latin American Constitutionalism

Since the beginning of the twentieth century, the situation in the entire region has suffered dramatic changes. The old scheme of order and progress, which had prevailed in Latin America since the mid-nineteenth century, and from which (particularly certain accommodated sectors of) Latin America greatly benefited, was now in crisis. The politically authoritarian regimes, which had managed to ensure economic development with peace, were increasingly struggling to maintain the old scheme intact. Now it was necessary to use greater levels of coercion to keep the old order stable. The serious political, economic, and social crises of those early years, which demanded profound political and economic changes, found immediate translation into the constitutional order (Halperín Donghi 2007). Constitutionalism attempted to dissipate these crises by incorporating the social questions that had been marginalized from constitutional discussions in the 1950s into the old constitutions (Gargarella 2013).

The start of this reformist wave was the approval of the Mexican constitution in 1917. This constitution, which followed a dramatic revolutionary movement, represented the first and most radical constitutional response to a crisis that was also a legal crisis. In order to respond to this crisis, it was decided to incorporate a long and robust list of social, economic, and political rights, which became a crucial feature of the new Latin American constitutionalism. For instance, Article 27 of the Mexican Constitution maintained:

> The Nation shall at all times have the right to impose on private property such limitations as the public interest may demand, as well as the right to regulate the utilization of natural resources, which are susceptible to appropriation, in order to conserve them and to ensure a more equitable distribution of public wealth. With this end in view, necessary measures shall be taken to divide up large landed estates; to develop small landed holdings in operation; to create new agricultural centers, with necessary lands and waters; to encourage agriculture in general and to prevent the destruction of natural resources, and to protect property from damage to the detriment of society. Centers of population which at present either have no lands or water or which do not possess them in sufficient quantities for the needs of their inhabitants, shall be entitled to grants thereof, which shall be taken from adjacent properties, the rights of small landed holdings in operation being respected at all times.

Another crucial clause was Article 123, which included wide protections for workers, recognized the role of trade unions, and regulated labor relations reaching very detailed issues, which in a way covered most of the topics that later would came to distinguish modern labor law. The clause referred, for example, to the maximum duration of work, the use of labor of minors, the rights of pregnant women, a minimum wage, the right to vacation, the right to equal wages, comfortable and hygienic labor conditions, workplace accidents, the right to strike and lockout, arbitrations, dismissal without cause, social security, and the right to association.

The Mexican constitution thus came to symbolize a new approach to constitutionalism, which began to emphasize the importance of social, economic, and political rights. Metaphorically speaking, or not, the "working class," some of the most disadvantaged members of society, in the end found their way into the new constitution: they entered in a peculiar way, it is true— that is, through the section on rights—but they found legal recognition in any case. The Mexican example was soon followed by almost all Latin American countries. We recognize constitutional changes in similar directions in the constitutions of Brazil (1937), Bolivia (1938), Cuba (1940), Ecuador (1945), and Argentina and Costa Rica (1949).

We are now in the third important wave of Latin American constitutionalism (the first wave appeared right after independence; the second, in the mid-nineteenth century with the liberal–conservative compact). More significantly, we have the second crucial moment in the life of Latin American constitutionalism.

The first fundamental moment of regional constitutionalism appeared in the mid-nineteenth century, a time when Latin America adopted its basic institutional "matrix," which defined its organization of powers from then to the present. The second fundamental moment of regional constitutionalism began in the early twentieth century and extended to the entire region after a few decades. At that second moment, Latin America defined its organization of rights, which marks its constitutions written since then.

Through these two moments we can recognize the two main characteristics that still distinguish Latin American constitutions. On the one hand, we have constitutions that organize power in a centralized way, imperfectly combining a scheme of checks and balances with a strong presidentialism. On the other hand, we see that those constitutions organize a system of rights in ways that stress the centrality of social, economic, and political rights.

## The Judiciary in Twentieth-Century Latin American Constitutionalism

Let us focus, in what follows, on the relevance of the renewed bill of rights in relation to the role of the judiciary. There are a few relevant issues to mention concerning the relationship between rights and the judiciary. First, this has been a difficult relationship. In fact, and at least until the last decades of the twentieth century, social rights ended up being transformed into "programmatic rights";[3] in other words, social rights were considered objects to be pursued by the political branches not as the proper object of judicial activity (Courtis 2005). Very commonly, judges said that they had neither the legal power nor the democratic legitimacy to enforce social rights; it was instead the task of political branches to define basic questions about the allocation of economic resources.

These results seemed surprising and required an explanation. How to explain the fact that all Latin American constitutions described, more or less at the same time, strong commitments to social rights (which they would only ratify or strengthen in the future), and that they all had serious difficulties in enforcing those rights through the judiciary? Why did the constitutional clauses establishing social rights suddenly become dormant clauses? How could this happen everywhere in light of such open and emphatic legal commitments to social rights? How could this anomaly persist for so long, for so many decades? These questions have to come together with a second set, with which I will deal in the next section. This second set of questions refers to the slow, gradual but clear coming to life of those social clauses by the end of the twentieth century. Again, why did this happen? Why and for what reasons? More precisely, why did so many different courts, in different countries, suddenly begin to take those social clauses seriously, after their early denial?

The explanation concerning why social rights became dormant clauses is undoubtedly complex and certainly difficult to untangle. In addition, it certainly goes well beyond the law, and here I am interested in the exploration of legal issues. In any case, let me mention a few things that could help us explain this phenomenon.

The first thing to do is to remember the profile of the organization of powers that has prevailed in Latin America's constitutional organization since the mid-nineteenth century. This was a counter-majoritarian structure, which reserved very little room for popular participation in politics, limited the role of external or popular controls, and made an explicit effort to separate the people from public officers. Within this structure, there was an explicit attempt to isolate the members of the judicial department, who were purposely placed "too far removed from the people to share much in their prepossessions" (Hamilton, Madison, Jay 1982, 10). The judiciary has epitomized since then the case of a counter-majoritarian power (Bickel 1962). Worse still, in Latin America, the organization of power became still more centralized, vertical, and isolated from popular pressures.

A second area merits consideration within that institutional context, namely that social rights were inserted into the new or reformed constitutions without the introduction of any significant change into the old, vertical, rather authoritarian organization of power. This point is extremely relevant for our purposes and allows us to detect perhaps the most crucial defect within Latin American constitutionalism. Latin America has once again accumulated rather than synthesized the different institutional demands and innovations that it came to acknowledge during its two hundred years of existence. And the main tension that has emerged within this way of proceeding is one that resulted from the juxtaposition of an old (eighteenth-century-style) vertical and rather authoritarian organization of power with a new (twenty-first-century-style) organization of rights, which aspired to provide legal recognition and support to all the relevant interests and social demands that existed within their societies. Remarkably, these new social rights were incorporated into the old constitutions without changing the organization of powers accordingly—that is, in the way suggested and required by those bold social commitments.

To put it more clearly: through the introduction of social rights, some of the most disadvantaged sectors of society found support for their demands and recognition of their identities; in other words, they found a place within the new constitutions. However, and in spite of this, the new constitutions incorporated no changes that would strengthen the political influence of those marginalized groups, that would bolster their capacity to decide and control those in power. Thus the working class came into the constitution, through the section on rights, while the doors to the engine room of the constitution remained closed to them.

Moreover, the fact is that not only did the most disadvantaged gain no constitutional power through these constitutional changes; it was also the case that their access to justice remained limited. In sum, no relevant changes were introduced to expand legal standing or reduce the costs of litigation.

Within the prevalent conditions, the future of those innovative social rights seemed unpromising: popular participation and mobilization, which, one could argue, were necessary for ensuring the vitality of social rights, were not promoted (or still discouraged); the engine room of the constitution remained hermetically sealed (unreached by the demands and direct pressures of the most disadvantaged); while the old judicial branch, that is to say, the least democratic branch of power, the most isolated and elitist branch, maintained primary responsibility for the enforcement of these social rights. In this context, was it finally surprising not to find the rights revolution realized during those years? (Epp 1998).

## The Bill of Rights in Twentieth-Century Latin American Constitutionalism II

Finally, we have to examine the fourth wave of Latin America's constitutional reforms, which took place during the late twentieth and early twenty-first centuries. Among the many relevant reforms during those years we can mention the following: Colombia (1991), Paraguay (1992), Argentina (1994), Venezuela (1999), Ecuador (2008), Bolivia (2009), and Mexico (2011).

These new reforms are rich and diverse and should be examined separately. However, it should still be possible to highlight some common notes about these processes and their relevance concerning the protection of rights and the role of the judiciary in this regard. Among the many different causes that motivated these later reforms, two were particularly noteworthy.

### Human Rights

First, many of these changes emerged at least in part as a response to a new social drama affecting the region during the 1970s, namely authoritarian regimes that carried out massive violations of human rights. The impact of those violent regimes was extraordinary in many different and tragic ways. In some cases, constitutional reforms were promoted in order to amend the authoritarian legal legacy left by the previous dictatorial governments. The 1988 constitution of Brazil, for example, can be read to a great extent as a response to the dictatorial constitution of 1967–69, which brought with it numerous undesirable legal changes (restricting political liberties, political participation, and so forth), and the same may be said about the constitutional changes introduced in Chile many years after the return of democracy, and against the background of General Pinochet's 1980 constitution. More generally, Latin American countries modified their legal order in those years, trying to affirm a renewed commitment to human rights.

These changes implied giving a special, sometimes constitutional status to different human rights treaties that the different countries had signed during the previous four or five decades: initiatives that came together with growing litigation in the area directed at punishing the massive violations of human rights committed by dictatorial governments (Acuña and Smulovitz 1991; Sikkink 2012). In some countries, such as Argentina and Bolivia, human rights treaties were explicitly awarded the status of constitutional laws. In other cases, such as Costa Rica and El Salvador, these treaties were awarded supralegal status (Rossi and Filippini 2010). In any case, the forms of incorporating international human rights law have been quite varied. Some constitutions, such as those of Peru and Colombia, included interpretive clauses in their texts, incorporating specific references to international law. Others, such as Brazil's, refer to the existence of non-enumerated rights, among which are those related to principles and treaties to which Brazil is party. The Guatemalan constitution refers to international human rights law by establishing guidelines for the country's foreign policy. The constitution of Chile assigns special duties in the area of human rights with which all state organs must comply.[4]

The decision to provide special legal status to diverse human rights treaties was extremely interesting, particularly so if one takes into account the fact that many of those who began to press for the introduction of these rights had previously, for lengthy periods, dismissed them as irrelevant or superficial. In the end, these initiatives expressed the reconciliation of certain parts of the Left with the issue of rights in particular and constitutionalism more generally. In addition, the fact that many constitutions granted human rights a new legal status caused an interesting effect among individuals of conservative convictions. Typically, in the face of these changes, many conservative judges for the first time began to take seriously arguments based on the value of human rights.

Moreover, two factors helped rethink the relationship between judges and social rights in general: the special status afforded to international human rights treaties, and the kind of legal activism that was promoted concerning human rights legislation and a renewal within legal doctrine, which helped recognize, among other things, that there were no good reasons for making strong distinctions—and thus treating substantially different—civil/political and social/human rights). Here we find, in the end, some of the reasons explaining the curious, perhaps unexpected awakening of the social clauses in Latin American constitutions that until those years appeared to be merely dormant clauses.

## Social Rights, Again

The second type of constitutional change that appeared during this new wave of reform concerns social rights. In effect, many countries have modified their constitutions, particularly since the beginning of the twenty-first century, to reaffirm or further expand their commitment to social, economic, and cultural rights. These changes reached in many instances groups that figured among the "marginalized among the marginalized"—typically, indigenous groups. They emerged after the second fundamental crisis of the period, which this time was related not to dictatorial regimes and massive violations of human rights but rather to democratic regimes and profound economic and social crises. These crises characteristically emerged after the application of so-called neoliberal reforms or programs of structural adjustment, which were very commonly applied without much concern for the fate of the most disadvantaged. As a consequence, most countries in the region faced sometimes violent social protests.

The protests referenced above included those that exploded in 2001 in Argentina, promoted by the *piqueteros* (usually unemployed people who blocked the national roads to call public attention to their demands following the adjustment programs of the 1990s); the consistent and powerful protests in defense of the right to land, promoted by the movement of the Sim Terra (MST) in Brazil; the wars for water and gas in Bolivia during 2000 and 2005; the "invasions" occurring in Peru; the taking of land in Chile, whether private or public; the protests of the young students (*pingüinos*) in Chile; the fights lead by the *mapuches* in Patagonia, Argentina, and the south of Chile in defense of indigenous rights; the numerous environmental disputes, particularly with mining companies, which occurred across the entire region over the last decades; and so forth. All of these protests received strong popular support and gained social legitimacy, even in their most extreme expressions.

The reforms that followed these social crises were numerous and took place in different countries, but those in Venezuela (1999), Ecuador (2008), and Bolivia (2009) were particularly salient: all three countries emphasized questions related to economic, social, and cultural rights, political participation, indigenous integration, and a mixed economy. These constitutions thus appeared as examples of anti-neoliberal reforms.

These approaches confronted numerous difficulties related to the general problems examined in the previous section. First, this new strengthening of the social aspects of the constitution was generally done, again, against the background of vertical rather authoritarian constitutions in what concerns the organization of power. Once again, the introduction of these social reforms in the section on rights was done without introducing any other corresponding changes in the organization of powers, which remained untouched. After so many decades, constitutional thinkers (in Latin America, as in other parts of the Western world) had not learned the lessons of the past: the engine rooms of the reformed constitutions were still closed. The renewed discourse favorable to the interests of disadvantaged groups did not seem to transcend the sphere of constitutional rights.

In the face of this situation, someone could say: "Latin American doctrinaires and constitutional delegates did what they could. They began their progressive task by introducing changes in the sphere of rights as a first step for the introduction of more advanced and extended changes." But this claim is problematic, at least for two reasons. First, they were insisting on the same methodology they had used before when introducing social rights for the first time without seeming to recognize that, after so many decades, the engine room of the constitution still remained untouched, and without seeming to care about the very limited progress achieved in social rights during those years. Second, and more importantly, legal reformers did not seem to realize that the two main areas of the constitution (rights and power) were not independent one from the other, but rather the contrary: what was done or not done in one area had an impact on the other. Moreover, they did not seem to realize that between the two parts of the constitution, the organization of power was the one that was more likely to determine what happened with the other.

Naturally, over-powerful presidents tended to see as a menace to their own power any attempt from disadvantaged groups to expand their decision-making powers, or—more generally—gain more autonomous powers. So it was not surprising, after all these years, to find that attractive, challenging reforms introduced in the area of rights were directly undermined or blocked by the forces of hyper-presidentialism. It was then common to find disappointing situations such as a new constitution (like those of Venezuela or Ecuador) that is particularly emphatic in regard to indigenous and participatory rights; indigenous groups clamoring for their participatory rights; repeated vetoes from the president, blocking those initiatives; and the leaders of those indigenous gróups put in jail by the same governments that had promoted those constitutional initiatives.

## Recent Developments: Access to Courts and Dialogic Justice

In the previous pages, we explored some constitutional changes that have taken place in the region over the last decades. Against those modifications we raise at least one significant charge, namely that most of these changes were directed at bills of rights while leaving the organization of powers basically untouched. This omission, we claimed, undermined the force of the very changes that were incorporated in the rights section of the constitution. Here I want to mention a more optimist viewpoint related to some seemingly modest constitutional changes that were also introduced during those years. The changes I am referring to were minor in appearance but had the potential to affect in a positive, inclusive way the organization of power. As an illustration, I refer to two such changes: one that appeared in Costa Rica, with the adoption of a new so-called Constitutional Chamber, and the other related to access to justice in Colombia.

In Costa Rica, the parliamentary discussion about the constitutional amendment that would modify the organization of judicial power took place without major polemics or snags. No one seemed to anticipate at all the changes that would take place in the high court's operation from then on. In effect, during the last fifty years, the court had received only a few cases (155) dealing with constitutional questions. Apart from that, the court record until that time had always been marked by a strong deference to political power (Wilson 2010). Hence when it was decided to annex a special chamber dealing with constitutional issues—the Constitutional Chamber, or Chamber IV—to the high court, no one paid very much attention. As might be expected, only the members of the court then seated on the bench showed any resistance to the creation of the new chamber.

Nevertheless, the reforms in question include some other details that ended up playing a decisive role in explaining what followed: hyperactive, socially conscious, and politically defiant behavior on the part of the new chamber. Conspicuous among the reforms is the extraordinary expansion granted in the legitimacy of standing before the court. This was accompanied by a break in the strict procedural formalism that had characterized court appearances. In addition, every person was granted standing to appear in Chamber IV without needing to resort to legal representation, without needing to pay any fee, and without having to stick to preestablished rules and arguments. A claim could be filed at any time of the day, in any language, and without any age requirements for the claimant, and could be written in any medium (Wilson 2010).

The results of these changes were swift and extraordinary. In its first year, 1990, the tribunal received two thousand cases. This increased to six thousand in 1996, thirteen thousand in 2002, and more than seventeen thousand in 2008. Over its first nineteen years, the court reviewed more than two hundred thousand cases, almost all related to seeking injunctions (*amparos*) (Wilson 2010, 68). Otherwise, this incremental dynamic was favored in the very operation of Chamber IV, which proved itself not only able to deal with the sheer number of cases but also to do so in a short time.

The situation described has significant parallels, and at least one significant difference, with what occurred at the highest levels of judicial power in Colombia in the 1991 constitutional reform. The difference is that this constitution was the product of a broad and heterogeneous group of representatives (which included figures from the political right, ex-guerillas from the M19 group, indigenous peoples, and religious minorities) working together over six months (García Villegas 2004, 14). The constitution seemed to be, finally, the product of a broad consensus, rather than a *carta de batalla*, or winner's document, according to the famed expression of Valencia Villa (Lemaitre Ripoll 2009, 124). This fact of plural representation would also explain, for example, how a profusion of social rights incorporated into the constitution arrived hand in hand with explicit constitutional declarations in defense of the free market.[5]

In any case, the fact is that in Colombia, as in Costa Rica, the creation of a new judicial organ—here, a constitutional court to be positioned alongside the already extant Supreme Court—also failed to generate serious preoccupation or resistance, except, as in Costa Rica, on the part of the magistrates then seated, who feared seeing their powers curtailed. Politically, the new court was not perceived as a threat in the context of a country where the tribunals were characterized by a long tradition of independence while displaying deference to political power. Nevertheless, and as can be seen in the Costa Rican example, the tribunal showed immediate signs of strength, activism, social calling, and defiance that surprised even its own creators (Gaviria Díaz 2002; Cepeda-Espinosa 2004; Bonilla and Iturralde 2005; Uprimny 2011; Lemaitre Ripoll 2009; Bonilla 2013).

Although, yet again, it is difficult to determine an explanation for this noteworthy development in the court, some apparently modest procedural reforms occurring since its creation seem to hold part of the answer. In Colombia, as in Costa Rica, judicial reform incorporated drastic changes to procedural issues—especially, for example, through the *acción de tutela*,[6] which grants any person recourse to the justice system without any formal experience, without the necessity of incurring economic costs, without the requirement of hiring a lawyer, and without having to demonstrate a concrete interest in the claim under litigation. This was a maximal expansion not easily matched in terms of access to the courts.

The results of the adoption of this mechanism were as explosive in Colombia as in Costa Rica. The new court decided 236 cases in 1992, its first year, and 10 years later it averaged was well above 1,100 (an increase of almost 500 percent). In the matter of *tutelas*, the court received some 8,000 *amparos* in its first year; in 2001, this number reached 133,273 (a more than sixteenfold increase). The average number of annual decisions by the Constitutional Court ended up also being 16 times higher than that of the Supreme Court prior to the arrival of the new tribunal (Cepeda-Espinosa 2004).

Finally, what happened in Costa Rica and Colombia—then later, more modestly, in Argentina and Brazil—was no more than the repetition of a phenomenon that had already occurred in far more distant and unexpected places, such as Hungary, India, and South Africa. Relatively minor changes to the law of standing, together with drastic reductions in the formal requirements customary for judicial proceedings, tended to produce radical changes in the relationship between individuals and the judicial system. These changes translated into an unequivocally significant rise of litigation rates and at the same time, notably, altered the behavior of the tribunals. Beset by an excessive burden of claims from the least advantaged sectors, which, thanks to the aforementioned changes, had access to opportunities for judicial redress, the tribunals tended to demonstrate greater acceptance of questions connected with social and economic rights (Gloppen et al. 2010). In the case of the Colombian court, contrary to the practice of a majority of similar tribunals, the new judicial organ would mostly end up resolving social rights cases. In fact, the majority of cases (55 percent) resolved by the tribunal between 1992 and 2005 were related to social rights (the remainder were related to civil or political rights). More importantly, in 66 percent of cases the magistracy was inclined to rule in favor of protecting the rights solicited by the claimant (García Villegas and Saffón 2005, 18).

The good news is that these changes came together with some new doc-
trinal innovations in the region concerning the scope and limits of judicial
review and judicial activism in the face of its limited democratic legitimacy.
Following these innovations, many judges and courts began to respond to
new and increased social demands in a more appealing way. Their traditional
responses, in those kinds of cases, oscillated between silence and imposition:
they either claimed not to have authority to act or simply imposed their own
preferred view on the political branches. At this time, however, their responses varied and acquired a more estimable profile: on many occasions,
courts opted for dialogic responses, recognizing that the types of problems
they faced required more nuanced responses over time rather than their traditional binary responses of yes or no, of validation or invalidation.

Let me illustrate the point with an example. Imagine that a group of individuals files a legal complain concerning the level of pollution affecting the
environment in the area where they live (imagine a river that is regularly polluted by dozens of corporations). Traditionally, in the face of such an immense social, economic, and political problem, which calls for structural
answers from the state, judges choose one of the following paths: most commonly, they declare that they have no competence or authority to intervene
in the case (say, given the amount of resources, actions, and decisions required to address such environmental problems); in other, more exceptional
circumstances, they choose to deal with the issue in a merely formal or le-
galistic way, leaving the structural problem untouched. Contrary to those
traditional responses, dialogic devices appear as a means to help judges engage more directly with those structural matters. The issue—say, the need to
clean up a polluted river—is now seen as a matter that affects fundamental
rights, which needs to be addressed by public authorities, cannot be solved
by a simple and formal judicial decision (the law is "valid" or "invalid"), and
requires the collaboration of different actors and institutions over time. Facing a serious environmental problem as such, a judicial dialogic response
could be that of calling successive public hearings where the actors (including, say, NGOs that represent the most directly affected groups; the corporations that are polluting the river; and public authorities) try to find a way
to resolve the matter (this is, for instance, what Argentina's Supreme Court
did in the well-known *Mendoza* case concerning the pollution of the Ria-
chuelo River, which affected more than one million people).[7]

In fact, in the last decades, all over the world, constitutional theory began to experience developments of this kind, which so far have been studied

under the rubric of dialogic constitutionalism, dialogic justice, and dialogic judicial review. In principle, this innovation appeared to represent only a modest legal development, but in fact it immediately triggered a fabulous academic debate.[8]

The alternatives that judges began to explore were many. We find, among other response: (a) courts that organized public hearings (or *audiencias*) with government officers and members of civil society, trying to obtain extended agreements, gain legitimacy for their decisions and/or obtain better information and arguments in the face of complex cases;[9] (b) courts that ordered the national government to present a coherent plan (in other words, in the face of an environmental or social catastrophe);[10] (c) courts that advised the government what decision to adopt in order to comply with its constitutional duties;[11] (d) courts that exhorted governments to correct their policies according to prevalent legal standards;[12] (e) courts that launched ambitious monitoring mechanisms to ensure the enforcement of their rulings;[13] (f) courts that requested reports from public or private institutions; and (g) my favorite example, courts that challenged the validity of a certain law because it was passed without proper legislative debate.[14] I should also add that, even though these innovations are not and should not be seen as limited to cases of social rights and structural litigation, it has been in those cases (this is to say, cases that involve massive violation of rights and implicate multiple government agencies) where the practice appeared to be more salient and interesting.[15]

Unfortunately, these reforms also tended to show some significant limitations in actual practice, particularly when the basic structure of political power remains untouched, as tends to be the case, and the organization and composition of the judiciary maintains its elitist bias. On the one hand, this double limitation hinders the citizen's capacity to actively participate in the reformist process, push for more significant changes, and contribute to their stability in time. On the other hand, judges tend to face severe difficulties for advancing changes in politically sensitive areas. Worse still, under present conditions, judges tend to feel more proximity with the interests and rights of certain groups, particularly the middle and upper classes (Sajo 2008; Ferraz 2011), and the citizenry finds scarce possibilities for controlling public officers and making them accountable.

The types of problems I am referring to mainly concern what we have already explored in previous sections, namely the presence of a system of checks and balances. That system was built to prevent and channel civil war. For this reason, the framers decided to provide "those who administer each department the necessary constitutional means and personal motives to resist encroachments of others" (Hamilton, Madison, Jay 1982, 264n51). In other words, their assumption was that public officers, mainly motivated by their self-interest, would fundamentally work for expanding their own power, which other public officers would tend to prevent with the help of the constitutional devices that were put at their disposal. These instruments included veto rights, impeachment powers, and judicial review, among others. These were, in other words, defensive tools, which would help public agents to resist the naturally expected encroachments of the other branches.

Now, the decision to create those particular defensive tools may have been reasonable at that time, and may still be found reasonable today. However, this is not good news for those of us who defend a more dialogic constitutionalism, and more particularly a dialogic justice. Simply put, those defensive tools may be appropriate for preventing civil war, but not for promoting public, collective dialogue.[16]

Notes

1. Following the Napoleonic example, the independence leader Simón Bolívar—whose work was enormously influential in the entire region—proposed for Bolivia an executive appointed for life and with the power to choose his successor. In his message to the Bolivian Congress (May 1826), he stated: "The President of the Republic, in our Constitution, becomes the sun which, fixed in its orbit, imparts life to the universe. This supreme authority must be perpetual, for in non-hierarchical systems, more than in others, a fixed point is needed about which leaders and citizens, men and affairs can revolve" (Bolívar 1976, 233).

2. In this way, liberals and conservatives were establishing the basis of a peculiar institutional system that, later on, Nino would characterize as hyper-presidentialist systems (Nino 1992; 1996).

3. "Programmatic rights" are rights that are "aspirational" in nature and are not directly operative through the courts (Glendon 1992, 519).

4. See these and other alternative types of incorporation in Dulitzky 1998.

5. Article 333, for example, sates that, "The state, by means of the law, will prevent impediments to or restrictions of economic freedom and will curb or control any abuses caused by individuals or enterprises due to their dominant position in the national marketplace."

6. Although the *tutela* represents the most well-known and influential of the new procedures for grievance created by the reform, it is not the only one; it is accompanied by a popular claim, a collective claim, and a noncompliance claim.

7. "Mendoza, Beatriz Silvia y otros c/Estado Nacional y otros daños y perjuicios (daños derivados de la contaminación ambiental del Río Matanza-Riachuelo)." *CSJN*, June 20, 2006.

8. See Bateup 2007; Hogg and Bushell 1997, 35; Hogg, Bushell, and Wright 2007; Langford 2009; Manfredi and Kelly 1999; Petter 2003; Roach 2004.

9. See, for example, a decision by the Brazilian Supreme Court, May 29, 2008, concerning the Biosafety Law.

10. See, for example, a decision by the Colombian Constitutional Court in *Corte Constitucional*, January 22, 2004, Sentencia T-025/04.

11. See, for example, a decision by the Argentine Supreme Court in *Corte Suprema de Justicia de la Nación*, August 8, 2006, "Badaro, Alfonso Valentín, c/ANSES s/reajustes varios."

12. Ibid.

13. See, for example, a decision by the Colombian Constitutional Court in Judgement T-025 of the Colombian Constitutional Court.

14. See, for example, a decision by the Colombian Constitutional Court in *Corte Constitucional*, Sentencia C-740/13. Of particular interest for the purposes of this chapter is the right to "meaningful engagement" in the way it was developed by the South African Constitutional Court. See, for example, Liebenberg 2014.

15. Courtis 2005; King 2012; Gargarella 2014a; Gloppen 2006.

16. Of course, there exist obvious disagreements concerning this claim. In fact, some scholars consider that the system of checks and balances is particularly apt for the promotion of dialogue See, for example, Holmes and Sunstein 1999. However, as I conclude this chapter, I cannot go into further details, so refer readers to Gargarella 2014b, where I have explored this issue at length.

## References

Acuña, C., and C. Smulovitz. 1991. "Ni olvido ni perdón? Derechos humanos y tensiones cívico militares en la transición argentina." Paper presented at the 16th Congress of the Latin American Studies Asociation, Washington D.C., April 4–6.

Alberdi, J. B. 1981 [1852]. *Bases y puntos de partida para la organización política de la República Argentina*. Buenos Aires: Plus Ultra.

Bateup, C. 2007. "Expanding the Conversation: American and Canadian Experiences of Constitutional Dialogue in Comparative Perspective." *Temple International and Comparative Law Journal* 21 (1): 1–57.

Bickel, A. 1962. *The Least Dangerous Branch*. New Haven, Conn.: Yale University Press.

Bolívar, S. 1976. *Doctrina del Libertador*. Caracas: Biblioteca Ayacucho.

Bonilla, D. 2013. *Constitutionalism on the Global South: The Activist Tribunals of India, South Africa, and Colombia*. Cambridge: Cambridge University Press.

Bonilla, D., and M. Iturralde. 2005. *Hacia un nuevo derecho constitucional*. Bogotá: Universidad de Los Andes.

Cepeda-Espinosa, M. 2004. "Judicial Activism in a Violent Context: The Origin, Role, and Impact of the Colombian Constituional Court." *Washington University Global Studies Law Review 529* 3 (4).

Courtis, C. 2005. "El caso 'Verbitsky': Nuevos rumbos en el control judicial de la actividad de los poderes politicos?" In *Colapso del sistema carcelario*, 91–120. Buenos Aires: Centro de Estudios Legales y Sociales (CELS)/Siglo XXI.

Dulitzky, A. 1998. "La aplicación de los tratados sobre derechos humanos por los tribunales locales: Un estudio comparado." In *La aplicación de los tratados internacionales sobre derechos humanos por los tribunales locales*, edited by M. Abregú and C. Courtis, 39–74. Buenos Aires: CELS.

Epp, C. 1998. *The Rights Revolution*. Chicago, Ill.: University of Chicago Press.

Ferraz, O. 2011. "Harming the Poor Through Social Rights Litigation: Lessons from Brazil." *Texas Law Review* 89 (7): 1643–68.

García Villegas, M. 2004. "Law as Hope: Constitutions, Courts and Social Change in Latin America." *Florida Journal of International Law* 16:133–159.

García Villegas, M., and M. Saffón. 2005. "Is There Hope in Judicial Activism in Social Rights? Assesing the Dimension of Judicial Activism in Social Rights in Colombia." Working paper prepared for Dejusticia.org, Bogotá, 2005.

Gargarella, R. 2013. *Latin American Constitutionalism*. Oxford: Oxford University Press.

———. 2014a. "Deliberative Democracy, Dialogic Justice and the Promise of Social and Economic Rights." In *Social and Economic Rights in Theory and Practice: A Critical Assessment*, edited by H. Alviar, L. Williams, and K. Klare, 105–20. London: Routledge.

———. 2014b. "We the People Outside of the Constitution: The Dialogic Model of Constitutionalism and the System of Checks and Balances." *Current Legal Problems* 67 (1): 1–47.

Gaviria Díaz, C. 2002. *Sentencias: Herejías constitucionales*. Bogotá: Fondo de Cultura Económica.

Glendon, M. 1992. "Rights in Twentieth-Century Constitutions." *University of Chicago Law Review* 59: 519–38.

Gloppen, S. 2006. "Analyzing the Role of Courts in Social Transformation." In *Courts and Social Transformation in New Democracies*, edited by Roberto Gargarella, Pilar Domingo, and Theunis Roux, 35–61. London: Ashgate.

Gloppen, S., B. M. Wilson, R. Gargarella, E. Skaar, and M. Kinander. 2010. *Courts and Power in Latin America and Africa*. London: Palgrave.

Habermas, J. 1996 [1992]. *Between Facts and Norms*. Translated by W. Rehg. Cambridge: MIT Press.

Halperín Donghi, T. 2007. *Historia contemporánea de América Latina*. Buenos Aires: Alianza.

Hamilton, A., J. Madison, and J. Jay. 1982 [1787]. *The Federalist Papers*. New York: Bantam Books.

Hogg, P. and A. Bushell. 1997. "The Charter Dialogue Between Courts and Legislatures." *Osgoode Hall Law Journal* 35 (1): 75–124.

Hogg, P., A. Bushell, and W. Wright. 2007. "Charter Dialogue Revisited: 'Or Much Ado About Metaphors.'" *Osgoode Hall Law Journal* 45 (1): 1–65.

Holmes, S., and C. Sunstein. 1999. *The Cost of Rights: Why Liberty Depends on Taxes.* New York: Norton.

King, J. 2012. *Judging Social Rights.* Cambridge: Cambridge University Press.

Langford, M. 2009. *Social Rights Jurisprudence: Emerging Trends in International and Comparative Law.* Cambridge: Cambridge University Press.

Lemaitre Ripoll, J. 2009. *El derecho como conjuro: Fetichismo legal, violencia y movimientos sociales.* Bogotá: Siglo del Hombre.

Liebenberg, S. 2014. "Deepening Democratic Transformation in South Africa through Participatory Constitutional Remedies." Manuscript, University of Stellenbosch Law.

Manfredi, C., and J. Kelly. 1999. "Six Degrees of Dialogue: A Response to Hogg and Bushell." *Osgoode Hall Law Journal* 37 (3): 513–27.

Manin, B. 1997. *The Principles of Representative Government.* Cambridge: Cambridge University Press.

Nino, C. S. 1992. *Fundamentos de derecho constitucional.* Buenos Aires: Astrea.

———. 1996. *The Constitution of Deliberative Democracy.* New Haven: Yale University Press.

Petter, A. 2003. "Twenty Years of Charter Justification: From Liberal Legalism to Dubious Dialogue." *University of New Brunswick Law Journal* 52:187–200.

Roach, K. 2004. "Dialogic Judicial Review and Its Critics." *Supreme Court Law Review* 23:49–104.

Rodríguez-Garavito, C. 2011. "Beyond the Courtroom: The Impact of Judicial Activism on Socioeconomic Rights in Latin America." *Texas Law Review* 89 (7): 1669–98.

Rosenn, K. 1990. "The Success of Constitutionalism in the United States and Its Failure in Latin America: An Explanation." *Inter-American Law Review* 22 (1): 1–39.

Rossi, J. and L. Filippini. 2010. In *Derechos sociales: Justicia, política y economía en América Latina,* edited by Pilar Arcidiácono, Nicolás Espejo Yaksic, and César Rodríguez Garavito, 34–57. Bogotá: Siglo del Hombre-Universidad de Los Andes.

Sajo, A. 1995. "Reading the Invisible Constitution: Judicial Review in Hungary." *Oxford Journal of Legal Studies* 15 (2): 253–68.

Sikkink, K. 2012. *The Justice Cascade: The Justice Cascade: How Human Rights Prosecutions Are Changing World Politics.* New York: Norton & Company.

Uprimny, R. 2011. "The Recent Transformation of Constitutional Law in Latin America: Trends and Challenges." *Texas Law Review* 89 (7): 1587–610.

Wilson, B. 2010. "Explaining the Rise of Accountability Functions of Costa Rica's Constitutional Court." In *Courts and Power in Latin America and Africa,* edited by E. Skaar, S. Gloppen, R. Gargarella, and B. Wilson, 63–82. New York: Palgrave.

# CHAPTER 10

# Agents of Neoliberalism? High Courts, Legal Preferences, and Rights in Latin America

Sandra Botero

## Introduction

Constitutional courts, like independent central banks, were seen by the international financial institutions and aid agencies fueling judicial reform in Latin America in the late 1980s and early 1990s as crucial to neoliberal economic development. Safe from the vicissitudes of representative democracy by virtue of their design, high courts were deemed ideally located to provide much-needed guarantees of legal predictability. Strengthening courts and the judicial system in general was seen as vital to promoting legal stability, providing access to justice for investors, increasing effectiveness, and safeguarding the neoliberal model (Carothers 2001; Rodríguez Garavito 2011). In this context, wide-ranging reforms often provided for the creation of constitutional tribunals where none existed or for the empowerment of those already existing.

Some of these new or recently reformed courts became assertive in the years that followed—that is, they exercised their power, making active use of the capacity for action conferred on them by institutional design. For instance, the Argentine, Brazilian, Colombian, and Costa Rican high tribunals became, to different extents, checks on their executives, but also enforcers of recently constitutionalized rights (Wilson 2009; Nunes 2010; Kapiszewski 2012). Their interventions safeguarded individual rights, often put a brake on the retrenchment of welfare benefits, sometimes expanded rights, and even resulted in greater involvement from the state in certain areas. Their rights activism was controversial and stood partly at odds with a neoliberal project. Following the breakdown of the Washington Consensus in the early 2000s, as Latin American countries continue to navigate the currents of democracy, these assertive high courts are entering a new stage. They remain important points for social policy and accountability discussions around rights, but the boundaries of their activism are being redefined. How are courts helping make effective new constitutional rights in Latin America, and what limits do these courts have?

In this chapter, I suggest constitutional courts have a complicated and evolving relationship with neoliberal reforms and neoconstitutionalism— that is, with the wave of constitutional reforms, also known as social constitutionalism, which swept the region just as market reforms did. Activist courts disappointed both neoliberal technocrats and progressive activists: they were neither perfect agents of neoliberalism nor perfect tools for social change. In the years that followed their empowerment, assertive young courts indeed helped safeguard new constitutional orders and became central to economic governance. They also, to the surprise of many, became central to the politics of rights in the region. In accordance with what second-generation neoliberal reforms wanted, high courts expanded and protected basic individual autonomy rights (negative rights). Simultaneously, they challenged neoliberalism when they protected some aspects of social provision and pushed back on the free market through enforcing newly constitutionalized economic and social rights (ESR, also associated with positive rights). Judicial leadership was central both to their activation and to the present and future of Latin American rights revolutions.

More than two decades later, as these courts grow older and more mature, they continue to be central to the politics of rights in the region. As a response to their own rights activism, however, they have become prized political booty and now enjoy a lesser degree of freedom than their younger selves did. The political backlash to their activism has taken two forms: first, political efforts have been made to reform them and shape the profile of the justices through the appointment process; and second, constituencies have been activated across the ideological spectrum mobilizing against the judicial enforcement of new rights. This backlash is consequential both today and going forward. On the one hand, changes to the profile of the justices in the region's rights-assertive courts may have implications for how the courts approach rights. On the other hand, mobilization around constitutional rights is no longer the sole purview of leftist movements, and courts are now embedded in the political efforts by groups of diverse ideological bents.

The growing importance of courts as checks and balances mechanisms and as sites for the political struggle around rights has been one of the most significant shifts in Latin American politics following the third wave of democratization. Several high courts in the region are playing key, new political roles. This rights activism cuts across ideological differences in national governments: we see assertive courts in countries whose governments were not key players in the post-neoliberal turn (such as Colombia, Costa Rica, or, increasingly, Mexico) and also in some that were (such as Argentina). Across the region, assertive courts are treading in new arenas and challenging our traditional conceptions of the role of courts and judges in democracy.

This chapter contributes to the literature on comparative judicial politics by explaining the political dynamics triggered by the active exercise of judicial power rather than why courts in new democracies are empowered. Our theoretical frameworks tend to assume that once courts become assertive they will remain assertive. Additionally, the implication is that rights activism is synonymous with a leftist or progressive stance. My research challenges these notions, building on recent research to show that the politics of appointments is crucial to understanding the profiles of these courts and the ongoing political struggle to define the ideas and legal preferences that the tribunals can act on. Judicial activism will trigger political and social mobilization across the ideological spectrum, which can directly impact the implementation of rulings and spur political backlash.

In the first part of this chapter I discuss why some high courts in the region, challenging the expectations of those who saw them strictly as neoliberal agents, became assertive enforcers of rights. Building on previous arguments I show that judicial leadership and, more specifically, the legal preferences of justices are crucial not only to the activation of courts but also to the sustainment of rights revolutions. Drawing on examples from different courts around the region, I describe the early trajectories of assertive young courts and explain how the political consequences of their activism can shape them. In the second part of this chapter I rely on interviews, fieldwork in Colombia, and secondary literature to illustrate this argument through a case study of Colombia's constitutional court. One of the first courts born out of the reform wave—and the most rights-activist in the region—the Colombian tribunal is ideal to study these trends.

## Neither Perfect Agents of Neoliberalism Nor Perfect Instruments of Social Change

During the 1980s and 1990s, neoliberal reforms unfolded in Latin American countries in two successive waves. The first wave brought with it a push for structural adjustment policies as a new free-market economic model was implanted, replacing the import-substitution industrialization economic model and redefining the political and structural foundations of the region. The second wave emphasized the slower process of institutionalizing reforms as "it became evident that merely rewriting key economic laws was of little use if the legal system was incapable of actually implementing and enforcing them" (Carothers 2001, 6). Hence judicial reform, the rule of law, and the performance of national judiciaries became part of the agenda of organizations such as the World Bank and the Inter-American Development Bank. Courts played two key roles in the push to deepen market reforms (Rodríguez Garavito 2011): on the one hand, more efficient civil and commercial courts that abstained from redistributive judicial activism contributed to maintaining the predictability of the norms regulating the economic market; on the other hand, efficient criminal courts were central to guaranteeing peace and order. From this perspective, high courts appear as agents of neoliberalism. Parallel to this second wave, another group of new constitutions or reforms to existing ones with an emphasis on social components was felt throughout the region in the 1990s and early 2000s. At the center of the reforms that were a part of this trend—known as neoconstitutionalism, or social constitutionalism—was facilitating access to justice, rights, and including provisions for stronger judicial review.

Eight Latin American countries drafted new charters between 1988, when Brazil inaugurated the series, and 2009, when Bolivia's constitution was approved.[1] Although not all countries promulgated new charters, several of those that did not do so still passed significant amendments to their constitutions—such as Argentina, Costa Rica, and Mexico. Despite national specificities, the majority of these constitutions share some common themes

(Uprimny 2011): they recognize multiethnic and multicultural nations, include diversity and religious equality, protect minorities (ethnic minorities in particular), redefine the state's role in the national economy, and entrench generous bills of rights, including economic and social rights.

Some saw these two currents as a single, unified neoliberal project. Hirschl (2004) famously argued that judicial review was the brainchild of self-serving elites who promoted it to protect their interests through a minority institution they could easily access. Constitutional rights were mere lip service. Critical law approaches suggested similarly cynical views. Rights rhetoric was a formalism that embodied yet another globalizing and hegemonic push—the judge conveniently took social conflicts out of the political realm and safely relocated them in the domain of legal expertise, unresolved (Kennedy 2006).

In hindsight, and on closer inspection of the empirical track record, however, we can see that rights-assertive courts have a more complicated and nuanced relationship to neoliberal reforms and to neoconstitutionalism than either Hirschl or any of the critical law approaches suggest. First, there was no single monolithic neoliberal view of the role of judicial systems and judicial review shared by all relevant actors; different actors had diverse agendas and emphasized different objectives for judicial reforms (Carothers 2001). Financial institutions were just one of many international and domestic actors with a stake in the process—overlapping, complex, and multiactor currents interacted in permanent tension (Rodríguez Garavito 2011). What proved decisive was these reform waves were contemporaneous, becoming closely associated.

Indeed, the track record of these courts suggests they were perfect agents neither of neoliberalism nor of neoconstitutionalism. Over the years, as both the neoliberal and neoconstitutional currents waxed and waned in the region, the crossing of their paths generated tensions in and around high courts. Reforms helped make these tribunals tools for protecting new institutional frameworks and economic governance, just as neoliberal reforms had intended. For example, Kapiszewski (2012) shows that both the Argentine and Brazilian high courts became pivotal actors in the critical realm of economic policy. Yet the strong social rights component of the constitutions also made assertive courts central to rights, and this generated significant tensions. Assertive courts often played key roles in augmenting the sphere of classic and new individual autonomy rights. These rights were in consonance with the cosmopolitan neoliberal project (Hirschl 2004), but their active enforcement upset the status quo. Notably, rights-assertive courts also went beyond what neoliberal reformers foresaw and became active defenders of newly constitutionalized economic and social rights. In safeguarding and defending ESR, they seemed to be going against strict neoliberalism.

The experiences of Costa Rica and Colombia illustrate the early trajectory of rights-assertive courts well. In both countries, constitutional reforms entrenched generous bills of rights and drastically lowered the barriers for accessing newly created high courts—the Sala Cuarta and Corte Constitucional, respectively. Citizens gained standing to challenge the constitutionality of laws directly, and a quick legal mechanism was created (*tutela/amparo*) to seek redress for rights violations. In Costa Rica, diverse groups and individuals (labor unions, private companies, citizens, students) used the growing accessibility of the tribunal to take the government to task with its social welfare constitutional commitments, thus constraining its ability to fully implement market reforms (Wilson, Rodríguez Cordero, and Handberg 2004). At the same time, the court began safeguarding the rights of sexual minorities. The Colombian Constitutional Court also quickly developed a notable rights track record, defending the civil and social rights of individuals (Cepeda 2005) but also expanding and safeguarding the right to health and the rights of indigenous minorities, among others.

Judicial rights activism in the region is closely intertwined with the actors in civil society who have relied on them since the mid-1990s. In Costa Rica, gay rights activists, AIDS patients, and labor unions have used the court to gain access to policymaking spaces and have thus made important strides in guaranteeing their constitutional rights (Wilson and Rodríguez Cordero 2006). In Colombia, gay-rights activists (Albarracín 2011), the indigenous movement (Uprimny and García Villegas 2004), women's rights organizations, and victims of the decades-long conflict (Sandoval Rojas 2013) have also repeatedly turned to the court since its creation. Activists and organizations throughout the region have engaged high courts as part of larger mobilization strategies that have included legislative efforts, political mobilization, community organizing and lobbying, seeking to protect constitutional rights, and resisting the retrenchment of the welfare state.

Decades after the neoliberal reforms, the judicialization of rights continues and received a boost as the Washington Consensus broke down and the region turned away from rigid free-market economics toward a new neodevelopmentalist approach (Brinks and Forbath 2014). Latin American high courts today vary greatly in how assertive they are. Those that are assertive play important roles in national debates regarding the limits, definition, and implementation of rights. Although several factors facilitated the activation of once dormant tribunals,[2] the legal preferences of their justices were a particularly important piece of why courts became active enforcers of rights. That was the case in both Costa Rica (Wilson 2007) and Colombia (Nunes 2010), for instance, where some justices imbued with less formalist approaches to the law took seriously the new rights provisions in the constitution. It is worth dwelling briefly on the importance of justices because they remain central to grasping how judicial rights activism is being redefined in the region as assertive courts mature.

## Why Judges and Legal Preferences Matter to Triggering and Sustaining Rights Activism

In his seminal piece on rights revolutions in the United States, India, and Canada, Epp (1998) argues that support structures in civil society (organized rights advocacy groups), not justices, are crucial to bringing about and sustaining rights revolutions. Indeed, the alliances between courts and civil society also mattered in Latin America. However, the legal preferences of justices themselves are central to understanding the present and future of political battles over constitutional rights in the region. This is so not only because it was the judges who took the new rights seriously, and in enforcing them activated the courts and forged alliances with organized groups in civil society, but also because the development and sustainability of the courts' approach to rights depends on them.

Justices' preferences help explain why some courts develop an activist profile while others do not (Woods and Hilbink 2009). We know that the Latin American judiciaries that remain wedded to formalist perspectives are less friendly to rights-based approaches (Hilbink 2007; Gonzalez Ocantos 2012). We also know, more specifically, that justices who were imbued with neoconstitutional, less formalist, and more rights-friendly approaches to the law were crucial to explaining the activation of courts in favor of economic and social rights (Wilson, Rodríguez Cordero, and Handberg 2004; Nunes 2010). Legal preferences matter not only for judges to favor ESR, but also in terms of how they conceive of their role more generally (Cifuentes 1995; Gillman 1999; Hilbink 2007). Dealing with the sustained judicialization of social policy confronts judges with challenges that are redefining their functions. Their outlook on rights, their willingness to redefine the boundaries of their role and go beyond the formalist prescription, or not, are crucial to the future of some procedural and institutional innovations they have devised to handle ESR cases.

Handling ESR cases confronts judges with social policy issues, an enterprise for which critics deem courts ill-equipped. Conventional wisdom on the intervention of courts in social policy claims that they cannot effectively intervene in this area because they lack institutional capacity for oversight, lack information, and lack the tools to understand and consider the consequences of their decisions (Horowitz 1977). This view, however, is largely based on the U.S. experience. More recently, high courts in Africa and Latin America have taken new, more creative and experimental approaches to how they intervene (Bergallo 2006). Some assertive high courts are handing down rulings that are more sensitive to the complexities of social policy, financial constraints, and the political dynamics of their realities (Brinks and Forbath 2014). They call attention to rights violations and redirect the matter to the government for it to determine how best to address the situation, trying to foster dialogue across different responsible parties (Abramovich 2005). They have also generated new institutional mechanisms to be able to monitor compliance with the implementation of these rulings, for example.

These cases take justices outside of the traditional boundaries of their role as defined by more formalist approaches: they put justices and courts at the center of complex public policy issues that involve many actors and often require their engagement, ideally as coordinating devices, over time (Botero 2015). A good example is Causa Mendoza, a landmark environmental ruling handed down by the Argentine Supreme Court in 2008. In it, the court ordered the federal, provincial, and local governments to work toward the environmental protection and recovery of Argentina's severely polluted primary fluvial artery, the Matanza-Riachuelo. The decision put the court at the center of an ambitious and controversial multiyear and multi-institutional effort to monitor the improvement of environmental and living conditions in the river basin (Merlinsky 2009). Initially, the court outlined some actions and general objectives that should be pursued to clean and protect the river basin, highlighting priority areas and deadlines. It left the drafting of a clean-up plan and the specifics of defining tasks and implementation to the authorities. In addition, it actively monitored compliance through a combination of different institutional mechanisms, including yearly public hearings (in which the involved parties report on progress), working with delegate lower courts, and creating a follow-up commission, including civil society organizations, which actively participates in monitoring. The Colombian constitutional court has relied on similar structural approaches to ESR issues with its decisions safeguarding the rights of internally displaced populations (Rodríguez Garavito and Rodríguez Franco 2010) and reforming the national health system (Yamin, Parra Vera, and Giannella 2011).

These new approaches require a certain kind of judge, one who is willing to rethink her role. Monitoring implementation over time, promoting interinstitutional coordination, or dialogue across government, private, and civil society actors are not the things that more readily come to mind when we think of describing justices—but they are increasingly part of the job description. Judges who lack the inclinations and interest to engage in intercultural dialogue and reduce the distance between themselves and those whose rights are being violated—often marginalized minorities—can seriously hamper already difficult processes (Gargarella 2015). This is why their profile was and remains crucial.

## Other Conditions That Facilitated Judicial Rights Activism

The rights activism that these justices engaged in through young high courts was unexpected. Actors' lack of experience with the new institutions put in place by constitutional reforms gave assertive young courts in democratic contexts significant room to maneuver. When these new or newly empowered courts first flexed their muscles, they took many in their political systems by surprise. Their activism has had political consequences: elites in Latin America are now watching courts closely and are increasingly aware that the justices' legal preferences matter. As a result, somewhat counterintuitively, assertive young courts at that time enjoyed a greater degree of freedom than they do today, even though they are older.

Two characteristics of the early years of assertive courts help to understand the leniency they were given. First, following reforms, all actors have to adapt to new institutions and frameworks with which they often have virtually no direct experience. Comprehensive constitutional reforms of the kind Latin America experienced, which tend to touch on several aspects of the national political architecture or at least entail major overhauls of one branch, alter the status quo of the entire political system. Although previous experience with judicial review probably gave some polities a better sense of what was coming, it was difficult for all involved to have foreseen all the consequences of the new institutional structures put in place.

Second, from early on, these courts were very responsive to societal demands as part of a strategy to build much needed legitimacy. Although some theories predict that young courts will not, for fear of retaliation, overstep the tolerance boundaries of other political institutions during these crucial early years (Epstein, Knight, and Shvetsova 2001), there are alternative routes to building legitimacy. Justices can choose to challenge other political powers in certain areas and also respond more directly to demands from citizens and organized civil society in others. A clerk in the Argentine Supreme Court, for example, recalls that in the early days of the new court, following Kirchner's key reforms in the mid-2000s, the new chief justice instructed the clerks precisely in this direction: "When Lorenzetti arrived in the court he gathered all the clerks and told us 'People, we are going to identify [and take on] cases with social impact, *causas sociales*, in five key topics, including consumer rights, environmental rights, and crimes against humanity. And we are going to hold public hearings on them.'"[3]

In contexts with significant political fragmentation and where courts are more easily accessible, such as in Latin America after the reforms, not only is "going social" viable, but it may also be sustainable in the long run. This mixed strategy can make courts politically relevant while they build public support and make allies of organized groups in civil society. The basic requirement for courts to act—namely, that there be cases they can decide on—is not difficult to come by in this scenario. Citizens and social organizations flocked to more easily accessible courts, particularly where justices gave early signals of being rights oriented and more open.

Early bursts of rights activism were not only unexpected; they were also controversial. Decisions on individual autonomy and civil rights, usually associated with more negative rights that require less action from the state—and were quite often countermajoritarian—upset the political status quo and certain groups specifically, such as the social conservatives. ESR activism in particular, usually associated with positive rights (which require action to be made effective), was also contentious. Additionally, ESR unearthed a deeper tension between neoliberalism and social constitutionalism: the simultaneous pull toward the retrenchment of the state on the one hand, and the defense of social provisions along with the expansion of ESR rights on the other. This was the case in Brazil, to name but one example, where the growing judicialization of health raised numerous questions regarding its fiscal sustainability and effectiveness (Ferraz 2011).

These tensions not only pulled courts and polities in opposite directions; they also had important political consequences. As assertive courts mature, they find they have to deal with the backlash from their own progressive activism. The sustained judicialization of rights has led to a political backlash that will increasingly shape the prospects of judicial activism around rights in the region in the years to come.

## Learning from Experience: The Political Consequences of Rights Activism and What Lies Ahead for Mature Courts

Political elites have developed two types of responses in their efforts to shape assertive high courts: on the one hand, occasional impulses to reform them or, conversely, to craft political alliances that protect them, while on the other, a keen interest in controlling the preferences of the courts via the appointment process, steering the profiles of justices away from neoconstitutionalism. As Smulovitz (1995) insightfully observed early on, as courts become an increasingly important part of the political process in Latin American democracies, they turn into prized political booty.

A second consequence of judicial rights activism is backlash in the form of mobilization and policy against the legal victories in favor of rights enforcement. Research on the aftermath of the U.S. rights revolution has suggested that the legal victories in civil rights and minority rights cases gave way to severe political backlash that ultimately took away more than was gained (Klarman 2004; Rosenberg 2008). This backlash consists of political and policy reactions (in terms of mobilization and public opinion) that can follow judicial decisions advancing rights. More recent approaches temper these negative conclusions (Keck 2009) and instead highlight the importance of understanding mobilization from both the Left and Right to get a full sense of how courts are used to advance strategies of change (Keck 2014). We are beginning to see similar phenomena in Latin America and need to study and understand them to get a full sense of the politics of constitutional rights in the twenty-first century. In what follows, I illustrate my argument by examining the trajectory and prospects of the Colombian Constitutional Court.

## Colombia

As the Colombian Constitutional Court enters its third decade, what are the forces shaping its role in the political struggle around constitutional rights? The court was created as part of the new 1991 constitution, supported by a president, César Gaviria, who saw in open access to the legal system and strong negative-rights protection a precondition for the successful establishment of the free market (Nunes 2010). As mentioned earlier, the newly created Colombian court quickly developed an assertive profile, both as a strong check on executive power and through a sustained interest in rights.

It is impossible to summarize in this short space the full breadth of the court's interventions advancing both negative and positive rights, along with their impact. The court has been particularly active in defending the right to health (Rodríguez Garavito 2012), an area in which it has not only handed down broad collective decisions but also dealt with a tidal wave of individual cases in the last decades. Throughout the years it has relied on judicial review to strike down the entire national mortgage system (Barreto Valderrama 2012) and it has also handed down broad, sweeping collective decisions favoring pensioners. Via *tutela*, it has played an important role in safeguarding the right to education and a clean environment, as well as the rights of women, children, LGBT, and indigenous minorities.

The court has established itself squarely at the center of political dynamics in Colombia. Its justices, particularly those who infused it with novel, less formalist legal perspectives, are paramount to this story (Uprimny and García Villegas 2004; Nunes 2010). Rights, and ESR especially, are central to their understanding of the court's role in Colombia. In the words of one of the former justices who sat on the bench during the court's early years:

> The Constitutional Court understood from the beginning that the most novel aspect of the [1991] constitution lay in the need to foster the effectiveness of the transformative norms within it: the idea that Colombia is an *Estado Social de Derecho*, the norm of social equality and ESR rights. In selecting tutelas [to rule on] the court privileged

those that allowed it to develop the *estado social de derecho*. . . . One has to bear in mind that these issues [inequality, social exclusion, ESR rights] are topics that are central to constitutionalism in Latin America. These concerns are not valid everywhere.[4]

Similar themes came up in interviews with justices who sat on the court at a later stage: "This constitutionalism is different, more inclusive. It's a constitutionalism that is looking for real equality. The protection of those who are less well-off is an explicit objective. . . . What is the function of a judge [in Colombia, in Latin America]? The search for true equality and real democracy."[5]

The Colombian Constitutional Court is known for the approach to rights and the progressive jurisprudence that resonate in the two quotes above. More recently it has developed a novel approach to collective ESR cases through a series of rulings in which, like the Argentine court in the Causa Mendoza example cited earlier, it seeks to safeguard rights by involving different institutions in long-term dialogue, planning, and monitoring efforts around a broad social policy issue. For former justice Juan Carlos Henao (2011), "taking on the monitoring [of compliance with] structural rulings is proof of an alternative way of thinking about the role of judges." One of his former colleagues was more specific in describing the challenges that implementing these new approaches entail for judges: "When does the job end? [structural rulings that require monitoring make it clear] this is not only about producing rulings. There's now a concern with the effective enjoyment of the right. The judge becomes accountable; there's greater responsibility. Also, the judge must tread into public policy. That is complex. It is a challenge to creativity."[6]

Not all justices share the same legal philosophy. Interestingly, however, the concern for rights and the awareness that the constitution's provisions on ESR and its own trajectory have led the court to play what can be perceived as a nontraditional role also came up in interviews with justices who are usually described as more ideologically conservative:

It is somewhat exotic that a tribunal turns to these issues. This is very questioned and the court is censured for taking on these tasks. We are told the court is co-administering and invading areas that belong to the executive or congress. What happens is that when you get to issues of such a magnitude that the court has to conclude there is an unconstitutional state of affairs it is because it's not only this right, that right, or Maria, Pedro, and Pablo's rights. No. It is the rights of many. Like in

the case of the internally displaced. Millions! . . . These are grave circumstances. It requires justices take it upon themselves to alleviate the
infringement of fundamental rights.[7]

The justices' legal preferences were crucial to shaping the court's activation
and trajectory. The court's assertiveness would have its own political consequences, to which I now turn.

## Reining in the Court

The court's activism generated fierce controversies and made it a political
target. As the next pages will show, politicians and mobilized groups learned
from the young court's intense activism and tried to rein it in via reform,
shape its profile, and mobilize in response to its rulings.

Although Colombia had previous experience with judicial review,[8] the extent of the court's early activism and the areas it touched on took President
Gaviria, the public, and political actors by surprise. Its rulings limiting the use
of extraordinary presidential powers, which had been abused by presidents
since the mid-twentieth century (Uprimny 2003), and early decisions defending individual rights unleashed political storms. A perfect example was the
decision to decriminalize "personal use," a ruling in early 1994 in which the
court legalized the personal possession of a minimum amount of narcotics.
This move generated strong reactions across the political spectrum, exemplified by a tense public exchange in which a government minister warned that
the court "was not infallible," to which the court responded by demanding respect for its independence.[9]

The first president to lead during the court's existence, César Gaviria, did
not publicly attack it, but economists, activists, and politicians engaged in
fierce debates about the court's actions that were mostly new in Colombia.[10]
ESR rights were also often at the center of the controversies. In 1999, for example, just eight years after being created and in the midst of an economic
crisis, the court handed down a series of rulings that found unconstitutional
and eventually dismantled the national mortgage system (known as UPAC).
Defending debtors' right to housing, the court ordered the executive and
Congress to create a new mortgage financing system, which had to follow
certain specifications. The political controversy was fierce: the situation was
described as a judicial dictatorship and justices as donkeys.[11] Whatever side

of the early discussions politicians found themselves on, they became acutely aware of the centrality of the court and started paying attention.

Over the next few years, different executives attempted reforms to curtail the powers of the court. Although the threats against the institutional integrity of the court did not result in concrete reforms—the fragmentation of the political spectrum and the support of organized civil society actors prevented these attempts from moving forward—it is worth mentioning them briefly to get a sense of the environment in which the court operated. President Samper's administration (1994–98), in reaction to the court's activism, was the first to officially threaten to curtail the court's powers: in 1996 and 1997 reform attempts threatened to limit the court's powers or do away with the tribunal. In both cases, according to Rubiano Galvis (2009), NGOs, academics, and political parties closed ranks in support of the court, and neither bill progressed.

Threats were made again and escalated during Alvaro Uribe's first presidency (2002–6). Uribe had been clear before his election that he intended to modify the constitution and especially the judicial branch. In late 2002, the Minister of Interior and Justice filed draft legislation that proposed to cut back severely on the powers of the court, and a second attempt was made in 2004. Although certain constituencies failed to formally reform the court, a parallel alternative strategy seems to have gained traction in more recent years: crafting a court that is decisively less activist and rights friendly.

A very brief qualitative overview of the profiles of the court's justices is helpful in identifying an important trend: the shift away from appointing[12] lawyers with academic profiles and an ideational commitment to the defense of rights. Nunes (2010), who focused on the young constitutional court, showed that the ideational character of individual justices determined their responses to rights claims. More specifically, appointees with a more academic profile had a common characteristic: "their commitment to human rights and to a proactive judicial role in protecting them, a commitment that was heavily influenced by their legal education" (Nunes 2010, 80). This was in contrast to the justices whose legal careers had been shaped by the traditional legal system, who sought to limit judicial involvement in rights issues.

Figure 10.1 summarizes key characteristics of appointees to the constitutional court, including a broad characterization of their background—a rough indicator of their "rights-friendliness" as measured by Nunes (see Appendix 1 for details). The justices with academic backgrounds and neoconstitutional legal philosophies were absolutely central to the development of the ESR jurisprudence of the court. Manuel José Cepeda, who wrote several of the land-

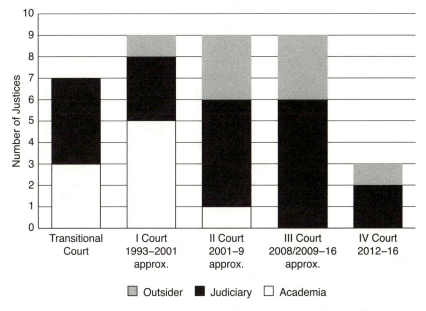

Figure 10.1. Transitional Court: Seven-member court 1992–93. The classification into eight-year periods is an approximation, following the original constitutional design. The resignation of some justices before their eight-year term expired has resulted in staggered appointments. See Appendix 1 for details.

mark decisions on ESR (T-760/08 and T-025/04, among others), was the last justice with an academic background to be appointed (in 2001). Efforts to appoint a similar academic figure in 2008 failed and look increasingly unlikely. It is also interesting to note that starting in the 2000s (II Court), as academic appointees stop, there is a rise in the appointment of outsider justices. I use this term to identify appointees with more explicitly partisan profiles as well as those who came from private practice and usually had no background within the judiciary or in constitutional law. Outsider appointees tend to be less prestigious legal figures. Because the tenure of justices in the court is only eight years, the absence of incoming justices who share rights-friendly ideational preferences is likely to have a great impact on its orientation.

## Women's Reproductive and Sexual Rights

The second phenomenon redefining the boundaries of judicial rights activism in Colombia is the mobilization that it has generated from constituencies who oppose its content. In this last section I focus on the backlash against recent legal victories with regards to women's reproductive and sexual rights and LGBT rights.

In 2006 the court declared unconstitutional the criminalization of abortion in Colombia under three specific circumstances: when the pregnancy endangers the physical or emotional health of the mother; when it is the result of rape or incest; and when grave fetal malformations make life outside the uterus nonviable. The court deemed the voluntary interruption of pregnancy a fundamental right of women, part of their sexual and reproductive rights. As such, this ruling also created obligations for the state, which must provide access to abortion services for the women who need them.

The original victory in 2006 (Case C-355) and those that reaffirmed it[13] generated political and social mobilization against the right to abortion, as well as policy impact (reversion or detraction from gains in terms of policy). Existing social conservative organizations came together under new umbrella organizations, such as Unidos por la Vida, with renewed purpose. At the same time, this also spurred the creation of smaller, explicitly pro-life organizations across the country, such as Red Futuro Colombia and Comité Antioquia Pro-Vida. These organizations have engaged in social, legal, and political mobilization geared at reinstating the status quo or stalling the implementation of C-355. Unidos por la Vida focuses its activities on legal and social mobilization: shortly after its inception in 2006, following the court's ruling, it led a two-year national effort promoting a referendum on abortion. The National Registrar cancelled the referendum for procedural reasons, but the organization's work continues. Along with other NGOs, it has promoted and participated in national pro-life marches held annually with the explicit "objective of voicing our rejection of the ruling that the constitutional court handed down in 2006 decriminalizing abortion."[14]

Red Futuro Colombia (RFC) and other social conservative groups, including the Catholic Church and its affiliated NGOs, have focused on filing legal challenges to the government's efforts at implementing the ruling. RFC successfully challenged the executive decree that regulated the provision of abortion services.[15] A lawsuit was filed in 2013 against efforts by the National Health Superintendent to provide guidelines for health providers on the provision of abortion services.[16] In its original ruling the court clarified that regulation was not necessary for abortion to stop being criminalized or for the service to be provided. In practice, the lack of regulation makes access difficult, exacerbating the confusion regarding obligations, rights, and correct procedures (Dalen 2013).

Part of the political reaction against C-355 also included the mobilization of key elite figures, some of them senior government officials. The national procurador, Alejandro Ordóñez, a social conservative and one of the key figures in the Conservative Party, publicly declared his opposition to the court rulings on abortion and gay rights. During his tenure (2009–16), Ordoñez used his office and its resources to restrict the right in question and openly challenge the court's jurisprudence on the matter (Dalen 2013). Not only did Ordoñez's high-profile political moves, in conjunction with the work of antiabortion groups, indicate a strong political reaction; they also had an important policy impact. Overall, they have succeeded in stalling the creation of a legal framework that clarifies the rights, procedures, and obligations of those involved in the provision of abortion services in Colombia.

## LGBT Rights (Same-Sex Marriage and Adoption)

In February 2007 the Constitutional Court started on the road to equalizing the rights of heterosexual and homosexual couples by recognizing the patrimonial rights of same-sex couples (C-075/07). It has since ruled favorably, piecemeal, on social welfare benefits, health, and alimony obligations, among others, until most rights and obligations have been equalized. In the last five years gay-rights activists throughout Colombia have escalated efforts to get the court to rule on rights to adoption and same-sex marriage.

Activists have secured important victories on both fronts, but the issues remain contested. The year 2011 was a turning point for same-sex marriage. That year the court ruled unanimously that it could not change the laws that defined marriage as the union between a man and a woman, but that this should not be understood as denying the rights of homosexuals to form a family. The court gave Congress two years to legislate, failing which same-sex couples could go before a judge or notary to formalize their unions. In April 2013, as the deadline approached, a bill allowing for same-sex unions died in the Senate. Amid huge national controversy the first same-sex marriage was celebrated the following July. A leading case on adoption slowly began making its way through the legal system in 2009 and lingered in the court for years, undecided, as pressure and controversy mounted. When the decision was finally handed down in early 2015, instead of the ruling grant-ing full adoption rights to gay couples that activists had hoped for,[17] a split court gave adoption rights only to couples in which one of the two is the biological parent of the child. These legal victories have generated a politi-cal backlash from increasingly organized and active constituencies that explicitly oppose the actions of the court.

Two initiatives stand out: first, the legal and political mobilization of so-cially conservative civil society organizations in opposition to same-sex marriage and adoption rights, as well as a ballot initiative on same-sex adop-tion rights. The NGO Fundación Marido y Mujer is a prime example of the types of organizations that are cropping up in strong opposition to the rec-ognition of same-sex marriage. The NGO was created shortly after the court's deadline to Congress passed in 2013; it is devoted to legally challenging gay marriages. In 2013 it initiated legal battles in different cities against mar-riages that had already taken place or were about to in efforts to declare them invalid. More recently, the director of the foundation (a former con-gressional candidate for the Conservative Party) has spoken out against the possibility that the court will decide in favor of same-sex adoption.[18]

On the other hand, the ballot initiative on same-sex adoption is spear-headed by Viviane Morales, a high-profile senator of the Liberal Party and also a member of an evangelical church. According to Morales, the decision to promote a referendum was made in late 2014 when the court decided in favor of a lesbian couple: "at that point we knew there was (another) consti-tutional challenge before the court and we concluded that the only thing that could counter this is a popular decision. That's why we opted for a referen-dum and began gathering the required signatures in October."[19] For the ballot initiative to go before voters, a number of requirements have to be met: (1) supporting signatures must be collected, (2) approval is needed by both chambers of congress, and (3) it must be reviewed by the constitutional court. By the time this book went to press, the first requirement had been met and the project had been approved in the Senate.

## Conclusions

In the wake of neoliberal and constitutional revolutions in Latin America, several new constitutional courts developed an assertive profile. The high courts that were born out of the reformist waves of the 1990s have a complex and evolving relationship with neoliberalism and social constitutionalism. From their early years, they were pivotal in maintaining new institutional orders, yet they also became active defenders of both negative and positive rights. Thirty years later, several Latin American high courts are still key players in their political systems, and they remain important focal points for discussions of rights and social policy. As they mature, they are grappling with the backlash from their own actions. To illustrate this trajectory, this chapter has focused on the case of the Colombian Constitutional Court, the most activist tribunal in the region. The experience of this tribunal offers interesting insights for the experiences of other activist courts in Latin America (the Argentine, Costa Rican, and increasingly, the Brazilian and Mexican) and other young democracies. Today, the court is closely watched by elites. Sitting squarely at the center of mobilization from across the political spectrum, the boundaries of its rights activism are being redefined.

The findings presented here raise interesting theoretical issues with regards to our understanding of judicial empowerment and what makes rights revolutions sustainable. We know precious little about the trajectory of recently empowered courts in new democracies. Our frameworks suggest that empowerment, if attained, leads to more assertive courts that remain assertive and, relatedly, progressive. The Colombian case challenges that narrative. The trajectory of this court from its early years through its present mature stage shows that the politics of appointment have to be included in any analysis of the aftermath of initial judicial empowerment. This is in accordance with recent research (Brinks and Blass 2014) that highlights the importance of the interaction of politics with institutional design to influence court behavior. The present research further specifies the mechanism: assertive courts can be shaped by strategic appointments that affect the legal preferences and ideas inside it, seeking (in this particular case) to make it less activist, less progressive.

Second and relatedly, the Latin American experience suggests that, aside from focusing on support structures (Epp 1998), we also need to look at justices and their legal preferences to understand how rights revolutions are sustained and evolve. Part of the backlash against judicial rights activism in the region involves the elite's growing interest in shaping the profile of these tribunals. Since judicial leadership was such a big part of the activation of young courts, the change in judicial profiles of these same tribunals decades later can have a big impact on their continued role. As the Colombian case indicates, if trends to shift the profile of the justices away from rights-friendly approaches continue, high courts in the future are likely to provide less leadership in realizing constitutional rights.

A second dimension of the backlash against judicial rights activism has been the activation of constituencies across the political spectrum, particularly social conservatives. The study of the Colombian experience indicates that once young courts become assertive, we can expect actors who oppose the courts' activism to become politically and socially energized and to seek to undermine or redirect it. We need more research on the politics of rights-based mobilization across the ideological spectrum—both on the newly mobilized groups who are reacting to leftist mobilization and also on the continued efforts of those who have a longer tradition of engaging courts. This is in line with that for which recent research on the politics of judicialization of rights in the United States also calls (Keck 2014). In choosing to "go social," assertive young courts in Latin America appealed to citizens and civil society organizations as part of a strategy to build legitimacy. Legal mobilization before courts became an important tool—along with political mobilization and sustained interest in the legislative avenue—on which (mostly) progressive rights advocacy groups could rely as part of a larger strategy for social and political change. Courts forged alliances with these organizations, creating constituencies that are invested in them. They also sparked other groups to organize and mobilize against their rulings. Political elites and very diverse groups of actors are now paying close attention. The struggle around the definition and enforcement of constitutional rights is far from over.

## Notes

Fieldwork was made possible with support from the SSRC International Dissertation Research Fellowship and a National Science Foundation DDRIG Grant. I am grateful to the editors, Juan Albarracín, Daniel Brinks, Laura Gamboa, Ezequiel Gonzalez Ocantos, and Rodrigo Nunes, for helpful feedback and to the Kellogg Institute for International Studies at the University of Notre Dame for support.

1. The six other countries to draft new charters were, Colombia (1991), Paraguay (1992), Peru (1993), Dominican Republic (1994), Ecuador (1998 and 2008), Venezuela (1999).

2. For an overview of the key arguments explaining judicial assertiveness and rights activism see Kapiszewski and Taylor 2008.

3. Author's interview with former clerk of the Argentine Supreme Court, Buenos Aires, March 3, 2013.

4. Author's interview with former justice of the Colombian Constitutional Court, Bogotá, August 14, 2012.

5. Author's interview with former justice of the Colombian Constitutional Court, Bogotá, August 15, 2012.

6. Author's interview with former justice of the Colombian Constitutional Court, Bogotá, August 21, 2012.

7. Author's interview with former justice of the Colombian Constitutional Court, Bogotá, July 24, 2012.

8. More limited judicial review used to be in the hands of the Supreme Court of Justice. After the 1991 reform, the SCJ is dedicated exclusively to criminal matters.

9. The ruling was C-221 1994. See: "Nueva fricción Gobierno-Corte," *El Tiempo*, May 24, 1994, http://www.eltiempo.com/archivo/documento/MAM-135406.

10. For a panorama of these early controversies and an excellent overview of Court-Executive relations in Colombia between 1994 and 2009, see Rubiano Galvis 2009. The next paragraphs rely on his account to identify key threats to reform the court.

11. "La dictadura de la corte," *Semana*, July 5, 1999; Rudolf Hommes, "Dictadura constitucional," *El Tiempo*, July 7, 1999.

12. Nine justices serve nonrenewable, nonstaggered, eight-year terms. Members of the court are elected by the Senate by a two-thirds majority from lists of candidates presented by the president, the Supreme Court of Justice, and the Council of State, each of whom nominates three candidates.

13. C-355/06, T-988/07, T-946/08, T-209/08, T-388/09, T-009/09, T-585/10, T-841/11, and T-627/12.

14. From the press release published by the Conferencia Episcopal de Colombia promoting the 2013 pro-life march: "Grupos pro vida convocan a la séptima versión de la Marcha por la Vida," April 29, 2013, on file with author.

15. Decree 444 of 2006 was challenged before the Council of State. In 2013, the Council initially suspended the decree and then nullified it.

16. One of the biggest private Catholic hospitals in Bogotá, San Ignacio Hospital, filed the lawsuit against the Circular 03 de 2013.

17. Justice Juan Carlos Henao, who had written a favorable decision, resigned in 2012 due to unforeseen circumstances, and the drafting of the decision had to be reassigned.

18. "Fundacion Marido y Mujer pide al papa intervenir en adopción gay," *El Colombiano*, January 26, 2015.

19. "Adoptar no es un derecho: Viviane Morales," *Semana*, February 17, 2015.

References

Abramovich, Victor E. 2005. "Courses of Action in Economics, Social and Cultural Rights: Instruments and Allies." *Sur International Journal on Human Rights* 2 (2): 180–206.

Albarracín, Mauricio. 2011. "Corte constitucional y movimientos sociales: El reconocimiento judicial de los derechos de las parejas del mismo sexo en Colombia." *Sur International Journal on Human Rights* 8 (14): 7–33.

Barreto Valderrama, Francisco. 2012. "La crisis del sistema UPAC como crisis social y su dimensión jurídica: Política, regulación y neoconstitucionalismo." In *Los actores en la crisis económica de fin de siglo*, edited by Miguel Urrutia and Jorge Llano, 101–62. Bogotá: Universidad de los Andes.

Bergallo, Paola. 2006. "Justicia y experimentalismo: La función remedial del poder judicial en el litigio de derecho público en Argentina." In *Derecho y Pobreza*, edited by Roberto Saba, 161–83. Buenos Aires: Seminario en Latinoamerica de Teoría Social y Democracia (SELA).

Botero, Sandra. 2015. "Courts That Matter: Judges, Litigants and the Politics of Rights Enforcement in Latin America." Ph.D. dissertation, University of Notre Dame, Indiana, United States.

Brinks, Daniel M., and Abby Blass. 2014. "Inclusion-exclusion: Designing judicial institutions in Latin America since 1975." Paper presented at the Latin American Studies Association International Conference, San Juan, Puerto Rico.

Brinks, Daniel M., and William Forbath. 2014. "The Role of Courts and Constitutions in the New Politics of Welfare in Latin America." In *Law and Development of Middle-Income Countries: Avoiding the Middle-Income Trap*, edited by R. P. Peerenboom and Tom Ginsburg, 221–45. New York: Cambridge University Press.

Carothers, Thomas. 2001. "The Many Agendas of Rule of Law Reform in Latin America." In *Rule of Law in Latin America: The International Promotion of Judicial Reform*, edited by Pilar Domingo and Rachel Sieder, 4–16. London: Institute of Latin American Studies.

Cepeda, Manuel José. 2005. "The Judicialization of Politics in Colombia: The Old and the New." In *The Judicialization of Politics in Latin America*, edited by Rachel Sieder, Line Schjolden, and Alan Angell, 67–103. New York: Palgrave Macmillan.

Cifuentes, Eduardo. 1995. "El constitucionalismo de la pobreza." *Direito* IV (2): 53–77.

Dalen, Annika. 2013. *La implementación de la despenalización parcial del aborto en Colombia*. Bogotá: Dejusticia.

Epp, Charles R. 1998. *The Rights Revolution: Lawyers, Activists, and Supreme Courts in Comparative Perspective*. Chicago, Ill.: University of Chicago Press.

Epstein, Lee, Jack Knight, and Olga Shvetsova. 2001. "The Role of Constitutional Courts in the Establishment and Maintenance of Democratic Systems of Government." *Law & Society Review* 35 (1): 117–64.

Ferraz, Octavio L. 2011. "Brazil: Health Inequalities, Rights, and Courts: The Social Impact of the 'Judicialization of Health.'" In *Litigating Health Rights: Can Courts Bring More Justice to Health?* edited by Alicia Ely Yamin and Siri Gloppen, 76–102. Cambridge, Mass.: Harvard University Press.

Gargarella, Roberto. 2015. "Deliberative Democracy, Dialogic Justice and the Promise of Social and Economic Rights." In *Social and Economic Rights in Theory and Practice: Critical Inquiries*, edited by Helena Alviar García, Karl E. Klare, and Lucy A. Williams, 105–20. New York: Routledge.

Gillman, Howard. 1999. "The Court as an Idea, Not a Building (or a Game): Interpretive Institutionalism and the Analysis of Supreme Court Decision-Making." In *Supreme Court Decision-Making: New Institutionalist Approaches*, edited by Cornell W. Clayton and Howard Gillman, 65–87. Chicago, Ill.: University of Chicago Press.

Gonzalez Ocantos, Ezequiel. 2012. "The Collapse of Impunity Regimes in Latin America: Legal Cultures, Strategic Litigation and Judicial Behavior." Ph.D. dissertation, University of Notre Dame, Indiana, United States.

Henao, Juan Carlos. 2011. "The Colombian Constitutional Court and Economic, Social and Cultural Rights." Paper presented at the conference Fairness, Justice and Human Rights: Realising Economic, Social and Cultural Rights, UK, November. http://just-fair.co.uk/hub/single/chief_justice_juan_carlos_henao_perez/.

Hilbink, Lisa. 2007. *Judges Beyond Politics in Democracy and Dictatorship: Lessons from Chile.* New York: Cambridge University Press.

Hirschl, Ran. 2004. *Towards Juristocracy: The Origins and Consequences of the New Constitutionalism.* Cambridge, Mass.: Harvard University Press.

Horowitz, Donald L. 1977. *The Courts and Social Policy.* Washington, D.C.: Brookings Institution.

Kapiszewski, Diana. 2012. *High Courts and Economic Governance in Argentina and Brazil.* Cambridge: Cambridge University Press.

Kapiszewski, Diana, and Matthew M. Taylor. 2008. "Doing Courts Justice? Studying Judicial Politics in Latin America." *Perspectives on Politics* 6 (4): 741–67.

Keck, Thomas M. 2009. "Beyond Backlash: Assessing the Impact of Judicial Decisions on LGBT Rights." *Law & Society Review* 43 (1): 151–86.

———. 2014. *Judicial Politics in Polarized Times.* Chicago, Ill.: University of Chicago Press.

Kennedy, Duncan. 2006. "Three Globalizations of Law and Legal Thought: 1850–2000." In *The New Law and Economic Development: A Critical Appraisal*, edited by David M. Trubek and Alvaro Santos, 19–73. Cambridge: Cambridge University Press.

Klarman, Michael J. 2004. *From Jim Crow to Civil Rights: The Supreme Court and the Struggle for Racial Equality.* New York: Oxford University Press.

Merlinsky, Maria Gabriela. 2009. "Atravesando el rio: La construcción social y política de la cuestión ambiental en Argentina." Ph.D. dissertation, Universidad de Buenos Aires / Paris 8.

Nunes, Rodrigo M. 2010. "Ideational Origins of Progressive Judicial Activism: The Colombian Constitutional Court and the Right to Health." *Latin American Politics and Society* 52 (3): 67–97.

Rodríguez Garavito, Cesar. 2011. "Toward a Sociolgy of the Global Rule of Law Field: Neoliberalism, Neoconstitutionalism, and the Contest over Judicial Reform in Latin America." In *Lawyers and the Rule of Law in an Era of Globalization*, edited by Yves Dezalay and Bryant G. Garth, 156–82. New York: Routledge.

———. 2012. "La judicialización de la salud: Síntomas, diagnósticos y prescripciones." In *La salud en Colombia: Logros, retos y recomendaciones*, edited by Oscar Bernal and Catalina Gutiérrez. Bogotá: Universidad de los Andes.

Rodríguez Garavito, Cesar, and Diana Rodríguez Franco. 2010. *Cortes y cambio social: Cómo la corte constitucional transformó el desplazamiento forzado en Colombia.* Bogotá: Dejusticia.

Rosenberg, Gerald N. 2008. *The Hollow Hope: Can Courts Bring About Social Change?* 2nd ed. American Politics and Political Economy. Chicago, Ill.: University of Chicago Press.

Rubiano Galvis, Sebastian. 2009. "La corte constitucional: Entre la independencia judicial y la captura política." In *Mayorías sin democracia: Desequilibrio de poderes y estado de derecho en Colombia, 2002–2009*, edited by Mauricio García Villegas and Javier Eduardo Revelo Rebolledo, 84–145. Bogotá: Dejusticia.

Sandoval Rojas, Nathalia. 2013. "La movilización social en tiempos de la constitución: Feministas, indígenas y víctimas de crímenes de estado ante la corte constitucional colombiana." *Colombia Internacional* 79:191–217.

Smulovitz, Catalina. 1995. "Constitución y poder judicial en la nueva democracia Argentina." In *La nueva matriz política argentina*, edited by Carlos Acuña, 71–114. Buenos Aires: Nueva Visión.

Uprimny, Rodrigo. 2003. "The Constitutional Court and Control of Presidential Extraordinary Powers in Colombia." *Democratization* 10 (4): 46–69.

———. 2011. "The Recent Transformation of Constitutional Law in Latin America: Trends and Challenges." *Texas Law Review* 89 (7): 1587–609.

Uprimny, Rodrigo, and Mauricio García Villegas. 2004. "Corte constitucional y emancipación social en Colombia." In *Emancipación social y violencia en Colombia*, edited by Boaventura de Sousa Santos and Mauricio García Villegas, 463–514. Bogotá: Norma.

Wilson, Bruce M. 2007. "Claiming Individual Rights Through a Constitutional Court: The Example of Gays in Costa Rica." *International Journal of Constitutional Law* 5 (2): 242–57.

———. 2009. "Institutional Reform and Rights Revolutions in Latin America: The Cases of Costa Rica and Colombia." *Journal of Politics in Latin America* 1 (2): 59–85.

Wilson, Bruce M., and Juan Carlos Rodríguez Cordero. 2006. "Legal Opportunity Structures and Social Movements: The Effects of Institutional Change on Costa Rican Politics." *Comparative Political Studies* 39 (3): 325–51.

Wilson, Bruce M., Juan Carlos Rodríguez Cordero, and Roger Handberg. 2004. "The Best Laid Schemes: Evidence from Costa Rica." *Journal of Latin American Studies* 36 (3): 507–31.

Woods, Patricia J., and Lisa Hilbink. 2009. "Comparative Sources of Judicial Empowerment: Ideas and Interests." *Political Research Quarterly* 62 (4): 745–52.

Yamin, Alicia Ely, Oscar Parra Vera, and Camila Giannella. 2011. "Colombia: Judicial Protection of the Right to Health: An Elusive Promise." In *Litigating Health Rights: Can Courts Bring More Justice to Health?*, edited by Alicia Ely Yamin and Siri Gloppen, 103–31. Cambridge, Mass.: Harvard University Press.

Appendix 1. Justices of the Colombian Constitutional Court

| Judge | Nominated by | Background | Background Aggregate | Term |
|---|---|---|---|---|
| Simon Rodriguez | Consejo de Estado | Consejo de Estado | Judiciary | (1992) |
| Jaime Sanin | Supreme Court | Supreme Court | Judiciary | (1992) |
| Ciro Angarita | President Gaviria | Academia | Academia | (1992) |
| José Gregorio Hernandez | Supreme Court | Supreme Court | Judiciary | (1992) |
| | | | | 1993–2001 |
| Fabio Morón | Supreme Court | Supreme Court | Judiciary | (1992) |
| | | | | 1993–2001 |
| Alejandro Martinez | President Gaviria | Academia and M-19 | Academia | (1992) |
| | | | | 1993–2001 |
| Eduardo Cifuentes | President Gaviria | Academia | Academia | (1992) |
| | | | | 1993–2000 |
| Hernando Herrera Vergara | President Gaviria | Academia and judiciary | Academia | 1993–99 |
| Jorge Arango Mejia | Supreme Court | Judiciary and politics | Outsider | 1993–98 |
| Carlos Gaviria | Consejo de Estado | Academia | Academia | 1993–2001 |
| Vladimiro Naranjo | Consejo de Estado | Academia | Academia | 1993–2000 |
| Antonio Barrera | Consejo de Estado | Judiciary and practicing lawyer | Judiciary | 1993–2000 |
| Manuel José Cepeda | President Pastrana | Academia | Academia | 2001–9 |

(Continued)

**Appendix 1. Continued**

| Judge | Nominated by | Background | Background Aggregate | Term |
|---|---|---|---|---|
| Alvaro Tafur | President Pastrana | Supreme Court | Judiciary | 1999–2007 |
| Marco Gerardo Monroy Cabra | President Pastrana | Supreme Court | Judiciary | 2001–9 |
| Alfredo Beltrán Sierra | Supreme Court | Supreme Court | Judiciary | 1998–2006 |
| Clara Inés Vargas | Supreme Court | Judiciary | Judiciary | 2001–9 |
| Jaime Cordoba Triviño | Supreme Court | Judiciary and politics | Judiciary | 2001–9 |
| Eduardo Montealegre | Consejo de Estado | Practicing lawyer (criminal law) and politics | Outsider | 2001–4 |
| Rodrigo Escobar Gil | Consejo de Estado | Private practice (administrative law) | Outsider | 2001–9 |
| Jaime Araujo Rentería | Consejo de Estado | Politics and judiciary | Outsider | 2001–9 |
| Maria Victoria Calle | President Uribe | Private practice (insurance) | Outsider | 2009–16 |
| Mauricio Gonzalez | President Uribe | Political profile | Outsider | 2008–15 |
| Jorge Pretelt | President Uribe | Political profile | Outsider | 2009–16 |
| Nilson Pinilla | Supreme Court | Supreme Court | Judiciary | 2006–14 |
| Jorge Iván Palacio | Supreme Court | Supreme Court | Judiciary | 2008–16 |
| Luis Ernesto Vargas | Supreme Court | Judiciary | Judiciary | 2008–16 |
| Humberto Sierra Porto | Consejo de Estado | Consejo de Estado | Judiciary | 2004–12 |
| Gabriel Eduardo Mendoza | Consejo de Estado | Consejo de Estado | Judiciary | 2008–16 |
| Juan Carlos Henao | Consejo de Estado | Consejo de Estado | Judiciary | 2008–12 |
| Luis Guillermo Guerrero | Consejo de Estado | Judiciary, Constitutional Court | Judiciary | 2012–20 |
| Alberto Rojas | Consejo de Estado | Political profile and private practice | Outsider | 2013–14 |
| Gloria Stella Ortiz | Consejo de Estado | Judiciary | Judiciary | 2012–20 |

Based on data presented in Nunes (2010) and Rubiano Galvis (2009), with author's additions.

# CHAPTER 11

# Experimenting with Participation and Deliberation in Latin America: Is Democracy Turning Pragmatic?

Thamy Pogrebinschi

## Introduction

The new democracies of Latin America that emerged with the third wave of democratization have now completed their transitions and reached an advanced stage of their consolidation processes, despite clientelism, corruption, populism, and the other alleged deficiencies taken as indicative of imperfect institutionalization and inadequate government performance (Diamond et al. 1999). According to the literature, Latin American governments' supposed inability to promote growth and development, reduce poverty and inequality, or control inflation and crime explains their successive failures and is symptomatic of poor state performance that has affected citizens' trust in political institutions and led to a crisis of representation in the region (Hagopian and Mainwaring 2005; Mainwaring 2006).

Although rises in levels of political satisfaction are expected to follow democratic consolidation, during the first two decades after the beginning of the third wave in Latin America, attitudinal indicators (a low level of political trust and a high level of dissatisfaction with democracy among citizens) and behavioral indicators (low electoral turnout, low party identification, and high electoral volatility) corroborated specialists' diagnoses of a widespread disenchantment with institutions of representative democracy, in particular political parties and legislatures (Mainwaring and Scully 1995; Hagopian 1998).

Democracy indices also led to critical assessments of the quality of democracy in Latin America. Even if the scholarship now agrees that transitions are complete and democracy is consolidated in almost all countries, disputes persist about how to adequately measure democracy in the region (Altman and Pérez-Liñán 2002; O'Donnell, Vargas Cullel, and Lazzetta 2004; Munck 2007; Levine and Molina 2011), as do diagnoses that only a few countries in the region have "met the challenge of governing both democratically and effectively" (Mainwaring and Scully 2009). Democracy in Latin America has been persistently defined as "pseudo" (Diamond, Linz, and Lipset 1999), "delegative" (O'Donnell 1993), or "defective" (Merkel 2004), among other deprecatory adjectives.

This critical assessment of democracy, emblematic of most of the scholarship on democratization in Latin America, has however already been deemed flawed for not taking into account the differences across the region and for being static (Hagopian 2005). Furthermore, efforts to evaluate democratic quality have been taken as insufficient to capture Latin America's cultural diversity and political identities (Van Cott 2008). In particular, forms of participation beyond elections, and political parties and spaces of deliberation beyond legislative bodies, escape analysis and are not taken into consideration by the traditional measurements of democracy and its quality.

In recent years it has become gradually acknowledged that participatory mechanisms and deliberative bodies are integral to Latin America's democratization process (Avritzer 2002). The speed with which participatory innovations are multiplied and institutionalized in several countries indicates an urge to incorporate them into existing measurements of democracy. A reassessment of redemocratization is imperative, taking account of the experimentation with participation and deliberation that increasingly characterizes democracy in the region.

In this chapter, I throw light on some positive cases of experimentation with participation and deliberation in Latin America. I argue that those experiments take place within the structure of representative democracy and do not compete with it; rather, participatory innovations would many times seek to correct some of the latter's purported deficiencies. I claim that in addition to strengthening the representative system, some participatory experiments aim at enhancing social equality, serving governments to promote inclusion and redistribution. These two main ends, fulfilled by the new means of participation, would indicate a pragmatic disposition of recent Latin American governments to experiment with politics, giving rise to what

I call a pragmatic turn of democracy. I conclude the chapter by asking whether, if such a turn is successfully taken, participatory innovations can eventually improve democracy in the region.

## From the Left Turn to a Pragmatic Turn

The expansion of experimentalist governments in Latin America may indicate that, in consolidating, a number of countries have taken a turn in their democratization processes. Such a turn, which can also be read as a detour from the path of consolidation expected by third-wave scholars, does not consist of hindering the stabilization of representative institutions. It also does not imply substituting them for alternative, participatory, or deliberative institutions. Rather, what I call the pragmatic turn of Latin America's democracy consists in the attempt to correct some of the alleged failures of representative institutions with participatory and deliberative innovations, and use the latter as a means to improve social equality.

Democracy's pragmatic turn shares some features in different countries: first, political experimentalism, defined as the combination of new participatory and deliberative practices with and within old representative institutions; second, institutional redesign, indicated by the creation of new deliberative bodies and participatory schemes, as well as the reconfiguration of representative institutions that accommodate them; and third, the interplay between political means and social ends, which leads governments to delegate authority and devolve power to new actors and institutions to achieve more inclusion and equality.

In assessing the context of the pragmatic turn, one can see how these three features have evolved mostly due to two overlapping conditions. The first condition is the so-called Left Turn, the series of electoral victories by left-leaning governments at both local and national levels throughout Latin America, starting in 1998. Second is the waves of constitution making, which comprise both the enactment of new constitutions and extensive constitutional reforms in numerous countries at various stages of their transition or consolidation processes. The first wave of constitution making, when constitutions were rewritten in most countries following their transitions to democracy, may have facilitated the Left Turn because many of the new constitutional documents opened the door to decentralization and to political parties to reenter the electoral arena. On the other hand, the most recent wave of constitution making, from 1999 onward—when some new constitutions were drafted or extensive constitutional reforms undertaken—can be seen as a product of the Left Turn.

The sequence of electoral victories following Hugo Chávez's 1998 victory in Venezuela led about two-thirds of Latin America's countries to be governed by left-leaning political parties. Parties with grassroots membership and close ties to labor unions and social organizations came to power, and former union and social movement leaders rose to presidential office. Although analysts agree that there is no single, homogeneous "left" (Panizza 2005; Castañeda 2006; Weyland 2009), its diversity seems to converge on at least three points: parties' programmatic objectives of reducing social inequality, their openness to civil society, and their willingness to experiment with politics.

The various newly elected local and national leftist governments have shown as much concern for participation and civil society as for equality and redistribution. Citizen participation has been enhanced through several innovative institutional designs, which have often been used to promote redistribution and improve equality. In several countries, participation and deliberation have been used to correct purported flaws of representative institutions and achieve social ends that the latter are deemed unable to accomplish alone.

As governments have expanded their redistributive role, they have engaged in an unprecedented policy experimentation that, as accurately put by Levitsky and Roberts (2011), has changed not only who governs in Latin America, but also how they govern. The Left seems to have developed a specific method of governing, which consists mainly in devising new political means to deliver social policies and public goods. New institutions have been designed within the state and in its interface with civil society, enabling more than simple dialogue between political and social actors.

Deliberative bodies involving the equal participation of representatives from government and civil society have acquired consultative or decisional power, in some cases making binding decisions. These bodies have expanded the scope of political representation, as well as its traditional spaces and actors, allowing citizens and civil society organizations' leaders to play representative roles and make representative claims. Even when not entitled to make binding decisions, these bodies sometimes achieve representativeness by allowing citizens and officials to sit together and deliberate on the design, implementation, and evaluation of public policy. Policy councils, conferences, workshops, commissions, and assemblies, composed of both government and nongovernment members at local and national levels, seem to be a recurrent innovation among Latin America's left-leaning parties, and they have been developed in political and social settings as diverse as Brazil, Bolivia, Chile, Ecuador, El Salvador, and Venezuela.

Concerned with the sustainability of these new institutional designs and aiming at turning participation into more than a programmatic party principle, several governments inscribed them in their countries' constitutions. Although most of the constitutions enacted or reformed during the transition in the 1980s and 1990s had already expanded the opportunities for participation in numerous countries, the new wave of constitution-making that started at the turn of the century had the clear scope of institutionalizing direct, participatory, and deliberative mechanisms. The method of using social participation as a means of reducing social and economic inequality has been, for example, inscribed in the new constitutions of Venezuela (1999), Ecuador (2008), and Bolivia (2009).

In Venezuela, participation has been expanded to "open forums and meetings of citizens whose decisions shall be binding among others" (Article 70). Communities and citizens are entitled to formulate investment proposals to be presented to municipal and state authorities, as well as to "participate in the execution, evaluation, and control of works projects, social programs, and public services within their jurisdiction" (Article 184.2). In Bolivia, the new constitution makes clear that the country has adopted a "participatory, representative, and communitarian form of democratic governance," which is "direct and participatory, by means of referendum, popular initiative, recall, assembly, native council, and prior consultation," besides still being "representative, by means of elections of representatives through universal suffrage and secret and direct voting" (Article 11). In Ecuador, participation is constitutionalized as a human right and a political principle, as "citizens, individually and collectively, shall participate as leading players in decision-making, planning and management of public affairs, and in the people's monitoring of state institutions and society and their representatives in an ongoing process of building citizen power." This right of participation "shall be exercised by means of mechanisms of representative, direct, and community democracy" (Article 95).

The appeal to constitution-making by the Latin American Left reflects the region's political experimentalism, combining the principles of representative, direct, participatory, and deliberative democracy, and creating new institutional designs to put them in practice. It also reflects a purpose to refound the political system, making room for an entirely new model of democracy intended to include traditionally unrepresented groups in decision-making and therewith extend to them access to social rights and public goods.

The intent of inaugurating a new pattern of democracy is not restricted to the Andes and does not rely solely on constitution making. The Brazilian Workers' Party (PT) started its third consecutive term of government in 2011 with President Dilma Rousseff declaring before the Congress the intention to continue "to adopt social participation as an important governmental tool for the design, implementation, and evaluation of public policies, assuring quality and feasibility to a project of development in the long term" (Brasil 2011). In 2013 the government enacted a national plan of participation, introducing a national system of participation connecting the hundreds of innovations created in Brazil in the previous years. Although this has faced resistance in the Congress, participatory mechanisms and bodies have become an integral part of decision-making.

Although citizen participation is not exclusive to the Left (neoliberal governments have fostered, especially over the 1990s, participation in the name of transparency and efficiency), using it as a tool, as a new means of making policy and delivering public goods, is something the Left turned into a method of governing, that of political experimentalism. Experiments such as the national dialogues in Bolivia, the national councils for equality in Ecuador, the local development committees in El Salvador, the national public policy conferences in Brazil, and the community councils in Venezuela aim, through different arrangements with and within representative institutions, at expanding the delivery of public services, increasing the distribution of public goods, and ensuring the enactment of social policies and rights, in addition to strengthening the voice of disadvantaged groups in the political process. Despite their varying degrees of success, those cases indicate a new form of government in which new participatory means are created to achieve inclusion and other desirable social ends. This new, experimental form of government is what I call pragmatic democracy.

To say that democracy in Latin America is turning pragmatic implies that it is engendering a new pattern of relations between state and civil society by changing the liberal institutions of representation. Such change takes place within the boundaries of representative democracy, by adapting its institutions to a nonliberal logic, a logic that assumes democracy has an intrinsic social meaning. Such a process of adaptation or adjustment, which

makes representative institutions combine with participatory and deliberative designs, and makes liberal institutions fit social ends, is the core of the
new, pragmatic democracies.

## Expanding the Means of Democracy

On the one hand, electoral volatility seems to remain high and electoral
turnout low in Latin America, making scholars worry that "citizens believe
that they are not well represented" (Mainwaring 2006, 15). On the other
hand, over two thousand cities on the continent as a whole had adopted a
form of participatory budgeting by 2007 (Goldfrank 2007), thirty-three
thousand community councils were active in Venezuela by late 2007 with
more than eight million citizens participating (Hawkins 2010), five thousand
health councils were reported to engage a hundred thousand people in 2004
in Brazil (Coelho 2004), and thirteen thousand community organizations
were enabled by the Law of Popular Participation in Bolivia to monitor local
spending and public works management by 2006 (Van Cott 2008). Altogether, these democratic innovations have mobilized millions of citizens on
the continent, and these are just a few examples. In Brazil alone, seven million people are reported to have participated in eighty-two national public
policy conferences between 2003 and 2011 (Pogrebinschi 2012). While the
number of Latin American citizens who vote in elections or identify with a
political party is decreasing, the number of participatory innovations and
the volume of citizens engaging in them seem to have increased extensively
and rapidly since 2000.

That representative democracy has limits is a fact even its most avid proponents admit. Przeworski (2010) acknowledges that among the main limits
of representative institutions is their incapacity to generate more social and
economic equality, as well as their inability to make political participation
more effective. It was the acknowledgment of the empirical limitations of
representative democracy to deliver the normative values on which it is
grounded that has led contemporary democratic theory to embrace participatory and deliberative accounts of democracy and advocate for a more comprehensive idea of representation, one that makes room for claims that cannot
be fulfilled by liberal representative institutions (Mansbridge 2003; Urbinati
2006). Latin America seems today to be the main laboratory where those
concepts and theories are being put to the test (Fung 2012; Pateman 2012).

Some Latin American governments since the Left Turn seem to have been aware of representative democracy's lack of means to achieve its purported ends. They have been creating more effective means of participation to generate more political and social equality. Citizens' opportunities to participate have been extended beyond elections, and democratic innovations allow citizens to deliberate and often even decide on how public services are managed, state resources allocated, and public goods distributed. That has been pursued with the intent not to undermine representation but rather to expand it to new bodies and actors. Despite the many participatory reforms, left-leaning governments have maintained all the basic institutions of representative democracy (Madrid, Hunter, and Weyland 2010, 141).

In Latin America as elsewhere, political disaffection leads to the intensification of citizens' demands. Widespread dissatisfaction with the democratic performance of representative institutions seems to have encouraged civil society organizations and political parties to align and jointly search for innovative ways of solving problems and have the desired policies delivered, especially at the local level. After decades of experience in the long struggle for democracy and against authoritarianism, civil society was ready to take a step further. Instead of participating against their governments, they would have the chance to participate with them, and somehow within them.

Along with civil society, governments design innovative institutions envisaging more effective means of participation. Beginning with participatory budgeting in Porto Alegre in Brazil in 1989, participatory innovations now include a wide range of local and national experiments that allow citizens to play a larger role in politics. Citizens have been gradually involved in the design, implementation, and monitoring of public policy. Citizens deliberate on policy preferences, set priorities together with government representatives, and manage resources, effectively taking part in decision-making.

A broad range of new institutional participatory designs has been put to work in Latin America in recent years: local and national policy councils, community councils, advisory councils, national policy conferences, municipal development councils, participatory urban planning, and a long list of less institutionalized practices, not to mention the hundreds of participatory budgeting initiatives that have spread all over the continent. The wide spectrum of activities performed by citizens and civil society organizations implies much more than mere social control. Citizens take part in drafting policies, have a role in the planning of their cities, decide on the allocation of municipal budgets, manage the delivery of public services, administer access to public goods, deliberate on governments' policy priorities, and make proposals and recommendations to policymakers, among other activities.

The degree of variation found among those forms of participation is very high. Not all participatory innovations involve deliberation. Not all of those that do involve deliberation result in decision-making; some consist simply of consultation. Not all decisions reached in participatory innovations that involve deliberation and decision-making are binding; some consist simply of policy recommendations. Some participatory innovations have reached the national level, but most of them take place only at a local level. Not all participatory innovations are initiated by the government, and not all of those initiated by civil society are supported by governments.

It is also important to note that not all participatory innovations are the product of left-leaning governments. The initial success of the participatory budgeting in 1989 seems to have persuaded center and right parties—as well as multilateral aid agencies such as the World Bank—that participatory innovations are useful to delivering efficient public services and providing better governance (Avritzer 2009; Hawkins 2010; Goldfrank 2011). Several new national participatory designs have been created and implemented by right-leaning parties, while many others are a product of left-leaning local governments in countries that had not taken the Left Turn. The ends of the new means of participation seem to adapt to the political context, with innovations aiming at social inclusion belonging more to the Left, while those aiming to correcting defects of the representative system through more accountability and responsiveness suit the Right's repertoire. All these are likewise facets of the pragmatic political experimentalism that has characterized democracy in Latin America since the beginning of the twenty-first century.

## Experimenting with Participation and Deliberation

Below I provide some examples of distinct institutional designs for participation and deliberation adopted in different Latin American countries. Some cases indicate how, by expanding democracy's means, innovations seek to correct some of representative democracy's limits by strengthening political participation to enhance government responsiveness and accountability. Other cases show how participatory innovations have been designed aiming at enhancing the redistribution of public goods and further including underrepresented and disadvantaged groups in the political process. What all

cases have in common is the experimentation of participatory and deliberative designs within the representative system, in many cases by adapting
liberal institutions to fit ends that are not exactly liberal.


## National Public Policy Conferences (Brazil)

In Brazil, the National Public Policy Conferences (NPPC), a national experiment promoted by the federal executive branch along with civil society, gather
together ordinary citizens, civil society organizations, private entrepreneurs,
public administrators, and elected representatives from all three levels of government to deliberate together and contribute suggestions to national policy in
several fields. Although NPPCs have existed longer, they are reported to have a
significant impact on policymaking and lawmaking, especially since the
Workers' Party took over the federal government in 2003. About 20 percent of
all legislative bills under discussion in the Brazilian federal legislature in 2009,
as well as 48 percent of all constitutional amendments enacted after the
country's redemocratization, have been deemed congruent with NPPC policy recommendations (Pogrebinschi and Santos 2011; Pogrebinschi 2012). In
particular, NPPCs have ensured the political and cultural inclusion of minority groups by promoting rights and developing corresponding policies to address matters of gender, race, ethnicity, and other cultural minority issues. The
number of national policies addressing minority and human rights increased
from 12 to 224 between 2003 and 2010, a growth of almost 2,000 percent. As a
result of the demands voiced in NPPCs, extensive national policy plans have
been enacted in this same period delivering specific policies to groups such as
women, the elderly, people with disabilities, and racial and ethic minorities
(Pogrebinschi 2012). On food and nutritional security, the NPPCs supported
the enactment of Brazil's first comprehensive policy in this area, the Food and
Nutritional Security National Plan (PLANSAN), which has been translated
into specific actions and programs impacting the lives of millions of Brazilians,
lifting them out of hunger and undernutrition (Pogrebinschi and Samuels 2014).


## Strategic Participatory Plan (El Salvador)

The municipality of Santa Tecla pioneered in El Salvador a highly developed
participatory system through several mechanisms, such as citizen assemblies

and citizen councils. One of the most relevant instruments deliberated to-gether by government and civil society has been a ten-year plan for local de-velopment, the so-called Strategic Participatory Plan (PEP). This initiative involved, in 2002–3, about 150 civil society representatives deliberating in 37 roundtables to elaborate the mission, vision, policies, and main projects to be developed in the municipality during the following decade (2002–12). Since 2000, Santa Tecla has been governed by the leftist Farabundo Martí National Liberation Front (Frente Farabundo Martí para la Liberación Na-cional; FMLN), and has kept its Mayor Oscar Órtiz in office for fourteen years. An evaluation of the PEP's implementation conducted in 2010 showed a high level of correspondence between the citizens' proposals and the de-veloped initiatives. Of 378 projects implemented, 63 percent were proposed by the participatory plan. The other 137 executed proposals resulted from the annual participatory budget process. Studies evidenced mixed results re-garding the impact of the participatory processes on the democratic govern-ability of Santa Tecla. Survey respondents underlined that participatory mechanisms contributed to a higher correspondence between government initiatives and the will of citizens, and also greater representation of citizens through participatory mechanisms, as in the case of a stronger perspective on gender equality (Alcaldía Municipal de Santa Tecla 2010). However, the survey also noted the lack of resources to attend the increase of citizens' demands over time, a delay in the development of accountability mecha-nisms, or the excessive control of the authorities over citizens' initiatives, which reduced the autonomy of citizen organizations (Alcaldía Municipal de Santa Tecla 2010). This shows how much adaptation is further required from representative institutions when they experiment with participation and deliberation.

## National Dialogues (Bolivia)

Since the late 1990s, the National Dialogues in Bolivia have served as a space for pacts and negotiations between the state and civil society organizations regarding the design and implementation of long-term public policies. The main purpose of the dialogues (1997, 2000, and 2004) was to develop a strat-egy to reduce poverty nationwide by employing funding from international donors. To have access to this financial aid, civil society organizations were required to be involved in formulating, implementing, and monitoring these policies. The idea behind this strategy was to increase the ownership of the policies by large parts of the population by fostering deliberation. Ultimately, the objectives were to increase popular satisfaction with the programs, the accountability of government performance, and the effectiveness of antipoverty policies. One of the most obvious achievements of the 1997 National Dialogue was the great participation of civil society organizations, with more than two thousand participants in three hundred municipalities involved in roundtables, conferences, and workshops to diagnose needs and propose initiatives (PNUD 2001). Participants managed to influence the final output, and some of the civil society organizations strengthened their capacities during the process (Molenaers and Renard 2003). Consensus was reached in many subjects and resulted in the creation of mechanisms of social control to increase monitoring of poverty reduction policies during implementation. The 2004 National Dialogue showed how the practice really made participation effective and became institutionalized, given that it engaged more than forty thousand organizations on policy deliberations at the local level. With the election of Evo Morales in 2005 turning Bolivia left, many participatory and deliberative designs created throughout the dialogues and during a period in which the Right was in power, have been effectively institutionalized, especially after the 2009 constitution turned Bolivia officially into a "participatory, representative, and communitarian democracy" (Article 11).

## Community Councils (Venezuela)

The community councils in Venezuela are part of a larger participatory system, designed by Hugo Chávez, that involves several initiatives designed to combat poverty and deliver social policies. Institutionalized by a law enacted by Venezuela's National Assembly in 2006, the community councils "permit the organized people to directly manage public policies and projects aimed at responding to the needs and aspirations of communities in the construction of equality and social justice" (Ley Orgánica de los Consejos Comunales, Article 2). Community councils can be formed by up to four hundred families, whose members share responsibilities in working committees concerned with several social and economic policies. Extraordinary revenues are transferred by the government to the community councils, which should then deliberate on needs and priorities, draft projects to address them, implement and monitor the desired measures, and manage the resources obtained. The autonomy and self-management model of community councils divides scholars, who offer a growing number of contested interpretations (Corrales and Penfold 2010; Hawkins 2010; McCarthy 2011; Smilde and Hellinger 2011). Despite pertinent criticisms, especially concerning community councils' political use and institutional design failures, comprehensive empirical studies assessing their impact on social equality are scarce. One must still investigate the actual role played by such councils, but one cannot disregard that while they were in full activity during Chávez's government, poverty decreased considerably and social spending increased significantly.

## Citizen Oversight Bodies (Colombia)

Since the 1990s hundreds of citizen oversight bodies have been created to monitor municipal governments under the recognition of Colombian Law 134 (1994). In 1995, in Bogotá alone four hundred participants were organized to monitor fifteen of the twenty districts, and in Cali around a thousand participants were involved in the Veedurías. These committees operationalize the regular monitoring of government performance by bringing together experts, civic and business leaders, lay citizens, and representative officials. In some cases, these experiences have evolved into permanent forums to discuss cities' strategic challenges by presenting academic studies, media analysis, and the evolution of quality of life indicators. As a result, administrations have more frequently used these forums as a space for their accountability before citizens and civil society organizations. The citizen oversight bodies are reported to have influenced the political agenda by introducing issues and problems from underrepresented communities (Velásquez 1998). Moreover, these new participatory institutions have become actual interlocutors between the state and unorganized citizens and have improved the means by which state institutions are held accountable by producing and communicating transparent information to citizens (El Ágora). In Colombia, pragmatic experimentations with participation within the representative system developed independently from a Left Turn in government, and it is interesting to notice how the new mechanisms designed for citizen participation are concerned less with redistributive policies or minority inclusion than they are with enhancing accountability and responsiveness.


## Neighborhood Improvement Community Program (Mexico)

The Neighborhood Improvement Community Program is a participatory policy program designed to fight the urban degradation of the most disadvantaged neighborhoods in Mexico City. The initiative was originated after the active work of social movements (especially the Urban Popular Movement), which appealed for a broader participation in housing and urban policies. The program aimed at improving housing conditions by increasing institutional interaction between government and society in strategic planning and management of resources. In short, promoters sought to create the conditions to make the city from the bottom up and provide a citizen-based perspective to urban projects. The program won an award for best practices in citizen participation from the International Observatory for Participatory Democracy, and an external evaluation showed successes after three years. Besides increasing community participation, one of the main achievements was creating links between social, civil, academic, and community organizations; neighborhood groups; and institutions of the government of Mexico City. These dynamics contributed to a stronger community appropriation and identification of the projects and evidenced an institutional effort to understand the importance of citizen participation (Inclusive Cities Observatory 2010).


## Indigenous Parties Innovations (Ecuador)

Evidence of the positive impact of participatory innovations on political parties and on the party system is found in Ecuador. Experiences of indigenous parties promoting institutional innovation in local government have helped mayors to establish personal bonds of loyalty and trust with voters. Implementing participatory and deliberative innovations, political parties based on indigenous movements achieved greater community control over elected authorities and greater transparency with respect to budgeting and spending (Van Cott 2008, 13–22). The institutional innovations implemented by Andean indigenous parties following their own cultural traditions includes regular, frequent, and open assemblies, where public spending preferences are freely exposed and jointly prioritized. Committees and working groups reuniting municipal government officials and representatives of civil society also take responsibility for decision-making and for overseeing and implementing policies. The participatory innovations have generated new sources of authority for weak local political institutions in the ethnically divided and politically unstable Andean countries (Van Cott 2008, 225).

### Community-Managed Schools Program (El Salvador)

In 1991 the Ministry of Education of El Salvador launched a program of community-managed schools in rural poor areas as a response to the urgent need for restoring basic school services after twelve years of civil war. The project, supported by the World Bank and other international organizations, delegated the management of preschools and primary schools to parents and community organizations, including NGOs. The government intended to build links among schools and communities, and new institutional channels to provide in a flexible and effective way school services and nutrition programs in underserved communities. The results were evidenced already in early stages. With financial support from the central government, communities managed to habilitate local infrastructure, where schools did not exist, and train and hire new teachers (Meza and Guzman 2004). By 1993 enrolment rates in rural areas had increased from 76 percent to 83 percent (World Bank 2003). The participation in the comanagement of resources not only effectively decentralized the education system but also empowered local communities. For example, parents under EDUCO schools were more involved in the education of their children and attended school meetings more frequently than in regular schools (Di Gropello 2006). There is also evidence of a growth in social capital in communities under this program by increasing parents' literacy and communication skills (Lindo 2000).

### Participatory Budget (Brazil)

Participatory budgeting is usually deemed by the literature as the most successful participatory innovation in Latin America precisely because of its demonstrated ability to generate greater equality through a more equitable redistribution of public goods, in addition to it having increased the participation of disadvantaged groups (in other words, the less-educated and lower-income citizens). Studies abound on participatory budgeting across Brazil and in numerous Latin American cities, although not all evidence supports an effective positive impact on social equality. Nevertheless, as Sousa Santos (1998, 484) has put it, "the redistributive efficacy of participatory budgeting has been fully confirmed"; the initial achievements of Porto Alegre—where between 1989 and 1996 participatory budgeting is considered to have doubled the number of children enrolled in schools and increased from 49 percent to 98 percent the number of households with access to water—would suffice to show that participatory budgeting is the "embryo of a redistributive democracy." Avritzer (2009), however, found that, depending on specific configurations of civil and political society, in some cities—such as São Paulo—the participatory budgeting displayed weaker distributive effects than in Porto Alegre and Belo Horizonte, where it benefited the cities as a whole. In all cases, the poor neighborhoods are those that have benefited the most, which confirms participatory budgeting's potential to favor the most disadvantaged and lowest-income citizens. This finding is also endorsed by Baiocchi (2003), who shows that the poor and uneducated are well represented in what he considers an efficient and redistributive decision-making procedure. Touchton and Wampler (2014) went a step further and have showed how participatory budgets are associated with increases in health care spending and decreases in infant mortality rates in Brazil's 253 largest cities.

Those many participatory and deliberative innovations vary in their impact and success. Even the most well-known and successful example, the participatory budget, varies enormously, has different results, and has achieved different degrees of success in the different cities and periods in which it has been implemented (Wampler 2007; Avritzer 2009; Peruzzotti 2009; Goldfrank 2011). Citizens also have different perceptions of the diverse participatory institutions in the various countries where they are implemented. As Gisela Zaremberg, Ernesto Isuna Vera, and Adrian Gurza Lavalle show in Chapter 12 of this volume, recent surveys in Mexico, for example, indicate that participatory institutions are actually irrelevant to citizens and provide only limited participation. In certain cases, a participatory institution may indeed not achieve the exact goal it was expected to, but it may still bring about positive impacts on democracy. In particular, those are cases in which, despite the level of success of the experiment itself or the number of citizens involved, the outcomes display the potential of participatory innovations to correct purported malfunctions of representative democracies or simply make representative institutions stronger.

But as the cases described above also show, political experimentalism embodies attempts to expand democracy's means so as to fulfill social ends. One important consequence of the Left Turn in Latin America has been to ascribe a clear social intent to democracy. But even before the successive election of left-leaning parties, democracy has been inscribed in post-transitional Latin American constitutions as aiming at social equality, which may have explained the design of certain participatory innovations in countries governed by the center-right. Brazil's 1988 constitution, for example, lists among the country's fundamental objectives that of "eradicating poverty and marginalization, and reducing social and regional inequalities" (Article 3, III). To restore order, consolidate representative institutions, and ensure civil and political rights was not enough. Democracy could not be achieved in Latin America without social justice.

Lack of social justice implies lack of citizenship—a critical component of Latin America's democratization, if not one of its main obstacles, if one endorses a more robust definition of democratization, such as the one advocated by Guillermo O'Donnell. As he once put it, "various forms of discrimination and extensive poverty and their correlate, extreme disparity in the distribution of (not only economic) resources, go hand in hand with low-intensity citizenship" (O'Donnell 1993, 72). O'Donnell knew that the brown areas of the new democracies could not be addressed simply with liberal rights. Several constitutional assemblies were also aware of this and have protected in their new constitutions social, economic, and, more recently, cultural rights, besides the classical civil and political rights. The search for social equality in Latin America is not simply a search for increased income and redistribution; it is also a search for political inclusion.

Along with the constitutionalization of social, economic, and cultural rights came the perception that, to make them more than fine words on a piece of paper, it was necessary to involve civil society in their attainment. With the extensive decentralization undergone by most of the continent, the delivery of basic social goods in several countries has been devolved to the municipalities, where new participatory institutions have begun to engage state and civil society actors in realizing rights. Empowering citizens and letting them play a role in resolving their own problems proved a valid method to further develop citizenship, and an effective means of implementing social policies on a local basis. Institutional innovations have been purposely designed to achieve political participation and social inclusion, two things that can barely be separated in Latin America.

It is still too early to evaluate whether the new means of democracy in Latin America contribute to achieving democracy's purported social end. It is very difficult to measure the redistributive impact of specific participatory innovations in the short term. The correlation between widespread political experimentalism and improving political and social indicators in the region must be properly investigated. Although several explanations concur, scholars must take seriously the interplay between participatory innovations and delivery of social policies to find out whether there is any causality in the fact that several improvements in political and social indices in Latin America have taken place while governments experimented with different combinations of representation, participation, and deliberation. In any event, while shedding light on the experimentation with new political means and ends, the notion of pragmatic democracy can at least offer a valid new analytical perspective from which to study Latin America's recent political history.

## Toward a New, Nonliberal Model of Democracy?

The "democracies with adjectives" (Collier and Levitsky 1997) that emerged in the third wave of democratization are being progressively displaced. The "delegative," "defective," or "pseudo" democracies of Latin America may gradually be giving way to pragmatic democracy, a new, experimental form of governance that combines representation, participation, and deliberation, enhancing accountability and responsiveness or achieving social ends. Whether this form of governance will prove sustainable and outlive the left-leaning governments that are associated with it, only the future will show.

The depth of institutional reforms undertaken in Latin America since 2000 is to a great extent the product of parties and presidents. As the latter with one hand have granted disadvantaged groups social and economic rights in unprecedented ways, while with the other awarding the executive branch considerable power, critics are quick to label those governments as populist. Some scholars believe the main challenge to be faced is the compatibility of new institutional designs for participation with strong presidential systems (Gargarella 2008 and in Chapter 9 of this volume; Cameron and Sharpe 2010). It is indeed an open question whether a strong executive branch encourages or discourages popular participation in the long term.

Pragmatic democracy is not a single and uniform phenomenon. That it is a specific form of governance does not imply that it evolves in the same way in different countries—or even within the same country in different times. The degree of decentralization, the role of political parties, social movements, and ethnic groups, among other possible conditions, might explain why each country relies more or less on one of the new democratic means. In all cases what one can see, however, is experimentation with those means, and a combination of political means and social ends that takes place with or within the institutions of representative democracy.

Furthermore, Latin America is a very heterogeneous continent. The interpretation offered in this chapter does not ignore the critical differences that separate South and Central America, for example, and does not dismiss the distinct historical, political, economic, social, and cultural narratives of each country. Pragmatic democracy also adapts to those differences, as well as benefiting from existing similarities, such as the Left Turn and the wave of constitution making that has taken place in most of Latin America's new democracies. The overwhelming inequality on the continent is also a crucial factor that might favor the adoption of new democratic means of government. After more than two decades expecting that the consolidation of liberal institutions of representation would not only restore democracy but also eradicate inequality, new means had to be sought.

Indeed, the increasing institutionalization of participatory and deliberative innovations within institutions of representative democracy seems to indicate that, three decades after the purported beginning of the third wave, Latin America may never conform to the liberal model of democracy. As I hope to have shown in this chapter, Latin America has taken a turn in its democratization, and the role of participatory and deliberative innovations can no longer be neglected in assessments of the performance of representative institutions and of the quality of democracy. The numerous democratic experimentations also need to be considered in public opinion surveys conducted in Latin American countries as a first step in future evaluations of how they really impact levels of political trust and satisfaction with democracy.

The intensification of political experimentalism raises important questions about assessments of the quality of democracy. The known measures and indices neither capture the institutional changes in Latin America, with the increasing adoption of participatory innovations, nor recognize that new forms of democracy can still be forged and that some democracies do not follow the liberal paradigm. New criteria are necessary to account for the democratic experimentation in Latin America and to evaluate it in accordance with its own principles and values in the context of its own process of democratization, not according to standards developed in other contexts and other times.

The use of measurements based on the procedural mechanisms of liberal democracy to evaluate Latin America is increasingly contested, as is the view that liberal democracy is a universal aspiration (Van Cott 2008; Buxton 2011). As López Maya and Lander (2011, 63) assert with regard to Venezuela, democracy is understood "not only as the enjoyment of civil liberties and the exercise of political rights but also, in a very emphatic way, as social justice and social equality." To dismiss Latin America's political experimentalism "is to deny plurality in democratic forms and also the legitimacy of endogenous democratic models" (Buxton 2011).

Only a proper appraisal of Latin America's experimentation with participation and deliberation and its interfaces with representative institutions may explain why the latter have supposedly constantly failed. Maybe, rather than persist in error, they work through a different logic, one that seeks to adapt liberal institutions to different means and ends. Scholarship on democratization in Latin America must be expanded to encompass new possibilities, such as the pragmatic turn described here. If the liberal paradigm is put to one side, and if the validity of this new, experimental model of democracy is recognized, Latin America might provide new and more creative recipes to make democracy fit less liberal times.

## References

Alcaldía Municipal de Santa Tecla. 2010. Plan estratégico participativo 2012–22.

Altman, D., and A. Pérez-Liñán. 2002. "Assessing the Quality of Democracy: Freedom, Competitiveness, and Participation in 18 Latin American Countries." *Democratization* 9 (2): 85–100.

Avritzer, L. 2002. *Democracy and the Public Space in Latin America*. Princeton, N.J.: Princeton University Press.

———. 2009. *Participatory Institutions in Democratic Brazil*. Baltimore, Md.: John Hopkins University Press.

Baiocchi G. 2003. *Radicals in Power: The Workers' Party and Experiments in Urban Democracy in Brazil*. London: Zed Books.

Buxton, J. 2011. "Foreword: Venezuela's Bolivarian Democracy." In Smilde and Hellinger, *Venezuela's Bolivarian Democracy*, xi.

Cameron, M. A., and K. E. Sharpe. 2010. "Andean Left Turns: Constituent Power and Constitution-Making." In *Latin America's Left Turns: Politics, Policies and Trajectories of Change*, edited by Maxwell A. Cameron and Eric Hershberg, 61–80. Boulder, Colo.: Lynne Rienner.

Castañeda, J. 2006. "Latin America's Left Turn." *Foreign Affairs*, May/June. https://www.foreignaffairs.com/articles/south-america/2006-05-01/latin-americas-left-turn.

Coelho, V. S. R. P. 2004. "Conselhos de saúde enquanto instituições políticas: O que está faltando?" In *Participação e Deliberação*, edited by Vera Schattan P. Coelho and Marcos Nobre, 255–69. São Paulo: 34 Letras.

Collier, D., and S. Levitsky. 1997. "Democracy with Adjectives: Conceptual Innovation in Comparative Research." *World Politics* 49 (3): 430–51.

Corrales, J., and M. Penfold. 2010. *Dragon in the Tropics: Hugo Chavez and the Political Economy of Revolution in Venezuela*. Washington, D.C.: Brookings Institution Press.

Diamond, L., J. J. Linz, and S. M. Lipset. 1999. *Democracy in Developing Countries: Latin America*. Boulder, Colo.: Lynne Rienner.

Di Gropello, E. 2006. "A Comparative Analysis of School-based Management in Central America." World Bank Working Paper No. 72. Washington, D.C.: World Bank.

El Ágora. n.d. "Del monitoreo de la gestión pública a la participación ciudadana: Dos modelos existentes en América Latina." El Agora. www.nuestracordoba.org.ar/sites/default/files/Estudio_Comparado_El_Agora.pdf.

Falleti, Tulia. 2010. *Decentralization and Subnational Politics in Latin America*. Cambridge: Cambridge University Press.

Fung, A. 2011. "Reinventing Democracy in Latin America." *Perspectives on Politics* 9 (4): 857–71.

Gargarella, R. 2008. "Cambiar la letra, cambiar el mundo." *Ecuador Debate* 75:93–95.

Goldfrank, B. 2011. *Deepening Local Democracy in Latin America: Participation, Decentralization and the Left*. University Park: Penn State University Press.

Hagopian, F. 1998. "Negotiating Economic Transitions in Liberalizing Polities: Political Representation and Economic Reform in Latin America." Working Paper No. 98-5 prepared for the Weatherhead Center for International Affairs, Harvard University.

———. 2005. "Conclusions: Government Performance, Political Representation, and Public Perceptions of Contemporary Democracy in Latin America." In *The Third Wave of Democratization in Latin America: Advances and Setbacks*, edited by F. Hagopian and S. Mainwaring, 319–62. Cambridge: Cambridge University Press.

Hagopian, F. and S. P. Mainwaring, eds. 2005. *The Third Wave of Democratization in Latin America: Advances and Setbacks*. Cambridge: Cambridge University Press.

Hawkins, K. A. 2010. *Venezuela's Chavismo and Populism in Comparative Perspective*. Cambridge: Cambridge University Press.

Inclusive Cities Observatory. 2010. "Social Inclusion and Participatory Democracy Report: From the Conceptual Discussion to Local Action." Barcelona: Universitat Autonoma de Barcelona.

Lindo, H. 2000. "Participación y comunidad en las escuelas EDUCO en El Salvador." Washington, D.C.: World Bank.

Levine, D. H. and J. E. Molina, eds. 2011. *The Quality of Democracy in Latin America.* Boulder, Colo.: Lynne Rienner.

Levitsky, S. and K. Roberts, eds. 2011. *The Resurgence of the Latin American Left.* Baltimore, Md.: Johns Hopkins University Press.

López Maya, M., and L. Lander. "Participatory Democracy in Venezuela: Origins, Ideas, and Implementation." In Smilde and Hellinger, *Venezuela's Bolivarian Democracy*, 58–79.

Madrid, R., W. Hunter, and K. Weyland, eds. 2010. *Leftist Governments in Latin America: Successes and Shortcomings.* Cambridge: Cambridge University Press.

Mainwaring, S. 2006. "The Crisis of Representation in the Andes." *Journal of Democracy* 17 (3): 13–27.

Mainwaring, S. and T. R. Scully, eds. 1995. *Building Democratic Institutions: Party Systems in Latin America.* Stanford, Calif.: Stanford University Press.

———. 2009. *Democratic Governance in Latin America.* Stanford, Calif.: Stanford University Press.

Mansbridge, J. 2003. "Rethinking Representation." *American Political Science Review* 97 (4): 515–28.

McCarthy, M. 2012. "The Possibilities and Limits of Politicized Participation: Community Councils, Coproduction and Poder Popular in Chávez's Venezuela." In *New Institutions for Participatory Democracy in Latin America*, edited by M. Cameron, E. Hershberg, and K. Sharp, 123–47. New York: Palgrave Macmillan.

Merkel, W. 2004. "Embedded and Defective Democracies." In "Consolidated or Defective Democracy?: Problems of Regime Change," edited by A. Croissant and W. Merkel, special issue, *Democratization* 11 (5): 33–58.

Meza, D. and J. Guzman. 2004. "EDUCO: A Community-managed Education Program in Rural Areas of El Salvador (1992–2003)." Paper prepared for the 2004 Shanghai Conference on Scaling-Up Poverty Reduction.

Molenaers, N. and R. Renard. 2003. "The World Bank, Participation and PRSP: The Bolivian Case Revisited." *European Journal of Development Research* 15 (2): 133–61.

Munck, G. L., ed. 2007. *Regimes and Democracy in Latin America: Theories and Methods.* Oxford: Oxford University Press.

O'Donnell, G. 1993. "Estado, democratización y ciudadanía." *Nueva Sociedad* 128:62–87.

O'Donnell, G., J. Vargas Cullell, and O. Iazzetta. 2004. *The Qualitf of Democracy: Theory and Applications.* Notre Dame, Ind.: University of Notre Dame Press.

Panizza, F. 2005. "Unarmed Utopia Revisited: The Resurgence of Left-of-Centre Politics in Latin America." *Political Studies* 53 (4): 716–34.

Pateman, C. 2012. "Participatory Democracy Revisited." *Perspectives on Politics* 10 (1): 7–19.

Peruzzotti, E. 2009. "The Politics of Institutional Innovation: The Implementation of Participatory Budgeting in the City of Buenos Aires." In *Participatory Innovation and Representative Democracy in Latin America*, edited by A. Selee and E. Peruzzotti, 40–61. Baltimore, Md.: Johns Hopkins University Press.

PNUD. 2001. Informe de diálogo nacional 2000.

Pogrebinschi, T. 2012. "Participation as Representation: Democratic Policymaking in Brazil." In *New Institutions for Participatory Democracy in Latin America: Voice and Consequence*, edited by M. Cameron, E. Hershberg, and K. Sharpe, 53–74. New York: Palgrave Macmillan.

Pogrebinschi, T. and D. Samuels. 2014. "The Impact of Participatory Democracy: Evidence from Brazil's National Public Policy Conferences." *Comparative Politics* 46 (3): 313–32.

Pogrebinschi, T., and F. Santos. 2011. "Participação como representação: O impacto das conferências nacionais de políticas públicas no Congresso Nacional." *Dados* 54 (3): 259–305.

Przeworski, Adam. 2010. *Democracy and the Limits of Self-government.* New York: Cambridge University Press.

Selee, A. D. 2009. "An Alternative to Clientelism? Participatory Innovation in Mexico." In *Participatory Innovation and Representative Democracy in Latin America*, edited by A. Selee and E. Peruzzotti. Baltimore, Md.: Johns Hopkins University Press.

Smilde, D. and D. Hellinger. 2011. *Venezuela's Bolivarian Democracy: Participation, Politics, and Culture Under Chávez.* Durham, N.C.: Duke University Press.

Sousa Santos, B. 1998. "Participatory Budgeting in Porto Alegre: Toward a Redistributive Democracy." *Politics & Society* 26:461–510.

Touchton, M., and B. Wampler. 2014. "Improving Social Well-Being Through New Democratic Institutions." *Comparative Political Studies* l47 (10): 1442–69.

Urbinati, N. 2006. *Representative Democracy: Principles and Genealogy.* Chicago: University of Chicago Press.

Van Cott, D. L. 2008. *Radical Democracy in the Andes.* Cambridge: Cambridge University Press.

Velásquez, F. 1998. "La veeduría ciudadana en Colombia: En busca de nuevas relaciones entre el estado y la sociedad civil." In *Lo publico no estatal en la reforma del estado*, edited by L. C. Bresser Pereira and N. Cunill Grau, 257–90. Buenos Aires: Paidos.

Wampler, B. 2007. *Participatory Budgeting in Brazil: Contestation, Cooperation, and Accountability.* University Park: Penn State University Press.

Weyland, K. 2009. "The Rise of Latin America's Two Lefts: Insights from Rentier State Theory." *Comparative Politics* 41 (2): 145–64.

World Bank. 2003. "Case Study 3: El Salvador: Participation in Macroeconomic Policymaking and Reform." Social Development Note No. 79, March 2003. Washington, D.C.: World Bank.

# CHAPTER 12

# The *Gattopardo* Era: Innovation and Representation in Mexico in Post-Neoliberal Times

Gisela Zaremberg, Ernesto Isunza Vera, and Adrian Gurza Lavalle

## Introduction

Over the last decades (1980s–2010s), the classic channels of representation in old and post-transition democracies, centered on political parties and labor unions, have been deeply transformed. The structural features of twentieth-century industrial societies have changed, among them the welfare state, mass democracy, the structure of labor markets, and the modes of production that accompany these political projects (Collier and Handlin 2009). Along with them, drastic changes have occurred in the social cleavages that supported labor unions and mass-based parties (Manin 1997; Novaro 2000; Gurza Lavalle and Araujo 2008).

In this context, two new trends have developed. First, innovative democratic institutions (IDIs) have multiplied in Latin America and the world, driving an expansion of representation (Smith 2009). Concepts such as deliberative and participative democracy, radical citizenship, and postliberal democracy have converged, at times contradictorily, in an attempt to understand processes aimed at the democratization of democracy (Santos de Sousa 2002).

The study field accounted for the existence of social-state interfaces (councils, committees, conferences, and so forth) as mechanisms of collective participation different from direct individual consultation in the form of referendums or assemblies. In this sense, the concept of participation itself has been redefined from the point of view of nonelectoral societal control (Gurza Lavalle and Isunza Vera 2010). In order to understand these phenomena the majority of studies have centered on these mechanisms (councils, committees, conferences, and so forth), with an emphasis on case studies.[1]

Second, analytical approaches have been refreshed in order to examine the new types of relations that exist between the urban popular classes, political parties, and unions. Based on research conducted in urban settings, these studies have suggested that there is a process of change in the organization of the popular classes. If in the past that relationship was based on a significant connection between labor unions and political parties (UP-Hub), today they are based on the preeminence of urban popular class associations (A-Nets) (Collier and Handlin 2009).

For Mexico, a country that has been characterized by a slow democratic transition with resistant authoritarian elements, a more detailed analysis of these new trends needs to be carried out. To what degree have the recently established IDIs influenced the expansion of representation channels? Can we agree with the studies that speak about the replacement of the UP-Hub by A-Nets in the Mexican case? Is it possible to talk about democratic innovation in a country in which we can hardly talk about the consolidation of electoral representation institutions?

In this chapter we examine from a different perspective the degree to which representation has expanded—that is, by shifting the focus of our observation from (case studies on) councils and committees to (survey on) citizens. For this purpose, based on the results of a recent survey, we use privileged information on contacts' networks that serve as intermediaries to help access citizens' rights. This is a survey statistically representative nationally and regionally for ten states, in which eleven thousand questionnaires were completed by Mexican men and women over the age of eighteen.[2] Based on this work, the main objective of this chapter is to identify which new and old elements, as well as mixed configurations, are present in the paths of intermediation, to which citizens turn to access rights. We argue that, at the individual level, the new interface institutions (the councils, committees, and so forth) seem irrelevant to the citizens, which would be in accordance with various research results that point to a democratization from above and limited participation in the Mexican case (Isunza Vera and Hevia 2012; Isunza Vera and Mendoza Moctezuma 2013).[3]

We suggest that, in *Gattopardo* style, the old ways change only to reappear with new garments. In other words, political parties, even though they have been reformed, and even though they are widely mistrusted by the population, appear to be key elements when people look for intermediation. We note, also, that although the labor unions seem to be ignored by survey participants, no new associations have taken their place. We also argue that the responses of survey participants indicate that association members are more likely to participate in nonelectoral activities (protests, taking over public buildings, and so forth) but less likely to have contacts for intermediation. In general, we maintain that the important legislative work around the creation of tools for democratic innovation in Mexico has been implemented weakly. It is the political parties, an element of the old system of representation, that have readapted to the new times.

We begin by presenting the conceptual and methodological tools on which the chapter is based. We then present the Mexican case in recent Latin American historical context, before analyzing the relevance of IDIs in the individual survey and examining the "old elements," especially the relevance of parties in the area of intermediation at the individual level. We end by evaluating our findings, with an emphasis on some of the implications that the Mexican case could have for a comparative study of the region.

## A Brief Conceptual and Methodological Framework

The concept of intermediation is fundamental for understanding the expansion of the level of representation. In Gurza Lavalle and Zaremberg (2014), we proposed that throughout a good part of the twentieth century the literature developed conceptual double reductionism between legitimate political intermediation and political representation, on the one hand, and between the latter and the notion of representative government on the other.

This resulted in a reduction of representation theories, centered exclusively on the electoral sphere (Castiglione and Warren 2006; Gurza Lavalle, Houtzager, and Castello 2006; Gurza Lavalle and Isunza Vera 2010). However, the world of representation was always wider and more diverse than that of electoral representation, although the latter has become the modality par excellence in representative government. The most notable exception in the twentieth century was functional representation via unions, whether in societal or state corporatist modalities (Schmitter 1992). Such reduction of the concept of representation restricted the development of theories of political, nonelectoral representation, prompting a persistent association between nonelectoral intermediation and informal modalities of mediation, often, and not surprisingly, with negative connotations. Clientelism is a term that better condenses those negative characteristics (Auyero 2002). Instead, we consider that the practices of intermediation go beyond simple reference to clientelism.

We thus proceed from two assumptions: first, we do not consider that electoral representation exhausts all possible forms of representation and, second, we maintain that not everything surrounding electoral representation, even in its informal modalities, should be attributed to clientelism. In this context, a language centered on the concept of broad intermediation increases the possibility of understanding the diversity of representation paths that exist from the actors' perspective (Long 2007). Based on the etymological meanings of the term intermediation, we define it as "being a way to" (a vehicle or a source) and, at the same time, "to be in the middle of" (being in between, in the exact measure). Intermediation refers to an activity that requires the capacity to measure with precision and, at the same time, to be the means for the creation of something new.

In this chapter, this definition relates to the measurement of contacts that act as intermediation links to access and guarantee rights (INE 2014). With this in mind, we begin by noting that relational capital is usually understood more in the sense of horizontal ties than of vertical ones (Smith 2013, 1). The former allude to relations between individuals in symmetrical positions in a community; the latter, to ties between citizens and persons in asymmetrical positions, as representatives of different areas, which are essential to access rights. At the individual level, we talk about intermediation when we refer to the various contacts mentioned by citizens as a way to access goods and services associated with rights.

The measurement of ties draws on relational data. The Encuesta de Calidad Ciudadana (Citizenship Quality Survey), conducted by the National Electoral Institute (INE) in 2013, included a special section of questions denominated "name generators," which asked the eleven thousand people surveyed if they knew any persons or "contacts" who could help them in different areas associated with rights. With each name generator, up to three nicknames or initials were obtained, and then the respondents were asked to specify different characteristics of each person they had mentioned.[4]

## *Gattopardo* in Mexico

The last decades of the twentieth century and the first decade of the twenty-first century witnessed important processes of change in Latin America. On the one hand, during the 1980s and 1990s most of the countries in the region underwent a democratic transition. On the other hand, in the context of economic constraints, they adopted reforms that deeply modified the limits between market and state. This had a profound negative impact on inequality indicators, as well as resulting in a sharp decline in the quality of attainable rights for wide sectors of the population. As a reaction to the negative effects of these structural reforms, in the first decade of this century voters in various countries elected presidents who, with varying degrees of radicalism, are on the Left.[5] Mexico stands out by not following this trend. The literature on democratic transitions finds it difficult to classify the Mexican case, especially because regime changes in this country were not the result of sociopolitical or economic collapses caused by either internal or external factors. Neither does the Mexican case fit into the category of transitions produced by elite pacts.[6]

In general, authors concur in defining the Mexican case as a prolonged transition (Einsestand and Loaeza 2004; Labastida and López Leyva 2004), referring to a process of gradual change, trench-warfare style, between groups in power and opposition parties so that changes are produced by marching and countermarching (Schedler 2001). This type of process occurred repeatedly over a long period, which some say lasted from the 1960s to 2000.

Therefore, after a seventy-year rule, it was only in 2000 that the Partido Revolucionario Institucional (Institutional Revolutionary Party, PRI) lost the presidency in a competitive election to the Partido Acción Nacional (National Action Party, PAN). After the PAN had held the presidency for twelve years, during which time democratic conditions and human security issues rapidly deteriorated in the country (Buscaglia 2012a; 2012b; Espinoza Valle and Monsiváis Carrillo 2012), in 2012 the PRI won the presidential election and returned as the ruling party.

With the PRI's return to power, several institutions, which were fundamental during that prolonged transition, were modified again. In this new context of reactions and countermarches the already fragile Mexican democratic institutions are rapidly becoming weaker.[7] A new pact between the three main Mexican political parties, the PRI, the PAN and the Partido de la Revolución Democrática (Party of the Democratic Revolution, PRD), has led to reforms that tend to reinforce guarantees for the political elite. While it cannot be said that a hegemonic party system was reinstalled, it is possible to argue that these oligopolistic agreements between the main political parties have led to a deterioration in the quality of the democratic contest.

Mexico is also unusual in the socioeconomic changes that it has experienced since the 1980s. The 1980s were known as Latin America's lost decade, with annual average growth only slightly higher than 1 percent and public finances weighed down by foreign debt. Toward the beginning of the 1990s, under pressure because of the debt they owed international financial institutions, Latin American countries accepted the conditions codified in the Washington Consensus and implemented far-reaching reforms that followed the principles of privatization, decentralization, and focalizing goods and public services, thus redefining the borders between the public and private spheres. Mexico was not alien to this process. However, in contrast to other Latin American countries, which implemented radical reforms (fast-paced and far-reaching), Mexico is usually classified as a cautious reformer, meaning reforms were partial and implemented gradually (Stallings and Peres 2000). Especially during the presidency of Carlos Salinas de Gortari (1988–94), goods and services (such as telecommunications) were privatized, and property rights (such as those prohibiting the sale of communal, or *ejidos'*, farm land) were liberalized. In addition, the rate of informal labor increased and wages deteriorated, further weakening labor unions, which had been the main source of support and loyalty to the PRI since the 1940s (Bensusán 2009; Temkin 2009). These reform processes continued slowly during the conservative PAN's period in government. Throughout both of PAN's six-year terms, the PRI exerted pressure in opposition to stop the reforms. Paradoxically, the same PRI, upon reoccupying the president's office, pushed to advance those same reforms, beginning with the new law regarding the oil industry.[8]

So while the rest of countries in the region, after decades of structural reforms, are moving toward a phase that has come to be known as post-neoliberal, in Mexico this process has developed according to a different logic and timing. We could say that following a fragile democratic situation, Mexico faces a new onslaught by monopolistic economic sectors, which have found a willing ear in a political leadership ready to further liberalize economic aspects of the market and delimit the state's role.

In this context, a series of important legislative reforms have taken place in Mexico, reforms that are in favor of IDIs. Among the most important and ambitious in the 1980s was the creation of Democratic Planning Councils (Consejos de Planeación Democrática), which, according to the law, were to be implemented in all the states and municipalities (COPLADE and COP-LADEMUN, respectively). These councils were part of the National System of Democratic Planning inaugurated in 1982 during the presidency of Miguel de la Madrid (1982–88). The formal intended function was to promote decentralization at the municipal level, which turned into a highly reactive process, including many marches and countermarches, as it was the object of dispute between federal, state, and municipal governments, which eroded considerably the councils' possibilities of effective implementation.

As we stated in Zaremberg et al. (2015), the reactive processes against political, administrative, and fiscal decentralization, along with the gradual democratization process described previously, constitute the contextual variables that are important to explain the existing gap between legislation and implementation of IDIs in Mexico.

Under the government of Carlos Salinas de Gortari (1988–94) various consultative councils on sectoral policies were created, among which the School Councils of Social Participation (Consejos Escolares de Participación Social-CEPS), deriving from the General Education Law (Ministry of Public Education—SEP 2011), and the Consultative Councils for Sustainable Development (SEMARNAT 2011) stand out. These were part of the efforts to gradually increase participation of voices within a political system that showed growing signs of deep fractures.[9]

It is important to mention that during Salinas's six-year term, the largest participatory project centered around the construction of Solidarity Committees (Comités de Solidaridad), generally headed by women residing in highly marginal regions, which were part of the National Solidarity Program (Programa Nacional Solidaridad) under the Ministry of Social Development (SEDESOL) and which, as shown by different studies, aimed at supporting the construction of a new party base for the PRI (Cornelius, Craig, and Fox 1994; Ziccardi 2004). This required that efforts concentrate on recentralizing those party bases in direct relation with the president and setting aside the old corporative structures of intermediation that supported the old PRI, which appeared to be a threat to the plan for economic and social liberalization, through which Salinas aimed to transform the country and the party that had ruled it by that time for sixty years.

After the first democratic alternation that occurred in the 2000 elections, everything looked ready for a new drive toward expanding electoral and nonelectoral institutions. At that time, new legislative and administrative reforms were adopted for the creation and regulation of IDIs, which, as will be shown in the next section, faced major obstacles. This resulted in an eroded and weakened implementation of IDIs vis-à-vis the normative ideals expressed in the reforms that created them.

In this context, an analysis of the new, old, and mixed configurations regarding the broadening of representation in Mexico must consider this situation of gradual changes and persistent elements of the old system.

## A Look at the New: Institutions of Participation at the Individual and Organizational Level

In 2000 the possibility of a PRI comeback seemed remote. When this party left the executive office after seventy years in power, it looked like a point of no return. In this context, civil society organizations acquired a certain importance (Olvera 2003).[10] It was expected that during Vicente Fox's presidency (2000–2006), there would be a drive for the development of a new relationship with civil society.

Although there were some accomplishments, the general picture was mixed. According to Hevia (2012) and Isunza Vera and Hevia (2012), during Fox's six-year term several systems established by previous legislation were preserved, including the aforementioned COPLADE and COPLADEMUN in all states and municipalities, as well as political consultative councils in areas such as education, social participation, and sustainable development.

The first PAN government formalized and refined the rules and regulations regarding these councils and created others in various policy areas, including gender equality, sustainable rural development, and strengthening civil society organizations.[11] The Sustainable Rural Development Law (Ley de Desarrollo Rural Sustentable) came into effect, indicating the construction of social-state interphases at the municipal level in the form of Municipal Councils for Sustainable Rural Development (Consejos Municipales de Desarrollo Rural Sustentable; CMDRS), whose implementation ended up being considerably different from the intended norm (Caire Martinez 2011).

The transformation of Solidarity Committees, which were part of the Ministry of Social Development during the Salinas government, deserves a special note. As mentioned in various studies, these bodies had been designed to support the creation of a new grassroots base for the PRI (Cornelius, Craig, and Fox 1994; Ziccardi 2004).

Thus, it is understandable that this structure was dismantled and replaced by another, which enabled mostly an individual type of relations between the state and poor populations who received cash transfers from the Programa Oportunidades (Opportunities Program), also dependent on the Ministry of Social Development.[12] As a whole, it can be said that during this period the prevalent attitude toward civil society was elitist and associated with an idea of individual citizen participation, or with the Third Sector concept, whose mission was conceived as a support for social entrepreneurial projects and as the outsourcing agent targeted to carry out programs initiated by the government.

For the following six-year term, after the most hard-fought elections in Mexico's recent history (2006), the new president from the PAN, Felipe Calderón, began his mandate with a serious legitimacy deficit. Shortly after taking office he declared a war against drug trafficking, which triggered a security and humanitarian crisis that continues to this day (Escalante 2011). In 2008 an economic crisis ensued, worsened by Mexico's commercial dependence on the United States. Within this climate of crisis, the Calderón government also pushed to create democratic innovation mechanisms, mostly at the discourse level. One of the main strategies of the Plan Nacional de Desarrollo 2007–12 (National Development Plan) was to establish citizens' participation councils in various areas of federal policy.

In 2008, after compiling and analyzing 253 federal laws, 131 operational rules, the list of transparency obligations of the Instituto Federal de Acceso a la Información (Federal Institute of Access to Information; IFAI), and secondary sources, Hevia, Vergara-Lope, and Ávila Landa (2011) found a total of 227 collegial institutions. This is no small number of IDIs in Mexico, considering their presence in norms or regulations at the federal level. With these findings in mind, the question is: To what degree are these new bodies "real" in the framework of efforts to broaden the scope of representation channels from the point of view of citizens?

An initial examination does not leave much room for optimism. In the INE Survey (INE 2014) there is practically no mention of these new institutions. The only significant allusion refers to the Asociaciones de Padres de Familia (Parents' Associations; APF). A relatively high percentage of Mexicans (19 percent) described themselves as either current or past active participants in associations at their children's schools. This is a high percentage if we take into account that the highest degree of participation (21 percent, according to INE 2014) is in religious organizations. However, parents' associations are not new. As mentioned before, according to Zurita Rivera (2011) they are part of the normative tools contained in the Ley General de Educación (General Education Law) approved in 1993, based on the 1992 Acuerdo Nacional para la Modernización de la Educación Básica (National Agreement for the Modernization of Basic Education; ANMEB) approved during Carlos Salinas de Gortari's presidency. This law also established Consejos Escolares de Participación Social (School Councils of Social Participation; CEPS).[13] Zurita Rivera (2011) also points out that the expansion of APF and CEPS is due to the fact that they are a prerequisite to receive other government funding. In addition, she found that their actual functions are limited.

These data are consistent with evidence provided by other researchers who note that the implementation of a substantial part of IDIs in Mexico has not evolved toward a significant increase in citizen representation. While the obligation to establish councils as a prerequisite to receive or implement other programs is not necessarily reproachable, the evidence tends to show serious difficulties in extending these practices toward broader citizen involvement or increased government openness in pursuit of planning and accountability (Caire Martinez 2011; Caldera Ortega 2013).[14] As to the aforementioned CMDRS, Caire Martinez (2011) shows that they ended up functioning as mechanisms for selection of microprojects called for by federal funds for rural municipal development. This is due to the express requirement by those programs to include CMDRS. Thus this task is imposed reluctantly on municipal leaders, the majority of whom control it informally. In practice, the CMDRS function more in an administrative protocol manner, far from the normative ideal that conceived them as an essential component of rural development planning.

Something similar happens with the COPLADEMUN. These municipal planning councils are barely mentioned by surveyed citizens, especially in light of the fact that they were conceived precisely in the spirit of bringing local government closer to citizens. Formally, the objective of these councils is to be an auxiliary organ in formulating, updating, enabling, and evaluating municipal administration plans. However, in practice the reality could not be more different. The composition of councils is usually controlled by the municipal president (who, at the same time, usually has influence over the local city council). In general, the role of council members is merely formal, attending meetings to sign the minutes as a prerequisite for the approval of budgets or resources (provided mostly by the federal government) needed to carry out projects.[15]

The weakness of the IDIs in the eyes of citizens is consistent with the evidence that arises in the current research. On the basis of thirty-nine institutions defined as Nonelectoral Democratic Controls, Isunza Vera and Mendoza Moctezuma (2013) point out that two out of three institutions have been created by the state and that the vast majority (seven out of ten) play a consultative role, which concurs with a model of delimited participation in the context of democratization from above (Isunza Vera and Mendoza Moctezuma 2013, 470).

Furthermore, a new study, which identified 139 IDIs in 22 municipalities and states, confirms these images (Isunza Vera 2015). At first analytical glance, it shows that the majority of institutional mechanisms are designed only as nonbinding, consultative (47 percent), or overseeing (23 percent) bodies, which does not mean, however, that they have the potential for democratic control, as their design does not allow for effective implementation of sanctions. Second, the majority of IDIs (54 percent) are composed of people invited by public officials and are not elected by the public. Third, there is a huge concentration of territorial areas of influence: 70 percent are national, meaning they work in a centralized manner around the Federal Public Administration's policy, program, or project. Last, these results are consistent with the findings of an exploratory survey carried out simultaneously in twelve municipalities concurrently with the individual survey sponsored by the INE. For lack of space we are unable to expound on these complementary results here, but out of a total of 419 contacts mentioned by the organizations, only 3 referred to an existing municipal IDI.[16]

The main findings mentioned in this section generate a new question to lead us to the next section: If the IDIs seem to be irrelevant, to what degree could new actors replace the old actors in the context of intermediation in Mexico?

## Examining the Old: The Role of Political Parties as Intermediaries for Access to Citizens' Rights

It is worth exploring the degree to which old main actors (UP-Hub) are still relevant at the level of intermediation, or whether the new organizations' networks (A-Nets) are today's main actors. In this respect, the results of the survey are conclusive. Political parties, in spite of being among the organizations that arouse the highest level of mistrust (more than 80 percent), are the key element to increase the probability of having contacts of intermediation to obtain goods and services related to rights.

Using a multinomial logistic regression model we tested three sets of theoretical-causal factors in order to understand the effect on the dependent variable constructed as the degree of relational capital for intermediation and measured at three levels for the first three name generators: no contacts, one contact, and two or more contacts.

The first causal set includes structural variables such as gender, educational level, and income; the second set, variables related to factors that we call political-instrumental. These refer to party membership, participation in electoral campaigns, and knowing someone who received money or gifts in return for his/her vote. A third set includes variables related to what we call cooperative altruism (in other words, trust in others and participation in volunteer organizations).

Our hypothesis was that the third set of factors, which are closer to the characteristics of an organizational network (A-Nets), would have the highest probability of increasing the individual's relational capital. However, this was not the case. The results show that all variables associated with party and electoral participation are consistently the more relevant factors. For reasons of space, we focus here mainly on this result, while briefly mentioning the variables related to the structural and cooperative altruist sets.

Thus when a person states s/he is currently an active member of or has belonged to a political party in the past the probability of not having any relation is notably reduced by 14 percentage points (see Table 12.1).

At the same time, those who collaborated in activities prior to and during electoral campaigns have a higher probability of having intermediation contacts for access to rights. When compared to someone who doesn't participate in electoral campaigns, the probability of not having any contact is reduced by 17 percentage points—the probability of having one contact

Table 12.1. Probability of Having an Intermediation Contact by Party Membership

| Party member | Probability of intermediation contacts | |
|---|---|---|
| No contacts | −0.14 | ** |
| One contact | 0.06 | ** |
| Two or more contacts | 0.08 | ** |

Source: Self-elaboration based on INE 2014. Probability calculated with Clarify.
**95% trust level.

Table 12.2. Probability of Having Intermediation Contacts
According to Collaboration in Electoral Campaigns

| Participation in political party activities | Probability of intermediation contacts | |
|---|---|---|
| No contacts | −0.17 | ** |
| One contact | 0.07 | ** |
| Two or more contacts | 0.10 | ** |

Source: Self-elaboration based on INE 2014. Probability calculated with Clarify.
**95% trust level.

Table 12.3. Probability of Having Intermediation Contacts
According to "Knowing Someone Who Receives Money or
Gifts in Return for Vote"

| Knows someone | Probability of intermediation contacts | |
|---|---|---|
| No contact | −0.09 | ** |
| One contact | 0.03 | ** |
| Two or more contacts | 0.06 | ** |

Source: Self-elaboration based on INE 2014. Probability calculated with Clarify.
**95% trust level.

increases by 7 percentage points, and by 10 points of having two or more (see Table 12.2). This tells us that collaboration in electoral campaigns is a key factor for increasing the probability of having relational capital for access to rights. In the case of "knowing someone who receives money or gifts in return for his/her vote," the probability of not having any contact is reduced by almost 9 percentage points. In addition, the probability of having one contact increases by 3 percentage points, and the probability of having two or more increases by 6 percentage points (see Table 12.3). Having established that party membership and participation in electoral activities are important for increasing the probability of having intermediation contacts, we can ask ourselves which party is the most convenient to belong to in terms of having such relations. Probability effects show that the probability of remaining isolated is lower when the party affiliation is the *Partido Revolucionario Institucional (PRI)*—4 percentage points lower when compared with no party membership, with a trust level of 95%.

In contrast with the relevance of all variables associated with the political-instrumental set, in the second causal set income level is the second most important variable. The probability of not having any relations is lower for people with a higher income. That is, they are less likely to be isolated. The highest income level reduces the probability of not having any contacts by 12 percentage points compared with the lowest income level. It also increases the probability of having one contact by 10 percentage points, and of having two or more contacts by 3 percentage points. In conclusion, people with a higher income have a higher probability of having contacts.

Examining the behavior of the variables related to party and electoral participation in people with low and high income in terms of the probability of having contacts, we discovered that not being close to a party environment has more severe consequences for low-income citizens in terms of the relational capital available for intermediation. In other words, when both high-income and low-income people are not party members, or have not participated in electoral campaigns, the probability of being isolated is higher for those with lower income.

Lastly, the findings regarding the set of *cooperative-altruist* factors were surprising. Being involved in an association increases the probability of having two or more contacts by 5 percentage points compared with noninvolvement. In comparison, the effect of belonging to a political party in terms of the probability of having intermediation contacts is much higher than that of membership in an association. Additionally, the results show that trust increases, albeit slightly, the probability of having intermediation contacts. When someone goes from trust to mistrust, the probability of being isolated increases by only 3 percentage points.

## Conclusion

The work carried out until now shows results that might seem strange to those accustomed to associating legislative reforms with real change. On the one hand, the Mexican case exhibits a profuse creation of society–state interface institutions, in the context of what has come to be known, in Latin America and the world, as democratic innovation. However, when analyzing the relevance of these mechanisms in terms of intermediation to concretely guarantee citizens' rights, neither the individuals nor the organizations report that they have achieved a significant relevance. There are only a few exceptions in this scenario, but they fail to meet the expectations of building a stronger democracy that arose at the time of the shift of power in the 2000 elections. On the other hand, the replacement of UP-Hubs by A-Nets, which was praised as a new form of interest intermediation for the popular classes in Mexico, does not resonate in an articulate way either.

While the evidence shows that political parties have disengaged from labor unions, those parties were not replaced by civil associations and they still increase the probability of having intermediation contacts. This is doubtless the most important change reflected in this study. Political parties are connecting directly to the citizens in the territories and are leaving out union ties as the most relevant pattern to obtain electoral adhesion. Parties no longer go through labor unions in pursuit of a loyal grassroots (as was the case during the hegemonic rule of the PRI in the 1950s); they do so, rather, through local contacts. As a result, civil organizations emerge as withdrawn, not engaged in individual citizens' intermediation but, at the same time, participating in nonelectoral activities, such as demonstrations, marches, taking over public facilities, and so forth.

In summary, this chapter shows that reforms in Mexico related to democratic innovation are still far from significant. Although it would be an exaggeration to say that nothing has changed (especially because we can see changes in the Mexican party system and in the new oligopolistic pacts), it would not be far from the truth to assert that, as in the play *Il Gattopardo*, much has changed but, structurally, nothing has changed too much.

## Notes

The *Gattopardo* (in English, *The Leopard*) is an Italian novel that tells the history of the Prince of Salina, a noble aristocrat who tries to preserve his family and class amid the tumultuous social upheavals of 1860s Sicily. A well-known quote from the novel is "If we want everything to remain the same, we need to change everything." This novel became a symbol of the capacity to change politics on the surface without changing the structure.

1. See, for instance, Chapter 14 of this volume.

2. This research also includes a survey conducted among organizations in a "snowball format" in four states, within which three municipalities were selected (a total of 12), which measured intermediation from the viewpoint of the organizations. Due to lack of space we cannot detail the results here. This study, at the organizational level, can be seen in INE 2014.

3. See INE 2014. In Zaremberg et al. 2015 we explain that, regarding Mexico, this is a result of an erosive sequence that pushed legislation regarding IDIs farther away from effective implementation. This is also due to the intersection of this sequence with two processes: a) a gradual democratization centered on electoral alternation, which resulted in an oligopolitization of the party system, and b) a reactive decentralization filled with marches and countermarches. In these processes, the actors had incentives to avoid innovating and expanding representation through IDIs.

4. See INE 2014, Chapter 6, Annex.

5. Venezuela (1999), Argentina (2003), Brazil (2003), Uruguay (2005), Bolivia (2006), and Ecuador (2007).

6. See O'Donnell and Schmitter 1986; Linz 1990.

7. We refer here especially to the reform of the *Instituto Federal Electoral* (Federal Electoral Institute, IFE), which became the INE, through which some powers were taken from the states and centralized at the national level; the reform that allows the reelection of congress members, senators, and municipal presidents; and various reforms that created numerous entities with autonomy, but with a doubtful capability for implementation.

8. This law needs the support of other laws. A debate is going on these days around the proposed New Law of National Waters, which, from some perspectives, seems likely to favor the advance of private fracking initiatives.

9. In 1988 a highly questionable presidential election took place, as the left wing presidential candidate of the PRD was ahead on the vote count until the computer system "crashed" and the PRI candidate was declared the winner. Various authors point at this event as the defining moment of the beginning of a democratic transition centered on the development and installation of more trustworthy electoral institutions. This process proved effective, but was questioned again in 2006.

10. That same year, the *Ejército de Liberación Nacional* (National Liberation Army, EZLN) triumphantly arrived in Mexico City and the Congress was discussing bills arising from the San Andres Agreement.

11. Such as the Technical Consultative Councils mandated by the Federal Law of Encouragement of Civil Society Organizations, advisory and social councils within the National Women's Institute, the Program of Social Conversion in the National Institute for Social Development (See Hevia 2012).

12. This program also established consultative, participatory, and comptroller's functions in the form of councils and committees. However, they carry significantly less weight than those held by Solidarity Councils.

13. The APF are essentially bodies that represent schoolchildren's parents vis-à-vis the authorities regarding various educational interests (Article 67, Ministry of Public Education, 1993). In contrast, the CEPS have "an inherent democratic vocation that enables society's intervention in actions aimed at strengthening and increasing the quality and range of education (Article 69, Ministry of Public Education, 1993)." Zurita 2011, 142.

14. Some policy areas show relatively more substantive progress in this scenario, such as the councils related to environmental policies put forth by SEMARNAT (Ministry of Environment) and those related to gender equality (Hevia 2012; Zaremberg 2012).

15. See Zaremberg 2012.

16. See INE 2014.

## References

Auyero, Javier. 2002. "Clientelismo politico en Argentina: Doble vida y negación colectiva." *Perfiles Latinoamericanos* 20:33–52.

Bensusán, Graciela. 2009. "Estándares laborales y calidad de los empleos en América Latina." *Perfiles Latinoamericanos* 17 (34): 13–49.

Buscaglia, Edgardo. 2012a. "Cooperación internacional: ¿Seguridad humana o pax mafiosa?" *Variopinto*, November.

———. 2012b. "Seguridad humana: La transición hacia una democracia con estado de derecho." *Variopinto*, December.

Caire Martinez, Georgina. 2011. "Descentralización participativa en ausencia de recursos: Los consejos municipales de desarrollo rural sustentable." Mexican Rural Development Research Report No. 18, Woodrow Wilson International Center for Scholars, Mexico.

Caldera Ortega, Alex. 2013. "Redes de política y diseño de estrategias para superar la crisis del agua: Los casos de los acuíferos del Valle de León, Guanajuato, y del Valle de Aguascalientes (México)." *Agua y Territorio* 2:56–66.

Castiglione, Dario and Mark Warren. 2006. "Rethinking Democratic Representation: Eight Theoretical Issues Prepared for Delivery to 'Rethinking Democratic Representation.'" Centre for the Study of Democratic Institutions, University of British Columbia, May 18–19.

Collier, Ruth Berins and Samuel Handlin. 2009. *Reorganizing Popular Politics Participation and the New Interest Regime in Latin America*. University Park: Penn State University Press.

Escalante, Fernando. 2011. "Homicidios 2008–2009: La muerte tiene permiso." *Nexos* 397:36–49.

Espinoza Valle, Víctor Alejandro, and Alejandro Monsiváis Carrillo. 2012. *El deterioro de la democracia: Consideraciones sobre el régimen político, lo público y la ciudadanía en México*. Tijuana: El Colegio de la Frontera Norte.

Gurza Lavalle, Adrián, and Cicero Araujo. 2008. "O debate sobre a representacaon politica no Brasil: Nota introdutoria." *Caderno CRH* 21 (52): 9–12.

Gurza Lavalle, Adrián, and Ernesto Isunza Vera. 2010. "Precisiones conceptuales para el debate contemporáneo sobre la innovación democrática." In *La innovación democrática en América Latina: Tramas y nudos de la representación, la partici-*

*pación y el control social,* edited by Ernesto Isunza Vera and Adrian Gurza Lavalle. México City: CIESAS/Universidad Veracruzana.

Gurza Lavalle, Adrián, and Gisela Zaremberg. 2014. "Más allá de la representación y del clientelismo: Hacia un lenguaje de la intermediación política." *Revista Mexicana de Ciencias Políticas y Sociales* 59 (221): 19–50.

Hevia, Felipe. 2012. "¿Cuándo y por qué funcionan los consejos consultivos? Patrones asociativos, voluntad política y diseño institucional en órganos colegiados de participación del poder ejecutivo federal mexicano." In *Redes y jerarquías: Representación, participación y gobernanza local en América Latina,* edited by Gisela Zaremberg, 124–46. Mexico City: Facultad Latinoamericana de Ciencias Sociales.

Hevia, Felipe, Samana Vergara-Lope, and Homero Ávila Landa. 2011. "Participación ciudadana en México: Consejos consultivos e instancias públicas de deliberación en el gobierno federal." *Perfiles Latinoamericanos* 38:65–88.

INE (Instituto Nacional Electoral). 2014. *Informe país sobre la calidad de la ciudadana en México.* Mexico City: Instituto Nacional Electoral.

Isunza Vera, Ernesto. 2015. "Mapeo de mecanismos de participación ciudadana en la administración pública federal de México." Working paper from the project "Hacia la construcción de los lineamientos para el impulso, la confirmación, la organización y el funcionamiento de los mecanismos de participación ciudadana de la Administración Pública Federal de México." Programa de las Naciones Unidas para el Desarrollo (PNUD), Mexico.

Isunza Vera, Ernesto, and Felipe Hevia. 2012. "Participación acotada: Consejos consultivos e incidencia en políticas públicas en el ámbito federal mexicano." In *Nuevas institucionaes de democracia participativa en América Latina: La voz y sus consecuencias,* edited by Maxwell Cameron, Eric Hershberg, and Ken E. Sharpe, 105–35. Mexico City: Facultad Latinoamericana de Ciencias Sociales.

Isunza Vera, Ernesto, and Vicente Mendoza Moctezuma. 2013. "México." In *Controles Democráticos no electorales y régimen de rendición de cuentas: En búsqueda de respuestas comparativas: México, Colombia, Brasil, China y Sudáfrica,* edited by Ernesto Isunza Vera, 459–523. Mexico City: Centro de Contraloría Social y Estudios de la Construcción Democrática.

Labastida, Julio Martín Del Campo, and Miguel Armando Leyva López. 2004. "México: Una transición prolongada (1988–1996/97)." *Revista Mexicana de Sociología* 66 (4): 749–806.

Linz, Juan J. 1990. "Transiciones a la democracia." *Revista Española de Investigaciones Sociológicas* 51:7–33.

Long, Norman. 2007. *Sociología del desarrollo: Una perspectiva centrada en el actor.* Mexico City: CIESAS/El Colegio de San Luis Potosí.

Manin, Bernard. 1997. *The Principles of Representative Government.* Cambridge: Cambridge University Press.

Novaro, Marcos. 2000. *Representación y liderazgo en las democracias contemporáneas.* Rosario: Homo Sapiens.

O'Donnell, Guillermo, and Philippe Schmitter. 1986. *Transitions from Authoritarian Rule: Tentative Conclusions About Uncertain Democracies*. Baltimore, Md.: Johns Hopkins University Press.

Olvera, Alberto. 2003. *Sociedad civil, esfera pública y democratización en América Latina*. Mexico City: Fondo de Cultura Económica.

Santos De Sousa, Boaventura, ed. 2002. *Democratizar la democracia: Los caminos de la democracia participativa*. Rio de Janeiro: Civilizacao Brasilera.

Schedler, Andreas. 2001. "Measuring Democratic Consolidation." *Studies in Comparative International Development* 36 (1): 66–92.

Schmitter, Phillipe. 1992. "Corporativismo (Corporatism)." In *Relaciones corporativas en un período de transición*, edited by Matilde Luna and Ricardo Pozas, 203–28. Mexico City: Instituto de Investigaciones Sociales.

Smith, Amy Erica. 2013. "Conexiones políticas en las Américas." *Perspectivas desde el barómetro de las Américas* 98. Nashville: Vanderbilt University Press, LAPOP.

Smith, Graham. 2009. *Democratic Innovations: Designing Institutions for Citizen Participation*. New York: Cambridge University Press.

Stallings, Bárbara, and Wilson Peres. 2000. *Growth, Employment, and Equity: The Impact of the Economic Reforms in Latin America*. Washington, D.C.: Brookings Institution Press.

Temkin, Benjamin. 2009. *Informal Self-Employment in Developing Countries: Entrepreneurship or Survivalist Strategy? Some Implications for Public Policy, Analyses of Social Issues and Public Policy* 9 (1): 135–56.

Zaremberg, Gisela. 2012. "Fuerza, proyecto, palabra y pueblo: Circuitos de representación en consejos de desarrollo municipal en América Latina (Nicaragua, Venezuela, México y Brasil)." In *Redes y jerarquías: Participación, representación y gobernanza local en América Latina*, vol. 1. Mexico City: Facultad Latinoamericana de Ciencias Sociales.

Zaremberg Gisela, Adrian Gurza, Ernesto Isunza, and Marcello Fragnano. 2015. "¿Control democrático o democratización del control? Innovación democrática en Brasil y México en perspectiva histórica comparada." Lecture given at the GT08, "Controles democráticos e participação política: Atores, instituições, dinâmicas e resultados," 39th annual meeting of ANPOS, Caxambú, Minas Gerais, Brazil, October 26–30, 2015.

Ziccardi, Alicia. 2004. *Participación ciudadana y políticas sociales del ámbito local*. UNAM-Instituto de Investigaciones Sociales/Instituto Nacional de Desarrollo Social/Consejo Mexicano de Ciencias Sociales.

Zurita Rivera, Úrsula. 2011 "Los desafíos del derecho a la educación en México: A propósito de la participación social y la violencia escolar." *Revista Mexicana de Investigación Educativa* 16 (48): 131–58.

# PART IV

## Race, Decolonization, and Violence

# Anti-imperial, But Not Decolonial? Vasconcelos on Race and Latin American Identity

Juliet Hooker

## Introduction

The Mexican philosopher José Vasconcelos (1882–1959) is known for having produced one of the most famous formulations of *mestizaje*, which is perhaps the dominant strand in Latin American thinking about race. Along with Brazilian Gilberto Freyre's notion of racial democracy, Vasconcelos articulated the core tenets of what has been described as Latin America's distinctive approach to race.[1] The key premises of Latin American theories of *mestizaje* are: (1) that Latin American national and regional identity are defined by long-standing and widespread practices of (cultural and biological) racial mixing; (2) that the principal result of a process of mixing that began in the colonial era was a national population that is homogeneous in its mixed-ness, to the point that the various groups that contributed to the mixing process (predominantly Spaniards and Indians, and to a less-acknowledged extent Africans) have disappeared as separate racial groups per se; and (3) that as a result of a racial system that blurs the boundaries between races and that did not include legally encoded racial segregation, the region has avoided the problems of racial stratification and discrimination that have plagued other countries, especially the United States. All of these tenets, which defined official state discourses and intellectual debates in the

region for much of the twentieth century, have been contested and critiqued by black and indigenous intellectuals in the region since their formulation. As scholars of racial politics in the region have shown, Latin
American racial systems were characterized by extralegal forms of racial discrimination that produced racially hierarchical societies with differential
access to citizenship, wealth, and so forth.[2] At the same time, as other
scholars have argued, national ideologies of racial inclusion narrowed elite
choices and made certain forms of outright exclusion untenable in Latin
America (de la Fuente 2001). Narratives of Latin American racial harmony
grounded in *mestizaje* such as that propounded by Vasconcelos have thus
been (and remain) enormously influential, not only in Latin America but
also in the United States. Indeed, Vasconcelos has been described as serving
as "an ideological standard-bearer for the Chicano movement that began in
[the 1960s] . . . and for pan-Latino thinkers through the 1990s" (Stavans and
Vasconcelos 2011, xiii).

As I have noted in Hooker (2014), however, Latino political theorists' positive recuperations of Vasconcelos tend to gloss over the more unsavory elements of the theory of *mestizaje* developed in his most well-known work, *The
Cosmic Race*, such as its reproduction of racist evaluations of nonwhites as
inferior and its obscuring of Latin American anti-black and anti-indigenous
racism. While engaging in selective reading in order to recuperate useful
theoretical tools from a thinker whose ideas might be problematic on certain fronts is certainly par for the course in political theory, paying careful
attention to the concrete political context in which ideas emerge is key to
developing a nuanced understanding of their potential normative implications. In Vasconcelos's case, the Latin American ideologies of *mestizaje* that
emerged and were consolidated in many countries in the region in the first
half of the twentieth century need to be understood in light of transnational
debates about race in the Americas at the time, particularly the rising threat
of U.S. imperialism and Latin American intellectuals' embrace of a certain
conception of regional identity in opposition to it. A key component of the
discourse of "our America" within which Vasconcelos's work is situated is
thus the fact that it was developed in direct conversation with U.S. racial politics through a consistent practice of comparison and juxtaposition. Like the
Cuban nationalist José Martí, Vasconcelos was ideally positioned to com-
ment on U.S. racial politics given that he lived in the country for extended
periods of time at various points in his life.[3]

I thus read Vasconcelos as the inheritor of an anticolonial strand within Latin American political thought that grappled with the question of Latin American identity in light of growing U.S. imperial policies toward the region. Like the Argentinean Domingo F. Sarmiento, Vasconcelos's ideas about race were shaped in key ways by the U.S., although unlike Sarmiento he did not seek to emulate them, but rather developed a critique of U.S. racism. The hemispheric intellectual frame adopted here is thus particularly appropriate for understanding Vasconcelos's ideas about race, not only because of how he has been appropriated by contemporary Chicano and Latino thinkers in the U.S. but also because his theorization of Latin American *mestizaje* was self-consciously formulated in light of domestic racial politics in the United States and the challenge of confronting global white supremacy.

Vasconcelos's extensive oeuvre is broad, thematically varied, disjointed, and often contradictory, but his arguments about race and Latin American identity are fairly consistent. As Ilan Stavans has noted, Vasconcelos is one of those thinkers who is often invoked but not closely read, or to be more precise, most understandings of his political thought focus only on the opening essay of *The Cosmic Race*, "Mestizaje," first published in 1925 and reissued in 1948 (Stavans and Vasconcelos 2011, 4–5). I focus instead on two of Vasconcelos's later, lesser-known works, *Indología* (1927) and *Bolivarismo y Monroísmo* (1934), which contain his most direct analysis of how Latin Americans should respond to the threat of U.S. imperialism. They thus allow us to situate Vasconcelos's work within an anticolonial strain of Latin American political thought that explicitly resorted to comparison with U.S. racial politics in order to assert Latin American superiority. Vasconcelos's project was thus antiracist insofar as it refuted negative assessments of the region because of its large multiracial population rooted in racist condemnations of racial mixture as leading to degeneration, a key tenet of the scientific racism that dominated intellectual circles in Europe and the United States (and which was also influential in Latin America) in the late nineteenth and early twentieth centuries.[4] There are important limits to Vasconcelos's conception of *mestizaje*, however, as it falls short of full-blown racial egalitarianism and obscures racism within Latin America (especially in *The Cosmic Race*). I conclude by juxtaposing Vasconcelos's ideas to contemporary Latin American thinkers' articulation of a "decolonial option" that shares his concern with the connections between race and coloniality at the same time as it seeks to formulate an alternative epistemology drawn from Latin America's racial "others."

## Vasconcelos and Sarmiento

As is true of many other Latin American thinkers, Vasconcelos undoubtedly drew on and was influenced by European ideas,[5] but I want to suggest that his arguments about *mestizaje* are best understood by placing him within a hemispheric intellectual lineage in which comparison between the United States and Latin America is a key methodological and rhetorical feature of debates about race. In particular, an unlikely, but key, reference point for Vasconcelos was Domingo F. Sarmiento (1811–88), the Argentinean statesman and *pensador*, who was one of the most influential Latin American thinkers of the second half of the nineteenth century. While Sarmiento is generally read as a thinker who advocated the Europeanization of Latin America, he also articulated a preoccupation with whether a horizontal relationship could be established between "Ambas Americas" or both Americas: the United States and Latin America. Sarmiento's successors, such as Martí and Vasconcelos, would take his concerns in a more radical antiimperialist direction. Like him they argued that the region needed to unite politically in order to counter U.S. hegemony, but they also rejected the United States as a model and focused entirely on the cultural/ethno-racial unity of "Our America" (i.e. Latin America). Vasconcelos theorized *mestizaje* more explicitly than Martí, but his arguments about race cannot be understood apart from the anticolonial impulse to challenge U.S. imperialism and the notion of global white supremacy underpinning it. The two are inextricably linked because the self-proclaimed aim of his arguments about *mestizaje* was to vindicate Latin America and contest white supremacy ideologically.

Vasconcelos's project was anticolonial and antiracist in this (limited) sense, even as it fell short of full-blown racial egalitarianism, particularly in a domestic Latin American context. It is precisely because of this underlying anticolonial impulse that racial homogeneity is such a fundamental element of Vasconcelos's conception of *mestizaje*. Unlike the conception of hybrid subjectivity developed by Chicana feminist Gloria Anzaldúa, for instance, Vasconcelos's conception of *mestizo* identity is decidedly not fluid, fractured, or multiple (Anzaldúa 1987). It is instead a seamless fusion or synthesis of various original elements. Vasconcelos's aim was not to deconstruct race, as we shall see, but rather to encourage Latin Americans to embrace a conception of their racial identity that he believed would allow them to unite politically in order to contest U.S. imperialism. In his conviction that the region's racial politics was crucial to Latin America's potential to assert itself as the United States' political equal and withstand its dominance in the hemisphere, Vasconcelos was indeed Sarmiento's heir, even as he embraced a thoroughly inverted conception of which region's racial system was more advantageous and who should serve as the political model where race was concerned.

There are numerous reasons to situate Vasconcelos's theorization of *mestizaje* within a strand of Latin American political thought that was deeply concerned with hemispheric power relations and U.S. imperialism. Vasconcelos viewed Sarmiento as a kind of model. His admiration is evident in the numerous occasions in which he referenced Sarmiento by name in his various works. Gabriella De Beer, one of Vasconcelos's biographers, suggests that he identified with him because: "In Sarmiento, Vasconcelos saw what he would have liked others to see in him. . . . Sarmiento symbolized the educated leader diametrically opposed to . . . the military chieftain" (De Beer 1966, 253). Vasconcelos shared Sarmiento's criticism of *caudillismo* and lauded his efforts to promote public education in Argentina. Referring to Sarmiento's educational reforms, Vasconcelos described him as "a type of victorious Quetzalcoatl."[6] He also condemned "those barbarous dictatorships that . . . do nothing more than continue the tradition of facundismo in a continent that generally lags in civilization" (Vasconcelos 1927, 147–48). He argued that if Latin America were able to "cast off the yoke of those barbarous caudillajes that are the reproach of some of our countries we will have eliminated at least half of the causes that threaten our destinies" (Vasconcelos 2011, 76). According to Vasconcelos, "America's glory days were not presided over by any absolute leader, they were the presidencies of Sarmiento . . . in Argentina . . . and Lincoln's administration in the United States" (Vasconcelos 1927, 18). Twentieth-century dictatorships, whether animated by right- or left-wing ideologies, were the modern legacy of *caudillismo*, according to Vasconcelos, and in the case of Mexico had resulted in the loss of half of its national territory. He further connected the dangerous localism of *caudillismo* with the kind of shortsighted nationalism that prevented the regional unity needed to oppose U.S. imperial encroachment. Vasconcelos sought to add weight to his call for Latin American unity by presenting it as a continuation of Sarmiento's views. He argued that nationalism was a European import that Latin Americans needed to move beyond: "[To] overcome European nationalism . . . is to proclaim with Sarmiento that the borders of Hispanic nations are not subject to the hazards of armed conflict" (Vasconcelos 1927, 23).

Vasconcelos completely disagreed with Sarmiento's critique of Spain's legacy in the Americas, however. Vasconcelos's views on the impact of the Spanish conquest and Catholicism were diametrically opposed to Sarmiento's. He valorized them, whereas Sarmiento rejected them. Vasconcelos vehemently disputed the view that the Spanish legacy was to blame for Latin American underdevelopment. He argued that U.S. imperial ambitions toward Latin America were legitimized by "the cultural doctrine propagated throughout the continent of the uselessness of whatever is Spanish. Not even our best have escaped this anti-Spanish phobia. Sarmiento falls prey to it, even though he does not want to be taken for an Indian either" (Vasconcelos 2011, 23). For Vasconcelos, the nineteenth-century critique of the Spanish legacy opened the doors to U.S. domination in the twentieth, encouraged by the "foreign-izing, Pan-Americanizing, Monroe-ist current fomented, without realizing its risks, by men of such eminent capacity as Sarmiento" (Vasconcelos 2011, 12). Vasconcelos and Sarmiento thus had widely disparate assessments of the impact of the Spanish legacy on Latin America.

Vasconcelos and Sarmiento also had very different views of the United States. While Vasconcelos admired some of the United States' achievements, he was a staunch critic of U.S. imperialism. During Vasconcelos's lifetime, U.S. intervention was at its height in Latin America, whereas Sarmiento wrote at a time when the threat was beginning to be perceived but had not yet fully manifested itself.[7] The shifts in Latin American views of the United States wrought by heightened unequal hemispheric power relations in the twentieth century are evident in Vasconcelos's emphasis on the need for regional unity, even when he placed this call in the context of a notion of egalitarian coexistence in the Americas that was reminiscent of Sarmiento's concept of "Ambas Americas." In 1927, for example, Vasconcelos asserted that Latin America needed to reaffirm and recover its "collective personality," but that doing so did not preclude recognizing "the worth and rights of the great race that shares with us the responsibilities for dominion over the New World. They and we represent . . . the two cultures of the New World. That is why it is urgent that . . . we find a way that these two cultures[,] rather than becoming spent and exhausted in conflict[,] reach an understanding and collaborate in progress" (Vasconcelos 1927, 17). In the prologue to *Indología*, which is a compilation of lectures delivered in Puerto Rico and the Dominican Republic, Vasconcelos suggested that ending the illegitimate U.S. occupation of that island (and of the Philippines and Panama) would go a long way toward resolving the widespread ill will it had provoked in Latin America and restoring friendly hemispheric relations: "True amity, which existed in the continent during the era of our independence, when all of our liberals turned to the U.S. in search of wisdom and advice, would be reestablished in an instant, to the advantage of both Americas" (Vasconcelos 1927, xxxiv).

The United States was thus never a political model for Latin America for Vasconcelos, as it was for Sarmiento, particularly in terms of race relations. Vasconcelos warned Latin Americans not to fall into the trap of following imported racial theories: "Let us remember that our mission is to unite all the races into a single one. Let us take care not to imitate other peoples who create barriers based on color. . . . Destiny has decreed that the races that live in Latin America should not be kept separate, but rather that they should continue to unite their blood. . . . No color barriers, no barriers of blood" (Vasconcelos 1927, 220–22). Vasconcelos and Sarmiento thus differed in their estimation of the United States. After 1847 Sarmiento turned away from Europe and argued that the United States should be the political model for Latin America. Vasconcelos agreed that intellectuals should look to the Americas rather than Europe for models, but in his case it was Latin America which he believed should be the political model, not only for the U.S., but the world. As Vasconcelos asserted in *Indología*: "Europe, [is] the continent where everything has already been tried . . . [America is] the continent where things are being done" (Vasconcelos 1927, xi). For Vasconcelos, Europe was the past, Latin America was the future, and that future was *mestizo* or mixed.

## *Mestizaje*, "A Doctrine That Nourished the Hopes of the Non-White Races"

When one compares the two texts in which Vasconcelos sketches his theory of *mestizaje* most directly, *The Cosmic Race* and *Indología*, it is striking how many more denigrating statements about nonwhites mar the former compared to the latter. To be sure, Vasconcelos continues to traffic in racial stereotypes in *Indología*, but *Indología* also contains a much more genuine appreciation for black and indigenous contributions to Latin American culture and identity, an appreciation that is missing from *The Cosmic Race*. When Vasconcelos laments his lack of black ancestry or refers to elements of preconquest indigenous peoples' cultures admiringly in *Indología*, the reader is persuaded that he is genuine, as opposed to the skepticism occasioned by statements such as: "Who has not a little of all this, or does not wish to have all?" in *The Cosmic Race* appended to a long list of negative attributes of non-whites.[8] Vasconcelos described *Indología* as "in a certain sense only an enlargement" of *The Cosmic Race*, but the difference in tone (at least) between the two texts raises important questions about the reason for the markedly different degree of racial egalitarianism in Vasconcelos's theory of *mestizaje* present in these two texts (Vasconcelos 1927, lv–lvi).

Vasconcelos undoubtedly remained committed to a notion of *mestizaje* as harmonious fusion in *Indología*, which is problematic for a variety of reasons (because it obscures the existence of racial hierarchy and inequality in Latin America, because it denies the existence of separate racial groups as such in the present, and so forth), but there are some key features of Vasconcelos's philosophical and political project that are stated more explicitly in *Indología* than in *The Cosmic Race*. Not only does Vasconcelos actually recognize the contributions of black and indigenous Latin Americans and critique the identification with whiteness of the region's elite in *Indología*, he also makes it clear that his aim was not to deconstruct race, but rather to urge Latin Americans to embrace a particular conception of their racial identity as nonwhites. There is an interesting moment in the prologue to *Indología* (which is mostly a travelogue of his experiences in Puerto Rico and the Dominican Republic giving the lectures that compose the book rather than an introduction to its content per se) when Vasconcelos recounts an exchange following the delivery of the lecture on race called "El hombre" in Puerto Rico. When he was praised by a fellow intellectual for the scientific soundness of his theory of *mestizaje*, he replied: "Doctor, it is just as arbitrary and as fragile as the idea of white supremacy. Scientific knowledge, at least certain types of it, is still that, a tool of combat, and our obligation is to make use of it" (Vasconcelos 1927, xx). This reply captures a key assumption underlying Vasconcelos's writings about race (one shared by W. E. B. Du Bois): while "race" may have been an arbitrary scientific construct, it was nevertheless absolutely necessary to not only challenge and debunk ideas of white supremacy, but to formulate "positive" conceptions of racial identity that could be embraced by Latin Americans.

One of the reasons that *Indología* is a less racist text than *The Cosmic Race* is that its challenge to white supremacy is not articulated solely on behalf of lighter-skinned Latin American elites. Instead, in it Vasconcelos at times explicitly presents his critique of ideologies of white supremacy as being rooted in or arising from the experiences of black and indigenous Latin Americans. Compared to the silences and denigrating statements about these groups in *The Cosmic Race*, in *Indología* Vasconcelos describes the African presence as a key component of Latin American identity, for example, and attributes positive qualities to his indigenous ancestry. Commenting on those who noted that a prominent Puerto Rican nationalist was a mulatto, he retorted:

> As if being a mulatto was not the most illustrious citizenship card in America! I believe even Bolivar was one. He was, if we are to believe the English descriptions, notwithstanding that today they would have him be the descendant of blue-blooded ancestors from I don't know which strain of pure Basque stock. Unfortunately I don't have black blood, but I have a small fraction of indigenous blood and I think that it is to this that I owe a greater breadth of feeling than most whites and a kernel of a culture that was already enlightened when Europe was still savage. (Vasconcelos 1927, xxv)

There are thus moments in *Indología* when Vasconcelos appears to critique Latin American antiblack and anti-indigenous racism. This is a departure from *The Cosmic Race*, where he fails to even acknowledge the internal racism practiced by Latin America's proto-white elites. Such moments of consistency in the application of the critique of the ideology of white supremacy lend a certain credence (by virtue of rendering it more universal and less self-serving) to the notion that Vasconcelos's theory of *mestizaje* could serve as "a doctrine that nourished the hopes of the non-white races" (Vasconcelos 1927, xxxi).

There are in fact multiple moments in *Indología* where Vasconcelos speaks positively of black and indigenous Latin Americans and condemns the pretensions to whiteness of Latin American elites. Describing the reception to his lectures on race in the Dominican Republic, for example, he reported that excerpts from *The Cosmic Race* (accompanied by commentaries) had been published in a local newspaper, and suggested that it was the preponderance of darker-skinned people in the country that accounted for the positive reception to his argument:

> Such a mixed-race country would have to welcome such a talk with interest. . . . I do not exaggerate when I say that in certain sites where people of color are plentiful I was received like a kind of Messiah. . . . I

noticed the most interest among the faces of the blacks, because they, in contrast to the mulatto, do not try to hide a truth that cannot be denied, nor do they renege of a color that was the aristocracy of the earth possibly five thousand years ago. . . . The white [man] was then like an albino rat, hidden in burrows or covered by the trees. (Vasconcelos 1927, xliv)

Similarly, *Indología* also contains positive statements about indigenous peoples. While Vasconcelos decried the despotism of the Aztecs and the Incas, he admired other indigenous cultures. Referring to the Mayas and Quechuas, he wrote that:

The great cities, the prodigious architecture, the splendid decorative art, the full arrangement of the constructions demonstrate that, when the Spaniards arrived in America calling themselves the bearers of civilization, in reality civilization, or at least one of the greatest manifestations of human civilization, not only had already manifested itself, but had already decayed in America . . . before the existence of Europe as a cultured region, there had already flourished in Central America and the Yucatan, empires and civilizations whose architecture, at least, has nothing to envy of and indeed in many aspects surpasses European architecture proper. (Vasconcelos 1927, 116–17)

America, according to Vasconcelos in *Indología*, was thus not empty land when the Europeans arrived; it already possessed cultures that were to leave their imprint on the region's inhabitants. Indeed, in *Indología* Vasconcelos argued that Latin American political thought was shaped by Spanish contact with indigenous cultures during the colonial era, and was influenced by both (Vasconcelos 1927, 125). *Indología*, however, is not exempt from the occasional stereotypical description of blacks or statements praising the Spanish conquest and minimizing the achievements of preconquest indigenous cultures.[9] But on balance the "racial eruptions" in this text are overshadowed by the other more positive references to black and indigenous Latin Americans, which represents a marked shift in tone from *The Cosmic Race*.[10]

In addition to acknowledging and even at times celebrating the presence of black and indigenous Latin Americans, in *Indología* Vasconcelos also challenged the aspirations to whiteness of the region's elite. He explicitly recognized *mulataje* and Afro-indigenous mixture as part of

Latin American *mestizaje*, for instance, and criticized those who sought to deny it:

> I do not advocate merely for the consolidation of a sense of caste among mestizos. . . . Let us continue with our mestizaje, without denying it, but also without boasting about its privileged openness of heart. . . . Let us also pay attention to the fact that alongside the older indo-Hispanic one another humbler mixing process has occurred, that is also important as a factor . . . and is also endowed with rare virtues: the mixing of Spaniard and black and of Portuguese and black, the mulatto, *which has given so many illustrious sons to our nations.* . . . Add to these mixtures . . . indigenous mixture, black mixture, and the combination of these two types . . . add even the Asian migration, located on the Pacific, and you will recognize that our America is already the continent of all the races. For the first time so many and such diverse peoples have united in the same vast region of the world on equal footing. (Vasconcelos 1927, 81–82, emphasis added)

While Vasconcelos clearly continued to portray *mestizaje* as occurring on equal terms in Latin America, two additional elements of this passage are striking: the explicit recognition of black participation in *mestizaje*, and the implication that Latin American elites should not try to deny or distance themselves from a nonwhite regional identity. This double theoretical move is characteristic of the limits of Vasconcelos's thinking about mixture (even in its most positive version in *Indología*) as an approach to antiracism. At the same time as it contains a criticism of the internalized racism of Latin American elites, his notion of *mestizaje* as harmonious fusion resulting in a homogeneous subject is incompatible with black and indigenous Latin Americans possessing their own distinct identities. We see this clearly in two moments in particular in *Indología*: in Vasconcelos's discussion of how to approach the education of indigenous peoples and in his refutation of U.S. eugenicist Madison Grant's pseudo-scientific defense of white (Nordic) supremacy.

In the essay in *Indología* on public education in Latin America, Vasconcelos praised the educational efforts of the Spanish missionaries, disputed the notion that the destruction of indigenous culture that accompanied the conquest was a loss, and rejected the creation of separate schools for indigenous education. Contradicting his recognition of antiblack and anti-indigenous racism in Latin America elsewhere in the text, Vasconcelos portrayed *mestizaje* as a harmonious process by which Spanish Catholic missionaries inducted willing Indians into a superior culture:

> Not a few Indians, as they became educated, entered fully to take advantage of social life in a civilization like ours, which never established barriers of color or blood.... The missionaries have been accused of ... extirpating the beliefs of the conquered people.... A conqueror who brings only violence, as he remains within the subjected people bears its influence and is absorbed, but for that [to occur] it is necessary that the subjected people possess a culture.... In our continent, material conquest was accompanied by the destruction of indigenous ideology; but the ideology that was destroyed was replaced [by another], and I do not believe anyone will seriously deny that the replacement was advantageous. (Vasconcelos 1927, 144)

Vasconcelos's denial of the existence of any preconquest indigenous culture worthy of survival contradicts other statements elsewhere in the text, but it is entirely consistent with the homogenizing imperative of his theory of *mestizaje*. Considering the alternatives to indigenous integration, for example, he argued that the U.S. model of creating reservations was "the path of death by isolation" (Vasconcelos 1927, 144). Nor did he believe that indigenous peoples could preserve their own cultures; instead, via *mestizaje* indigenous Latin Americans were able to become the "co-author of a great culture" (Vasconcelos 1927, 145). As Minister of Education, Vasconcelos also rejected the creation of separate Indian schools, a policy that was later pursued by some of his successors.[11] Separate education was a mistake, he argued. For its proponents in Mexico, moreover, it "might end up being difficult to pin down who should fall within it and who should not, as many of those who favor the American system would have been interned as Indians, if they were to present themselves in the U.S." (Vasconcelos 1927, 160). Perhaps because he was blinded by his fervent adherence to Catholicism and the Spanish legacy, Vasconcelos was unable to envision indigenous Latin Americans as anything except (at best) co-contributors to *mestizaje*. But he also critiqued the propensity of Latin American elites to imitate "foreign methods, poorly understood," and their delusions of whiteness.

Vasconcelos's criticism of the racial self-hatred of Latin American elites is clearest in the appendix to the essay "El hombre," which is devoted to a discussion of Madison Grant's arguments in favor of white supremacy and racial segregation in *The Passing of the Great Race*.[12] Vasconcelos debunked the empirical soundness of Grant's claims, and then quickly moved to a scathing criticism of Latin American elites who failed to see the threat posed by global white supremacy:

> Because of the little white blood we have, we think as if we were an outpost of colonization among the Indians. . . . This spiritual servility is what leads me to renege of some of our own and to say once and for all that we are not white. This assertion is particularly scandalous to the semi-whites who gad about Europe pretending to be Parisian. Very well, let them hide behind the door of any of the luxury hotels they tend to frequent off of the sweat of the Indian slaves and they will see how they, who lord it over the Indians, are treated by any of these citizens of France; immediately they will hear themselves being called mixed. The white Argentinean . . . as much as the dark Mexican or the Dominican or the Cuban. . . . We belong to a colonial, semi-independent population threatened by the white imperialisms of Europe and the United States . . . *our greatest hope of salvation lies in the fact that we are not a pure race, but a mixed one, a bridge to future races, an aggregate of races in formation . . . that can create a more powerful race than those that emanate from a single tree.* (Vasconcelos 1927, 104–5)

Vasconcelos's frustration with Latin American elites' aspirations to whiteness is palpable in this passage. Moreover, it is noteworthy that in it the strategy of racial comparison functions not to obscure Latin American racism but rather to demonstrate the need for an anticolonial critique of global white supremacy.

In this Vasconcelos was very much in sync with his African American contemporary, Du Bois. Indeed, both Vasconcelos and Du Bois recognized the need to formulate anticolonial movements that could challenge global white supremacy and unfettered capitalism. Vasconcelos believed that his theory of *mestizaje* had a positive role to play in the reconstitution of a Latin American identity that could be more than a servile imitator of European or U.S. ideas. It is thus a mistake to view Vasconcelos's and Du Bois's ideas about race as fundamentally at odds.[13] Vasconcelos's aim was certainly not to deconstruct or disavow the notion of race, but rather to encourage Latin Americans to embrace a particular conception of their racial identity as nonwhite, mixed-race peoples.[14] In order to confront U.S. imperialism,

Vasconcelos argued that Latin America needed to develop its racial unity, as well as unite politically. He argued that while the region was viewed as a dispersed set of twenty nations, the truth was that: "Latin America [exists], not as a vague geographic category, but rather as a perfectly homogeneous ethnic group. . . . We constitute a homogeneous racial whole, as homogeneous as any other homogeneous race on earth, and this single race, the Iberian-American race inhabits a large and continuous area of the New World" (Vasconcelos 1927, 16). It was this sense of common racial identity that would allow "the Iberian-American race" to regain "consciousness of its unity" and move toward "spiritual fusion and political confederation" (Vasconcelos 1927, 26). Vasconcelos thus criticized those Latin American intellectuals (such as Martí) who claimed that race did not exist.[15] In order to demonstrate that it did, he turned to examples of the heightened racist climate in the United States during "the nadir" era, and more specifically, to how it affected Latinos.

### Latinos and U.S. Racial Politics During "the Nadir" Era

Despite his assertion in 1926 that he had no intention of writing any more about "these trite issues of race and Iberoamericanism," Vasconcelos continued to do so (Vasconcelos 1927, lvii). *Bolivarismo y Monroísmo* (published in 1934) contains his most extensive discussions of Latinos and U.S. racial politics. There are numerous references to U.S. racism in *The Cosmic Race* that function as a foil in comparison to which Latin America's superior racial harmony is revealed, but they are not about the experiences of Latinos. In contrast, *Bolivarismo y Monroísmo*, written after he lost his bid for the presidency in 1929 and during his second period of exile between 1930 and 1940 (a significant portion of which was spent in the United States), contains a number of references to the racial politics confronted by Mexican American communities in the Southwest and by Latin American immigrants. Analyses of Vasconcelos's writings about *mestizaje* have not sufficiently considered the extent to which he may have been influenced by the heightened racism and racial terror that characterized "the nadir" era of U.S. race relations during the early twentieth century, which also coincided with heightened anti-immigrant sentiment.[16] Writing for a Latin American audience prone to dismiss the significance of race, Vasconcelos felt the need to justify the continued salience of racism. Against adherents of both liberalism (for whom race was not a legitimate political category) and Marxism (who believed that the relevant category was international class struggle), he argued that in the 1930s there existed at a global level, a "policy firmly rooted in the fact of the inequality between men on the basis of color and race. . . . Race may be debatable as a biological thesis, but that does not render any less true the fact that race produces important and notable socio-economic consequences everywhere" (Vasconcelos 2011, 57). The aim of Vasconcelos's analysis of domestic U.S. racial politics in *Bolivarismo y Monroísmo* was thus not to assert Latin America's greater racial harmony but to persuade the region's intellectuals about racism's continued salience.

Unlike Sarmiento, who lived in the United States during Reconstruction, a period during which the country seemed committed to racial justice, Vasconcelos lived and wrote during the post-Reconstruction era, when white supremacy was explicitly codified as the law (and ideology) of the land. *Bolivarismo y Monroísmo* in particular reveals that Vasconcelos was very much aware of the heightened racial terror and anti-immigrant sentiment that characterized the United States during "the nadir" era. The text contains numerous references to the Ku Klux Klan, for example, and to lynching and racial segregation. Many of Vasconcelos's descriptions of U.S. racism are aimed at showing the contradiction between the United States' self-conception as a democracy and the reality of racial subordination. "Black freedom is a myth in the U.S. South," he wrote, "and the killings due to racial hatred, the lynchings, tell us that our Indians would have nothing to gain" by being incorporated into such a system (Vasconcelos 2011, 28). Indeed, the almost casual way in which Vasconcelos incorporates information about lynching into the text speaks to how ubiquitous racial terror was during this era, and to how widespread knowledge of it was. In a discussion of the influence of U.S. business interests on reporting in Latin American newspapers, for example, he suggested that were the reverse to occur, the newspaper in question "would last as long as a lynching does, that is two or three hours" (Vasconcelos 2011, 92). Moreover, Vasconcelos did not portray racism as something that was restricted to the South; he described segregation as a feature of the entire country. There is a "chasm that in North America separates the white Methodist from the black Methodist. Not even to pray do Anglo-Saxons and blacks gather together in the same church" (Vasconcelos 2011, 69).

In *Bolivarismo y Monroísmo* Vasconcelos reiterated his criticism of Latin American intellectuals' tendency to deny race and to identify with whiteness.

He suggested that too many Latin American intellectuals were willing adherents of notions of white supremacy. In Latin America, he argued, "the doctrine of the Ku-Klux-Klan has been broadcast with the endorsement of our intellectual heroes. . . . Preaching the survival of the fittest was satisfying to many of our brown professors, as if by proclaiming it they could escape the supposed penalty of their color" (Vasconcelos 2011, 23). Of course, part of Vasconcelos's criticism was directed at those who decried the effect of the Spanish legacy on Latin America, but his criticism was also aimed at those who affirmed (like Martí) that race did not exist. To refute this claim, Vasconcelos argued that race relations within the region could not be understood outside the context of global white supremacy:

> Race does not exist, habitually shouts the [Latin American] pariah forced to serve as a wage laborer, now to the English, tomorrow to the French. But the French, the English, the Germans, the oppressors, practice caste within their territories . . . [we can believe race does not exist] when we see the English sharing a table with the Hindus, their co-nationals within the [British] Empire, or the day that the Yankees share a railroad car with their black compatriots. The warning I am formulating does not seek to establish among us petty distinctions, but rather to demonstrate the extent to which we live deceived. (Vasconcelos 2011, 61)

As a result of this repeated insistence that race relations within Latin America were not taking place in a vacuum, in *Bolivarismo y Monroísmo* the comparison between the United States and Latin America functions not as a foil to demonstrate Latin America's more egalitarian racial politics (as it does in *The Cosmic Race)*, but rather as the grounds for a criticism of mistaken Latin American racial self-conceptions that sought to align the region with whiteness. Vasconcelos was thus quite clear that Latin American elites were often blind to their actual subordinate position within global white supremacy. A key component of this argument was an analysis of where Latin Americans were situated within domestic racial hierarchies in Europe and in the United States: "The super-white criollos of our continent tend to smirk at North American racial distinctions, believing that they are beyond the reach of the metric that is applied to the Indians, the rule that affects the Chinese and the blacks. If the occasion allows, they will learn right away that light skin bestows a rank that lasts only as long as their pesos.

The instant they search for work, they will learn that racism places the Spaniard . . . in a similar category as the Berber" (Vasconcelos 2011, 58). Because even white Latin Americans were viewed as at best "pseudo-whites" in the United States, the region's elite should abandon its futile aspirations to whiteness, Vasconcelos argued.

In fact, *Bolivarismo y Monroísmo* contains Vasconcelos's most extensive analysis of anti-Latino racism in the United States. In addition to prefiguring contemporary discourses about Latinos who claim to "discover" race once they arrive in the United States, Vasconcelos was also an acute observer of the treatment of Latin American populations who had become part of the United States as a result of imperial expansion, such as Puerto Ricans and Mexican Americans in the Southwest. The latter, he argued, represented a warning for what awaited Latin America if U.S. imperialism continued unchecked: "The example of Texas, conquered forty years ago, shows us what the Latin American could expect from such an advance of racial imperialism. The entire Mexican population, that is Hispanic-American, of California and Texas, a population the majority of which is as white as the whitest Argentinean criollo, as the whitest Spaniard from Castile, now finds itself subordinated, dispossessed of its property, its language bastardized, proletarianized in body and soul" (Vasconcelos 2011, 52). Vasconcelos not only observed the forced assimilation of Mexican Americans but also noted that all Latinos faced racial discrimination in employment: "Every worker from Argentina or Mexico that offers his labor in the sweatshops of Yankeeland discovers, right away, that the nature of his blood bars him from the best jobs." And this fact could not be attributed to Latinos suffering from a language barrier, as "Jews and blacks speak good English" (Vasconcelos 2011, 58).

A constant theme in Vasconcelos's analysis in *Bolivarismo y Monroísmo* of Latinos' place in the U.S. racial order is the claim that all Latin Americans were equally subject to racism once they reached the United States, whatever their skin color:

There is no race, we think, until the day that crossing the U.S. border reveals that we have already been classified, and before being given the opportunity to define ourselves. And it will be totally pointless at that moment to recall the vague lineages and literary opinions that want to situate us in the Mediterranean or Scotland . . . the foolish and naïve Latin American who in his country believed that race had been abolished and that all men are equal discovers, shortly after moving to the U.S., that there is a rigid unwritten hierarchy that determines one's place in society and also one's salary. And if he digs a bit more deeply he will verify that the highest positions in the land ... all are in the hands of the aristocracy of the pure bloods of New England. (Vasconcelos 2011, 62–63)

According to Vasconcelos there was a salary scale that matched "the racial classifications of the Department of Immigration," with Northern Europeans at the top followed by Southern Europeans and the Irish, "blacks with U.S. or British citizenship, the Chinese, and at the bottom of the scale, South Americans and Mexicans" (Vasconcelos 2011, 63–64). There are certainly important caveats to be raised about Vasconcelos's claim that Latinos were at the bottom of the U.S. racial order during the nadir era. African Americans, for example, also suffered from racial discrimination in employment, in addition to being the objects of racial violence. What is most interesting about his claim, however, is that it was intended to persuade Latin Americans to embrace a racial identity as nonwhites. It was a direct rebuttal of Latin American arguments "against race":

Tell us then, messieurs theorists, that the problem of race does not exist in America; tell that to the Mexicans expelled after they had forged patrimonies in territories such as Texas and California that used to be theirs and where a treaty guarantees them asylum. Preach it to the South American workers[,] who to find a decent job in the United States would have to join Unions that *do not admit them*, because, despite their socialist ideology, they do not reserve places within their ranks neither for blacks nor negroids nor Mexicans or South Americans. That is reality as it exists. (Vasconcelos 2011, 65)

Arguments about U.S. racial politics in *Bolivarismo y Monroísmo* thus served to disabuse Latin Americans of their mistaken belief that racism did not exist, not to reassure them about their superior racial politics.

Vasconcelos's solution to U.S. imperialism, which was for Latin Americans to embrace nonwhiteness, was not one that was necessarily shared by other Latin Americans at the time, however, or even by U.S. Latinos. As Vasconcelos observed, Latin American denials of race functioned as pleas for inclusion into whiteness, not as a challenge to it: "Our snobbery points in the direction of the strong . . . it obscures the servile desire to reject the ethnic reality that constitutes us. The timidity and mimicry of an inferior species leads our Europeanizers and Saxon-izers to view themselves bovaristically as different from what they are. But such a false, ineffective posture precipitates ruin instead, it does not prevent it" (Vasconcelos 2011, 59).[17] Mexican Americans in the United States also sought to avoid the heightened racism of the nadir era by means of inclusion into whiteness. When the U.S. census introduced "Mexican" into the "race or color" category in 1930, for example, the Mexican government and its representatives in the United States, along with Mexican American organizations such as LULAC (the League of United Latin American Citizens), "all vigorously protested the exclusion from whiteness" and succeeded in having Mexicans reclassified as white in the census (Hochschild and Powell 2008, 81). While Mexican Americans at this time did not heed Vasconcelos's call to embrace nonwhiteness, later Chicano activists in the 1960s found inspiration and support for their efforts in Vasconcelos's ideas.

A final assessment of the anticolonial elements of Vasconcelos's call in the 1920s and 1930s for Latin Americans to embrace a nonwhite racial identity might best be arrived at by situating it in light of contemporary Latin American decolonial thought, however. As formulated by Anibal Quijano (2000) and Walter Mignolo (1995), among others, decolonial theory in Latin America is fundamentally concerned with the question of "modernity/coloniality," or the idea that coloniality is constitutive to modernity. This concern with the "coloniality of power" has led decolonial thinkers to criticize both the historical organization of political power in Latin America and the way in which Latin American political thought remains Eurocentric and reproduces Western modes of knowing and epistemological hierarchies that discount or ignore "the critical thinking produced by indigenous, Afro, and *mestizos* whose thinking finds its roots in other logics, concerns, and realities that depart not from modernity alone but also from the long horizon of coloniality" (Walsh 2007, 224). Even though Vasconcelos's valorization of *mestizaje* during the first half of the twentieth century was part of an anticolonial philosophical and political project, Vasconcelos would certainly not be embraced as a precursor by contemporary decolonial thinkers, for very good reasons.

While he did at times formulate an important critique of Latin American aspirations to whiteness that anticipates some elements of contemporary decolonial thought, Vasconcelos's conceptualization of *mestizaje* as an anti-imperial answer to global white supremacy and U.S. imperialism falls short of being fully decolonial in a variety of ways. Vasconcelos did not fully envision the dual project of decolonizing Latin American political thought and power relations articulated by contemporary decolonial thinkers. He continued to operate within the epistemic logic of the "coloniality of power" that privileges European sources over knowledge produced by black and indigenous Latin Americans, for instance. Thus, although he challenged certain elements of the scientific racism of his time, he never sought to fully decolonize Latin American political thought. Despite his criticism of Latin American elites' aspirations to whiteness articulated in texts such as *Indología* and *Bolivarismo y Monroísmo*, Vasconcelos also did not formulate a consistent challenge to neocolonial power relations within Latin America. His homogeneous conception of mixed-race subjectivity cannot encompass multiple, overlapping, simultaneous identities, nor did it fundamentally challenge the reification of colonial racial hierarchies in postindependence Latin America. Rather than being read as a thinker who articulated a conception of mestizaje that can serve as the basis for anti-racist politics in Latin America then, Vasconcelos is more aptly viewed as an anti-imperial thinker who at times sought to challenge global white supremacy. His project was anticolonial in a hemispheric context, insofar as it challenged U.S. imperialism, but it was not truly decolonial.

## Notes

This chapter is an earlier version of "'A Doctrine That Nourished the Hopes of the Non-White Races': Vasconcelos, Mestizaje's Travels, and U.S. Latino Politics," in Hooker 2017.

1. Von Vacano (2012), for example, has argued that Vasconcelos's theory of racial mixing is emblematic of a "synthetic paradigm" of race that is both one of multiple strands of thinking about race in Latin American political thought, and one that is distinctive to this tradition (particularly when compared to European and American political thought, which respectively produced "domination" and "dualistic" paradigms of race).

2. The literature on race in Latin America is vast, but recent empirical studies have shown the persistence of skin color hierarchies in the region that determine the distribution of rights and opportunities; see Telles and PERLA 2014.

3. Vasconcelos visited or lived in the United States at different periods in his life. As a child he lived in the United States–Mexico border region and attended elementary school in Texas. Later, as a young man he was in and out of exile and lived in New York, Washington, D.C. (where he served as an official representative of different

Mexican governments), San Antonio, and California at various points between 1913 and 1920. In 1926–1927 he taught at the University of Chicago and lectured at other U.S. universities. After losing his bid for the presidency he again lived in the U.S. for short periods, principally in Texas in the 1930s (De Beer 1966, 90–125).

4. Von Vacano 2012 for example, has (rightly) traced how approaches to aesthetics and notions of synthesis derived from Nietzsche informed Vasconcelos's understanding of *mestizaje*.

5. See Aline Helg, "Race in Argentina and Cuba, 1880–1930: Theory, Policies, and Popular Reaction," in Graham et al. 1990, 37–69.

6. The reference to Quetzalcoatl alludes to an Aztec myth about the struggle for primacy between two gods, one warlike and the other intellectual and dedicated to science and the arts, which according to Vasconcelos showed that the effort to bring education to Latin America was of long standing. Vasconcelos and Sarmiento were both educational reformers credited with building the foundations of the public education system in their respective countries.

7. Between 1890 and 1925 there were thirty-five different instances of United States military intervention (in other words, troops on the ground) in Latin America.

8. Preceding Vasconcelos's rhetorical question is the following: "This infinite quietude [of indigenous peoples' souls] is stirred with the drop put in our blood by the Black, eager for sensual joy, intoxicated with dances and unbridled lust. There also appears the Mongol, with the mystery of his slanted eyes that see everything according to a strange angle. . . . The clear mind of the White, that resembles his skin and his dreams, also intervenes. Judaic striations that were hidden within Castilian blood since the days of the cruel expulsion now reveal themselves; the melancholy of the Arab, which is a reminder of sickly Muslim sensuality. Who has not a little of all this, or does not wish to have all?" (Vasconcelos 1997, 61–62).

9. There are moments when Vasconcelos refers to "the lubricious cry of the black" in a discussion of music or to the presence of a "seductive mulatta" among a group of women, for example, and when he praises the "missionary spirit of Catholicism" as the dominant force that forged Latin American identity (Vasconcelos 1927, liii, liv, 80, 124).

10. I borrow the concept of racial eruptions from Charles R. Hale, "Racial Eruptions: The Awkward Place of Blackness in Indian-centered Spaces of Mestizaje." Paper presented at the Conference, Race and Politics in Central America, University of Texas at Austin, February 24–25, 2006.

11. *Indigenismo* was a type of nationalist ideology that glorified some aspects of indigenous cultural heritage, primarily as a relic of the past, which became influential in various countries in Latin America during the first half of the twentieth century. It was a construct of *mestizo* elites, not indigenous people themselves, and was characterized by nostalgia for an imagined, folklorized notion of indigeneity. *Indigenismo* became official state policy in Mexico after the Revolution of 1910–1920, with the aim of integrating indigenous peoples, not their autonomous development. Alan Knight

has argued that *mestizaje* and *indigenismo* coexisted as official ideologies during the Mexican Revolution (See Knight, "Racism, Revolution, and Indigenismo: Mexico, 1910–1940," in Graham et al. 1990, 71–114.

12. Grant's book originally appeared in 1916, but Vasconcelos cites the French translation published in 1926. In line with the book's thesis that the superior Nordic race needed to be defended against the threat of inferior races, Grant was an advocate of restricting immigration to the United States from Southern and Eastern Europe and Asia, and of racial classification/anti-miscegenation laws that helped codify the "one-drop rule" in Virginia in the 1920s, which became a model for other segregation statutes in the South.

13. Greg Carter (2013), for example, points to Vasconcelos's celebration of mixture as a foil to what he sees as Du Bois's advocacy of a monoracial conception of African-American identity. The distinction between a monoracial (which may recognize mixture but highlights a unified result) and a mixed-race approach to identity (which attempts to emphasize membership in multiple groups) is useful for clarifying the similarities between Du Bois's and Vasconcelos's racial projects. While Vasconcelos is often lauded as a proponent of the mixed-race approach, his theory of *mestizaje* in fact emphasized the achievement of a uniformly mixed and homogeneous *mestizo* subject among Latin Americans. The publishers' guide to *The Prophet of Race* also connects the two thinkers, suggesting that: "Vasconcelos is to Latinos what W. E. B. Du Bois is to African Americans—a controversial scholar who fostered an alternative view of the future."

14. For the argument that Latin Americans historically "dismantled" race through *mestizaje*, see Mendieta 2000.

15. Martí famously argued that "there are no races" (1999, 119).

16. This is widely understood by scholars as the period after 1890 (when Northern Republicans ceased supporting the rights of Southern blacks) through the early twentieth century, extending until around 1940. It was characterized by open adherence to white supremacy, heightened anti-black violence, lynching, segregation, and legal racial discrimination.

17. Vasconcelos appears to be referencing "collective Bovarism," a term coined by the Haitian intellectual and politician Jean Price-Mars (1876–1969), an advocate of Negritude, who used it to describe the way the predominantly-mixed Haitian elite embraced their European ancestry while denying any ties to their African legacy. It is based on Flaubert's famous character Emma Bovary.

## References

Anzaldúa, Gloria. 1987. *Borderlands/La Frontera: The New Mestiza*. San Francisco, Calif.: Spinsters/Aunt Lute.

Carter, Greg. 2013. *The United States of the United Races: A Utopian History of Racial Mixing*. New York: New York University Press.

De Beer, Gabriella. 1966. *José Vasconcelos and his World*. New York: Las Americas.

De la Fuente, Alejandro. 2001. *A Nation for All: Race, Inequality, and Politics in Twentieth-Century Cuba*. Chapel Hill: University of North Carolina Press.

Graham, Richard, Thomas E. Skidmore, Aline Helg, and Alan Knight. 1990. *The Idea of Race in Latin America, 1870–1940*. Austin: University of Texas Press.

Hochschild, Jennifer L., and Brenna Marea Powell. 2008. "Racial Reorganization and the United States Census, 1850–1930: Mulattoes, Half-Breeds, Mixed Parentage, Hindoos, and the Mexican Race." *Studies in American Political Development* 22 (1): 59–96.

Hooker, Juliet. 2014. "Hybrid Subjectivities, Latin American Mestizaje, and Latino Political Thought on Race." *Politics, Groups, and Identities* 2 (2): 188–201.

———. 2017. *Theorizing Race in the Americas: Douglass, Sarmiento, DuBois and Vasconcelos*. New York: Oxford University Press.

Martí, José. 1999. "Our America." In *José Martí Reader: Writings on the Americas*, edited by Deborah Shnookal and Mirta Muníz, 111–20. New York: Ocean Press.

Mendieta, Eduardo. 2000. "The Making of New Peoples: Hispanicizing Race." In *Hispanics/Latinos in the United States*, edited by Jorge J. E. Gracia and Pablo de Greiff, 44–59. New York: Routledge.

Mignolo, Walter. 1995. *The Darker Side of the Renaissance: Literacy, Territoriality, and Colonization*. Ann Arbor: University of Michigan Press.

Quijano, Anibal. 2000. "Coloniality of Power, Eurocentrism, and Latin America." *Neplanta* 1 (3): 533–80.

Stavans, Ilan, and José Vasconcelos. 2011. *José Vasconcelos: The Prophet of Race*. New Brunswick, NJ: Rutgers University Press.

Telles, Edward, and PERLA (Project on Ethnicity and Race in Latin America). 2014. *Pigmentocracies: Ethnicity, Race, and Color in Latin America*. Chapel Hill: University of North Carolina Press.

Vasconcelos, José. 1927. *Indología: una interpretación de la cultura Ibero-Americana*. Paris: Agencia Mundial de Librería.

———. 1997. *The Cosmic Race/La Raza Cósmica: A Bilingual Edition*. Translated by Didier T. Jaén. Baltimore, Md.: Johns Hopkins University Press.

———. 2011 [1934]. *Bolivarismo y Monroísmo: temas Iberoamericanos*. Mexico City: Trillas.

Von Vacano, Diego A. 2012. *The Color of Citizenship: Race, Modernity and Latin American/Hispanic Political Thought*. New York: Oxford University Press.

Walsh, Catherine. 2007. "Shifting the Geopolitics of Critical Knowledge." *Cultural Studies* 21 (2–3): 224–39.

CHAPTER 14

# Decolonization and Plurinationality

Oscar Vega Camacho

My final prayer:
O my body, make of me always a man who questions!
Frantz Fanon, 2008

I have decided on the title "Decolonization and Plurinationality" for this chapter because both terms could help us grasp what kind of problematization takes place in social and indigenous movements, institutional practices, and constitutional challenges in Latin American, or, as I prefer to call it, South American thought. The reason is that it is more a geopolitical daring than a linguistic option. Remember that talking about Latin Americans is mostly a way of reassembling the legacies of the Spanish and Portuguese colonial empires, and what is being disputed here is the division of the North and South as a global system and a civilizing project. These are the reasons to bring up decolonization as a central problematization for politics today.

In view of the vast amount of literature on decolonization, I will not define it here, nor do I pretend to close the debate about this topic. On the contrary, the invitation will be to keep the debate open and to further extend the discussion of what could be the implications of reworking the subjects of decolonization. In a certain way, we will try to understand what kind of thought this poses and try to argue when social and indigenous movements demand decolonization as a cultural and social challenge for the democratization of society.

We are starting to acknowledge that the demands for decolonization from social and indigenous movements are diverse and different even though they will be using the same term. However, we also know that this is no surprise in political confrontations, because the battleground is about their use and meaning, and the object of the struggle will be the appropriation of names. Terms such as "democracy," "legitimacy," and "dignity," used extensively in the movements mentioned, are not only the political battleground but also the principle tools for demanding and opening an expanding space of struggle.[1]

We are interested more in how these terms work than in how they are defined. It is more an exploration of conditions of possibilities than the definition of a possible condition. This may sound as if we are avoiding the debate, or as though we have no position in the debate, but it is necessary first to think what kind of debate is going on, what is at stake, and why it is being risked, to think why we think that way or what makes it possible to think that way. Let us begin by trying to understand the ways in which we think about politics or political terms and political struggles, and in talking about decolonization we could introduce a way of reframing our categories and narratives: the frameworks of understanding and acting. At the very least, we could begin to question and inquire about why we think that way, under what assumptions we establish the known, knowledge, and understanding, and why we take for granted certain situations and behaviors, since this is the legacy of colonial power. Not only can we trace it as part of economic, political, and social systems, but also this legacy still works as a dispositive of power in the partition of social, cultural, and gender divisions in our societies, even though, supposedly, there are no more colonial states or settlements in our recent world interstate system. But that is another matter.

Let us start with decolonization as the struggle against and resistance to colonial power relations in multiple scales in a historical process for emancipation and liberation. Of course, this struggle takes place within a modern world system, as Wallerstein and others have researched, always understanding modernity and colonialism as two sides of the same coin (Wallerstein 2014). This could help in understanding why anticolonial demands are usually against modernity, or at least against a certain modernity and modernism that we have to comprehend historically. In Frantz Fanon's words:

Decolonization, which sets out to change the order of the world, is, obviously, a program of complete disorder. However, it cannot come as a result of magical practices, or of a natural shock, nor of a friendly understanding. Decolonization, as we know, is a historical process: that is to say it cannot be understood, it cannot become intelligible nor clear to itself except in the exact measure that we can discern the movements which give it historical form and content. Decolonization is the meeting of two forces, opposed to each other by their very nature, which in fact owe their originality to that sort of substantification which results from and is nourished by the situation in the colonies. (Fanon 1968, 35)

Quoting Fanon is a strategic approach for the discussion of decolonization because his work is a hinge between philosophy and history, and between capitalism and racism, but mostly between Marxism and psychoanalysis, allowing us to escape the essentialism and substantialism that are so dear to monism and theological thinking. To grasp Fanon's words is to seize the violence involved in the colonial situation; overcoming the difficulties in the struggle for decolonization will be presented, not surprisingly, as a violent event or one that triggers violent acts. "Violence" would be the key word for misunderstanding and condemning any attempt to challenge and confront a colonial situation and tame the emancipatory initiatives. Fanon has said: "National liberation, national renaissance, the restoration of nationhood to the people, commonwealth: whatever may be the headings used or the new formulas introduced, decolonization is always a violent phenomenon" (Fanon 1968, 30). So it will depend on what situation is encountered and how one reacts to it. It is always a political and historical decision.

But let us return to Fanon's first quote and underline this "program of complete disorder," because the order they confront and destroy is lived as normal and is naturalized by society. That is, how to behave, act, speak, or think has to be invented; it has to inaugurate a new beginning, be reborn socially. In a way, it is like a monster or a monstrous challenge because the confronted postcolonial order is normality and is presented as natural. Therefore, other ways, other possibilities or alternatives, will be seen as unnatural—as disorder, and of course, as a specter of monstrosity, fury, and violence. There is quite vast literature about the latent and unpredictable movements of anticolonial attempts and battles, bringing out the deepest fears and what is feared.

And Fanon is specific: "It cannot be understood, it cannot become intelligible nor clear to itself." So he says very carefully that they need "the exact measure that we can discern the movements which give it historical form and context"—that is, historical contextualization in power relations, for Fanon lived during the Cold War and the national liberation of the people and the state. He was thinking beyond third-world states and underdeveloped societies, as they were called, and even "thought" was read as part or product of these tendencies. But maybe that is why his work is so relevant to social movements in the twenty-first century.

In the Bolivian process during 2006, when the Constituent Assembly was officially installed, the main social and indigenous organizations, through the so-called Pact of Unity coalition, presented a document as their proposal to refound Bolivia. It says in its preamble: "We understand that the Plurinational State is a model of political organization for the decolonization of our nations and peoples, reaffirming, restoring and strengthening our territorial autonomy to achieve full life, to live well, with a solidarity vision; thus be the motors of the unity and welfare of all Bolivians, ensuring full exercise of all rights."[2]

This document was central for the debates and for the formulation of our actual version of the Constitution, and it was created and defended by those who were silenced and invisible publicly and politically, those who were designated as incompetent, ignorant, and illiterate according to Western standards in past centuries, even in democratic republican states. Since the creation of Bolivia in 1825, the universal rights of citizenship are very recent. They were recognized as Bolivians and paid a tribute, but they had no citizenship or civilian rights until 1952, as a result of the National Revolution. It then took forty-two years, until the constitutional reform of 1994, for the nation to be recognized as a multicultural and multilingual society in a neoliberal framework, and it would take fifty-four years, until the Constituent Assembly, for community and collective rights to be formulated within a pluralistic framework.

So we can begin to understand why they say that it is a demand with a very long duration and their memories of the past are pathways to understanding. In the Andes, there is a saying that if you want to find the road, you have to look at the walked path and not turn your back. As if the future could only shine lights from the past without denying or ignoring it. This will be the main point of this chapter, as will be developed below.

A few warnings. Taking a recent publication by Sandro Mezzadra and Bret Neilson, titled *Border as Method, or The Multiplication of Labor*, their intention is to build conceptual tools for a changing world and an unstable or mutant system lived as migratory, precarious, and impoverished on a daily basis. They argue: "we can say that method for us is as much about acting on the world as it is about knowing it. More accurately, it is about the relation of action to knowledge in a situation where many different knowledge regimes and practices come into conflict. Border as a method involves negotiating the boundaries between different kinds of knowledge that come to bear on the border and, in doing so, aims to throw light on the subjectivities that come into being through such conflicts" (Mezzadra and Neilson 2014, 17–18).

This will introduce us to border thinking as a method for negotiating the boundaries and creating or inventing new kinds of unity, such as the Pact of Unity in Bolivia mentioned above. Or it could lead us to work for common goals in our lives or to understand life forms and life organizations as negotiating within a commonality. In the Bolivian Constitution, this thinking was called "Vivir Bien," which translates as good living or living well. This will be our second main point in this chapter.

First it is necessary to make explicit the other term in the title, plurinationality, and its importance to the kind of state that is reflected in the Bolivian Constitution. As we have said, it is closely related to how decolonization is formulated, at least in the Pact of Unity. What kind of state are they trying to establish? It is a difficult question because they are not thinking just to reform or reformulate a state where different cultural identities and forms of organization could fit, or achieve state recognition for their cultural practices and institutions. The wager was much more profound and disorderly for what we understand as state organization and institutions, at least different from what we know and from what our culture informs us about the form of the state and nation-state. Moreover, the Pact of Unity was formulated by people who lack training and experience of working within the state; they are illiterate about state affairs. What is worse, they have always been apart from the life of the state and were continually plotting and struggling against state demands when they were not fighting against the state itself.

Maybe this sketch will sound exaggerated and Manichaean, but it should illustrate how our fears are expressed when the people who had no importance begin to have a political impact. It is when those who were politically irrelevant become political subjects. This fact will change not only political affairs but also the state of politics and what it is that we understand about political matters and new political subjects. In Bolivia we have called it the indigenous irruption or plebeian subversion because the major political protagonists were the people left behind, not taken into account, or not being a part of the public space and state institutions, in effect a colonial order in the twenty-first century (García Linera et al. 2000).

Plurinationality is to be understood by the second article of the Constitution. This article affects the form of state and how we work in terms of state structure and organization, because this state is not the beginning of the nation and culture in a territory with a population as all republican and liberal constitutions declare the birth of the national state form. On the contrary, in this constitution, the state form will be where they meet, confronting and negotiating with the preexisting nations and peoples, with their "own ways" and practices, languages, traditions, institutions, and authorities. This new perspective on a state form changes role and function in relations of society with the state, the public and the private, the law and its practices, and authority and social responsibilities, for example. This constitution calls for a new understanding and practice of building up the state form, and maybe because there are no existing models it will take an experimental form, with continuous tests and errors.

The key concept in this constitutional article is self-determination within the framework of the unity of the state—that is, the rights to autonomy, self-government, one's own culture, recognition of self-institutions, and consolidation of indigenous territory. Thus plurinationality will be the objective for rebuilding nations and peoples (as "pueblos") after the oblivion and destruction of the postcolonial order, and after the attempts to impose a monocultural and unique state form as the national state form, following the pattern preconceived in Western societies or, more precisely, in Eurocentric modern history. This is what I mean by the decolonization of the state form. Plurinationality is the right of preexisting indigenous nations and peoples to leave their imprint, and it is their way to make the state a more flexible form to meet their needs.

How is plurinationality related to the form of the state or state formation? It means above all to find a way of building a new form of state that responds to a pluralistic society and that assumes that within this new state condition, it will be able to politically negotiate and settle differences and disagreements, but with an understanding that these state conditions are constantly and repeatedly rearranged and reordered by changes and transformations of society as a perpetual movement of creation of pluralist forms of living and life organizations. In a certain way, the aim is to transform state conditions as needed.

Of course, to accept this supposition of the transformation of the conditions of the state, we need to question our beliefs and knowledge about politics, law, and history, or how we have learned to think for centuries, at least since we started to consider ourselves as moderns and began to divide how, where, or who was not modern. Try to imagine how collectivities and "pueblos" for centuries have been characterized and designated as nonmodern, as wild, barbaric, ignorant, and idiotic. It is not that they do not know about politics, law, and history; but their experience brings another perspective on the order of things—they have to deal with it every day; they are constituted by these institutions, norms, and languages, but it does not mean that they do not know it, that they do not understand what is going on. So when they begin to talk, to express and formulate what kind of politics, law, and history they are referring to, it is not necessarily the same thing, the same order of things. We are changing perspectives, changing the meaning of order and what we are calling things. This is a way to approach decolonization, to accept the possibility of other lives, other worlds. In James Clifford's words: "From my perch in the new millennium, I understand the last half century as the interaction of two linked historical energies: decolonization and globalization. Neither process is linear or guaranteed. Neither can subsume the other. Both are contradictory and open ended. And both have worked to decenter the West, to 'provincialize Europe,' in Dipesh Chakrabarty's words. This is an unfinished but irreversible project" (Clifford 2013, 5).

So they are proposing a new state form, the plurinational state, perceiving that institutions, norms, and authorities are plastic, flexible, and moldable so that they can respond more effectively to a pluralistic society, one that is complex and transforming; so they are thinking of a persistent transformation of state conditions. This challenges many approaches and opens many questions, but it promises to rethink globalization and the new forms of capitalism.

Plurinationality is closely related to autonomy, self-government, and territoriality. It asks how, under what conditions, it is possible to have self-determination as "pueblo" and nation for the Constitution and reproduction of a collective decision and to strengthen and cultivate the common aim through the new state form. It is not a simple matter, and they will understand it as the decolonization of the state, an opportunity for rearranging and building political conditions from their perspectives, a possible space of negotiation and agreements, and a possible time for learning and experiencing other lives, other worlds.

In other terms, we can trace in Arturo Escobar's new book, *Sentipensar con la tierra*, something like "Feel-think with the Earth." In the preface he writes: "The essay proposes that the rights of indigenous peoples, peasants, and afro-descendent to their territories can be seen in terms of two interlocking processes: the problematization of "national" identities, with the concomitant emergence of indigenous knowledge and identities, afro-descendants and peasants; and the problematization of life, in relation to a biodiversity crisis, climate change and the increasing rate of environmental devastation by extractive industries" (Escobar 2014, 19).

Even though he is not arguing directly about the state as a form, both of the problematizations have to do with the state, or how the state will handle demands in the dispute of the rights of indigenous peoples, peasants, and afro-descendants in their territories. This makes us see more visible conflicts and demands that are taking place on a multidimensional scale. It also allows a glimpse of the new configuration of conflicts and demands for the plurinational state of Bolivia and how they are managed and driven, because the problematization of life, to paraphrase Escobar, is a geopolitical and global issue. Even though plurinationality tries to answer or experiment with the problematizing of "national" identities, both are, as Escobar points out, interlocking processes. But state conditions are far different for the political conflict and the dispute of rights, even though the challenge they face is the same. It is a global issue and needs a geopolitical quest.

Pluralism is at the core of this political proposal and it is necessary to try to raise it, to understand how the formulation of a plurinational state arose. In politics there is no pluralism per se or, to put it more explicitly, in politics we have working social relations within power diagrams. Politics arise as a way to stir, manage, or negotiate these relations; it does not replace the conflict, disagreement, or dispute, but it does affect the social partition and will even try to suppress it, transform it, or at least modify it. So social relations could be changed if they are able to modify the correlations of power. This could happen—it is not so simple; it is never so abstract—politically or as a violent armed confrontation. As we mentioned, violence will arise as a way to neutralize, denounce, or disqualify the opponent; violence is latent because of social divisions and it will continue as long as this social partition exists. What is at stake is not violence in general or in an abstract way; rather it is the social conditions that confront it politically or through armed struggle to suppress the opposition: disappearances, killings, or complete elimination. The past centuries of modern history, as we are taught to call it, have been a gallery of massacres in the name of religion, reason, state, and politics. Creating and building political ways to confront these perilous times is not an individual decision, but it will compromise authorities and institutions and throw into question social capacities and legitimization processes.

These are the kinds of events that have brought about the changes in Bolivia since 2000. The Water Wars in Cochabamba, against water privatization, unleashed it. By blocking roads, the principal peasant and indigenous organization, CTSUB, demanded diverse collective rights. From 2000 to 22 January 2006, when Evo Morales was elected president in a resounding electoral victory, Bolivia was living in perilous and uncertain times. Depending on your point of view, it was either an opportunity or a danger for the status quo in Bolivia; it meant either the possible destruction of the political institutional order or the emergence of a "deep Bolivia," either to strive to maintain the success of neoliberal democracy or to accept the need for a constituent assembly to refound Bolivia or establish a new Bolivia. In those long and intensive years there emerged numerous alternatives or possibilities to redirect the political crisis, but it was a national crisis that required rethinking and reframing a new state form. By 2003, after the uprising of the Gas Wars, the October Agenda emerged, synthesizing the social and cultural demands under three points: the nationalization of hydrocarbons, a call for a constituent assembly, and the bringing to trial of the responsible national authorities (García Linera, Prada, and Tapia 2004).

Evo Morales's overwhelming victory in the presidential elections of December 2005 cannot be understood if he had not assumed entirely the October Agenda as the political proposal of his candidacy rather than his political party program. So the Democratic and Cultural Revolution, as the government named their leadership, is the result of the polls; but to be fair, the political elections took place at a time of a political crisis, a national crisis, which could not necessarily be resolved by polls because the electoral system was part of the problem. But it was an institutional policy that was to produce social discontent and it would meet new challenges in the first months after the new Morales government made its first move: a call to elect representatives to the Constituent Assembly in 2006.

The indigenous and peasant organizations refused to approve this method of election of representatives to the Constituent Assembly because it ignored their own ways or traditional ways for electing authorities. The dilemma was that if this call were ignored, it would threaten the future of the Morales government. Alternatively, they had to create enough political power in order to have some effect in the Constituent Assembly and to induce the support of the Morales government. That is how for the first time in Bolivian history different indigenous and peasant organizations were brought together to create a single political program with a common aim and goal. For the first time they had the opportunity to meet, learn, and discuss their political objectives, to try to produce a unified meaning, language, and strategy. Pluralism was brought into play, by political opportunity and necessity, and that is briefly how the Pact of Unity began.

These were not recent experiences in the social and indigenous movements in building consensus from pluralism. Look, for example, at the Water Wars that brought together multiple social and cultural sectors in the city of Cochabamba and the nearby rural areas. The visible head of the movement was called Coordination for Water and Life (an entity that would administer and coordinate this social movement), making it clear that they were asking for new types of organizations and new structures that could take in diverse forms of organization and participation (Olivera 2004). Or look at the Gas Wars in El Alto, where the confluence of neighborhood organizations, local unions, immigrants, and peasant organizations took over the reins and decision-making in the youngest city in Bolivia (García Linera, Prada, and Tapia 2004; Gómez 2004). In a certain form, the creation of Morales's party, the MAS-IPSP, is also a convergence of different sectors: the emergent platform of "cocaleros" (migrant farmworkers) and indigenous organizations in the lowlands of Bolivia in the 1990s (Stefanoni 2006). We can trace this to the march for life in the 1990s of lowland indigenous organizations, which for the first time in Bolivia's history gave visibility and presence to the diverse nations and peoples, and established plurality, both cultural and political, as their demand (Regalsky 2006).

We can note the different opportunities for bringing pluralism as a political platform, but with the Pact of Unity these were challenged to propose a new state form, which was unprecedented, and they had only a few months to build a proposal to create the chance for common goals and needs. Each organization produced its own proposal—some organizations had been submitting proposals for decades—but the core of this moment was to build a proposal among the different organizations as a Pact of Unity. This was an unprecedented political experience, and to the extent that it could be implemented, it could become a social mandate for the government and the country as a whole.

Both terms, decolonization and plurinationality, in Bolivia are intimately associated with state transformation, with seeking a new state form through

a constitutional process. State transformation was, admittedly, a very difficult and long process, involving much debate in the Constitutional Assembly and protracted negotiations with diverse state and society actors, such as
the parliament, executive negotiators, and the traditional empowerment
strata. It took from August 2006 to February 2008 to be officially promulgated, finally being approved by referendum, which was unprecedented in
Bolivia's constitutional history.

For the first time there was a feeling of pride in this new constitution and,
at the same time, there was also awe and fear for what might transpire. Socially
there was a tense situation and high expectations of how this constitutional
text will be used and put into practice, but the new plurinational polls of
December 2008 had reached again an unprecedented voting result of
64 percent for Evo Morales—a strong demonstration of political support for
Morales and the new constitutional text. The political configuration of power
in Bolivia started to change again, to modify its alliances and oppositions,
not only as political parties or organizations but mostly by holding strategic
political posts and representatives from the different states and regions. So it
would not be long before intense social conflicts appeared, especially in indigenous sectors that were supposedly supporting the transformation of the
Bolivian state, such as the Tipnis conflict, which exposed internal debates as
a geopolitical issue and a conflict of interest. A few months earlier, there was
very strong opposition by social organizations against the surprising government decision to raise the price of petroleum-based fuels during the holiday
season in December 2009. In a matter of days the government was forced to
rescind its decision and forget any attempt to raise prices in the future. These
two examples illustrate the tendencies of new social struggles in Bolivia, but
most of all, how such struggles took hold in the state, or at least at the beginning of the plurinational state. From then on, the disjunctions were wider,
with sides accusing each other of treason and regression. For now, there is a
wound that is difficult to heal.

Another way to approach this political process is by accepting democracy
as a permanent conflict that needs or is nourished by these differences, and
the political action is the capacity to negotiate and agree on possible solutions or modifications of the parts. We could say that it is the institutional
way or, at least, when possible, or just to enforce an institutional agreement.
I think I gave several Bolivian illustrations of this understanding of democracy, which some might call a radical democracy, but in Bolivia it is certainly
a process of decolonization (Exeni 2015).

So this point gets us back to the debate on decolonization, at least to try to understand the thinking that picks up decolonization as a gesture of rupture and affirmation of nations and peoples in the global South, and in this way, I will try to introduce the importance of pluralism in all dimensions of life.

In this second part of the chapter, I introduce three concepts that I think are not sufficiently considered in discussions of the Bolivian process and that are important in the decolonization debate: social movements, constitutional politics, and social economy efforts. I do not mean to say that these concepts are not already part of the debate; rather, they have been insufficiently problematized considering the profound changes of the past fifteen years, and of the ten years of the Morales government. We should see it not as a straight road but as multiple roads and branches that make political orientation and demands tougher, creating other political debates, and not viewed or categorized as pro or against governments policies and decisions. It calls for a political debate in social scales of decisions and without the pressure from government or opposition that monopolizes the public sphere. A possible alternative could be to approach with strategic positions in the turbulent times of transformation of state and a very fast social and economic enlargement. In a certain way, I think the relation between time and politics is central to the Bolivian process and to the potential for decolonization in our societies.

Understanding social movements means understanding that these movements include indigenous movements. They were not considered political subjects; it took several political events to start regarding old-new ways of organization and participation and allow us to begin to grasp the tendencies in our changing societies. In our experience in Bolivia, only after the victories of the social movements in 2000 were the decisive political presence and demands of these groups being discussed, even if people were opposed to them. From the indigenous viewpoint, this was a big opportunity to forge their different capacities and memories as modes of resisting power and of proposing other alternatives and possibilities, to assert that indigenous identity is not uniform and homogeneous, but a unique identity.

It is not until the 1990s that strong movements from Bolivia's lowlands began. At this time, regional organizations organized several marches to demand their collective rights and began to connect with Andean indigenous organizations and build strategic relations with them. It is in these movements that pluralistic politics and organizations begin to be produced, because their particular circumstances made them very vulnerable and dispossessed. Just imagine if today's constitution recognized thirty-two official languages. This gives you an idea of the existing cultural diversity in Bolivia: only three languages are used in the Andean region, while the other twenty-nine are found in Bolivia's lowlands, which occupy two-thirds of Bolivia's territory. Decolonization is therefore also a challenge for Andean indigenous organizations. Most of the time, this is not explicit. In other South American contexts they maintain this kind of cultural and linguistic hierarchy within so-called indigenous organizations and movements, and there is an enormous population of Afro-Americans who are struggling for their collective rights (Walsh 2010). And there were not always connections and collaborative roles within political and social movements.

The importance of women's rights and gender demands are present crosswise in most of the social movements of the region, driven by rapid and intense change in domestic structures and roles in economic production and reproduction. More women entered the labor force in disadvantaged situations, and more women are head of households in single-parent domestic units, assuming all responsibilities for subsistence. In past decades we have incorporated women in the economic and social cycle but in ways that were uneven and hierarchical. In Bolivia, this is part of confronting a patriarchal system and, according to government declarations, this also forms part of the movement for decolonization. This demand was also presented during the Constituent Assembly to make a statement against certain political positions about sexuality, body politics, and marriage. Though some legislation was passed in support of women's rights, implementation has been very slow, entangled in bureaucracy. The demands remain, and an explosion seems imminent.

Generational issues are also about to explode. Just consider that more than half of the population in South America is made up of minorities, and this is a population estimated at half a billion. The next years will be challenging in terms of education, labor, and communication, taking into account this large percentage of young people. Are we prepared? Are we taking this into account? I'm not sure; we're already much too absorbed with problems and dilemmas of the present.

But mostly for the Bolivian experience, the capabilities of an indigenous presence in state quarters and their participation in state decisions have modified their own organizational structures and forms. In short, how much have social and indigenous organizations changed in the past years in their capabilities to move toward and even occupy positions of leadership in state offices? Obviously this was their political objective, but once that is reached, how will it affect their organization? What changes will take place inside their organization? Relations with leaders and organizational structures could start to be tightened and become an ambiguous relationship. How will organizations deal with it? Perhaps it is time to examine the discussions and conflicts inside organizations to see what its tendencies and configurations might be. This is a fast-moving panorama in Bolivia of social and cultural affirmations, of social mobility and identity pride; but it could turn out as a riddle if the point of view is from some indigenous minority, women's position, or children's perspectives.

These are the challenges of constitutional politics and the transformation of the state, and I put it this way because it is a challenge concerning constitutional power, in its political sense. Because to think that the effort to discuss and change a constitutional text is done once the text is promulgated is to think that the text is the new reality. If it says, like in Bolivia, we have a constitutional plurinational state, then there is a new state, and we are forgetting, or at least underestimating the process of transformation underway in a changing state form. And how is this transformation achievable and what kind of process will help this transition? To answer these questions, a new time or temporalities and politics will be decisive here.

The social debates around the transition are not as relevant for the media as the diverse consultations and elections of state authorities that we have had in the past ten years. The media concentrate on scandals and victories in the political arena, even though we could confirm that there are strong debates in organizations and everyday spaces. The difficulty lies in the capacity to impact and enforce these issues at the institutional level. If we had to evaluate recent legislation after the approved Constitution, we will find that most of the laws are called into question, not necessarily because they could be unconstitutional, as some declared, but because they are incomplete or improperly treated. We can try to explain these odd situations by the continuous change in the correlation of power relations in Bolivia, but it will not be satisfactory if we do not take note of new points of conflict and how they affect social organizations and even determine state entities and authorities.

The image of the state as a battlefield could help understand the kind of political conditions that are displayed in the discussions of the transformation and transition of the state as mentioned. We must accept this image in order to understand the state not as a single, homogeneous entity but as a decentralized configuration of power, authority, and law; to comprehend the state as a historical form of a dynamic assemblage of institutions, norms, and authorities coexisting in a struggle defined by the correlations of power relations. This brief characterization is highly debatable, but it is quite effective for discussing state conditions and constitutional issues in our post-neoliberal politics, and in Bolivia's case, for reworking the potentials and limits of the aims of the plurinational state (Vega Camacho 2014).

Evaluating constitutional politics from 2009, when the Constitution was promulgated, to today would be difficult because institutional changes can take much longer. However, in terms of new laws and so-called organic laws, these have been considered more conservative with the established order or less propitious to collective and indigenous rights. Even though there is an important indigenous presence in state offices, this does not necessarily mean that indigenous demands are given priority. Remember that there is an enormous heterogeneity within indigenous organizations.

This panorama brings skepticism in different social sectors or to opponents of government initiatives and attempts, and because of the short life of this constitution, there is not enough time and space to pose active and critical actions. But there is political discussion and constitutional politics in organizations and social movements. Some of the changes in their structure and role, as we have mentioned, are rooted in these issues. And the strategies with a long history of resisting colonial orders have arisen once again, in a more subterranean way or low-voice activity. Another way of channeling this increasing discontent is to form new movements demanding new urban rights and necessities such as gas or water services, public transportation, and public safety.

Finally, socioeconomic efforts could allow us to visualize the biggest transformation in socioeconomic criteria. I mean that if there is a successful change in the role of the state, it is in its economic policies by the democratization of economic access by the population. Some will call this the creation of a middle class because of the decrease in extreme poverty and an expansion of the market and money, increasing consumption and savings, which are important for national economic policies. "Middle class" might be helpful as a self-definition of social mobility, but it makes invisible the complex ensemble of markets and economies that are made viable by a diversity of producers and traders, services, and immaterial work that compose this new urban labor.

That is why I chose the term "social economy": it gathers different efforts to respond to social necessities and urgencies, and I describe these as efforts because they could be state initiatives or other types of social actions that arise from community bonds or social initiatives. Economic prospects as social economics has not been the object of much research, nor have state policies concerning bonuses and other economic support to certain sectors of the population, such as nursing mothers, school children, and senior citizens.[3]

The combination of economic growth, democratization of access to markets and money, and a strong state role has repercussions in discussions of the plural economy inspired by the Constitution and its interpretations. This is a strong argument for the government together with the social feeling of being at last removed from the list of poorest countries. But indeed, for the first time in Bolivia there is democratization in having access to opportunities. On the other hand, intensive dynamics of accumulation and dispossession create new inequalities that challenge the capabilities of social policies, organization, and forms of life to build alternatives.

These three topics, changing social movements, constitutional politics, and socioeconomic efforts, allow us to glimpse the challenging times in Bolivia. It is not necessarily a negative or skeptical view, because the goal of a plurinational state is increasingly discredited. Public media paint only one side or the other as black or white, which is very convenient for electoral polls and for overwhelming political debate and discussion. So the impression of the Bolivian process will reflect only those options again as a problem of two Bolivias, as was done before in terms of nationalistic ideals for seeking a racial mixture (mestizaje) or in terms of proposing a purely indigenous republic. This was something that was overcome when indigenous organizations assumed their plurality and differences and proposed a new state form: the plurinational state. Their political participation was to stand up for a plurinational state as the strategic place from which to negotiate and settle the indifference that colonial order and liberal-republican norms had imposed on them.

The relationship between time and politics could enable us to broaden the problematization of the political process in Bolivia and the geopolitical region, allowing us to understand the multiscale levels of politics and to take a strategic approach to experimenting with alternatives in a geopolitical sense and to building connections where social movements are the triggers for state transformations to support the germinating pluralism and common social spaces (commonalities).

As I opened this inquiry with Fanon's words of 1952 as a final prayer to his body to allow him to remain a man who questions, in closing I would like to quote Rancière from an intervention during the 2012 Venice Bienniale: "I would like to counter these analyses of the reign of the present from a completely different perspective: that of a time that is not framed by the sole speed of the development of capital. This perspective is framed in relation to the institutions that make temporal coincidence and non-coincidence their main affair. Our world does not function according to a homogeneous process of presentification and acceleration. It functions according to the regulation of the convergence and divergence of times" (Rancière 2012, 23).

## Notes

1. "I think the proper in political notions is not to be or not polysemic: is proper that are the subject of a struggle. The political struggle is also the struggle for the appropriation of words" (Rancière 2010, 99).
2. El Pacto de Unidad y el Proceso de Construcción de una Propuesta de Constitución Política del Estado (Garcés 2010, 145).
3. For notable exceptions see Wanderley 2009; Loza Tellería 2013; Gago 2014.

## References

Clifford, James. 2013. *Returns: Becoming Indigenous in the Twenty-First Century*. Cambridge, Mass.: Harvard University Press.
Escobar, Arturo. 2014. *Sentipensar con la tierra*. Medellín: UNAULA.
Exeni, José Luis, ed. 2015. *La larga marcha: El proceso de autonomías indígenas en Bolivia*. La Paz: Fundación Rosa Luxemburgo.
Fanon, Frantz. 1968 [1961]. *The Wretched of the World*. Translated by C. Farrington. New York: Grove Press.
———. 2008 [1952]. *Black Skin, White Mask*. Translated by C. L. Markmann. London: Pluto Press.
Gago, Verónica. 2014. *La razón neoliberal: Economías barrocas y pragmática popular*. Buenos Aires: Tinta Limón.
Garcés, Fernando, ed. 2010. *El pacto de unidad y el proceso de construcción de una propuesta de constitución política del estado: Sistematización de la experiencia*. La Paz: Programa NINA.
García Linera, Alvaro, Raquel Gutierrez, Raúl Prada, and Luis Tapia. 2000. *El retorno de la Bolivia plebeya*. La Paz: Muela del Diablo.

García Linera, Alvaro, Raúl Prada, and Luis Tapia. 2004. *Memorias de octubre*. La Paz: Muela del Diablo.

Gómez, L. 2004. *El alto de pie: Una insurrección aymara en Bolivia*. La Paz: Comuna.

Loza Tellería, Gabriel. 2013. *Bolivia: El modelo de economía plural*. La Paz: Editorial Vínculos.

Mezzadra, Sandro and Brett Neilson. 2013. *Border as Method, or, the Multiplication of Labor*. Durham, N.C.: Duke University Press.

Olivera, Oscar. 2004. *Cochabamba! Water War in Bolivia*. In collaboration with Tom Lewis. New York: South End Press.

Rancière, Jacques. 2010. "Las democracias contra la democracia." In *Democracia en suspenso*, edited by Giorgio Agamben, Alain Badiou, Daniel Bensaid, Wendy Brown, Jean Lu-Nancy, Jacques Rancière, Kristin Ross, Slavoj Zizec, 97–102. Madrid: Casus Belli.

———. 2012. "In What Time Do We Live?" In *The State of Things*, edited by Marta Kuzma, Pablo Lafuente, and Peter Osborne, 9–38. London: Koenig Books.

Regalsky, Pablo. 2006. "Bolivia indígena y campesina: Una larga marcha para liberar sus territorios y un contexto para el gobierno de Evo Morales." *Revista Herramienta* 31 (3).

Stefanoni, Pablo. 2006. *La revolución de Evo Morales: De la coca al palacio*. Buenos Aires: Capital Intelectual Editores.

Vega Camacho, Oscar. 2014. "¿Qué hacer con el estado?" In *Dar Staat in Lateinamerika Kolonialität, Gewalt, Transformation*, edited by Alke Jenss and Stefan Pimmer, 171–202. Munster: Westfälisches Dampfboot.

Wallerstein, Immanuel. 2014. *World-Systems Analysis: An Introduction*. Durham, N.C.: Duke University Press.

Walsh, Catherine. 2010. "Interculturalidad y (de)colonidad: Diferencia y nación de otro modo." In *Construyendo interculturalidad crítica*, coauthored by Jorge Viaña and Luis Tapia, 75–96. La Paz: Convenio Andrés Bello.

Wanderley, Fernanda. 2009. *Crecimiento, empleo y bienestar: ¿Por qué Bolivia es tan desigual?* La Paz: CIDES-UMSA.

# CHAPTER 15

# Postwar El Salvador: Entangled Aftermaths

Irina Carlota (Lotti) Silber

## Introduction

During the summer of 2014, United States President Barack Obama declared the unaccompanied border crossings of minors an "urgent humanitarian situation" as the number of detentions was dramatic and on the rise (Semple 2014). Indeed, Customs and Border Protection (CBP) of the Department of Homeland Security reported the capture of 68,541 unaccompanied minors in 2014, a 77 percent increase since 2013. Of these children, 75 percent are from what policymakers describe as the Northern Triangle—the Central American countries of El Salvador, Guatemala, and Honduras (Stinchcomb and Hershberg 2014, 6). In this way, for the first time in decades, news about Salvadoran processes and bodies entered the front pages of mainstream media. With this reporting came the images of disheveled, dirty, and panicked children along with the squalor of their shelters. This framed unaccompanied Central American youth, in part, within a conception of vulnerable humanity rooted in what Didier Fassin illuminates as the moral compassion of our time (2012). For others, however, in the heated politics of immigration reform and border security, these same bodies are read within a continuum of dehumanizing illegality spawned both by neglectful, amoral parents—who allow their children to travel alone despite the well-known dangers of the desert and La Bestia, where they can be raped, trafficked for sex, kidnapped, and murdered—and by President Obama's compromised immigration reform of June 2012 for undocumented youth. Deferred Action for Childhood Arrivals (DACA), which granted liminal legality and deportation relief to a generation of undocumented youth between the ages of 16 and 30, supposedly has opened the floodgates (Lopez and Krogstad 2014). Data compiled by the U.S. Citizenship and Immigration Services indicate that 18,700 Salvadoran youth received this status from August 2012 to September 2013 (USCIS 2014).

By the spring of 2015 another set of numbers dominated the international public sphere through the trope of more alarming numbers. There were 635 homicides in El Salvador during May (Guardian 2015a), 667 in June (Malkin 2015), and 911 in August (Guardian 2015b). Reports highlight that these numbers illuminate a peak in the violence, the highest since the end of the Salvadoran civil war (1980–92), with one murder every hour. At the time, analysts were consumed by these numbers, prognosticating that if the homicide rate continued in this trend it would exceed 90 per 100,000 people in 2015, the highest in the world (Watts 2015). To analyze this surge of violence, significant discussion focuses on gang violence. Reports note the failure of a truce between the leading gangs Mara Salvatrucha (MS-13) and Barrio 18 and former FMLN President Mauricio Funes's administration as escalating the violence (Valencia 2015). Gangs have been compared to ISIS (Dickey 2015), though less coverage exposes the hidden violence aimed at gangs perpetrated by El Salvador's police forces (Valencia, Martínez, and Caravantes 2015). Overwhelmingly, accounts highlight the immediacy of everyday anger and insecurity felt by so many Salvadorans who see no solution outside of historically right-wing Mano Dura policies (Alarcón 2015). Unlike those unaccompanied minors, there is no humanitarian project here, though ample reporting clearly illuminates the forced conscription of minors into gangs throughout El Salvador (for example, Kennedy 2014).

What to make of these numbers and the binary in this juxtaposition of the violent and the vulnerable? How have these embodied numbers come to represent postwar El Salvador? For across perspectives, consistently, resoundingly, El Salvador is depicted as a contemporary, bloody, terrifying, and insecure place more than twenty years into the postwar period. Most importantly, this chaos threatens to "leak" into the United States—those disheveled and panicked kids and the transnational gangs organizing crime and violence across borders (see also Coutin 2007).

This chapter seeks to complicate narratives of postwar life that ultimately flatten regional histories, erase both lived experience and larger geopolitical forces, and condemn a nation and a people for the production of outlawed bodies. It asks what other narratives can be told about El Salvador's prolific and proliferating violence and insecurity. El Salvador has become a key case study in the analysis of comparative peace processes (for example, Hayner 2011) and is heralded as a model of disarmament, demobilization, and reintegration (DDR). Qualitative research, particularly ethnographic, has expanded macro level findings and analysis with an attention to the everyday meanings and experiences of postwar rebuilding and reconciliation across a range of social, political, and economic locations. A significant amount of this work has been gendered and focuses on the postwar trajectories of former insurgents. This chapter builds on more than twenty years of longitudinal, ethnographic research in the Department of Chalatenango, a former war zone, and with the diaspora as it argues against a facile account of a Salvadoran culture of violence as a legacy of war. It acknowledges, however, the politics of this violence, names it as impunity, and points to the ways in which people live through the everyday of aftermaths and violence.

It is in this daily "living through" that the entanglements of violence, security, and practices of reconciliation emerge. In order to elucidate these entanglements it is helpful to consider the cultural production of postwar subjects. Anthropologist John Jackson elsewhere asks us to consider the always already racialized and embodied "overdetermined markers" (2012, 480) that are deployed to tell a story. For the Salvadoran case I suggest that we explore how violence has become one such "overdetermined marker" for Salvadoran postrevolutionary and postwar bodies. Specifically, in the chapter I argue that cultural work takes place through the production of the Salvadoran biopolitical body. Salvadorans' quantified perceptions of violence and insecurity, as well as the national counting of the dead,[1] rub up against unexpected spaces of forgiveness, still laden with violence and still without reconciliation.

The chapter first contextualizes the war and postwar period and locates the ethnographic context of Chalatenango. Second, it points to research on security and insecurity as it intersects with the statistical data that is ever unfolding on El Salvador's crime and violence. Third, it introduces entangled and diasporic ethnographic vignettes of postwar life across families and across borders. In doing so it troubles the narratives on the surge of violence in El Salvador and interrogates what insecurity means in the long postwar period and how people live in the aftermath. As a result, the chapter offers a way to think about modalities of postwar truth-telling in the *longue durée* and intimacy of ever-shifting postwar life.

## Contexts of War and Postwar

The Salvadoran civil war (1980–1992) claimed the lives of seventy-five thousand people, disappeared another seven thousand Salvadorans, and displaced five hundred thousand civilians (Montgomery 1995). Research shows that the United States supported the counterinsurgency with $6 billion of military aid over a decade (Murray 1997, 15). The war officially ended on 16 January 1992 with the signing of the United Nations-brokered peace accords between insurgent forces (FMLN, Fabundo Martí National Liberation Front) and the right-wing ARENA (National Republican Alliance) government. Much scholarship and policy has addressed this period, as El Salvador's "negotiated revolution" (Karl 1992) quickly became the model and success story for how to mediate a civil war. The peace accords were extraordinary in many respects, from reforming the military and police forces to legalizing the insurgent FMLN into an official political party. With demobilization and reintegration, scholars began to explore El Salvador's democratization within larger Latin American shifts away from authoritarian regimes to democracies. While an earlier literature was concerned with the transition to democracy and then its consolidation (Mainwaring 1992; O'Donnell et al. 1986), work on El Salvador began to move beyond a focus on electoral politics in an attempt to understand the relationship between peace making and democratization (Popkin 2000; Hayner 2011; Boyce 2002).

Qualitative research increased significantly during the 1990s and led to important work that reframed the conceptualization and periodization of peace building as evidenced in what anthropologist Ellen Moodie discusses as the "aftermath of peace" (2010). For Moodie, El Salvador after war is characterized by an anxious and depoliticized uncertainty that resignifies violence discursively into common crime. Much of this research has focused on theorizing postwar reconstruction and local transitions to democracy. For instance, political scientist Elisabeth Wood has explored the role of peasant insurgent activism and agrarian processes in peace building from below (2000; 2003). Leigh Binford, too, has long explored wartime processes in a war zone (Morazán) and theorized the binds of collective action (1996; 1998).

Much of this research has highlighted the role of women in the insurgency and beyond, pointing to their critical and varied role in military-political structures, as well as to the multiple gendered challenges encountered during the postwar period in both urban and rural communities (Kampwirth 2002, 2004; Shayne 2004; Silber 2011; Viterna 2013). This gendered perspective is crucial because women accounted for approximately 30 percent of FMLN forces, yet reintegration programs often did not consider or meet their particular needs (Segovia 2009, 8, 18).

My own research has focused on northern El Salvador, in the Department of Chalatenango, a rural, mountainous, and poor region of the country where historically most people were small-scale peasant farmers who migrated seasonally for wage labor in order to survive. This was an area where the 1970s teachings of the progressive Catholic Church, known as liberation theology, ran deep alongside other movements for social justice. By the late 1970s repression by paramilitary, military, and police forces was brutal, and Chalatenango became a key site of wartime oppositional organizing and an area that was destroyed by military conflict. The war was marked by a back and forth in people's degree of participation. Men, women, the young, and the old fled through hills in *guindas*,[2] leaving just about everything in their communities in order to escape state-sponsored violence. Many joined the FMLN guerilla forces for a time or crossed borders into refugee camps, smuggled guns, medicine, and the injured, and sometimes transported the dead.[3] In 1987, many civilians left Honduran refugee camps and repopulated their destroyed communities, all the while supporting insurgent forces.[4]

Specifically, I have conducted ethnographic research in the municipality of Las Vueltas[5] and in a community that I call El Rancho.[6] This region comprised former militants and their community supporters. As such, these repopulated communities were politically quite homogeneous and from the early to mid-1990s found themselves targets of international and national development efforts to reincorporate excluded and marginalized citizens into the nation, into the productive economy. Chalatenango became the site of a flurry of postwar "reconstruction and development" attention (for example, potable water, electrification, new roads, microcredit programs, cement-block houses, arts and crafts, and cattle, pig, and hen farming aimed at "gendering" development). Much of this was handled through new forms of governmentality, through an explosion of nongovernmental organizations (NGOs), many deeply politicized, in the early throes of professionalization and emerging from insurgent collective action (see Silber 2011).

In this early period—postwar, postconflict—all things "post" were actually experienced as temporally very present. Salvadorans were in the midst of transition, and the meaning and practices of *la transición* and everyday trust in the path toward and possibilities of democratization were newly unfolding and lived differently across scales. For some sectors of the population who had struggled militarily and politically for social change, the FMLN *en poder* "in power," meaning winning the presidency, was still a rallying cry, not an institutional reality as it is today with the election of two FMLN presidents: Mauricio Funes in 2009 and former FPL Comandante Salvador Sánchez Cerén in 2014. It was the time of reconstruction and development as democracy, of the reintegration of insurgents into civil society.

Recall that Chalatecos and Chalatecas[7] in these communities had been off the grid, long-excluded from national policies, and then agents in the rejection of local and national governments during the war as political, social, and economic life was organized through popular and armed organizations. Indeed, new research indicates just how powerful political military organizations (PMOs) were in this region (Sprenkels 2014). As Sprenkels illuminates, PMOs organized all aspects of community life—and continued to do so well into the postwar period. This pushes us to think through what he terms a "social field of 'post-insurgency'" and beyond a politics of reintegration (Sprenkels 2014).

## Reintegration, Reconciliation, and Impunity

Reintegration is something that my own ethnography has challenged, most eloquently illuminated during an interview with a former insurgent turned mayor. Aquilino theorized reintegration and reconciliation as spectral, as "una reconciliación fantasma. . . . Reintegration has not been resolved because the problems continue. We organized because of these; it is what motivated us, what drove us to an armed struggle, for issues that are still not resolved" (Silber 2011, 2). For in this long postwar period, the politics of opposition was rooted in a local history of martyred leaders, wounded bodies, heroic narratives, and a vision of the revolution as one that would fundamentally result in economic justice, which has not occurred. In neoliberal El Salvador, at least for the everyday rank-and-file Chalateco and Chalateca, the backbone of the insurgency, that search for economic justice, along with a call for truth and accountability (for human rights abuses) was trumped by a national and local experience of postwar life as reconstruction—development as democracy. After twenty-five years of postwar life, it is clear that this model of reconstruction produced unintended consequences, with a nation territorially unmoored.

By the late 1990s across El Salvador, but dramatically in former war zones, the torrent of reconstruction aid was over and the global peace industry shifted to new sites.[8] With internationally funded projects dwindling, an agricultural economy marginalized, and a series of "natural disasters,"[9] ten years into the "transition," Chalatecos and Chalatecas began an unprecedented migration to the United States, joining the now more than two million Salvadorans estimated to live in the U.S., who send remittances home and keep the nation afloat.[10] Salvadorans in the U.S. sent $3.6 billion dollars in remittances back home in 2011, making up 16.5 percent of the gross domestic product. As a UNDP country report makes clear, the municipality of Las Vueltas was altered by this new migration that erupted between 2001 and 2004; it was a response to a crisis in the agricultural sector (2005, 222) and ultimately a product of the violence of neoliberal economic policies already underway before the peace accords (Moodie 2010).

In my larger work I have come to understand postwar processes through the metaphor of entanglement. In doing so I theorize how Chalatecos and Chalatecas live with their past, speaking for a generation lost to war and for the next generation socialized through it. I argue that the struggles of war are entangled first with the disillusionment of peace despite political gains and some economic benefits, and second in the precarious hope for the future that takes shape in what I have come to understand as the unanticipated obligation of migration by the protagonist generation, those insurgents of the past and their now adult children who find themselves pushed and pulled across borders (Silber 2011).[11] In doing so, residents of repopulated communities join a longer and older wave of Salvadoran migrants in the United States whose labor and remittances are estimated to have reduced the national poverty rate by 7 percent. Indeed, scholars argue that migration has become a key aspect of El Salvador's national development plan (Gammage 2006). However, the everyday narratives and testimonies of former insurgents from Chalatenango clearly indicate that emigration was not an aspiration of war, or of postwar life, or of securing justice and equality.

Unexpectedly then, during the postwar period, many Salvadorans continue to move through clandestinity and through new forms of displacement. In 2008 there were an estimated five hundred and seventy thousand unauthorized Salvadoran migrants in the United States. Through these post-war circulations of bodies, development, migration, and democracy are linked. How is this relationship lived? What do these numbers tell us about reconciliation after war? Is this postwar displacement of Salvadoran citizens producing spaces for new kinds of postwar truth-telling that disrupt vulnerable lives? Or is the everyday violence and insecurity exacerbated? These are not only academic questions. For instance, it is catching that the discourse of reintegration has come full circle or is reemergent in the Salvadoran political landscape twenty-five years into the postwar period. What is the meaning of these waves of reintegration?

Interestingly, by 2015, a politics of *reinserción*, or reintegration, was called upon for a new generation of outlawed bodies, for those Salvadorans deported from the United States, or "removed," as discursively constructed by the Department of Homeland Security. In El Salvador they are called *los retornados*, the returned. As the Director of the Dirección de General de Migración y Extranjería stated on a Salvadoran government website, the work ahead involves facilitating their reintegration: "to work so that the returned understand our economic environment so that we can facilitate their reintegration. We are in a very different context then what they had in the United States. That requires an adaptation."[12] In July 2015, preliminary ethnographic research with retornados in the municipality of Las Vueltas indeed points to the diversity of experiences, and the difficulty of "integrating" often urban, service sector skills—a bartender in downtown Washington, D.C.—into the rural spatial and temporal geography. The numbers have been consistent: 20,848 Salvadorans were removed in 2009 with a slight dip in 2011 when 17,308 Salvadorans were deported from the United States back to their country of origin (Simanski and Sapp 2012). In comparison, the reintegration of former combatants took place in the early 1990s. Demobilization figures indicate that 15,009 FMLN combatants and political cadre demobilized with the peace accord, as did more than twenty thousand from various units of the Salvadoran Armed Forces (FAES) (Segovia 2009, 7, 9). Analyst Alexander Segovia situates these numbers by noting that of these demobilized, "a significant number subsequently became part of the new National Civilian Police [Policía Nacional Civil] (PNC). In effect, the peace accords provided for their incorporation so long as demobilized individuals met the requirements for entrance to the National Public Security Academy (ANSP) . . . in subsequent agreements it was decided that each of the two demobilized forces could account for up to 20 percent of the members of the PNC" (Segovia 2009, 9).

Across generations this rhetoric of *reinserción* takes place in obviously different contexts, from the immediate postwar laying down of guns, the UN-facilitated roll-out of development programs, and political power still in the hands of the ARENA government, to the *long durée* of the postwar period, with two FMLN presidents, and the now quite institutionalized discourse of "estamos peor que antes" (Moodie 2010) that circulates across the nation as impunity persists. Recall that an aspect of the peace process involved the publication of the United Nation's Truth Commission Report. Of the twenty-two thousand investigated cases of human rights violations, close to 95 percent were attributed to the Salvadoran Armed Forces and to paramilitary groups and death squads clearly linked to the state. Five percent were attributed to the FMLN forces. However, by March 1993, a law was passed that granted amnesty to all those involved in crimes against humanity (on the right and left) during the war, and thus a window was dramatically closed in the search for truth and justice, for redress. The Salvadoran national discourse has emphasized that it was critical to forget the war, to forget the past violence in order to move beyond it, in order to forgive and reconcile the nation. For remembering the bloodshed would create festering wounds and deepen a polarized political field, the body politic toxic.

However, across sectors in El Salvador and internationally, the pressure mounted to remove the amnesty law. Key efforts include the Inter-American Commission on Human Rights, internationally from the Spanish National Court and its pursuit of the "Jesuit Massacre Case," and domestically through the 2013 challenge by the Human Rights Institute of Central American University (IDUCA) that contests the constitutionality of the amnesty law (Thale 2013). Noted was the January 2013 public apology by then FMLN President Mauricio Funes for the El Mozote massacre and the acknowledgement that the military committed serious human rights violations.[13] Historic, indeed, in July 2016, El Salvador's Constitutional Chamber of the Supreme Court ruled that the 1993 Amnesty Law was unconstitutional. This has opened a legal path for the investigation and prosecution of major human rights abuses during the civil war. Still, in El Salvador perpetrators have not been prosecuted, reparations programs have not been institutionalized, and many argue that there is no justice (ICTJ 2013). As Sprenkels reminds us, the amnesty law not only benefited the leadership on the right and the FMLN, but also the human rights organizations that were historically closely aligned with the FMLN (2012, 77). Thus the unintended limitations of the Truth Commission can also be read, as provocatively suggested by historians Rey Tristán and Lazo, as "el modelo de 'reconciliación' vía impunidad" (a model of reconciliation via impunity) that spawns "una reconciliación sin reconciliados" (a reconciliation without the reconciled) (2011). This framing is extremely compelling. What does it mean to have reconciliation without the reconciled?

## Insecurity in the Long Postwar Period

A way to think through this question is to analyze Salvadoran public opinion polls about violence, policy research on the "prevention of violence," and census data on violent deaths. The internationally recognized Instituto de Derechos Humanos of the Universidad Centroamericana (IDHUCA) José Simeón Cañas explains: "Prevention is always better than to cure; when the disease is present, in this case, violence, it should also be addressed so that preventive measures are able to reduce or eliminate the risk of appearance of violent events."[14] What interests me most about this opening passage is the metaphor of the diseased nation to be cured, in part, the report suggests, by the government's "strong political will" to combat the multiple causes of delinquency (IDHUCA n.d.). A diseased nation comprised of delinquents and the unreconciled?

It is true, violence is rampant, ranging from everyday extortion in neighborhoods, assassinations, and gender-based violence to the assault of local buses. Recall the numbers referenced at the opening of this chapter. The response has been decades of zero-tolerance anti-gang laws in El Salvador known as Mano Dura, which was passed in 1993 and Super Mano Dura of 2004. However, critical scholarship continues to expose the deep contradictions and unexpected consequences of these policies. As Seelke demonstrates, this restriction on the rights of suspected criminals made gang membership illegal, compromised fair trials, and dramatically, in a reversal of the peace accords, introduced the military into everyday policing (Seelke 2009, 10). Significantly, between 2004 and 2005, of the fourteen thousand Salvadoran youth arrested, ten thousand were released. Reports indicated that it was during their incarceration that youth were subsequently recruited into gangs (Seelke 2009, 9). And while homicides decreased during a controversial truce between gangs and the Salvadoran government led by Funes, the homicide rate has always remained at what the World Health Organization terms epidemic levels.[15] In 2015, according to the National Civilian Police (the police force instituted as part of the peace accords), 60 percent of homicides in El Salvador were committed by gangs (Martínez 2015).[16] And the legacy of the Mano Dura remains. For as Alisha Holland illuminates, a key aspect of this ARENA policy was security (2013). Elana Zilberg expands this analysis as she highlights the relationship between the history of U.S.-supported counterinsurgency and new "transnational security agreements" in order to explode facile discussions on transnational gangs (2011, 2).

At the national and regional level, security remains a top priority. Note the 2015 "Plan El Salvador Seguro" (Safe El Salvador Plan) worth $2 billion and created by President Salvador Sánchez Cerén through the direction of the Consejo Nacional de Seguridad Ciudadana y Convivencia, which was facilitated by the United Nations. Citizen security and "convivencia," or "co-existence," are rhetorically linked. What does this mean, living with, living together, well and in harmony? The plan, to be instituted in the country's fifty most violent municipalities, focuses on prevention and the creation of employment opportunities, with a projected $500 million directed toward two hundred and fifty thousand jobs for youth. The plan details immediate (within six months) to long-term plans (ten years) and includes significant rhetorical interventions. For example, it acknowledges the existence of structural violence in its enumeration of the structural causes underscoring El Salvador's generalized insecurity. Further, it identifies the normalization and routinization of these causes, generating institutional weakness across sectors of society, which ultimately produces the current context of impunity (Consejo Nacional 2015, 3). The plan is not without its critics, who note its similarities with former ARENA President Antonio Saca's "País Seguro" of more than a decade ago (Zablah 2015).

Additionally, regionally, and in response to at the time U.S. President Barack Obama's insistence that the countries of the Northern Triangle devise a concerted plan to stem the tide of unaccompanied minors, El Salvador, Guatemala, and Honduras put forth the "Plan of the Alliance for Prosperity in the Northern Triangle: A Road Map" (2014). The opening lines of the executive summary state: "Nearly 9% of our population *has decided to leave*, resulting in a major loss of human capital. For the most part, this flight of our people stems from the lack of economic and job opportunities in our countries, growing violence, and the departure of those who want to reunite with relatives living abroad" (2014, i; emphasis added). Theirs is a call to action: "we have taken immediate measures to ensure the human rights of our minors, help people who have returned to reintegrate into society, and dis-

mantle human trafficking rings" (2014, i). The document is rife with strategies to improve, stimulate, develop, and strengthen economic sectors with
the aim to further attract foreign investment, global markets, and so on. One
could surely argue that this regional plan reinscribes neoliberal global politics within the region and fails to address people's everyday experiences with
the very insecurity that many argue propels emigration. As remarked by a
former police officer turned migrant, who felt "obligated" to join the new civilian police force (PNC) as a way to rebuild a polarized society, and "obligated once again" to emigrate: "So, the pressure gets closer and obligates us
to migrate to the United States. I'm telling you, when you go visit the communities you won't see old, familiar faces. They've all come here. . . . Why did
they come? Because you can't find work. And everything is expensive. *Se ob-
liga. Uno se siente obligado.* (One feels obligated.) You say, 'I don't have any
options; I don't have any opportunities.' So the only option, the only dream
that awakens is to come to the United States" (Silber 2011, 174–75). This is a
complicated relationship between "desire" and a chronic sense of burden.
And Avel is correct, the silence in sending communities is palpable.

More pointedly, a discourse of insecurity is often deployed within con-
versations not only about a Salvadoran culture of violence but also about a
"culture of democracy" as pursued in a 2012 USAID-funded project (Córdova Macias, Cruz, and Seligson 2013). What is it about the possibility of the
one for the other? In these studies (Observatorio de Seguridad Ciudadana
2013; Fundaungo 2013), insecurity is the lens through which El Salvador is
understood. Córdova Macias, Cruz, and Seligson's (2013) public opinion
polls, for example, indicate that political tolerance is actually lower than in
2004 (seen as a sign of a healthy democracy) and that Salvadorans list insecurity as one of the key fundamental problems across the nation. Indeed,
38 percent of the population described insecurity as the most urgent issue in
their community (34). Researchers based at FUNDAUNGO[17] have followed
up with a series of studies on crime and violence that continue to produce a
biopolitical population through this reporting. The numbers are, again, dramatic in terms of pointing to the degree of people's everyday concerns. For
example, 52.5 percent of Salvadorans in the study reported that violence and
delinquency are at the heart of national problems. Six out of ten Salvadorans
say that crime is the country's main problem (Observatorio de Seguridad
Ciudadana 2013, 15).

Disaggregating this opinion poll data is crucial. For instance, the study
further points to a rural/urban divide. Crime is noted as the primary factor

generating insecurity in urban areas, whereas it is the economy that creates an everyday insecurity for Salvadorans in the rural countryside (Observatorio de Seguridad Ciudadana 2013, 20). This supports my ethnographic findings on the unanticipated obligation of migration for so many of the Chalatecos and Chalatecas I have interviewed. People's perception of insecurity also appears to be strongly linked to their feelings of confidence in various institutions. Thus, whereas 81 percent of the Salvadorans interviewed felt the highest level of confidence in churches, followed by the Instituto Salvadoreña para el Desarrollo de la Mujer (73 percent—a striking number—perhaps indicating success in gendered issues), they were least confident in those institutions actually charged with ensuring citizen security (in other words, the Policía Nacional Civil—61.6 percent—and the Corte Suprema de Justicia—61.4 percent) (Observatorio de Seguridad Ciudadana 2013, 63).

Yet, it is the *Atlas de Violencia en El Salvador (2009–2012)*, the third atlas produced since the turn of the twenty-first century, that yields some striking data. The atlas, a collection of tables and charts and glossy colored maps rigorously compiled from a range of national sources, provides a detailed statistical breakdown of homicides at the national, departmental, and municipal levels.[18] Accordingly, we know nationally that in 2011 and 2012 the most vulnerable age group was 15–19. In 2011 this age group constituted 20 percent of the nation's homicides, followed by youth between the ages of 20–24, comprising 19 percent. Twenty-five to twenty-nine year olds and thirty to thirty-four year-olds each comprised 14 percent of homicides in 2011 and 2012 (Fundaungo 2013, 37). Gendered data is also available as reproduced in Figure 15.1 (Fundaungo 2013, 33). Comparative district data is available as well, in Table 15.1 (Fundaungo 2013, 51).

Reproducing these charts is instructive because of their work of documentation. They can push us to ask questions about the geographies of postwar violence. For example, why is it that Chalatenango and Morazán, two districts that compete in ranking for poverty, marginalization, destruction from war, and war organization (Morazán via the ERP and Chalatenango as FPL), have the least number of homicides, ranking thirteenth and fourteenth respectively? Is organizational capacity, despite disillusionment, a contributing factor? Is it, as Garni and Weyher suggest in their comparative study of two Salvadoran towns, that it is the "kind" of experiences of wartime violence that matter? They offer that "direct" wartime violence leads to more cohesion in the postwar period (Garni and Weyher 2013, 641). These experiences, they theorize, can confront the individualizing violent processes of

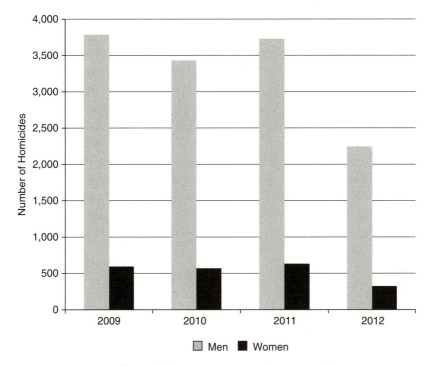

Figure 15.1. Number of homicides by sex, 2009–12. Author's own elaboration using data from IML. 2010 and 2012 exclude 4 and 9 cases, respectively, with unspecified sex.

neoliberalism (in other words, the inequalities produced by CAFTA), the "estrangement" that casts violence in the bodies of individuals rather than in "situations" (Garni and Weyher 2013, 624). This ranking remains consistent when we disaggregate for gendered data. Women were killed proportionately less in Chalatenango and Morazán. In 2012, 3.7 women were killed out of 100,000 inhabitants in Chalatenango, compared to 16.7 per 100,000 in San Vicente (the highest for the nation) (Fundaungo 2013, 59). After a peak in homicides in 2010, there has been a steady decline in Chalatenango (Fundaungo 2013, 85).[19]

The *Atlas* also provides further breakdowns for each department, tracking homicides at the municipal level from 2009 to 2012. Here, too, analysis of these data indicates that former organized conflict zones, the repopulated communities at the heart of much theorizing on the war and the postwar period, have remarkably low homicide rates. For instance, the oft-touted model insurgent municipality of Las Flores has no recorded murders. Compare this to the region

Table 15.1. Number of Homicides and Rates By Department, 2009-12

|  | 2009 | | | 2010 | | |
|---|---|---|---|---|---|---|
|  | *Number of Homicides* | *Population* | *Rate* | *Number of Homicides* | *Population* | *Rate* |
| Ahuachapán | 158 | 324,578 | 48.7 | 151 | 326,524 | 46.2 |
| Santa Ana | 468 | 557,530 | 83.9 | 392 | 560,398 | 70.0 |
| Sonsonate | 460 | 457,065 | 100.6 | 404 | 458,558 | 88.1 |
| Chalatenango | 72 | 200,916 | 35.8 | 91 | 201,844 | 45.1 |
| La Libertad | 647 | 719,405 | 89.9 | 579 | 724,651 | 79.9 |
| San Salvador | 1,487 | 1,728,851 | 86.0 | 1,350 | 1,732,703 | 77.9 |
| Cuscatlán | 105 | 237,572 | 44.2 | 121 | 240,911 | 50.2 |
| La Paz | 157 | 319,440 | 49.1 | 190 | 321,551 | 59.1 |
| Cabañas | 67 | 161,820 | 41.4 | 73 | 162,916 | 44.8 |
| San Vicente | 108 | 168,964 | 63.9 | 66 | 170,028 | 38.8 |
| Usulután | 162 | 355,358 | 45.6 | 139 | 357,767 | 38.9 |
| San Miguel | 331 | 467,935 | 70.7 | 290 | 470,176 | 61.7 |
| Morazán | 38 | 194,818 | 19.5 | 37 | 195,886 | 18.9 |
| La Unión | 122 | 258,319 | 47.2 | 121 | 259,082 | 46.7 |
| Country total | 4,382 | 6,152,571 | 71.2 | 4,004 | 6,182,995 | 64.8 |

Source: IML and DIGESTC.

of Nueva Concepcion, which has the highest murder rate in Chalatenango (Fundaungo 2013, 101) and is known as a key narcotrafficking route (*el caminito*). In the municipality of Las Vueltas where I have conducted my research, no one was killed in 2009, 2010, or 2011, though one person was killed in 2012. Upon careful review of my ethnographic field notes I am unable to identify the victim; however, what emerges is the clouded story of the near murder of a former insurgent. Like so many, his story and that of his kin does not quite fit the graphics outlined above. He is "lucky" in that he does not become a statistic in the *Atlas* and survives a coma. As his story reveals, he embodies the entanglements of victim, perpetrator, past, and present in the interstices of insecure Salvadoran spaces.

## A Critical Anthropology of Security

Anthropologist Daniel Goldstein suggests that we theorize this moment, even in "post-neoliberal" Latin America,[20] through what he defines as "a crit-

Table 15.1. Number of Homicides and Rates By Department, 2009–12, *cont'd.*

| 2011 | | | 2012 | | |
|---|---|---|---|---|---|
| *Number of Homicides* | *Population* | *Rate* | *Number of Homicides* | *Population* | *Rate* |
| 140 | 328,812 | 42.6 | 92 | 331,396 | 27.8 |
| 445 | 563,821 | 78.9 | 256 | 567,768 | 45.1 |
| 502 | 459,905 | 109.2 | 237 | 461,471 | 51.4 |
| 66 | 202,842 | 32.5 | 53 | 203,874 | 26.0 |
| 524 | 731,114 | 71.7 | 274 | 738,842 | 37.1 |
| 1,445 | 1,736,011 | 83.2 | 745 | 1,738,665 | 42.8 |
| 111 | 244,549 | 45.4 | 92 | 248,417 | 37.0 |
| 221 | 323,740 | 68.3 | 156 | 325,967 | 47.9 |
| 82 | 163,995 | 50.0 | 61 | 164,877 | 37.0 |
| 139 | 171,218 | 81.2 | 88 | 172,544 | 51.0 |
| 171 | 360,447 | 47.4 | 147 | 363,196 | 40.5 |
| 292 | 472,833 | 61.8 | 190 | 475,713 | 39.9 |
| 58 | 197,093 | 29.4 | 53 | 198,341 | 26.7 |
| 164 | 259,756 | 63.1 | 132 | 260,421 | 50.7 |
| 4,360 | 6,216,136 | 70.1 | 2,576 | 6,251,492 | 41.2 |

Source: IML and DIGESTC.

*ical* security anthropology, one that recognizes the centrality of security discourses and practices to the global and local contexts in which cultural anthropology operates" (2010, 489, emphasis in original). Security discourses certainly remain key to postwar Salvadoran processes across scales and are, as Goldstein offers about his research in Bolivia, "fundamentally social and in a sense performative" (2010, 492). Security in El Salvador as referenced in state and regional plans emphasizes economic security in the service of global capitalism (see also Goldstein 2010, 493). Alongside this focus is the eruption across the region of "citizen security," which Goldstein summarizes as the everyday "protection against crime, now seen as one of the greatest obstacles to the peace and happiness of rich and poor men, women, and children in a variety of Latin American countries" (2010, 496). In his larger ethnographic work, *Outlawed: Between Security and Rights in a Bolivian City*, Goldstein further elaborates that this "everyday insecurity" exists as people "occupy a habitus of fear and uncertainty that is at once social, psychological and material." And where insecurity is "a sense that the world is unpredictable, out of control, and inherently dangerous, and that within this chaos the individual must struggle desperately just to survive" (2012, 4–5). As a result, this citizen security constructs naturalized evil criminals and delinquents to be cleansed.

Ethnography can help us theorize Salvadorans' insecure and precarious lives and link the interpersonal and the structural. As Goldstein observes, we can understand the "disposition of the neoliberal subject in this security society" as "one of perpetual alertness" where citizens are always on guard, ready for emergencies and for threats around every literal and figurative bend (2012, 14). For the variously positioned protagonists of the Salvadoran struggle I wonder if we also need to think about embodied experiences of agentive alertness. Here I am thinking of Fanon's discussion where "the colonized subject is always on his guard . . . the muscles of the colonized are always tensed . . . it is not that he is anxious or terrorized, but he is always ready to change his role as game for that of hunter" (2004 [1963], 16–17). For the Chalateco self-identified revolutionary combatant and supporter, this alertness was linked to a revolutionary security—a security of territory, a control over geographical perimeters. The securing of insurgent spaces was scaled up by the disciplining and regulating of obedient bodies (Silber 2011). These bodies were indeed targets of violence but also agentive actors. This is a key tension, which in turn raises questions around the legacy of postwar violence. What happens to obedient bodies in disobedient times? In a context of reconciliation without the reconciled, are there spaces to contest embodied insecurity across generations and geographies?[21]

### Esmeralda After War

In February 2012 I returned to Chalatenango and engaged in follow-up visits with many women and men I had not seen in fifteen years—though in many cases I had met their kin in the United States. A significant number of women were still single heads of households; others had left their partners or had been left by them because of migration. For instance, Esmeralda was in a new home, displaced from her former house and plot of land when she left her husband, a local *curandero* (folk healer). She told me he had gone crazy again, from war, from drink. There were just too many beatings. I was unclear if she meant hers or his from the war. Esmeralda had a brood of children, all of them with deep, almond, wide-set eyes, just like hers. The youngest was cognitively disabled and motor impaired, and really no longer very small. When I stopped by Esmeralda's home, he was at the center of social and familial life, sitting in a hammock between two sisters. Esmeralda has nurtured ten children. Remarkably, none died during the war or during infancy. Only two of her adult children live in the United States. I saw her eldest last when he was twelve, a wiry, strong little thing working his father's carpentry wheel. He is a man now, in Kentucky of all places. Esmeralda's third child, Raquel, her first girl, had a six-month-old baby boy who was round faced and with a hearty cry. As we visited, she asked my advice about when it would be best to cross the border with her baby. With the infant's father already in the United States, she surmised it was only time before the relationship ended. "When would it be best to cross?" She had heard that when infants turn one, border crossings separate mother and child. Younger infants can travel with the mother, but are heavily sedated, limp and loose on their sides.

I don't know if Raquel crossed alone or with her baby. It is often difficult to keep in touch with Salvadoran migrants, many of whom are always on the move. However, I did learn about Raquel's father, the local *curandero*, carpenter, and artist, whose vibrant paintings depict military attacks against rural communities on smoothed slabs of wood. He produced these in the early 1990s for the wave of postwar solidarity delegations in search of recently retired revolutionaries. His art still graces my office wall. His name is Julio.

News in the diaspora travels. Only six months later, while I was conducting ethnographic research in the diasporic community in New Jersey, stories about Julio emerged. Rumor had it that Julio was consorting with some odd elements in El Rancho, not really *maras*, but this too is unclear. A former neighbor, now living in New Jersey, had heard that Esmeralda had kicked him out of their home. According to the narrative, he was seeking revenge and planned to kidnap her for ransom. While extortion is common across El Salvador, it is much less prevalent in repopulated communities. As the story goes, Julio had planned the kidnapping with some local youth and "unos muchachos Hondureños" (there is illicit movement of Hondurans escaping the law into this region of Chalatenango). However, rather than capture Esmeralda, the "muchachos" (also a term used to denote the insurgents of the past) turned on Julio and brutally assaulted him with knives, leaving him for dead in a pit originally dug for his wife. A farmer discovered Julio on his way to his own field. After months in a coma in the department hospital, Julio was released, minus one eye.

Julio's story of postwar violence doesn't fit so neatly into the rubrics that quantify and seek to measure how, where, and why people feel insecure or what deaths and near-deaths matter. Why did this story—true, fictional, or more than likely somewhere in between—move across borders, through former kin and neighborhood ties? I suggest that Julio's circulated story of near death embodies those always already overdetermined markers that do the cultural work of packaging El Salvador as simultaneously violent and vulnerable, comprised of bodies to be contained and disciplined at borders and checkpoints, or counted in atlases of the dead. As Michael Taussig offers, "sometimes when you write field notes time stands still and an image takes its place" (2012, 500). Clearly Taussig does not suggest an analytic paralysis, but that is a concern. For there are so many halting images of the postwar period: migrants' desolate homes in El Rancho that cost over thirty-five thousand dollars to build; Julio, as I imagine him, one-eyed and crazy *(enloquecido)* without kin; his severely impaired son laying on a hammock rocked by his mother. Time does not stand still, and these insecure lives, as Deborah Thomas (2011) suggests, perhaps too can be read as an archive of counternarratives.

### In the After

I conclude with another migrant story, a counternarrative to precarity, insecurity, and injustice as lived through the frictions of postwar life (Tsing 2005). In my complicated work and friendship with Salvadorans in the diaspora (Gay y Blasco and Hernández 2012), I am struck by the everyday, intimate negotiations that unexpectedly rub against the profound lack of accountability in postwar life. This is the everyday of the unreconciled who reterritorialize reconciliation through practices of forgiveness, without justice, in the aftermath of war. These practices of forgiveness take place in the interstices of daily life, across generations, and across polarized political fields of the past. These practices trouble the insecurity that structures transmigrant's lives.

When I was last in Los Angeles, in the summer of 2012, I visited Flor, whom I had first met in Chalatenango when she was nine years old. Her mother was a local, everyday women's organizer. I have written about Flor in the past because she blazed the trail for her family, as now all of her siblings live in the United States—some faring better than others. I have written about the ways in which her life trajectory embodies waves of clandestinity, agentive yet pained in the chronic unfolding of her multiple losses (Silber 2011). Her life could be historically framed through the humanitarian logics of our contemporary period, which commingle repression and compassion (Fassin 2012). For anthropologist Didier Fassin, today's global governance is marked by a moral politics of compassion that in fact masks and elides deep inequalities (2012), of which there are many. Indeed, Flor's migrant moves do not match the images of those disheveled kids, the rhetoric of the Dreamers and DACA, though she came to the United States young and alone.

I have traced the cycles of Flor's ever-changing insecurity—her clandestinity as a child of the FMLN and as an unauthorized migrant. She has lived through multiple losses, from the death of her insurgent father to the violent death of her first-born son when she was only sixteen; a stray bullet killed him during a gang-related bus holdup. And I have also discussed her "transborder mothering" (Stephen 2007). Flor has been separated for more than ten years from her now-teen boy in El Salvador because of her inability to return home. In the meantime, she has built a home in California, created ritual kinship ties within the diasporic Salvadoran community, and has two U.S.-born children, although their father was recently deported.

From Flor's vulnerable space, it may be the configurations of ritual kin that provide respite from insecurity. During our visit in 2012, as I shared with Flor photographs of her son's birthday party, which I had attended during my time in El Salvador, photographs that she had already seen posted on Facebook, I was struck by an unexpected and hopeful story made possible through migration. Like so many Salvadorans, Flor and her partner worked multiple jobs and long hours. They shared a home with a Salvadoran couple who had become their daughter's godparents, *compadres*. In talking about daily life and how she juggled what we would call the gendered work–family balance, Flor shared a compelling story about making family. Specifically, one of her daughter's kindergarten assignments was to draw a picture representing her family. According to Flor, young Jennifer drew a picture of herself with her "two moms" and her "two dads": the parents who took her to school in the morning and the ones who picked her up at the end of the day (in other words, her biological parents and her godparents). Only later, during another conversation, I learned that Jennifer's godfather had served in the Salvadoran military during the war. In fact, he had been stationed in the northeast of Chalatenango, at around the same time that Flor's insurgent, platoon-leader father was ambushed and killed.

Institutional, historic enemies in the past, both Flor and her *compadre* claimed that the past, the war, and their war stories never came up. Jennifer's godfather explained that Flor was simply too young to remember. I don't believe this is the case. Among the first objects Flor requested from El Salvador, many years ago now, was a copy of a picture of her father in olive green with two guns strapped on his back. Like other stories, this one is silenced, and in that space there emerges a way to survive and make sense of an everyday insecurity, away from what Sprenkels describes as "militant memories" that are complicit in maintaining a polarized political field (2011). I offer that these intimate spaces between former warring bodies erupt with new negotiated postwar truth-tellings. This everyday reality contests humanitarian logic's emphasis on urgent, bounded crises and on the suffering body (Redfield 2013). For the Salvadoran case points instead to suffering that, to quote Philippe Bourgois and Jeff Schonberg, is "chronic and cumulative" and both personal and structural (2009, 16). Ultimately, this is living in the after despite or because of memories of war, across generations, across geographies, so that a little girl can have two moms and two dads, at least for a while.

## Notes

1. Winifred Tate provides a critical analysis of the production of statistics for deaths in Colombia, exploring, for example, the ways in which deaths are catalogued, commodified, and thus made legible in this way (2007).

2. A local term used to describe the arduous escapes through the hills, on foot, en masse during a military bombardment and attack.

3. FMLN (Farabundo Martí National Liberation Front) comprised of five political and armed forces. Officially becomes a political party with the peace accords. ARENA (National Republican Alliance) was the ruling party of the government of El Salvador during the negotiated peace until March 2009.

4. For classic work on the region see the work of Pearce 1986 and books written within a solidarity movement such as Doljanin 1982 and Metzi 1988, about the repatriation movement itself, Schrading 1991, and those that are explicitly faith-based, such as Classen 1992.

5. 2005 census indicates that there are 2,101 people living in the municipality.

6. Preliminary research took place during the summers of 1993 and 1994. Fourteen months of research were conducted during 1996–97 funded by Fulbright-Hays, IAF, and OAS fellowships. I am careful with the use of pseudonyms for people and for specific communities or *caseríos* due to the politicized nature of this material, and ultimately because of issues of migration. However, since the beginning of this project,

new technologies have indeed made the transparency and mapping of research sites an important topic of ethical concern.

7. What residents from the Department of Chalatenango call themselves.

8. Van der Borgh provides a cogent summary of the role of the international community in peace building and how early on policymakers linked security and development and structural reforms as key to peace building (2009, 303). Ultimately, this review critiques assumptions that underscore "liberal peace" models that are universalizing, decontextualizing and Eurocentric.

9. Hurricane Mitch (1998), earthquakes (2001).

10. The Pew Research Center cites the 2011 Census Bureau's American Community Survey, which places the estimated 2 million Salvadorans in the United States as the third largest population of Hispanic origin (Anna Brown and Eileen Patten, "Hispanics of Salvadoran Origin in the United States, 2011," Hispanic Trends, Pew Research Center, June 19, 2013, http://www.pewhispanic.org/2013/06/19/hispanics-of -salvadoran-origin-in-the-united-states-2011/).

11. It is beyond the scope of this chapter to address the ever growing literature on Salvadoran migration that addresses questions such as belonging (Coutin 2007); fragmented communities (Menjívar 2000); the making of transnational family (Abrego 2014); the state and migration (Baker-Cristales 2004); the hegemonic circulation of the Salvadoran as entrepreneur (Pederson 2013), and much more.

12. Author translation of: "trabajar para que los retornados conozcan bien nuestro entorno económico y poderles facilitar su inserción, estamos en otro contexto muy diferente como el que tenía en Estados Unidos, ello nos exige una adaptación." By February 2017, under a new political climate in the United States, the Dirección de General de Migración y Extranjería held a forum on the "protection of migrants and the reintegration of migrants [foro para protección de migrantes y reinserción de retornados]" (https://www.migracion.gob.sv/noticias/realizan-foro-para-proteccion-de -migrantes-y-reinsercion-de-retornados/

13. See Binford 1996 for an analysis of the massacre.

14. Translation of original: "Prevenir es siempre mejor que curar; cuando la enfermedad se encuentra presente—en este caso, la violencia—debe igualmente ser abordada para permitir que las medidas preventivas puedan disminuir o eliminar el riesgo de aparecimiento de eventos de violencia."

15. Defined as 10 homicides per 100,000 people.

16. Salvadoran journalist Martínez frames these deaths comparatively, one could almost say alluding to the violence of humanitarian inaction in two disparate cases. He remarks: "La epidemia de homicidios fue tan expandida en 2014 que quedamos a poco más de 1,000 cadáveres de alcanzar la epidemia de ébola del año pasado. Con un matiz: esa epidemia mató a unas 5,000 personas, pero en seis países africanos" (2015).

17. This is a well-respected public policy organization founded in January 1992. They consistently produce critical public policy research aimed at promoting "development

and democratic governance in El Salvador" ("Perfil Institucional," FUNDAUNGO, http://www.fundaungo.org.sv/index.php?option=com_content&view=article&id =3&Itemid=8).

18. Sources include La Fiscalia General de la Republica, FGR, Policia Nacional Civil, Instituto de Medicina Legal.

19. Currently there is significant pressure, both national and international, organizing to end the violence of anti-abortion laws in El Salvador. This chapter does not address El Salvador's extreme law.

20. For a cogent review see the work of Yates and Bakker 2014.

21. See also Yashar 2013 for a discussion on the role of the "illicit" in the creation of new regimes of citizenship within neoliberal governments that propels citizens to take on new choices, such as unauthorized migration.

## References

Abrego, Leisy. 2014. *Sacrificing Families: Navigating Laws, Labor, and Love Across Borders*. Stanford, Calif.: Stanford University Press.

Alarcón, Daniel. 2015. "The Executioners of El Salvador." *New Yorker*, August 4. http://www.newyorker.com/news/news-desk/the-executioners-of-el-salvador.

Baker-Cristales, Beth. 2004. *Salvadoran Migration to Southern California: Redefining el Hermano Lejano*. Gainesville: University Press of Florida.

Binford, Leigh. 1996. *The El Mozote Massacre: Anthropology and Human Rights*. Tucson: University of Arizona Press.

———. 1998. "Hegemony in the Interior of the Salvadoran Revolution: The ERP in Northern Morazán." *Journal of Latin American Anthropology* 4 (1): 2–45.

Bourgois, Philippe, and Jeff Schonberg. 2009. *Righteous Dopefiend*. Berkeley: University of California Press.

Boyce, James K. 2002. *Investing in Peace: Aid and Conditionality After Civil Wars*. London: Oxford University Press.

Classen, Susan. 1992. *Vultures and Butterflies: Living the Contradictions*. Eugene, Oreg.: Wipf and Stock.

Consejo Nacional de Seguridad Ciudadana y Convivencia. 2015. *Plan El Salvador Seguro*. El Salvador: Gobierno de El Salvador Programa de las Naciones Unidas para el Desarrollo San Salvador.

Córdova Macias, Ricardo, José Miguel Cruz, and Mitchell A. Seligson. 2013. "Cultura política de la democracia en El Salvador y en las Américas, 2012: Hacia la igualdad de oportunidades." Report prepared for the Latin American Public Opinion Project, Vanderbilt University, Nashville, Tennessee, March.

Coutin, Susan Bibler. 2007. *Nations of Emigrants: Shifting Boundaries of Citizenship in El Salvador and the United States*. Ithaca, N.Y.: Cornell University Press.

Dickey, Christopher. 2015. "Street Gangs More Vicious Than ISIS." *Daily Beast*, July 31. http://www.thedailybeast.com/articles/2015/07/31/the-street-gangs-more-vicious-than-isis.html.

Doljanin, Nicolas. 1982. *Chalatenango la guerra descalza: Reportaje sobre El Salvador*. Mexico City: El Día.

Fanon, Frantz. 2004 [1963]. *The Wretched of the Earth*. New York: Grove Press.

Fassin, Didier. 2012. *Humanitarian Reason: A Moral History of the Present*. Berkeley: University of California Press.

Fundaungo [2013]. *Atlas de la violencia en El Salvador (2009–2012)*. San Salvador: FUNDAUNGO.

Gammage, Sarah. 2006. "Exporting People and Recruiting Remittances: A Development Strategy for El Salvador?" *Latin American Perspectives* 33 (6): 75–100.

Garni, Alisa and L. Frank Weyher. 2013. "Neoliberal Mystification: Crime and Estrangement in El Salvador." *Sociological Perspectives* 56 (4): 623–45.

Gay y Blasco, Paloma and Liria de la Cruz Hernández. 2012. "Friendship, Anthropology." *Anthropology and Humanism* 37 (1): 1–14.

Goldstein, Daniel. 2010. "Toward a Critical Anthropology of Security." *Current Anthropology* 51 (4): 487–517.

———. 2012. *Outlawed: Between Security and Rights in a Bolivian City*. Durham, N. C.: Duke University Press.

*Guardian*. 2015a. "El Salvador's 'Most Violent Month': Homicide Rate Hits Record High in May." June 3. https://www.theguardian.com/world/2015/jun/03/el-salvador-homicide-killings-gangs.

———. 2015b. "El Salvador Gang Violence Pushes Murder Rate to Postwar Record." September 2. http://www.theguardian.com/world/2015/sep/02/el-salvador-gang-violence-murder-rate-record.

Hayner, Priscilla. 2011. *Unspeakable Truths: Transitional Justice and the Challenge of Truth Comissions*, 2nd Edition. New York: Routledge.

Holland, Alisha C. 2013. "Right on Crime?: Conservative Party Politics and *Mano Dura* Policies in El Salvador." *Latin American Research Review* 48 (1): 44–67.

ICTJ. 2013. "Twenty Years Later, A Chance for Accountability in El Salvador." October 1. www.ictj.org/news/twenty-years-later-chance-accountability-el-salvador.

IDHUCA. n.d. *Elementos para una política de prevención de violencia*. San Salvador: UCA. http://uca.edu.sv/publica/idhuca/propuestas.html#politica (accessed February 7, 2015).

Jackson Jr., John L. 2012. "Ethnography Is, Ethnography Ain't." *Cultural Anthropology* 27 (3): 480–97.

Kampwirth, Karen. 2002. *Women and Guerrilla Movements: Nicaragua, El Salvador, Chiapas, Cuba*. University Park: Pennsylvania State University Press.

———. 2004. *Feminisms and the Legacy of Revolution: Nicaragua, El Salvador, Chiapas*. Athens: Ohio University Press.

Karl, Terry L. 1992. "El Salvador's Negotiated Revolution." *Foreign Affairs* 71 (2): 147–64.

Kennedy, Elizabeth. 2014. *No Childhood Here: Why Central American Children Are Fleeing Their Homes.* Washington, D.C.: American Immigration Council.

Lopez, Mark Hugo, and Jens Manuel Krogstad. 2014. "5 Facts About the Deferred Action for Childhood Arrivals Program." Pew Research Center. http://www.pewresearch .org/fact-tank/2014/08/15/5-facts-about-the-deferred-action-for-childhood -arrivals-program/.

Mainwaring, Scott. 1992. "Transitions to Democracy and Democratic Consolidation: Theoretical and Comparative Issues." In *Issues in Democratic Consolidation: The New South American Democracies in Comparative Perspective*, edited by Scott Mainwaring, Guillermo O'Donnell, and J. Samuel Valenzuela, 294–341. Notre Dame, Ind.: University of Notre Dame Press/Kellogg Institute.

Malkin, Elisabeth. 2015. "El Salvador Cracks Down on Crime, but Gangs Remain Unbowed." *New York Times*, August 11. www.nytimes.com/2015/08/12/world /americas/el-salvador-cracks-down-on-crime-but-gangs-remain-unbowed.html.

Martínez, Óscar. 2015. "Palabra De Pandillero: '24 Muertos O Más'" *El Faro*, January 15. http://www.salanegra.elfaro.net/es/201501/bitacora/16479/Palabra-de-pan dillero-24-muertos-o-más.htm.

Menjívar, Cecilia. 2000. *Fragmented Ties: Salvadoran Immigrant Networks in America.* Berkeley: University of California Press.

Metzi, Francisco. 1988. *Por los caminos de Chalatenango: Con la salud en la mochila.* San Salvador: UCA Editores.

Montgomery, Tommie Sue. 1995. *Revolution in El Salvador: From Civil Strife to Civil Peace.* Boulder, Colo.: Westview.

Moodie, Ellen. 2010. *El Salvador in the Aftermath of Peace: Crime, Uncertainty, and the Transition to Democracy.* Philadelphia: University of Pennsylvania Press.

Murray, Kevin. 1997. *El Salvador: Peace on Trial.* London: Oxfam UK and Ireland.

Observatorio de Seguridad Ciudadana. 2013. *Percepción de inseguridad y victimización por crimen en El Salvador 2012.* San Salvador: FUNDAUNGO, FLACSO Programa El Salvador y UTEC.

O'Donnell, Guillermo, Philippe C. Schmitter, and Laurence Whitehead. 1986. *Transitions from Authoritarian Rule: Latin America.* Baltimore, Md.: Johns Hopkins University Press.

Pearce, Jenny. 1986. *Promised Land: Peasant Revolution in Chalatenango, El Salvador.* London: Latin America Bureau.

Pederson, David. 2013. *American Value: Migrants, Money, and Meaning in El Salvador and the United States.* Chicago, Ill.: University of Chicago Press.

"Plan of the Alliance for Prosperity in the Northern Triangle: A Road Map." 2014. Regional plan prepared by El Salvador, Guatemala, and Honduras, September. Inter-American Development Bank. http://idbdocs.iadb.org/wsdocs/getdocument.aspx ?docnum=39224238.

Popkin, Margaret. 2000. *Peace Without Justice: Obstacles to Building the Rule of Law in El Salvador.* University Park: Pennsylvania State University Press.

Redfield, Peter. 2013. *Life in Crisis: The Ethical Journey of Doctors Without Borders.* Berkeley: University of California Press.

Rey Tristán, Eduardo, and Xiomara Lazo. 2011. "¿Es la justicia el precio de la paz? Logros y limitaciones del proceso de paz salvadoreño." In *Conflicto, memoria y pasados traumáticos: El Salvador contemporáneo,* edited by Eduardo Rey Tristán and Pilar Cagiao Vila, 211–40. Santiago: Universidad de Santiago de Compostela.

Schrading, Roger. 1991. *Exodus en América Latina: El movimiento de repoblación en El Salvador.* San José: Instituto Interamericano de Derechos Humanos (IIDH).

Seelke, Clare Ribando. 2009. *Gangs in Central America.* Congressional Research Service.

Segovia, Alexander. 2009. *Transitional Justice and DDR: The Case of El Salvador.* New York: ICTJ.

Semple, Kirk. 2014. "Surge in Child Migrants Reaches New York, Overwhelming Advocates." *New York Times,* June 17. www.nytimes.com/2014/06/18/nyregion/immigration-child-migrant-surge-in-New-York-City.html.

Shayne, Julie. 2004. *The Revolution Question: Feminisms in El Salvador, Chile, and Cuba.* New Brunswick, N.J.: Rutgers University Press.

Silber, Irina Carlota. 2011. *Everyday Revolutionaries: Gender, Violence, and Disillusionment in Postwar El Salvador.* New Brunswick, N.J.: Rutgers University Press.

Simanski, John, and Lesley M. Sapp. 2012. "Annual Report: Immigration Enforcement Actions: 2011." Department of Homeland Security. www.dhs.gov/sites/default/files/publications/immigration-statistics/enforcement_ar_2011.pdf.

Sprenkels, Ralph. 2005. *The Price of Peace: The Human Rights Movement in Postwar El Salvador.* Amsterdam: CEDLA Publications.

———. 2011. "Roberto d'Aubuisson vs Schafik Handal: Militancy, Memory Work and Human Rights." *European Review of Latin American and Caribbean Studies* 91:15–30.

———. 2012. "La guerra como controversia: Una reflexión sobre las secuelas políticas del informe de la Comisión de la Verdad para El Salvador." *Identidades* 2 (4): 68–92.

———. 2014. *Revolution and Accommodation: The Social Genealogy of Postinsurgency in El Salvador.* Ph.D. thesis, Utrecht University, Amsterdam.

Stephen, Lynn. 2007. *Transborder Lives: Indigenous Oaxacans in Mexico, California, and Oregon.* Durham, N.C.: Duke University Press.

Stinchcomb, Dennis and Eric Hershberg. 2014. *Unaccompanied Migrant Children from Central America: Context, Causes, and Responses.* Washington, D.C.: American University.

Tate, Winifred. 2007. *Counting the Dead: The Culture and Politics of Human Rights Activism in Colombia.* Berkeley: University of California Press.

Taussig, Michael. 2012. "Excelente zona social." *Cultural Anthropology* 27 (3): 498–517.

Thale, Geoff. 2013. "Amnesty Under Fire in El Salvador: Legal Challenges and Political Implications" WOLA. October 21, 2013. www.wola.org/commentary/amnesty _under_fire_in_el_salvador_legal_challenges_and_political_implications.

Thomas, Deborah. 2011. *Exceptional Violence: Embodied Citizenship in Transnational Jamaica*. Durham, N.C.: Duke University Press.

Tsing, Anna Lowenhaupt. 2005. *Friction: An Ethnography of Global Connection*. Princeton, N.J.: Princeton University Press.

UNDP. 2005. "Informe sobre desarrollo humano de El Salvador 2005: Una mirada al nuevo nosotros. El impacto de las migraciones." Human Development Report prepared for the United Nations Development Programme.

USCIS. 2014. Characteristics of Individuals Requesting and Approved for Deferred Action for Childhood Arrivals (DACA). www.uscis.gov/sites/default/files/USCIS /Humanitarian/Deferred%20Action%20for%20Childhood%20Arrivals/USCIS -DACA-Characteristics-Data-2014-7-10.pdf.

Valencia, Roberto. 2015. "La Tregua redefinió el mapa de asesinatos de El Salvador." *El Faro*, March 9. www.salanegra.elfaro.net/es/201503/cronicas/16490/La-Tregua -redefini%C3%B3-el-mapa-de-asesinatos-de-El-Salvador.htm.

Valencia, Roberto, Óscar Martínez, and Daniel Valencia Caravantes. 2015. "La policía masacró en la finca San Blas." *El Faro*, June 22. www.salanegra.elfaro.net/es/201507 /cronicas/17205/La-Polic%C3%ADa-masacró-en-la-finca-San-Blas.htm.

Van der Borgh, Chris. 2009. "Post-War Peace-Building: What Role for International Organizations?" In *Doing Good or Doing Better: Development Polices in a Globalizing World*, edited by Monique Kremer, Peter van Lieshout, and Robert Went, 303–20. Amsterdam: Amsterdam University Press.

Viterna, Jocelyn. 2013. *Women in War: The Micro-processes of Mobilization in El Salvador*. New York: Oxford University Press.

Wood, Elisabeth Jean. 2000. *Forging Democracy from Below: Insurgent Transitions in South Africa and El Salvador*. New York: Cambridge University Press.

———. 2003. *Insurgent Collective Action and Civil War in El Salvador*. Cambridge: Cambridge University Press.

Yashar, Deborah. 2013. "Institutions and Citizenship: Reflections on the Illicit." In *Shifting Fronteirs of Citizenship: The Latin American Experience*. Mario Sznajder, Luis Roniger and Carolos A. Forment, 431–58. Leiden: Brill.

Yates, Julia S., and Karen Bakker. 2014. "Debating the 'Post-Neoliberal Turn' in Latin America." *Progress in Human Geography* 38 (1): 62–90.

Zablah, Nelson Rauda. 2015. "Gobierno recicla ideas y estena el plan El Salvador Seguro." *El Faro*, July 16. www.elfaro.net/es/201507/noticias/17195/Gobierno-recicla -ideas-y-estrena-el-plan-El-Salvador-Seguro.htm.

Zilberg, Elana. 2011. *Space of Detention: The Making of a Transnational Gang Crisis Between Los Angeles and San Salvador*. Durham, N.C.: Duke University Press.

CONTRIBUTORS

Isabella Alcañiz is the Dr. Horace V. and Wilma E. Harrison Distinguished Professor in Environmental Politics and Assistant Professor in the Department of Government and Politics at the University of Maryland.

Sandra Botero is Assistant Professor at the Facultad de Ciencia Política, Gobierno y Relaciones Internacionales, Universidad del Rosario, Bogotá, Colombia.

Marcela Cerrutti is a sociologist and demographer and Senior Researcher at the Center for Population Studies (CENEP) and the National Council for Scientific and Technical Research (CONICET) of Argentina.

George Ciccariello-Maher is Associate Professor of Politics and Global Studies at Drexel University and Visiting Researcher at the Instituto de Investigaciones Sociales, Universidad Nacional Autónoma de México (UNAM).

Tulia G. Falleti is the Class of 1965 Term Associate Professor of Political Science, Director of the Latin American and Latino Studies Program, and Senior Fellow of the Leonard Davis Institute for Health Economics at the University of Pennsylvania.

Roberto Gargarella is Professor at the Law School of the University Torcuato Di Tella, Buenos Aires, Argentina.

Adrian Gurza Lavalle is Professor in the Department of Political Science at the University of São Paulo and Researcher at the Center of Metropolitan Studies (CEM), São Paulo, Brazil.

Juliet Hooker is Professor of Political Science at Brown University.

**Evelyne Huber** is Distinguished Professor of Political Science at the University of North Carolina, Chapel Hill.

**Ernesto Isunza Vera** is Professor at CIESAS-Golfo and Director of the Center for Social Accountability and Studies on Democracy, Veracruz, Mexico.

**Nora Lustig** is Professor of Latin American Economics at Tulane University and Director of the Commitment to Equity Initiative.

**Paulina Ochoa Espejo** is Associate Professor of Political Science at Haverford College.

**Emilio A. Parrado** is Professor and Chair in the Department of Sociology and Director of the Latin American and Latino Studies Program at the University of Pennsylvania.

**Claudiney Pereira** is Professor of Economics in the W. P. Carey School of Business at Arizona State University.

**Thamy Pogrebinschi** is Senior Researcher at the WZB Berlin Social Science Center, Democracy and Democratization Research Unit.

**Irina Carlota (Lotti) Silber** is Associate Professor of Anthropology at City College of New York/CUNY.

**David Smilde** is the Charles A. and Leo M. Favrot Professor of Human Relations at Tulane University.

**John D. Stephens** is the Gerhard E. Lenski, Jr. Distinguished Professor of Political Science and Sociology and Director of the Center for European Studies, European Union Center for Excellence, Trans-Atlantic Masters Program, University of North Carolina, Chapel Hill.

**Maristella Svampa** is Professor at the University of La Plata and Researcher at the National Council for Scientific and Technical Research (CONICET) of Argentina.

**Oscar Vega Camacho** is an independent writer and researcher and Guest Scholar at University of San Andres (UMSA), La Paz, Bolivia.

**Gisela Zaremberg** is Professor of Social Politics and Social Sciences, FLACSO, Mexico.

# INDEX

Page numbers followed by *f* and *t* indicate figures and tables.

ABACC (Brazilian-Argentine Agency for Accounting and Control of Nuclear Materials), 78

Abizadeh, A., 174

abortion, 230, 231

academic appointees to activist courts, 224, 228–29, 229*f*

Acción Democrática (AD), 153

*acción de tutela,* 207, 210n6, 219

Act for Brazilian-Argentine Integration, 77

activist courts: academic appointees to, 224, 228–29, 229*f*; challenges to abortion and reproductive rights decisions, 230–32; ideational character of judges, 224, 228–29, 229*f*, 239–40(Appendix 1); as political targets, 215, 224, 227

Acuerdo Nacional para la Modernización Básica (National Agreement for the Modernization of Basic Education, ANMEB), 273

adoption rights, 231–32

African Americans, 292, 297, 306n13

African presence in Latin American identity, 293

Afro-indigenous peoples, 294–95

agentive alertness, 341–42

agribusiness, 14, 18, 19, 25, 147, 149, 250, 329

Agrifood Strategic Plan (Argentina), 19

ALADI (Latin America Integration Association), 74, 75

ALALC (Latin American Free Trade Association), 70, 74, 75

Alberdi, Juan Bautista, 190–91, 192

Alfonsín, Raul, 72, 73, 76, 77

Almagro, Luis, 160

Ambas Americas, 288, 290

*amicus curiae,* 195

amnesty laws, 334

*amparos,* 206, 207, 219

ANC (National Constituent Assembly), 122, 123, 124, 134n4

Andean Community. *See* Bolivia; Colombia; Ecuador; Peru

Andrés Perez, Carlos, 134n3

A-Nets (urban popular class associations), 265, 274, 275, 278

Angra I (nuclear power plant, Brazil), 77, 79

ANMEB (Acuerdo Nacional para la Modernización Básica), 273

antiabortion activism, 230–31

Antonelli, Mirta, 21

Anzaldúa, Gloria, 288

APF (Asociaciones de Padres de Familia), 272, 273, 279n13

Aramar Experimental Center (Brazil), 77

Aratirí megamining project (Uruguay), 20

Araujo, Cicero, 266

Arditi, B., 182

ARENA (National Republican Alliance), 329, 334, 336

Arendt, Hannah, 133n1, 134n5

Argentina: Alfonsín government, 72, 73, 76, 77; anti-megamining initiatives in, 19, 20, 21; banking in, 80–82; Catholicism in, 191, 192; de la Ruá administration, 81–82; education in, 38*t*, 55*f*, 55*f*, 57*t*, 62, 289; food distribution, 19, 28; foreign debt of, 75, 81–82; GDP of, 37, 38*t*, 44; Gini coefficient for, 40*f*, 41*f*; government spending and revenue, 38*t*; health care, 39; human rights treaties, 202; income inequality in, 42–43, 62; Kirschner administration, 20, 21, 139,

Argentina: Alfonsín government (continued)
223; migration patterns in, 90, 92, 95,
97–99, 102–3; new charter in, 217; nuclear
treaties with Brazil, 5, 69, 73–79; poverty
in, 42f, 44–45, 57t; Residence Agreement
(2002), 5; social protests, 19, 20, 203; taxation in, 38t, 39, 44
Argentine-Brazilian nuclear integration, 5,
69, 73–79
Argentine constitution, 191–92, 217
Argentine National Commission of Atomic
Energy (CNEA), 76
Argentine Supreme Court, 218, 221, 223, 226
Article 16 of the Rights of Man, 120
Article 27 (Mexican Constitution [1917]),
197
Article 60 (Ecuadorian constitution [1869]),
196
Article 62 (1999 Constitution [Venezuela]),
125, 127
Article 70 (1999 Constitution [Venezuela]),
125
Article 123 (Mexican Constitution [1917]),
197–98
Article 333 (Colombia Constitution), 206,
210n5
Asociaciones de Padres de Familia (APF),
272, 273, 279n13
assertive courts, 216–21, 233. See also Co-
lombian Constitutional Court
Asunción Treaty, 69
Atlas de Violencia en El Salvador, 338, 339,
340
Atucha II (nuclear power plant, Argentina),
77, 79
audiencias (public hearings), 209
Avritzer, L., 256

BancoSur, 71, 80–81
banking, 71, 80–83, 118, 123, 139, 144t, 147,
155, 217, 249
Barrio 18 (gang), 327
Barro-Lee Educational Attainment Dataset
(1950–2010), 51–52
Belo Horizonte, Brazil, 256
Belo Monte mega-dam (Brazil), 19, 20
Betancourt, Rómulo, 116
Big Industrial Leap (Bolivia), 19
Binford, Leigh, 329
Boirgois, Philippe, 346

Bolivar, Simón, 210n1
Bolivarian movement, 6, 113–16, 121,
131–32, 145–46, 151–52, 298–301
Bolivarismo y Monroismo (Vasconcelos), 287,
298, 299, 301
Bolivia: BancoSur, 80; Big Industrial Leap, 19;
Buen Vivir (Living Well) in, 9, 16; Commodities Concensus in, 16; constitution in,
18, 217, 311, 322; constitution of, 311–13,
317–18; democracy in, 9, 318; education
spending, 38t, 39, 57t; Gas Wars (Bolivia),
316, 317; GDP of, 38t, 43; Gini coefficient
for, 40f, 41f; government spending and
revenue, 38t; human rights in, 95, 202,
203, 320–21; media in, 321, 323; Morales
government, 3, 139, 316–17, 318, 319;
national dialogues in, 246, 251–52; NGOs
in, 20; Pact of Unity, 311, 312, 317; participation opportunities in, 16, 245, 246, 247,
251–52; plurinationality of, 9, 16, 319–20,
322–23; population growth in, 320–21;
poverty in, 42, 42f, 43–45, 57t; Residence
Agreement (2002), 5; taxation in, 38t, 39;
Tipnis conflict, 3, 19, 20; Water Wars in
Cochabamba, 316, 317
Bolivian Alliance for the Peoples of Our
America (ALBA), 71
Bolivian Circles (study groups), 124
Border as Method, or The Multiplication of
Labor (Mezzadra & Neilson), 311–12
border crossings, 326–27, 330, 336
Brazil: banking in, 80; Belo Monte mega-dam,
19, 20; Bilateral Agreement, 78; citizen
participation in, 246, 247, 248, 255–56;
constitution (1988), 257; critical geogra-
phers of, 25; education in, 55f, 55f, 57t, 62;
Food and Nutritional Security National
Plan (PLANSAN), 250; foreign debt, 75;
GDP of, 37, 38t; Gini coefficient for, 40f,
41f; government spending and revenue,
38t; Growth Acceleration Plan, 19; health
care in, 223, 247; IBSA Dialogue Forum,
81; income inequality in, 42–43; migrant
rights in, 95; National Public Policy Conferences (NPPC), 250; new charter in, 217;
NGOs in, 20; noncontributory pensions in,
39; non-Mercosur commerce in, 68; NPT
(Nonproliferation Treaty), 73–74; nuclear
agreements with Argentina, 5, 69, 73–79;
oil industry in, 28; participatory budgeting

in, 248, 255–56; poverty in, 42f, 44–45, 57t; redistributive effect, 43; reduction of final income inequality, 43; Residence Agreement (2002), 5; Sarney administration, 76, 77; social equality in, 257; social protests, 203; taxation in, 38t, 44; Tlatelolco (Latin America Tlatelolco Treaty), 74, 78; trade relations with China, 28, 71; Workers' Party (PT), 246. *See also* citizen participation

Brazilian-Argentine Agency for Accounting and Control of Nuclear Materials (ABACC), 78

Bresser Pereira, Luiz Carlos, 24

Brewer-Carías, Allan R., 119, 133n1

Brics countries, 71, 81, 83

Bridas group (Argentina), 28

Bruckmann, Monica, 29

Bruhn, K., 178, 179, 180

budgeting, participatory, 248–49, 250–51, 255–56

Buen Vivir (Living Well), 3, 9, 13, 16, 25, 27, 312

Burke, Edmund, 193

Cabello, Diodado, 158

*Cadena Capriles,* 158

CAFTA, 339

Caire Martinez, Georgina, 273

Calderón government (Mexico), 272

Cañas, José Simeón, 335

Caracazo rebellion *(el Caracazo),* 116, 134n4, 157–58

Caravan for Freedom, 155

Carmona, Pedro, 152

Cartagena Concensus (1984), 72–73, 75

Carter, Greg, 306n13

Case C-355 (abortion rights), 230–31

cash transfers, 35f, 38t, 41f, 43–45, 47–48, 59, 62–63, 272

Casteñeda, Jorge, 1

Catholic Church, 144t, 146, 150–51, 191–92, 230, 295–96, 305n8, 330

*caudillismo,* 289

causal primacy, 140–41, 142

Causa Mendoza (Argentine Supreme Court), 221, 226

CBP (Customs and Border Protection), 326

CEABAN (Coordinating Commmittee of Argentine-Brazilian Business in the Nuclear Field), 77–78, 79

CELAC (Community of Latin American and Caribbean States), 144t, 150

CENCOEX (exchange control board), 144t

Centro de Cristo para las Naciones, 146

CEPAL (UN Economic Commission for Latin America), 70, 74–75, 78, 80

Cepeda, Manuel José, 228–29

CEPS (Consejos Escolares de Participación Social), 273, 279n13

Cerro Dragon (Argentine oil field), 28

Chakrabarty, Dipesh, 314

Chalatenango (El Salvador): FMLN (Frente Farabundo Martí para la Liberación Nacional) in, 327, 329, 330, 331, 333, 345; historic memories in, 345–46; homicides in, 339–40, 340t; Los Vueltas, 330, 332–33, 340; migration to the United States, 332, 343; postwar reconstruction in, 330; *reinserción* (reintegration), 331, 333–34; self-identified revolutionary combatant and supporter, 337, 342; spaces of forgiveness, 328, 344–45; women as heads of households in, 342

Chamber IV (Constitutional Chamber), 205–6

Chávez, Hugo: administration of, 139–40; ANC (National Constituent Assembly), 122, 123, 124, 134n4; Bolivarian Revolution, 6, 113–16, 121, 131–32, 145–46, 151–52, 298–301; Bolivarian universities, 144t, 146, 151–52; Caracazo rebellion *(el Caracazo),* 116, 134n4, 157–58; Catholic Church relations with, 144t, 146, 150–51, 305n8; and the communal state, 128–29; concentration of power, 124, 134n6, 139–40; decline of liberal democratic institutions, 139; economic policy of, 156–58; enabling law (2001), 118–19, 134n3; export-oriented populism, 147; judicial appointments to Supreme Justice Tribunal, 149; Kléber Ramírez Rojas and, 128–29; media controled by, 145–46, 151, 152; military background of, 148; militia under, 150; Mission System, 123, 144t, 148; National Assembly elections (December, 2015), 133, 159–60; oil industry, 118, 123, 144t, 146–47; opposition to, 133, 146, 151–54, 159–60; participatory system of, 252–53; party system and rise of, 149–50, 153–54; public autonomous universities,

Chávez, Hugo: administration (continued)
tensions with, 146, 151–52, 154; public
opinion on, 124; on regional unity, 150;
voter registration, 131. *See also* Venezuela
Chavismo (Venezuela): anti-neoliberalism of,
156; Catholic Church opposition to, 144*t*,
146, 150–51, 305n8; Communes Law, 128;
dominion theology, 146; political power
networks under, 144*t*, 149; public autonomous universities, tensions with, 146,
151–52, 154; Radical Cause on Chavismo,
134n6; revolutionary tourism, 146; rise of,
139–40
checks and balances, 159, 193–94, 195, 196,
209–10, 216
Chicano activism, 286, 303
Chile: constitution, 192, 196, 201; human
rights law in, 202; judicial appointments
in, 196; Mercosur and, 80, 94, 95; migrant
rights in, 95; migration patterns, 90, 92;
mining projects, 20; Residence Agreement
(2002), 5; social protests, 203; trade relations with China, 28
China, 4, 16, 24, 27–29, 71
citizen participation: in achieving social
justice, 257–58; A-Nets (urban popular
class associations), 265, 274, 275, 278;
Brazil's national plan of participation,
246; budgeting, 248–49, 250–51, 255–56;
community councils, 125–27, 132, 134n6,
150, 245–47, 246–47, 252–53; community-
managed schools in El Salvador, 254; in
education policy, 254, 256, 271, 273; in
IDIs (innovative democratic institutions),
264, 271, 272, 273, 279n33; in militias,
150; in municipal governments, 1, 161,
243–44, 249, 253–55, 273–74, 317; in
national dialogues, 246, 251–52; National
Public Policy Conferences (NPPC), 250;
natural resources management, 256; 1999
Constitution (Venezuela), 6, 18, 120,
121–22; 1999 Constitution (Venezuela) on,
6, 123–26, 130; participatory innovations,
250; popular sovereignty, 121–22, 123,
134n4, 173, 174; in public policy decision-
making, 8, 205–7, 210n6, 251–52
Citizenship Quality Survey (Encuesta de
Calidad Ciudadana), 267
Civil Society, 126–27
civil war in El Salvador (1980–1992), 329–46

clientelism, 140, 154, 267, 275*t*
Clifford, James, 314
CMDRS (Consejos Municipale de Desarrollo
Rural Sustenable), 271
CNEA (National Commission of Atomic
Energy), 76, 77–78
CNEN (National Commission of Nuclear
Energy), 77–78
Coalición por el Bien Todos, 177
cocaleros (migrant farm workers), 317
cognitive skills, 62–63, 91; among secondary
school students, 54, 55*f*, 56; cognitive test
scores, 54*t*, 55*f*, 56*t*, 57*t*; data for, 51–53,
63–64, 64*f*; educational expenditures
impact, 55*f*, 56*t*, 57*t*; educational expenditures' impact on, 54*t*; inequality and
development of, 50–51, 53–54; in Latin
American teenage school population, 52;
skill-biased technology change, 62
Collor de Mello, Fernando, 78
Colombia: citizen oversight of municipal
governments, 1, 161, 243–44, 249, 253–54;
constitutional reform (1991), 206, 210n5;
education in, 55*f*, 55*f*, 57*t*; Gaviria government, 225, 227, 239(Appendix 1); judicial
reforms in, 205–6; migration patterns,
90–91, 99; national mortgage system
(UPAC), 225, 227; reproductive rights in,
230–31; rights-assertive courts in, 219–20;
trade relations with China, 28
Colombia Law 134 (1994), 253
Colombian Constitutional Court: creation
of, 225; ESR (economic and social rights)
in, 222, 225–26, 227–28; as *Estado Social
de Derecho,* 225–26; on health rights, 225;
human rights, 219; justices of, 239–40(Appendix 1); political sanctions against, 228;
on reproductive rights, 230–31
colonialism, 16, 20, 129, 287–88, 297, 303–4,
309–10
Comité Antioquia ProVida, 230
Comité de Organización Política Electoral
Independiente (COPEI), 154
Commodities Consensus: collective resistance to, 16; comparative advantage, 17;
development narratives, 22; dynamic of
dispossession, 15; ECLAC on, 20–21;
first phase of, 19; neoextractivism, 13, 15,
17–18, 20; neoliberal narratives revised
by, 23; reprimarization of Latin American

economies, 13–14; revision of, 20–21; state funding of social programs, 16. *See also* Washington Concensus

Common System of Accounting and Control of Nuclear Materials (SCCC), 78

communal states, 128–29, 133

communes, 126, 127–28

community councils, 125–27, 132, 134n6, 150, 245–47, 252–53

Community of Latin American and Caribbean States (CELAC), 144*t*, 150

Confederación de Trabajadores de Venezuela (CTV), 153

conflict theory, 140, 142

Conga mine (Peru), 20

conjunctural causality, 141, 142, 143

Consejo Nacionla de Seguridad Ciudadana y Convivencia, 336

Consejos Escolares de Participación Social (CEPS), 273, 279n13

Consejos Municipale de Desarrollo Rural Sustenable (CMDRS), 271

conservatism, 20–21, 191–92, 202, 210n1, 223, 226–27, 230–32, 269, 322

Constituent Assembly (Bolivia), 311, 317, 318, 320

Constitutional Chamber (Chamber IV), 205–6

constitutional crises, 167, 168, 176, 182n1

constitutionalism: defects in, 199; dialogic constitutionalism, 208–9, 210, 222; origins of, 190–91; in Venezuela, 6, 18, 120, 121–23

constitutions: anti-neoliberal reforms in, 203–4; Constitutional Chamber, 205–6; constitutional crises, 167, 168, 182n1; constitutional tribunal enforcement of positive rights, 215; dialogic constitutionalism, 208–9, 210, 222; innovations in, 205–6, 217–18; political capacities of the people, 192–93; principle of distinction in, 192–93; social participation in, 245; vertical hierarchies in, 189, 190, 199, 200, 204

Coordinating Commmittee of Argentine-Brazilian Business in the Nuclear Field (CEABAN), 77–78, 79

Coordination for Water and Life, 316, 317

COPEI (Comité de Organización Política Electoral Independiente), 154

COPLADE, 270, 271

COPLADEMUN (municipal planning councils), 270, 271, 273–74

Coppedge, Michael, 121–22

corporate social responsibility (CSR), 23

Correa, Rafael, 3, 139

Corte Constitucional (high court, Colombia), 219

Corte Suprema de Justicia, 338

*The Cosmic Race* (Vasconcelos), 286, 291, 292, 293, 298, 300, 305nn8, 9

Costa Rica: assertive courts in, 220; Constitutional Chamber, 205–6; human rights treaties, 202; judicial reforms in, 205–7, 210n6; judicial rights activism in, 220; new charter in, 217; results from educational expenditures, 54*t*; rights-assertive courts in, 219; trade relations with China, 28

CSR (corporate social responsibility), 23, 24, 25

CTSUB, 316

CTV (Confederación de Trabajadores de Venezuela), 153

Cuba, 286, 288, 297, 298, 300

currency devaluation, 81, 82

Customs and Border Protection (CBP), 326

CVG, 144*t*

DACA (Deferred Action for Childhood Arrivals), 326, 345

dams, 17–18, 19, 20

DDR (disarmament, demobilization, and reintegration), 328

De Beer, Gabriella, 289

debt crises, 4–5, 71, 72–73, 75–76, 81–82

December 2001 crisis (Argentina), 81–82

Declaration of Iguaçu, 77, 78

decolonization, 8, 129, 303–4, 309, 310, 312–14, 317–18

Deferred Action for Childhood Arrivals (DACA), 326, 345

demobilizations, postwar in El Salvador, 333

democracy: accountability, 122; Bolivarian government, 113–14; Chavismo (Venezuela), 6, 115–16, 128; community, 128; critical assessment of, 241–42; decolonization, 318; "the democracy paradox," 172; El Salvador, 331; fomation of, 125–26; indigenous movements, 309; Left Turn and, 1, 3, 161, 243–44, 249, 253–54, 257–58; limits of, 21–22, 29–30; the military compared

democracy (continued)
  with, 148; as a permanent conflict, 318;
  populism, 165–66, 175–76; pragmatic turn
  of, 243; reconstruction of, 73; regionalization, 79; separation of powers in, 119–21,
  123; social equality, 61t, 62, 257. See also
  citizen participation; liberal democracy;
  poverty
Democratic and Cultural Revolution (Bolivia), 316
Democratic Planning Councils (Consejos de
  Planeación Democrática), 270
Department of Homeland Security, 333
dialogic justice, 208–9, 210, 222
"Dialogue and Political Pluralism" (Catholic
  Church in Venezuela), 151
Dirección de General de Migración, 333
direct identification method (survey methodology), 36–37
direct transfers, 35f, 41f
disarmament, demobilization, and reintegration (DDR), 328
disposable income, 34, 35f, 40f, 41f, 41t, 42f
domestic violence, 343–44
Dominican Republic, 293
dominion theology, 146
drug trafficking, 149, 227, 272, 340
Du Bois, W. E. B., 292, 297, 306n13
Dussel, Enrique, 115, 125–26, 129, 132
"Dutch disease," 147

ECLAC (Economic Commission for Latin
  America and the Caribbean), 20–21, 22,
  24, 59
Economic Commission for Latin America
  and the Caribbean (ECLAC). See ECLAC
  (Economic Commission for Latin America
  and the Caribbean)
economic power networks, 141, 142–43,
  144t, 146–48
Ecuador, 1; academic achievement, 56;
  Andean indigenous parties in, 254–55; autonomy in, 16; banking in, 80; Buen Vivir
  in, 16; Chinese investments in, 28; citizen
  participation in municipal government,
  254–55; Commodities Concensus in, 16;
  constitution in, 18, 196; criminalization
  of social struggles, 22; environmentalism,
  20; institutional innovation in, 254–55;
  megamining, 19, 20; migration patterns,

90; national councils for equality, 246;
  participation opportunities in, 245; participatory processes in, 16; plurinational state
  in, 16; political experimentalism in, 246;
  reaction to dynamics of dispossession, 20;
  Rights of Nature in, 16; social protests in,
  203; terrorism in, 22; trade relations with
  China, 28; Yasuni Project, 3, 19, 20
education: access to, 225; achievement gap of
  disadvantaged students, 49–50; Acuerdo
  Nacional para la Modernización Básica
  (National Agreement for the Modernization of Basic Education, ANMEB), 273;
  adult literacy, 52, 58f, 254; Barro-Lee Educational Attainment Dataset (1950–2010),
  51–52; CEPS (Consejos Escolares de
  Participación Social), 273; child labor, 50;
  citizen participation in educational policy,
  254, 256, 271, 272–73, 279n13; educational
  achievement, 50, 61t; family factors in
  educational success, 49–50; human capital,
  48, 50, 53, 56, 58, 59, 62; and indigenous
  integration, 295; inequalities in educational achievement, 50; inequality, 50,
  53–54, 61t, 62; migrant access to, 92, 97,
  101; missionary education, 295–96; parent
  participation in, 254, 272–73; poverty, 4,
  53–54, 58f, 60t, 61t; preschool education,
  47; School Councils of Social Participation
  (Consejos Escolares de Participación Social), 273; skill-biased technology change,
  62; socialization and educational success,
  49–50; spending on, 34, 35f, 36, 38t, 39, 45,
  51, 53–54, 54t, 55f, 56t, 57t, 61t; surveys
  on, 51; test scores, 50, 53, 54t, 55f, 56t, 57t;
  years of education, 51, 54, 55f, 58–59, 58t,
  60t, 61t, 63
EDUCO schools (El Salvador), 254
Eisenstadt, T., 179
El Alto, Bolivia: Gas Wars (Bolivia), 316, 317
elections: challenges to, 177, 178–81, 179,
  180–81; participation as nonelectoral societal control, 265; the people as electorate,
  173, 177, 180, 265; presidential elections
  in Mexico, 177, 178, 179, 180–81; results
  challenged, 178, 179; voter registration,
  131
Electoral Authority (Venezuela), 150
electoral campaigns, 266–67, 275t, 276t, 276t,
  277–78

elites: as corrupt, 169, 177–78; court decisions monitored by, 222, 227–28, 232, 233; on judicial review, 218; mobilization against abortion and same-sex marriage, 231, 232; on nonwhite regional identity, 294–95; out-migration of, 152; racial identity of Latin American elites, 292–93; racial self-hatred of, 292–93, 296–97; relations with assertive courts, 224; their subordinate position within global white supremacy, 300–301

El Mozote massacre, 334

El Salvador: ARENA (National Republican Alliance) government, 329, 334, 336; churches in, 338; community-managed schools in, 254; democratization in, 329, 331; FMLN (Frente Farabundo Martí para la Liberación Nacional), 251, 327, 329, 330, 331, 333, 345; Funes government, 327, 331, 334, 335; gang violence, 327–28, 335–36; homicides in, 338, 340t; human rights in, 202, 330, 334–35; *la transición*, 331; local development in, 246, 251–52; Mano Dura policies, 327; in the media, 327; NGOs in, 330; opinion polls on quality of life in, 337–38; peace accords in, 329; *reinserción* (reintegration), 331, 333–34; remittances, 332; security in, 337–38, 340–41, 343–44; spaces of forgiveness, 328, 344–45. *See also* postwar El Salvador

enabling law (2001), 118–19, 134n3

Encuesta de Calidad Ciudadana (Citizenship Quality Survey), 267–68, 278n2

Engels, Friedrich, 127

environmentalism, 16, 20–22, 25, 30, 203, 208, 221, 316–17

Epp, Charles R., 220

Escobar, Arturo, 26–27, 315

Esmeralda (research subject), 342–43

Esping-Andersen, Gøsta, 49

ESR (economic and social rights), 215, 219, 220, 221–24, 225–26, 228–29, 239–40(Appendix 1)

*Estado Social de Derecho:* Colombian Constitutional Court as, 225–26

"estamos peor que antes," 334

ethnographic research, 330, 346n6

European nationalism, 289–90

evangelicalism, 146

expatriate communities, 155, 332–33, 347n10

extractivism: agribusiness, 14, 18, 19, 25, 147, 149, 250, 329; mining, 14, 20, 28; new developmentalism, 16, 19; revenues, 24. *See also* water resources

FAES (Salvadoran Armed Forces), 333

Famatina revolt, 19, 20

Fanon, Franz, 129, 310–11, 324, 342

Farabundo Martí National Liberation Front (Frente Farabundo Martí para la Liberación Nacional), 251

Fassin, Didier, 326, 345

Fedecamaras (Venezuelan Federation of Chambers of Commerce), 152, 153

Federal Law of Encouragement of Civil Society Organizations, 178, 279n8

Filgueira, Fernando, 160

final income, 34, 35f, 40f, 41f, 43

Flor (research subject), 344–46

FMLN (Frente Farabundo Martí para la Liberación Nacional), 251, 327, 329, 330, 331, 333, 345

food distribution, 19, 28, 149, 152, 250

foreign debt, 4–5, 71, 72–73, 75–76, 79, 81–82

forgiveness, practices of, 344–45

Foro por al Vida, 154

Fox, Vicente, 271

FPL, 331

fracking, 17, 19, 21, 28, 279n8

Frank, Jason, 135n7

free markets, 206, 210n5, 219

Free Trade Association of the Americas (FTAA), 80, 83

French, John D., 161

Frente Farabundo Martí para la Liberación Nacional (Farabundo Martí National Liberation Front), 251

Freyre, Gilberto, 25, 285, 304n1

FTAA (Free Trade Association of the Americas), 80, 83

Fukuyama, Francis, 115

Fundación Marido y Mujer, 232

FUNDAUNGO, 337, 347n17

Funes, Maurio, 327, 331, 334, 335

Galvis, Rubiano, 228

gang violence in El Salvador, 327, 335–36

García Guadilla, María Pilar, 129–30, 132

García Serra, Mario J., 134n3

Garni, Alisa, 338
Gas Wars (Bolivia), 316, 317
Gavira, César, 225, 227
gay rights, 131, 219, 225, 231–32
gender, 131, 171, 251, 320, 330, 339f
General Education Law (Ley General de
    Educación), 273
general will (volunté générale), 166, 167, 168,
    169, 179
Giddens, Anthony, 48
Gini coefficient, 34, 37, 40f, 52, 56t
Gini index: cognitive test scores, 54t
Giordani, Jorge, 156
Globovisión (Venezuela), 158
Goldstein, Daniel, 340–42
Gomez Mera, L., 82
government performance: citizen monitoring
    of, 1, 161, 243–44, 249, 252–54
Gramsci, Antonio, 115, 116, 117, 120–21,
    126, 131
Grant, Madison, 295, 297, 306n12
grassroots movements, 127, 128, 134n6
gross income, 61t
Growth Acceleration Plan (Brazil), 19
Guatemala, 202, 326, 336
Gurza Lavalle, Adrián, 266
Guyana, 80, 153

Hands Off Venezuela, 146
Hanushek, Eric A., 63
Hardt, Michael, 126
Harvey, David, 15
headcount index, 40–41, 41f, 42f
health and health care, 48; citizen participa-
    tion in, 247; impact on human capital,
    59–61; long-run commitments to, 59;
    migrant access to, 92, 97, 101; reproduc-
    tive rights, 230–31; rights to, 225; sickness
    pay, 47; spending on, 34, 35f, 36, 38t, 39,
    45, 255–56
Hegel, Georg Wilhelm Friedrich, 115, 130
Henao, Juan Carlos, 226
Hirschl, Ran, 218
Holland, Alisha, 336
"El Hombre" (Vasconcelos), 296–97
homicide rates, 335–36, 337–39, 339f, 340t,
    341, 347n16
Honduras, 1, 28, 56, 139, 326, 336
horizontalism, 122, 128, 145, 267, 288
housing: discrimination against immigrants

in, 92, 97, 101
Humala, Ollanta (Peru), 20
human rights: IACHR (Inter-American Com-
    mission on Human Rights), 154, 155, 334;
    international immigrants, 89; in national
    charters, 217–18; 1999 Constitution on,
    124; NPPC (National Public Policy Confer-
    ences) on, 250; participation in democratic
    government as, 245; sexual rights, 8, 197,
    219, 225, 230–31; violations of, 17, 201–2
human rights advocacy, 94, 97–101, 154–55,
    202, 217–19, 334, 334–35
Human Rights Institute of Central American
    University (IDUCA), 334
hyperpresidentialism, 7, 194–96, 204

IACHR (Inter-American Commission on
    Human Rights), 154, 155, 334
IAEA (International Atomic Energy Agency),
    74, 77, 78
IALS (International Adult Literacy Survey),
    52
IBSA Dialogue Forum, 81, 83
ideological power networks, 141–42, 144t,
    145–46, 150–52
IDHUCA (Instituto de Derechos Humanos
    pf the Uniersidad Centroamerica), 335
IDIs (innovative democratic institutions),
    264, 271, 272, 273–74, 279n33
Iglesia Renacer, 146
ILO Convention 169, 21
IMF (International Monetary Fund), 81–82
immigrants and immigration: advocacy
    groups, 102; border crossings, 326–27, 330,
    336, 343–44; deportations, 333; discrimi-
    nation against, 92–93; Salvadoran migrants
    in the United States, 332–33, 347n10; self-
    perception of, 103; social status of, 103
imperialism, U.S., 9, 288–91, 297–98, 302
import-substituting industrialization (ISI),
    74–75, 78
income: gross income, 61t; household sur-
    veys on, 36; inequality, 4, 41t, 42f, 43, 61t,
    62, 91; market income, 35f, 40f, 41t, 44,
    59–60; net market income, 34, 35f, 40f, 41f;
    redistribution of, 47
indeterminancy, 172–73, 174, 175–76
India, 71, 74, 81
indigenous populations, 312, 315; Afro-
    indigenous peoples, 294–95; Andean

indigenous parties, 254–55, 320; consolidation of indigenous territory, 313; ILO Convention 169, 21; *indigenismo,* 305n11; indigenous organizations in Bolivia, 316–17, 320–21, 322–23; *Indolgía* (Vasconcelos) on, 294; institutional innovation promoted by indigenous parties, 254–55; judicial rights activism, 219; rights of, 203, 204–5, 219; suffrage for, 225, 321

indirect subsidies, 35*f*

*Indolgía* (Vasconcelos), 290–91, 292–93, 294, 295

inequality: development of cognitive skills, 50–51, 57*t*; in educational achievement, 50, 61*t*; income, 4, 41*t*, 43, 61*t*, 62, 91; moral politics of compassion, 344–46; test scores impacted by, 53, 57*t*. *See also* poverty

Institutional Revolutionary Party (Partido Revolucionario Institucional), 268–69

Instituto de Derechos Humanos of the Uniersidad Centroamerica (IDHUCA), 335

Instituto Salvadoreña para el Desarrollo de la Mujer, 338

Inter-American Commission on Human Rights (IACHR), 154, 155, 334

Inter-American Court on Human Rights, 21, 155

Inter American Democratic Charter, 160

Inter-American Development Bank, 217

intermediation, 266–68, 267, 275*t*, 276*t*, 276*t*, 277–78, 278n2

International Adult Literacy Survey (IALS), 52

International Chamber of Commerce, 155

International Convention on the Protection of the Rights of All Migrant Workers and Members of Their Families, 98

ISI (import-substituting industrialization), 74–75, 78, 217

Isunza Vera, Ernesto, 274

Iturriza, Reinaldo, 127

Jackson, John, 328

James, C. L. R., 127

Jameson, Fredric, 124

Jenson, Jane, 48

Jesuit Massacre Case, 334

Jiménez, Atenea, 132

judges: accountability of, 226–27; backlash to judicialization of rights, 223–24, 227–28, 231–32; confidence in intellectual abilities of, 195; dialogic devices used by, 208–9, 210; educational backgrounds of, 228–29, 229*f*, 239–40(Appendix 1); ideational character of, 220, 224, 228–29, 229*f*, 239–40(Appendix 1); implementation of rulings by, 221–22, 226; legal preferences of, 220–21, 221–22; and the people, 195–96

judicial appointments, 229*f*, 239–40(Appendix 1); Article 60 (Ecuadorian Constitution [1869]), 196; Article 82 (Chilean Constitution [1833]), 196; backlash to judicialization of rights, 223–24, 230–32; to constitutional tribunals, 215, 216; to Supreme Justice Tribunal (Venenzuelan Supreme Court), 149

judicial system: access to, 205–9, 210n6, 219, 223; checks and balances, 159, 191–92, 193–94, 195, 196, 209–10, 216; hyperpresidentialism, 196; litigation rates, 205–7; social rights, 199, 202–3, 219–20

Julio (research subject), 343–44

Kapiszewski, Diana, 218

Kirchner, Cristina, 20, 21, 139, 223

Knight, Alan, 305n11

Ku Klux Klan, 299, 300

labor: average years of education, 58*t*; child labor, 50; determinants of inequality, 61*t*; in development, 22; employment levels of, 47; informal labor, 60*t*, 62, 269; legislation, 101, 197–98; migration for, 90, 92, 101, 317; raising skill levels, 47; unemployment, 47, 81, 203, 336–37; unions, 92, 148, 153, 197, 246, 250, 266, 267, 278; wages, 56, 90, 92; women in, 47, 58, 92, 320. *See also* cognitive skills

Laclau, Ernesto, 126

Lander, L., 260

land rights, 123, 197, 269

Las Flores, 339

Las Vueltas, El Salvador, 330, 332–33, 340

Latin America Integration Association (ALADI), 74, 75

Latin American Free Trade Association (ALALC), 70, 74, 75

Latin America Tlatelolco Treaty (Tlatelolco), 74, 78

*la transición,* 331
Law 25.871 (Argentina), 97–99
Lee, Cheol-Sung, 62
Leff, Enrique, 25–26
the Left: appeal to constitution-making, 244–46; FMLN (Frente Farabundo Martí para la Liberación Nacional [Farabundo Martí National Liberation Front]), 251; governance methods of, 244; rise of, 161. *See also* political experimentalism
Left Turn, 1, 3, 161, 243–44, 249, 253–54, 257
Leninism, 145
Levine, Daniel, 133n1
Levitsky, S., 244
Ley de Desarrollo Rural Sustenable (Sustainable Rural Development Law), 271
Ley General de Educación (General Education Law), 273
liberal democracy: Bolivarian Revolution, 6, 113–16, 121, 131–32, 145–46, 151–52, 298–301; constitutional crises, 169; enabling law (2001), 118–19, 134n3; on institutions, 181; the people as changing, 181; pluralism, 138; popular sovereignty, 121–22, 134n4; populist movement compared with, 165–66; pure people v. corrupt elite, 169, 177–78, 180; self-limitation in, 6–7, 170–71, 172, 175–76; separation of powers in, 119–20, 123; stability of, 116–17; in Venezuela, 114, 115, 116–18
liberalism, 115–16; Argentine constitution, 192; causal primacy, 140–41; exclusionary practices, 129–32; Gramsci on, 121; origins of constitutionalism, 191; popular sovereignty, 121–22, 123, 134n4, 173, 174; recognition of rights, 169; separation of powers in, 119–20, 123; in times of crises, 171; universality, 129–30
liberal peace models, 347n8
liberation theology, 330
Linera, Garcia, 18
Living Well (Buen Vivir). *See* Buen Vivir (Living Well)
Loaeza, S., 180
Locke, John, 140, 141
López-Calva, Luis Felipe, 51, 62
López Maya, Margarita, 260
López Obrador, Andrés Manuel (AMLO), 177–81
Lord Rebel, 155

Luna, Juan Pablo, 160
Lustig, Nora, 51, 62

Macri, Mauricio, 4
Madison, James, 193, 194, 195
Maduro, Nicolás, 6, 122, 128, 133, 139, 148–49, 156–60
Mancano Fernandes, Bernardo, 25
Maneiro, Alfredo, 134n6
Mann, Michael, 138, 140, 141, 143, 162n2
Mano Dura policies, 327, 335
*mapuches,* 203
Mara Salvatrucha (MS-13) (gang), 327
market income, 35f, 40f, 41t, 44, 59–60
market reform, 217, 219
Martí, José, 286, 288, 298, 300
Martínez, Óscar, 347n16
Marxism, 121, 127, 130, 132, 139–40, 143, 299
MAS-IPSP (Morales political party), 317
Matanza-Riachuelo river, 221
McCoy, Jennifer, 133n1
media, 81, 144t, 145–47, 151–52, 155, 158, 321, 323
megamining: Aratirí megamining project (Uruguay), 20; in Argentina, 19, 20, 21; Ecuador, 19, 20; employment, 15; La Colosa mining megaproject (Colombia), 20; open-pit, 17; popular opposition to, 21; resistance movements against, 19, 20; resistance to, 19, 20, 21; revolts against, 20; support for, 20, 21–22
Mendoza Moctezuma, Vicente, 274
Menem, Carlos S., 78
Mercosur: Asunción Treaty creating, 69; China's presence in Latin America, 71; December 2001 crisis (Argentina), 81–82; declining interest in, 68–71; foreign debt, 81–82; gradualism as basis of, 79; migration rights, 5, 94–95, 104; regionalization, 69, 70–72, 79–80, 84; relations with Venezuela, 160; Residence Agreement for the Mercosur States, 95–96; third-party negotiations, 78, 82. *See also* Unasur (Union of South American Nations)
Merentes, Nelson, 156
Mesa de la Unidad Democratica (MUD), 153
messianic presidentialism, 128–29
*mestizaje:* Afro-indigenous peoples, 294–95; black participation in, 294–95; *indigenismo,*

305n11; missionary education, 295; *mulataje*, 294–95; racial egalitarianism, 292. *See also* race and racism; Vasconcelos, José
Mexican Americans, 298
Mexican Revolution, 180
Mexico: anti-drug trafficking legislation, 272; Calderón government, 272; Cartagena Concensus (1984), 72–73; China trade, 28; constitution (1917), 197–98, 217; democratic innovation in, 265; Democratic Planning Councils (Consejos de Planeación Democrática), 270; education in, 55f, 55f, 57t, 62, 272–73, 295; foreign debt of, 75; Gini coefficient for, 40f, 41f; government spending, 38t; income inequality in, 42–43, 62; *indigenismo* in, 305n11; informal labor in, 269; land tenure law in, 197; natural resources management, 279n8; oil industry in, 269; participatory institutions in, 256; pensions in, 39; poverty in, 42f, 44–45; presidential elections in, 177, 178, 179, 272, 279n8; Revolutionary Nationalism, 180; social protests in, 22; taxation in, 34; United States relations with, 272
Mezzadra, Sandro, 311–12
Michels, Roberto, 140
Mignolo, Walter, 303
migrants and migration: Caravan for Freedom, 155; deportations, 97, 333; as human right, 89, 97–99; insecurity, 327–28, 333, 336–38, 341–42, 343–46; integration of, 81, 92–93, 101; labor, 90, 92, 101; 317; legal recognition of, 93–96, 101–3; legislation, 89, 97–99; national security policies, 91–92, 333; remittances, 332; ritual kin, 345; Salvadoran communities in the United States, 332–33, 347n10; transborder mothering, 345; unaccompanied border crossings of minors, 326–27, 336, 343, 345; Venezuelan expatriates in Florida, 155
military power networks, 69, 118, 131, 141–43, 144t, 148–49, 148–50, 153, 158–59, 331, 334–35
mining, 14, 20, 21, 28
Ministry of Economy and Finances (Venezuela), 147
Ministry of Social Development, 271–72, 279n12
minors, border crossings of, 326–27, 336, 343
Miquilena, Luis, 124

Mission System (Venezuela), 123, 144t, 148
Mondero, Juan Carlos, 140
Montevideo Treaty (1960), 75
Moodie, Ellen, 329
Morales, Evo, 3, 139, 316–17, 318, 319
Morales, Viviane, 232
Mosca, Gaetano, 140
MST (Sim Terra), 203
MUD (Mesa de la Unidad Democratica), 153, 154
Mudde, Cas, 166, 168, 176, 177–78, 182n2
Municipal Councils for Sustainable Rural Development (Consejos Municipale de Desarrollo Rural Sustenable), 271
municipal governments: citizen participation in, 1, 161, 243–44, 249, 253–55, 273–74, 317
murder rates, 335–36, 337–39, 339f, 340t, 341, 347n16
Myers, David, 133n1

name generators: in surveys, 267–68
narcotrafficking routes (*el caminito*), 340
National Action Party (Partido Acción Nacional), 269, 271
National Agreement for the Modernization of Basic Education (Acuerdo Nacional para la Modernización Básica), 273
National China Petroleum Corporation [CNPC], 28
National Civilian Police (Policía Nacional Civil, PNC), 333, 335–36
National Commission of Atomic Energy (CNEA), 76, 77–78
National Commission of Nuclear Energy (CNEN), 77–78
National Commoners' Network, 132
National Constituent Assembly (ANC), 122, 123, 124, 134n4, 122122
National Development Plan (Plan Nacional de Desarrollo), 272
National Dialogues (Bolivia), 246, 251–52
National Electoral Institute (INE), 267
National Intelligence Council of the United States, 27–28
national mortgage system (UPAC), 225, 227
National Public Policy Conferences (NPPC), 250
National Public Security Academy (ANSP), 333

National Republican Alliance (ARENA), 329, 334, 336
National Revolution, 311
National Women's Institute, 178, 279n8
Negri, Antonio, 126
Negritude, 306n17
Neilson, Bret, 311–12
neoextractivism, 13, 15, 17–18, 20
neoliberalism, 22, 80; anti-neoliberal reforms in constitutions, 203–4; Chavismo on, 156; colonial domination, 129; constitutional tribunal challenges to, 215; corporate social responsibility (CSR) in neoliberal narrative, 23, 24; courts as agents of, 217; CSR (corporate social responsibility), 23, 24, 25; ESR (economic and social rights), 215, 219, 220, 221–24, 225–26, 228–29, 239–40(Appendix 1); Left Turn, 1, 3, 161, 243–44, 249, 253–54, 257; neodevelopmentalism, 16–17, 22, 161; neoextractivism, 13, 15, 17–18, 20; plurinationalism, 9, 13, 16, 312–15, 321, 323; reforms, 8, 145, 203–4, 215, 217–19; rights-assertive courts, 218–19; security, 337, 339–42; social constitutionalism, 206–9, 215, 217, 223; violence, 332, 337, 339–42; Washington Concensus, 1, 3, 14–16, 18, 62, 219, 269; weak view of sustainable development, 23–24. *See also* activist courts; citizen participation; Commodities Concensus; judicial appointments; judicial system; populism
neo-Marxism, 139–40, 143
neo-Weberian conflict theory, 6–7, 140, 141, 142, 161
net market income, 34, 35*f*, 40*f*, 41*f*
New Development Bank, 71
New Law of National Waters, 279n8
Nicaragua, 22
Nidera (grain production), 28
1968 Nonproliferation Treaty (NPT), 73
1999 Constitution (Venezuela), 6, 18, 120, 121–22, 123–26, 130
Nino, C. S., 210n2
Nonproliferation Treaty (NPT), 73–74, 78
nonwhiteness, 294–95, 302, 303
NPPC (National Public Policy Conferences), 250
NPT (Nonproliferation Treaty), 73–74, 78
nuclear agreements, 5, 69, 73–74, 76–77, 78

nuclear energy: Argentine-Brazil nuclear treaties, 5, 69, 73–79; regional nuclear integration, 76–77; site inspections, 74, 78; technology transfers to non-nuclear countries, 72, 73; U.S. economic aid, 74
Nueva Concepcion, 340
Nunes, Rodrigo M., 228

Obama, Barak, 326–27, 336
October Agenda (Bolivia), 316
O'Donnell, Guillermo, 257
OECD (Organisation for Economic Co-operation and Development), 4, 45, 71, 79
Oelsner, A., 79, 80
oil industry, 118, 123, 144*t*, 146–47, 155–57, 269, 316
Ojeda, Fabricio, 117
OLS regressions, 52–53
opinion polls, 335, 337–38
Opportunities Program (Programa Oportunidades), 272, 279n12
Ordóñez, Alejandro, 231
Organization of American States, 155, 160
Ortíz, Oscar, 251
"Our Common Future," 22

Pact of Unity, 311, 312, 317
País Seguro, 336
Panama, 28, 56, 291
Pan American Energy, 28
panel-connected standard errors, 52–53
PAN (Partido Acción Nacional), 269, 271, 272
Paraguay, 1, 3, 5, 28, 68, 80, 82, 84–85, 92, 95, 99, 101, 103, 201, 234n1
parents, 53, 56, 272–73, 279n13, 345–46
Parents' Associations (Asociaciones de Padres de Familia), 272
Parsons, Talcott, 141
participatory budgeting, 248–49, 250–51, 255–56
Partido Acción Nacional (PAN), 269, 271
Partido Comunista de Venezuela, 149
Partido de la Revolución Democrática (Party of the Democratic Revolution, PRD), 269
Partido Revolucionario Institucional (Institutional Revolutionary Party), 268–69
Pascua-Lama binational mining project (Chile), 20
*The Passing of the Great Race* (Grant), 297

Patagonia, 203
Patria Para Todos (Venezuelan political party), 149
PDVSA (Petroleos de Venezuela), 28, 118, 123, 144*t*, 146–47
peasant organizations, 316–17, 329
People's Ombudsman (Venezuela), 150
PEP (Strategic Participatory Plan), 251
Pérez, Carlos Andres, 157
Pérez Jiménez, Marcos, 117
Peru, 37, 39, 99; Chinese investments in, 28; education in, 38*t*, 55*f*, 55*f*, 57*t*, 62; Gini coefficient for, 40*f*, 41*f*; government spending and revenue, 38*t*; income inequality, 43, 62; income inequality in, 42–43; mining in, 15, 20, 28; out-migration to Argentina, 92; poverty in, 42*f*, 44–45; social protests, 22, 203; taxation in, 34, 38*t*; violence in, 20
Petroleos de Venezuela (PDVSA), 28
petroleum industry, 17, 19, 21, 28, 39, 118, 123, 144*t*, 146–47, 318
Pilcaniyeu uranium enrichment plant (Argentina), 77
Plan El Salvador Seguro (Safe El Salvador Plan), 336
Plan Nacional de Desarrollo (National Development Plan), 272
PLANSAN (Food and Nutritional Security National Plan), 250
pluralism: liberal democracy, 138; people as unchanging, 180–81; people defining, 173–75; popular indeterminancy, 174
plurinationalism, 9, 13, 16, 312–15, 321, 323
PNC (Policía Nacional Civil), 333, 335–36, 337
Polanyian social resistance, 161
Polar Industries (Venezuela), 15
Policía Nacional Civil (PNC), 333, 335–36, 337, 338
political ecology, 22, 25–27
political experimentalism: community councils in Venezuela, 125–27, 132, 134n6, 150, 246–47, 252–53; national councils for equality in Ecuador, 246; national dialogues in Bolivia, 246, 251–52; National Public Policy Conferences (NPPC), 250
political military organizations (PMOs), 331
political power networks, 142–43, 153–56
political representation
popular sovereignty, 121–22, 123, 134n4, 174

populism, 125–26; communal councils, 127; definition of, 166–67, 171; democracy compared with, 165–66; institutions rejected by, 178–80; liberal democracy compared with, 165–66; López Obrador's characterization of the people, 179–80; on the people as always right, 180–81; perception of people in, 171; presidential elections in Mexico, 177; pure people v. corrupt elite, 166, 167, 168, 169, 177–78, 180; self-limitation in, 6–7, 170–71, 172, 175–76; in times of crises, 171; *volunté générale*, 166, 167, 168, 169
Porto Alegre, Brazil: participatory budgeting in, 248, 256
Porto Goncalves, Carlos, 25
positive rights: ESR (economic and social rights), 215, 219, 220, 221–24, 225–26, 227
post-fiscal income, 34, 35*f*, 40*f*, 41*f*
postwar El Salvador: accountability in postwar life, 334–35; amnesty laws, 334–35; *reinserción* (reintegration), 331, 333–34; Salvadoran communities in the United States, 332–33, 347n10; spaces of forgiveness, 328, 344–45
poverty: cash transfers for the poor, 35*f*, 38*t*, 40*f*, 41*f*, 43–45, 47–48, 59, 62–63, 272; child labor, 50; communal councils on, 127; data sources, 41*f*, 42*f*, 43, 60*t*; development of cognitive skills, 50–51, 57*t*; education, 4, 53–54, 56, 57*t*, 58–59, 58*f*, 60*t*, 61*t*; exclusion of the poor, 92, 101, 129–32; extreme poverty, 40, 42*f*, 44; food security policies, 250; influenced by length of democratic record, 60–62, 65; informal sector employment, 60*t*; media coverage of, 152; poverty reduction, 4–5, 34, 41*f*, 42*f*, 43, 47, 61*t*, 88, 153, 252; social justice for, 257; suffrage for, 131–32; taxation, 34, 42, 44; welfare expenditures, 59, 60*t*; years of education, 51, 54, 55*f*, 58–59, 58*t*, 60*t*, 61*t*
power networks, 141, 142–43
pragmatic democracy, 246–47, 258, 259
Prais-Winsten regressions, 52–53
PRD (leftist party in Mexico), 177, 178, 279n8
PRD (Partido de la Revolución Democrática), 269
Prebisch, Raúl, 24, 74–75

presidency: compatibility of new institutional designs, 258; constitutional president who can assume the faculties of a King, 192; elections in Mexico, 177, 178, 179, 180–81; hyperpresidentialism, 7, 194–96, 204; institutional power of, 122, 178–80; messianic presidentialism, 128–29; military intervention in the affairs of local states, 194; power to declare a state of siege, 194

PRI (Partido Revolucionario Institucional), 177–78, 179, 268–69, 271–72, 276t, 278, 279n8

Price-Mars, Jean, 306n17

principle of distinction (constitutions in Latin America), 192–93

pro-government collectives in Venezuela, 150

Programa Oportunidades (Opportunities Program), 272, 279n12

programmatic rights, 199, 210n3

Program of Social Conversion, 178, 279n8

pro-life organizations, 230

protests, 6, 20, 122–24, 146, 151–52, 154, 158, 203–4, 230, 316–17, 319

Przeworski, Adam, 247

PSUV (United Socialist Party of Venezuela), 144t, 149–50

public hearings (audiencias), 209, 223

pueblos, 313, 314

Puerto Rican nationalism, 293

Puerto Rico, 290, 292, 293, 301

Quadripartite Agreement, 78

Quijano, Anibal, 303

race and racism, 304n2; African Americans, 292, 297, 306n13, 320; African presence in Latin American identity, 293; afro-descendents, 315; Afro-indigenous peoples, 294–95; classism, 130; denial of existence of, 298, 300; eugenics, 295, 306n12; extralegal forms of racial discrimination in Latin America, 285–86; Ku Klux Klan, 299, 300; Madison Grant on, 295, 297, 306n12; mulatto identity, 293; myth of black freedom, 299; one-drop rule, 306n12; racial imperialism, 301–2; racial unity in Latin America, 297–98; in United States, 286–87, 298–99, 301–3, 306n16; white supremacy, 9, 288, 292–93, 295, 296–97, 299–300, 306n12. See also mestizaje

racial democracy, 25, 285

racial eruptions, 294, 305n10

racial identity: indigenismo, 305n11; of Mexican Americans, 298, 303; one-drop rule, 306n12; skin color, 301–2; in United States, 301–2. See also whiteness

Radical Cause on Chavismo, 134n6

Ramirez, Rafael, 156

Ramírez Rojas, Kléber, 128–29

Rancière, Jacques, 324

Raquel (research subject), 343

Real News Venezuela, 146

reconciliation, 331, 333, 335, 347n11

Red Futuro Colombia (RFC), 230

red revolutions (1848), 193

regional citizenship, 95–97

regionalization, 69, 70, 71–72, 74–77, 79–80, 84, 319–20

regional strategies for economic development, 74–75

reinserción (reintegration), 331, 333–34

religious tolerance: Article 14 (Argentine constitution), 192

representative democracy, 125, 126, 127–28, 135n7, 243–44, 246–47

reprimarization of Latin American economies, 3, 13–14, 24

reproductive rights of women, 197, 230

Repsol (Brazil), 19, 28

Residence Agreement (2002), 5

Residence Agreement for the Mercosur States, 95–96, 98

Resolution 8610 (Venezuela), 158

los retornados (the returned), 331, 333–34

reverse migration, 336–37

Revolutionary Nationalism, 180

revolutionary tourism, 146

RFC (Red Futuro Colombia), 230

rights activism, judicial, 214–20, 223–26, 231–32

Rights of Man, Article 16, 120

Rights of Nature, 13, 16, 27

Rio+20 Summit, 24

ritual kin, 345–46

Rivera, Zurita, 273

Roberts, K., 244

Rousseau, Jean Jacques, 120, 167, 120133n1

Rousseff, Dilma, 1, 246

Rubiano Galvis, Sebastian, 228

Saca, Antonio, 336
Sala Cuarta (high court, Costa Rica), 219
Salinas de Gortari, Carlos, 269, 273
Salvadoran Armed Forces (FAES), 333
Salvadoran migrants, 332–33, 347n11
same-sex marriage, 231
Samper, Ernesto, 228
Sanchez Cerén, Salvador, 331, 336
Santa Tecla (El Salvador), 250–51
Santos, Milton, 25
São Paulo, Brazil, 256
Sarmiento, Domingo F.: Ambas Americas,
    288, 290; on caudillismo, 289; on education
    in Argentina, 289; on the United States,
    290, 291; Vasconcelos' identification with,
    287, 289
Sarney, José, 76, 77
SCCC (Common System of Accounting and
    Control of Nuclear Materials), 78
Schmitt, Carl, 115, 116, 119–21, 123
Schonberg, Jeff, 346
school systems. See education
Scott, David, 116
second article of the Bolivian Constitution,
    313
secondary school students, 52, 53, 54t
secondary students in Latin America, 52
security, 8, 335–36, 337–38, 340–41, 343–44
Seelke, Clare Ribando, 335
Segovia, Alexander, 333
self-limitation, 6–7, 170–71, 172, 175–76,
    179–80
Sentipensar con la tierra (Escobar), 315
Serrano, Alfredo, 157
sexual rights, 8, 197, 219, 225, 230–33
Sim Terra (MST), 203
SMEs (small and medium-sized enterprises),
    28–29
Smulovitz, Catalina, 224
social class: bourgeoisie's role in the com-
    mune, 132–33; Catholic culture, 150–51;
    class-based political polarization, 131;
    communal councils, 127; constitutional
    rights of, 197–200; inclusion in policy
    development, 250; indigenous rights, 203;
    inequality in the quality of education, 53;
    isolation and nonparticipation in electoral
    campaigns, 277; and leisure industry,
    152–53; middle class, 131; probability for
    having contacts, 277; rights of, 203–4;

universal inclusion, 131–32; the wealthy
    (boliburgueses), 144t, 148
social investment. See education; health and
    health care
"Socialism of the Twenty First Century," 6
Social Policy in Latin America and Carib-
    bean Dataset (1960–2006), 51
Solidarity Committees in Mexico, 271–72
Sources of Social Power (Mann), 141
Sousa Santos, B., 256
Southern Common Market. See Mercosur
Spain in Latin America, 290, 294, 295, 334
Sprenkels, Ralph, 331, 334, 346
Statoil Brazil, 28
Stavans, Ilan, 287
Strategic Participatory Plan (PEP), 251–52
Strategic Plan for the Production of Petro-
    leum (Venezuela), 19
structural economics, 70, 74–75, 78, 80
structural functionalism (Parsons), 141
student movements, 146, 151–52, 154
Summit in Rio (1992), 22
Sunkel, Osvaldo, 75
Supreme Judicial Tribunal (TSJ), 150, 159–60
Suriname, 80
survey methodology, 34, 36–37, 40f, 51–53,
    52, 54t, 56t, 267–68, 275, 278n2
Sustainable Rural Development Law (Ley de
    Desarrollo Rural Sustenable), 271

Tate, Winifred, 346n1
Taussig, Michael, 344
taxation, 38t; in Argentina, 44; commodity
    prices, 44; consumption taxes, 36, 44, 45;
    distortionary taxes, 44; effect of consump-
    tion taxes on the poor, 44; export tax, 44;
    household surveys on, 36; indirect taxa-
    tion, 34, 35f, 35f; indirect taxes, 34, 35f;
    payroll taxes, 36; poverty reduction, 34, 42,
    44; redistribution of income, 47; SENIAT
    (state tax collecting agency), 144t; as share
    of GDP, 35f, 37; standard benefit-tax inci-
    dence analysis, 33
Technical Consultative Councils, 177, 178,
    279n8
technology transfers to non-nuclear coun-
    tries, 72
test scores, 50, 53, 54t, 55f, 56t, 57t
Texas: Mexican American population in, 301
Third Way, 47, 48

Thomas, Deborah, 344
Tipnis conflict, 3, 19, 20, 318
Tlatelolco (Latin America Tlatelolco Treaty),
74, 78
TNCs (Transnational corporations), 24, 28
Toro, Francisco, 133n1
Touchton, M., 256
transborder mothering, 345
Transnational corporations (TNCs), 24, 28
Transparency International, 154
Treaty for Integration, Cooperation, and
Development, 76
Treaty of Asunción, 76
Tristán, Rey, 334–35
Truth Commission Report (United Nations),
334–35
TSJ (Supreme Judicial Tribunal), 150, 159–60
tutela, 207, 210n6, 219, 225

Unasur (Union of South American Nations),
144t; ALALC (Latin American Free Trade
Association), 70, 74, 75; ECLAC extractiv-
ist pact, 20–21, 24; exports from, 15; Mer-
casur and, 70, 80, 83; neostructuralism, 24;
relations with Venezuela, 160; Venezuela
and, 150, 160
UNCTAD (United Nations Conference on
Trade and Development), 15
UN Economic Commission for Latin Ameri-
ca (CEPAL), 70, 74, 78, 80
UNEFA (National Experimental University
of the Armed Forces), 146
unemployment, 47, 203, 336–37
Unger, Roberto, 193
Unidos por la Vida, 230
Union of South American Nations (Unasur).
See Unasur (Union of South American
Nations)
United Nations, 15, 70, 74, 78, 80, 154,
334–35
United States: deportations, 331, 333–34;
imperialism, 9, 288–91, 297–98, 302; Latin
American populations in, 298, 301, 302;
Mexico's commerical dependence on, 272;
model of organized powers, 194; nuclear
foreign policy, 72, 73, 74; race relations in,
286–87, 298–99, 301–3, 306n16; relations
with Venezuela, 155, 159; Salvadoran
communities in, 332–33, 337, 343–45,
347n10; support for counterinsurgency in

El Salvador, 329; Venezuelan expatriates in
Florida, 155
Universal Child Allowance program (Asig-
nación Universal por Hijo [AUH]), 101
Universal Family Allowance, 44
universities in Venezuela, 146, 151–52, 154
university student movements, 144t, 146,
151–52, 154
UNO (Un Nuevo Orden), 144t, 153, 155
UP-Hub, 265, 274, 278
urban popular class associations (A-Nets),
265, 274, 275, 278
Urbinati, Nadia, 135n7
Uribe, Alvaro, 228, 231
Uruguay: academic achievement, 54t,
56; Aratirí megamining project, 20;
BancoSur, 80; education in, 55f, 55f, 57t;
GDP of, 43; Gini coefficient for, 40f, 41f;
government spending and revenue, 38t;
income inequality in, 42–43; migrant
rights in, 95; poverty in, 4, 42, 42f, 44–45,
57t, 63; reduction of final income inequality, 43; Residence Agreement (2002),
5; taxation in, 38t; trade relations with
China, 28

Van der Borgh, Chris, 347n8
Vasconcelos, José: biography, 304n2; on caudillismo, 289; on European nationalism,
289–90; identification with Sarmiento,
289; on indigenous education, 295; on
mestizaje identity, 9, 285–86, 287, 288–89,
292–93, 303, 305n4; on mulatto identity,
293; on racial mixing, 285, 304n1; on
racial self-hatred of Latin American elites,
296–97; on racism, 298–99, 305nn8, 9; on
regional unity, 289, 290; on the Spanish
legacy in Latin America, 290, 295–96;
on U.S. racial politics, 287–88, 290, 291,
298–99; W. E. B. Du Bois and, 292, 297,
306n13; on white supremacy, 288; works
of: Bolivarismo y Monroismo, 287, 298,
299, 301; The Cosmic Race, 286, 291, 292,
293, 298, 300, 305nn8, 9; Indolgía, 290–91,
292–93, 294, 295
Venezuela: agroindustry in, 152; armed forces in, 144t, 145; banking in, 80, 118, 123,
139, 144t, 147; Betancourt administration,
116; Bolivarian Revolution, 6, 113–16, 121,
131–32, 145–46, 151–52, 298–301; Cara-

cazo rebellion *(el Caracazo)*, 116, 134n4, 157–58; community councils in, 125–27, 132, 134n6, 150, 245–47, 252–53; corruption networks in, 147–49; democracy in, 6, 113–14, 115–18, 133n1; disappeared persons in, 116; education in, 54*t*, 55*f*, 55*f*, 57*t*, 146, 151–52, 154; enabling law (2001), 118–19, 134n3; gun control, 150; international commerce, 28, 155–56; judicial system, 149; liberal democracy, 114, 115, 116–18; Maduro government, 6, 122, 128, 133, 139, 148–49, 156–60; military in, 118, 144*t*, 148–49, 150, 153, 155, 158; Mission System (Venezuela), 123, 144*t*, 148; multilateral agencies' relations with, 155–56, 160; National Assembly elections (December, 2015), 133, 159–60; 1999 Constitution, 6, 18, 120, 121–22, 123–26, 130; oil industry in, 19, 28, 118, 123, 144*t*, 146–47, 155–56, 159; opposition leaders in municipal and state offices, 154; political parties, 144*t*, 149–50, 153–54; private sector in, 148, 152–53; protest movements, 122–24, 158, 203; PSUV (United Socialist Party of Venezuela), 144*t*, 149–50; relations with the United States, 155, 159; state-controled media, 145–46, 151, 152, 158; state control over economy, 118, 147–48; university student movements, 146, 151–52, 154
Venezuela Defense of Human Rights and Civil Society Act (2014), 155
Venezuelan Central Bank, 144*t*, 147
Venezuelan Federation of Chambers of Commerce (Fedecamaras), 152, 153
Venezuela Solidarity Network, 146
Videla Law, 97
violence, 8, 315–16; in the aftermath of peace, 329; agentive alertness, 341–42; Caracazo rebellion *(el Caracazo)*, 116, 134n4, 157–58; in colonialism, 310; as common crime, 329; demographics of, 338–39; disappeared persons, 116, 329; domestic violence, 343–44; gangs, 335–36; homicides, 335–36, 337–39, 339*f*, 340*t*, 341, 347n16; humanitarian inaction, 347n16; insecurity, 327–28, 333, 336–38, 341–42, 343–46; Jesuit Massacre Case, 334; lynchings, 299; migration, 90; public opinion polls on, 335
Virno, Pablo, 126

*volunté générale* of common people, 166, 167, 168, 169
Von Vacano, Diego, 304n1, 305n4

wages, 56, 90, 92
Wallerstein, Immanuel, 309
Wampler, B., 256
war: Amnesty Law (1993), 334; bordercrossings of minors, 326–27, 336, 343; emigration after, 332, 347n11; insecurity, 327–28, 333, 336–38, 341–42, 343–46; memories of, 345–46; moral politics of compassion, 344–46; postwar reintegration, 330–33, 334, 347n12
Washington Concensus, 1, 3, 14–16, 18, 62, 219, 269
water resources: dams, 17–18, 19, 20; management of, 21, 256, 279n8; participatory budgeting impact on, 256; privatization of, 316, 317; Water Wars in Cochabamba, 316, 317
Weber, Max, 6–7, 140, 141, 142, 161
welfare spending, 59, 62, 215; constitutional commitments to, 219; dependence on redistribution, 47; determinants of inequality, 61*t*; family allowances, 47–48; income inequality, 62; post-World War II, 48; poverty, 59, 60*t*; Universal Child Allowance program (Asignación Universal por Hijo [AUH]), 101; Universal Family Allowance, 44
Weyer, L. Frank, 338
Weyland, Kyurt, 139
whiteness: Latin American elites aspirations to, 292–93, 296–97; of Mexican Americans, 301, 303; racial identity in United States, 301–2; racial identity of Latin American elites, 292–93, 300–301
white supremacy, 9, 288, 292–93, 295, 296–97, 299–300, 306n12
Wilpert, Gregory, 125
Woessmann, Ludger, 63
women: advocacy groups for, 219; average years of education, 58*t*; Bolivian socialism on, 131; as heads of households, 320, 342; in insurgency, 330; in labor force, 92, 320; in migrant populations, 92, 344–46; postwar reintegration programs, 330; reproductive rights, 8, 197, 230–33; rights activism, 225; social services supporting,

women: advocacy groups for continued
    47; violence towards, 339*f*, 343–44; in the
    work force, 47, 92
Wood, Elisabeth, 329
World Bank, 82, 155, 217, 249
World Health Organization, 335

Yasuni Project (Ecuador), 3, 19, 20
youth population: determinants of inequality,
    61*t*

Zelaya, Manuel, 139
Zilberg, Elana, 336

# ACKNOWLEDGMENTS

This book is the result of ongoing discussions within the Program on Democracy, Citizenship, and Constitutionalism (DCC) at the University of Pennsylvania. Since 2007, DCC has fostered interdisciplinary scholarship on the related and globally pressing topics of democratic participation, the rights of citizens, and formal frameworks of governance. It was fitting to include a regional approach, in our case Latin America, for the discussion of these issues. Accordingly, our most special thanks go to our dear colleague Professor Rogers Smith, who as Director of the DCC Program provided intellectual leadership, unwavering support, and encouragement for this project. The financial support of the DCC was essential to commissioning the contributions included in this volume and fostering the interdisciplinary discussions of the individual chapters. The Latin American focus within the DCC was inaugurated with an outstanding lecture by former Bolivian president Carlos Mesa Gisbert, who graciously and humbly joined us at Penn to reflect on the recent politics and economics of the region. We are also indebted to our Penn colleagues Sigal Ben-Porath, Ann Farnsworth-Alvear, and Deborah Thomas, with whom we selected the themes and the contributors to this volume, and to Mason Moseley, who as postdoctoral fellow of the DCC program in 2014–15 was an active and engaged participant in the project.

Furthermore, we were extremely fortunate to enlist an outstanding group of commentators and reviewers, who provided pointed and constructive comments to the first drafts of these chapters. They are Randall Collins, Camilo García-Jimeno, Maria Victoria Murillo, Anne Norton, Rogers Smith, Deborah Thomas, and Tukufu Zuberi. Deborah Yashar also participated, linking her scholarship with the discussion and thinking on institutions, citizenship, violence, and democracy in Latin America. Once the manuscript was completed, we benefited enormously from the support of the University of Pennsylvania Press editor-in-chief, Peter Agree, and from the comments of two anonymous Press reviewers. Last, but certainly not least, the effective and efficient administrative support of Matthew Roth of the DCC Program was essential to completing the project. To all of these colleagues and friends and to the contributors to the volume: Thank you!

*The Editors*